In Defence of Lenin

Rob Sewell at the London office where
Lenin edited *Iskra* in 1902-3

Alan Woods speaking in
London in 2023

Rob Sewell and Alan Woods were brought up in South Wales in a Communist household. As young teenagers, they became committed Marxists and are now leading members of the International Marxist Tendency (IMT).

Rob Sewell is the political editor of *The Communist* (communist.red) – the organ of the British section of the IMT – and has written extensively on revolutionary theory and history. He is the author of *Socialism or Barbarism: Germany 1918-1933*; *Chartist Revolution*; *In the Cause of Labour – A History of British Trade Unionism*; *Revolution and Counter-revolution in Germany*; *What is Marxism?* with Alan Woods and *Understanding Marx's Capital: A Reader's Guide* with Adam Booth.

Alan Woods is the political editor of the IMT's flagship *In Defence of Marxism* website (marxist.com) and has written many books covering a wide spectrum of topics. These include *Lenin and Trotsky: What They Really Stood For* and *Reason in Revolt: Marxist Philosophy and Modern Science* – both in conjunction with the late Ted Grant; *Bolshevism: The Road to Revolution*; *Spain's Revolution Against Franco: The Great Betrayal*; *Marxism and the USA*; *Reformism or Revolution*; *The Ideas of Karl Marx* and *The Venezuelan Revolution: A Marxist Perspective*.

In Defence of Lenin

Rob Sewell *and* Alan Woods

Volume One

Wellred Books
London

Dedicated to the memory of Steve Jones (1955 – 2022),
who devoted his life to the socialist revolution.

In Defence of Lenin
Rob Sewell and Alan Woods

Volume 1 of 2

First edition
Wellred Books, January 2024

UK distribution: Wellred Books Britain, wellredbooks.co.uk
152-160 Kemp House, City Road
London
EC1V 2NX
contact@wellredbooks.co.uk

USA distribution: Marxist Books, marxistbooks.com
WR Books
250 44th Street #208
Brooklyn
New York
NY 11232
sales@marxistbooks.com

DK distribution: Forlaget Marx, forlagetmarx.dk
Degnestavnen 19, st. tv.
2400 København NV
forlag@forlagetmarx.dk

Front cover: Lenin in Gorki, 1922
Back cover: Lenin in his office in the Kremlin, 1922
  – colourised by Olga Shirnina

Cover design by Jesse Murray-Dean

Layout by Wellred Books

ISBN:
Volume 1 – 978 1 913026 95 0
Volume 2 – 978 1 913026 96 7

Contents

VOLUME ONE

VOLUME TWO

Preface

It is good to be alive at a time when the
masses begin to stir with political life.
– Lenin, 27 May 1906[1]

The idea for this book arose from discussions of how best to commemorate
the centenary of Lenin's death. This was a most important and urgent task,
but it faced a number of difficulties. For the best part of a century, the memory
of that great man has been subjected to a constant campaign of vilification.
This is no accident. Nor does it lack historical precedents.

Despite being buried under a deluge of lies and slanders, Lenin's name still
resonates with millions of people as the founder of the Soviet Union and the
standard bearer of communism.

For Marxists, the October Revolution is the most important event in world
history. For the first time, the working class had come to power and held on
to it. Whatever anyone may say about the Revolution, it is impossible to deny
the fact that it had a profound worldwide impact. More than any other single
event, it changed the whole course of world history. And, in the last analysis,
that great event was only possible thanks to the work of one man: Vladimir
Ilyich Lenin. He therefore deserves our utmost attention.

Lenin's entire life was devoted to the cause of communism and building a
revolutionary party. Nadezhda Krupskaya, Lenin's lifelong companion and
comrade, wrote: "Struggle and study, study and scientific work were always
for Ilyich strongly bound together."[2] In the course of this book, we shall see
just how true those words were.

Why now?

For a long time, the enemies of communism believed that they had successfully exorcised the ghosts of October. The collapse of the Soviet Union seemed to confirm their suspicion that communism was dead and buried. "The Cold War is over", they gloated, "and we won."

But as Berthold Brecht once said: he who laughs has not yet heard the bad news. Contrary to the legend so persistently repeated by the enemies of socialism, it was not communism that collapsed in the 1980s, but Stalinism – a horrible bureaucratic and totalitarian caricature that bore no relation to the regime of workers' democracy established by Lenin and the Bolsheviks in 1917. As we shall show, Stalinism and Bolshevism, far from being identical, are not only different in kind. They are mutually exclusive and mortal enemies.

Today, with the capitalist system in crisis, the ideas associated with Lenin have become increasingly attractive, especially for the youth. In an article in the *Financial Times* from 2017 called 'From Lenin to Lehman', which marked two anniversaries, the October Revolution and the beginning of the global financial crisis, it gloomily states:

> The stultifying communism that the Soviet bloc had evolved to by the 1980s collapsed [...] The political turmoil of the last year demonstrated that we are now watching to see whether open market economies will suffer the same fate.

The reason, the article states, is that the system "betrayed the dream it had promised."[3] The author of these lines is one of the more serious strategists of capital.

Yet this staunch defender of the 'open market', is now openly pondering the collapse of capitalism. That is hardly surprising. The growing backlash against the so-called free market economy has terrified the apologists of capitalism. They are looking with dread towards an uncertain and turbulent future. A later editorial in the *Financial Times* states:

> Since the global financial crisis, this sense of betrayal has fuelled a political backlash against globalisation and the institutions of liberal democracy. Right-wing populism may thrive on this backlash whilst leaving capitalist markets in place. But as it cannot deliver on its promises to the economically frustrated, it is just a matter of time before the pitchforks come out for capitalism itself, and for the wealth of those who benefit from it.[4]

The word "pitchforks" here is nothing more than a synonym for revolution.

Together with this pervading mood of pessimism, the more thoughtful representatives of the bourgeoisie are beginning to discover uncomfortable parallels with the world of 1917. The fall of the Soviet Union was a great historical drama. But in retrospect, it will be seen as only the prelude to a far greater drama – the terminal crisis of capitalism.

The name of Lenin now begins to re-emerge as a powerful image and a point of reference. Evidence for this can be found even in the most unlikely places. Orn Svavarsson, a bankrupt businessman, demonstrating outside of the Icelandic Parliament in December 2008, was quoted as saying: "For the first time in my life I have sympathy with the Bolsheviks; [and] with the French revolutionaries who put up the guillotine."[5]

The decade of austerity that followed, with a further slump in 2020, has only added to this mounting discontent and anger. An ever-growing number of people are beginning to draw revolutionary conclusions.

This applies particularly to young people, even in countries like the USA, where many now call themselves communists and stand for the overthrow of capitalism. After so many decades of enforced silence, the voice of Lenin reaches them loud and clear. In the writings of Lenin, they find a concrete and convincing expression of their burning desire to change society.

A word on sources

The main source for this book is Lenin's *Collected Works*, the English edition of which embraces some forty-five volumes. These books are a goldmine of information, facts, letters, articles and documents, as well as several important books, such as *Materialism and Empirio-criticism* and *Imperialism, the Highest Stage of Capitalism*. It would be well worth the effort to study every volume of these works, which are essential reading for anyone with a serious interest in Marxism.

Lenin's *Collected Works* are a real revelation. One is immediately struck by how rich and relevant they are. They are a treasure-house of the theory and practice of Marxism and we hope that, on reading this book, many more people will find the encouragement to explore these incredibly valuable writings for themselves.

However, we are also aware that such an enterprise would seem too ambitious for most people. It is really the work of a lifetime. We therefore see no need to apologise for producing a book about Lenin, which aims to present his ideas and their relevance for today in a relatively concise and concentrated form.

However, here we were faced with a problem. The vast scope of his life's work and ideas could not be contained adequately in a single volume. It is therefore necessary to present the reader with an overview of the contents.

The first volume covers the years from Lenin's youth to the February Revolution in 1917. These are the years in which Lenin developed into a revolutionary Marxist and where Bolshevism took shape, from its theoretical beginnings among the first Russian Marxists to a professional revolutionary organisation, enriched by the experiences of the 1905 Revolution and the First World War.

The second volume spans from Lenin's return to Russia in April 1917 to his death in 1924. In this period, we see the working class, under the leadership of the Bolshevik Party, seizing power in October 1917. This is followed by the struggle to survive in a country racked by civil war and imperialist intervention, and the measures taken to protect the gains of the Revolution. It ends with Lenin's final struggle against the emerging Soviet bureaucracy.

Rob Sewell and Alan Woods
London, December 2023

*

In addition to the pleasant task of reading Lenin's *Collected Works*, it was regrettably necessary to suffer the penance of ploughing through the scribblings of bourgeois historians whose hatred of Lenin and communism knows no rational bounds.

These hired servants of the ruling class commerce in calumnies and lies with the same alacrity as the merchants who trade in shoddy, mass-produced goods for the bargain basements of disreputable stores.

All one can say about this vast heap of falsehoods, falsifications and fabrications is that reading most of them is a complete waste of time. They will add nothing to your understanding of Lenin and Bolshevism, but may do some damage to your digestive system.

Yet for every rule, there is always an exception. We refer to Edward Hallett Carr, the well-known British political scientist and historian specialising in modern Russian history, who was assistant editor of *The Times* during 1941-46.

Although he had all the credentials of a respectable figure of the British Establishment, Carr stands out for his fearless honesty in his treatment of the Russian Revolution and the leaders of the Bolshevik party. If he makes some mistakes (which he does) they are not the product of spite or malice, which is ever-present in other anti-Bolshevik authors, but merely of genuine misunderstanding or lack of knowledge of Marxism.

His serious attempts to arrive at an objective understanding of the Revolution earned him the undying hatred of the anti-communist mob. David Bowes-Lyon, a director of the paper, chipped in remarking that *The New York Times* called *The Times* the final edition of the *Daily Worker*.[6] As its lead writer and assistant editor, EH Carr was called 'The Red Professor of Printing House Square'.

Such views were not confined to Americans. Carr's enemies at the very top of the British establishment read like a veritable rogue's gallery of scoundrels, including Winston Churchill, his son Randolph and the right-wing Labour Foreign Secretary, Ernest Bevin.

Acknowledgements

The production of this book would not have been possible without the help of others. Fred Weston made valuable suggestions which helped improve the original manuscript. We would like to thank Kevin Ramage for his input, comments and suggestions, which were always very helpful. Many thanks to Jesse Murray-Dean, who not only did a wonderful job in laying out and designing the book, but he also made a host of useful suggestions to improve the text for which we are most grateful. Thanks also to Manon Powrie, who helped guide the whole project and patiently made the numerous corrections to the book, amazingly deciphering some handwriting in the bargain. We would like to wholeheartedly thank the proofreaders for their sterling work: Joseph Attard, Oliver Brotherton, Haydn Curran, Mia Foley Doyle, Jonathan Hinckley, Sean Hodges, Piotr Kwasiborski, John Peterson, Nye Shaw, Maarten Vanheuverswyn, Jonathan Wellsted and Jack Tye Wilson. In particular, we are very grateful to Su Norris for her work, not only proofreading but also for all of her helpful suggestions. Lastly, thanks also goes to the staff at the Marx Memorial Library for their assistance.

Of course, as the ones with the last say on things, we take full responsibility for any errors that may have crept in. Hopefully not too many.

Note on Dates

Tsarist Russia used the Old Style, Julian calendar, which was different to the New Style, Gregorian calendar used in the West and which is standard today. There is a discrepancy between the two systems. For example, the October Revolution took place on 25 October 1917 in the Old Style, but on 7 November in the New.

For clarity, the dates given in this volume are in the New Style, which are twelve days ahead during the nineteenth century, and thirteen days ahead of the Old Style in the twentieth century. When both dates are given, the earlier date given in brackets is in the Old Style.

The Soviet government adopted the New Style calendar used in the West on 14 February 1918, which would have been 1 February in the Old Style.

Introduction

The Great October Revolution! Today, they're calling it a military coup,
the Bolshevik conspiracy... The Russian catastrophe... Saying Lenin was
a German agent, and the Revolution was brought about by deserters and
drunken sailors. I cover my ears. I don't want to hear it!
— Margarita Pogrebitskaya, a medical doctor[1]

But the things I remember... I remember people with fire in their eyes. Our
hearts were on fire! No one believes me... I'll die with Lenin in my heart!
— Vasily Petrovich, who joined the Communist Party in 1922[2]

The publication of this book is timed to coincide with the centenary of
Lenin's death, one of the greatest revolutionaries who has ever lived.

Its aim is not to walk the tightrope of a non-existent "impartiality", a myth
used by bourgeois historians to disguise their own class prejudices, but to
offer an unapologetic defence of Lenin and answer the mountain of lies and
falsehoods about him.

John Reed, the author of *Ten Days That Shook the World*, once tried to sum
up Lenin in a few words. He wrote: "Lenin, simplest, most human, and yet
most far-seeing and immovable."[3] These were certainly some of his finest
qualities, although he had many others, as we shall see. Needless to say, the
hack historians attempt to bury such features, all the better to attack him.

Lenin burst onto the world stage following the successful October
Revolution, which inspired ordinary millions, but attracted the wrath of the
ruling classes everywhere. Ever since then, and right up to today, he has been
subjected to a deluge of vilification and slander.

When he was alive the capitalist press poured out a daily stream of abuse against him. Reports would regularly appear in the newspapers that either Lenin had shot Trotsky, or Trotsky had murdered Lenin, in a drunken brawl. Nothing was too crude for them. Several American newspapers even reported that the Bolsheviks had set up an electrically operated guillotine in Petrograd, capable of chopping off 500 heads an hour. Hundreds of stories were published about supposed decrees on free love. One alleged decree, which was reported in *The New York Times*, was said to require all women over the age of eighteen to register with a 'Bureau of Free Love', who were then parcelled out to each man.[4]

These horror stories were used to frighten their respectable middle-class readers about the Russian Revolution. They were roughly on the same level as the stories of hobgoblins told to frighten little children before they go to bed. The then head of the FBI, the notorious J Edgar Hoover, chilled his audience with tales of the bloodthirsty Lenin so as to make them faint with fright at the mere thought of revolutionary change:

> Revolutions cannot be won by clean hands or in white shirts; only by blood, sweat and the burning torch... The skill of Lenin cannot be overestimated. He introduced into human relations a new dimension of evil and depravity not surpassed by Genghis Khan or Attila.[5]

"His [Lenin's] sympathies, cold and wide as the Arctic Ocean; his hatreds, tight as the hangman's noose", wrote the fascist-loving Winston Churchill.[6]

Today, it must be said that the propaganda is little changed. Every year, the bourgeois historians churn out piles of books and articles, each one more absurd than the other, which represent no more than hack-work. The theme is always the same: Lenin was a 'dictator', 'psychopath', and 'bloodthirsty murderer'.

The lengths to which some of them go beggars belief. Some have discovered monstrous traits in Lenin, even as a baby in his cradle, in the way he looked, and especially his eyes. "But the eyes always gave him away: they were quick and shrewd, and betrayed his speed of thought", writes Helen Rappaport. "They also projected a certain craftiness of manner, and, as time went on, a cruel glint."[7] Simon Sebeg Montefiore also describes Lenin "with a bulging, intense forehead and piercing, slanted eyes."[8] The Russian writer, Kuprin, discovered Lenin had green eyes "like a monkey".[9]

There is nothing new in these attempts to demonise the leader of October, having been repeated a thousand times without any visible improvement.

But these days, it comes with the seal of approval from 'respected' bourgeois historians who have, they claim, 'researched' the subject. However, despite all their academic pretensions, most of them come from the same stable as the common hack journalists who wallow in distortion and invention and are incapable of understanding what they are criticising. What is more, they are anti-communists, and therefore hostile to revolution and to Lenin. These historians have built their careers and reputations sifting through dusty archives for any small scraps of incriminating 'evidence' that can be used to discredit Lenin and the Bolsheviks.

The collapse of the Soviet Union in 1991 ushered in a crescendo of bourgeois triumphalism, 'the end of history' and the final victory of the wonders of capitalism. As a result, the ideas of Lenin and the Bolsheviks were to be consigned to the dustbin of history, out of sight and out of mind. But the spectre of Lenin, the personification of world revolution, has continued to haunt them.

As the capitalist system began to enter into a deep crisis – particularly after the economic collapse of 2008 – the triumphalism of the bourgeoisie began to turn sour as the ideas of communism experienced a revival, especially among the new generations. "Life teaches", was a phrase Lenin was fond of repeating, and the only life that young people today have ever known is one of austerity and capitalist crisis. This, at a time when the class struggle, long considered dead, has experienced a rebirth in one country after another.

Of course, Stalinism has also played a pernicious role in denigrating Lenin by twisting his words to justify all kinds of crimes in the interests of the ruling bureaucracy in Moscow. Stalinism emerged after the death of Lenin, when, given the prolonged isolation of the revolution in backward conditions, a caste of bureaucrats seized power behind the backs of the working class. Stalin was their figurehead and the gravedigger of the revolution.

By murdering all those in the Bolshevik Party with any connection to Lenin, a river of blood separated the regime of Lenin from Stalin. While presiding over a nationalised planned economy, every element of workers' democracy was eradicated under Stalinism and world revolution was abandoned for 'socialism in one country' and 'peaceful co-existence'. It is no accident that Lenin's last struggle prior to his death was against Stalin and the dangers of bureaucratic degeneration.

The task of writing a genuine biography of Lenin is to unearth and explain his ideas, which have been subjected to so much distortion and calumny. When Thomas Carlyle wrote his work about Oliver Cromwell, he said he had to rescue his ideas, "fish them up from the foul Lethean quagmires where they lay buried."[10] We are now presented with a similar task in dealing with Lenin.

The centenary of his death is an appropriate time to answer this Niagara of lies and establish the truth, namely that the man called Vladimir Ilyich Ulyanov, known to the world as Lenin, stands out as the architect, chief organiser and guiding spirit of the October Revolution and one of the most remarkable revolutionary leaders in world history.

Some historians, such as Ian Kershaw, are forced to admit this: "Lenin made a greater impact on history than any other individual of his era."[11] Dmitri Volkogonov, a biographer and former Stalinist turned bourgeois liberal, who had a personal distaste for Lenin, nevertheless says the following: "Very few people in history have had influence of a global order: a few conquerors, some great philosophers and religious figures. Among them, undoubtedly, Lenin and Trotsky have a place."[12] Thus, even some of the most diehard of reactionaries are compelled to recognise Lenin's importance as a fact, whatever their point of view.

Prior to 1917, Lenin was known to very few people outside those in the Russian revolutionary movement and a handful in the leading bodies of the Second International. This body, which grouped together all the socialist parties internationally, formally adhered to Marxism, at least in words. Lenin stood on its 'extreme left-wing' along with his well-known contemporary, Rosa Luxemburg. His political intransigence earned him the title of a 'fanatic' from the other leaders, who looked with disdain at what they saw as 'theoretical squabbling' among the Russians. But Lenin was simply defending the fundamental ideas of Marxism against the opportunists and revisionists.

Under the pressure of the prolonged capitalist upswing before the First World War, the 'socialist' leaders of the Second International had succumbed to opportunism and had adapted to capitalism. Their 'revolutionary' speeches were reserved for May Day celebrations and other such holidays. This accommodation to capitalism would end in the betrayal of August 1914, when they chose to side with their own ruling classes in war. The Russian Social-Democrats, and a few others, were the exceptions who stood out against the imperialist war and in defence of socialist internationalism.

Lenin came to worldwide prominence following the success of the Bolshevik Revolution of October 1917. For those fighting for the emancipation of the working class, it was the greatest event in human history. For the first time, the working class, under the leadership of Lenin and the Bolsheviks, successfully seized power, expropriated the capitalists and landlords and established a proletarian state.

This explains why Lenin was considered "the most hated and most loved man on earth", to quote the words of John Reed – hated by the rich and powerful, but loved by the oppressed masses, who were inspired by the ideals of the October Revolution.

Victor Serge, who at the time was an anarchist, was so attracted by the October Revolution that he broke with anarchism and came over to Bolshevism. He relates an interesting conversation with his friend, Salvador Seguí: "Bolshevism", Serge said, "is the unity of word and deed. Lenin's entire merit consists in his will to carry out his programme… Land to the peasants, factories to the workers, power to those who toil. These words have often been spoken, but no one has ever thought seriously of passing from theory to practice. Lenin seems to be on the way…"

"You mean", Seguí replied, bantering and incredulous, "that socialists are going to apply their programme? Such a thing has never been seen…"[13]

This was a truly astonishing, unbelievable fact: socialists who actually did what they said they would do! Breathtaking! But Lenin and the Bolsheviks were a special breed – *real communists* – who dared to turn the world upside down and placed socialist revolution, for the first time, on the agenda.

"The entire first phase of the Russian Revolution", continues Serge, "seems to me today to have been dominated by the utter honesty of Lenin and his group. It was this that attracted all of us to him."[14]

This attraction was universal, including in the United States, the citadel of world capitalism. "The mention of Lenin and Trotsky was wildly cheered by the audience", stated a report of a mass meeting in support of the Russian Revolution held at Carnegie Hall in New York, December 1917.[15]

The same was true in Glasgow, at a meeting of the Russian Political Refugees Defence Committee addressed by the great Scottish revolutionary, John Maclean. "When Maclean referred to Russia and to the supreme efforts of Lenin and Trotsky in the cause of socialism, the hall thundered with fervent applause", wrote Nan Milton, Maclean's daughter.[16]

The strategists of capitalism, on the other hand, were very alarmed. "Every day the situation grows worse, until many people are ready to declare that the United States will be the next victim of this dangerous malady", recorded *The New York Times*.[17] The "malady" they refer to was Bolshevism. With its growing attraction, according to the *The Washington Post*, "indignation in the Senate reached boiling point over the 'red' meetings…"[18]

The victory of Lenin and the Bolsheviks had created a revolutionary wave that swept across the world. In Germany, the most important country in the heart of Europe, workers and sailors rose up and overthrew the Kaiser and established councils, or soviets, in November 1918, and in doing so they brought the slaughter of the First World War to an end. The following year, short-lived Soviet Republics were founded in Bavaria and Hungary. There were unprecedented mutinies in the British and French armies. At Dover, Folkestone and Calais, soldiers' committees were formed on similar lines to the Russian Soviets. This fact was not lost on General Sir Henry Wilson, who stated: "The soldiers' delegation bore a dangerous resemblance to a Soviet. If such a practice were to spread, the consequences would be disastrous."[19]

Mutinous sailors had seized the HMS *Kilbride* at Milford Haven in South Wales and hoisted the red flag. On 8 January 1919, thousands of armed soldiers based at Park Royal in West London marched on Downing Street demanding to be demobilised. In the same month, a mass strike gripped Clydeside, as the government stationed tanks in George Square, Glasgow, and John Maclean hailed the Russian Revolution. A political general strike swept France with posters in every town proclaiming:

I strike to demand
First, the eight-hour day;
Second, total amnesty;
Third, rapid demobilisation;
Fourth, a just peace and disarmament.
I strike to protest against
First, intervention in Russia;
Second, income taxes on wages;
Third, martial law;
Fourth, the censorship.[20]

"We are running a race with Bolshevism, and the world is on fire", complained the American President Woodrow Wilson, as he saw the revolutionary wave spreading ever wider.[21]

Such were the effects of the Russian Revolution, that following a visit to Russia and a meeting with Lenin, the American journalist Lincoln Steffens said on his return: "I have been over into the future, and it works."[22] "It is the most tremendous movement of the human spirit in centuries", wrote another American, Albert Rhys Williams in 1919, who was also present in Russia.[23]

The Russian Revolution shook the world, embracing millions of ordinary workers worldwide, including those war-weary soldiers fighting in the trenches. It glowingly inspired those traditionally excluded from everyday politics and raised them to their feet. Its popularity also spread beyond the working class. One such unusual source of support for the revolution came from the silent movies. Lenin had admired Charlie Chaplin for his portrayal of down-and-out characters in films like *The Tramp* (1915). However, what is little known is that Chaplin also admired Lenin.

In September 1921, when Chaplin returned to London from the United States after becoming world famous, he was mobbed by well-wishers and asked questions by the press, the first one being:

"Are you a Bolshevik?"

"An artist", says Chaplin.

"Why do you want to visit Russia?"

"Because I am interested in any new idea", he replies.

"What do you think of Lenin?"

"I think him a very remarkable man", says Chaplin.

"Why?"

"Because he is expressing a new idea."[24]

In the same year, when Chaplin was working on *The Kid* (1921), one of his finest films, he met with the actor Buster Keaton. According to Keaton, Charlie talked "about something called communism which he just heard about…" "Communism", explained Chaplin, "was going to change everything, abolish poverty." He then banged on the table and said: "What I want is that every child should have enough to eat, shoes on his feet and a roof over his head."[25] This is just one small example of the impact of Lenin and the Russian Revolution, even on prominent figures from the world of culture.

Arthur Ransome, an English journalist who came from a middle-class background and who later became famous for writing children's books, was present in Russia in 1917 and personally witnessed the scenes in the soviets:

> I do not think I shall ever again be so happy in my life as I was during those first days when I saw working men and peasant soldiers sending representatives of their class and not mine. I remembered Shelley's,
>
> "Shake your chains to earth like dew
> Which in sleep had fallen on you –
> Ye are many – they are few"
>
> and wondered that this thing had not come to pass before.[26]

He continued:

> I felt I would willingly give the rest of my life if it could be divided into minutes and given to men in England and France so that those of little faith who say that the Russian Revolution is discredited could share for one minute each that wonderful experience.
>
> Of course no one who was able, as we were able, to watch the men of the revolution at close quarters could believe for a moment that they were the mere paid agents of the very power which more than all others represented the stronghold they had set out to destroy. We had the knowledge of the injustice being done to these men to urge us in their defence. But there was more in it than that. There was the feeling, from which we could never escape, of the creative effort of the revolution. There was the thing that distinguishes the creative from other artists, the living, vivifying expression of something hitherto hidden in the consciousness of humanity. If this book were to be an accurate record of my own impressions, all the drudgery, gossip, quarrels, arguments, events and experiences it contains would have to be set against a background of that extraordinary vitality which obstinately persists in Moscow even in these dark days of discomfort, disillusion, pestilence, starvation and unwanted war.[27]

"Whatever else they may think of him, not even his enemies deny that Vladimir Ilyich Ulyanov (Lenin) is one of the greatest personalities of his time", explained Ransome.[28]

As it turned out, Lenin was at the head of the Soviet Republic for only a relatively short period. He famously described Russia as a "besieged fortress", where the young Republic was continually under attack from all sides. Lenin was the victim of a failed assassination attempt at the end of August 1918, which lodged two bullets into his body and almost killed him. A few days after this attempt on his life, the *Manchester Guardian* jumped the gun and announced that Lenin had "died from his wounds", adding, "his murder was expected, for he had enemies in his own country." The article sneered: "No kind words will be wasted on his memory…"[29]

But Lenin survived his wounds and soon recovered. Nevertheless, following a punishing work schedule, Lenin suffered a series of strokes from May 1922 onwards, which incapacitated him and then robbed him of his speech. He finally passed away at the age of fifty-three on Monday 21 January 1924 from atherosclerosis, a restriction of the arteries. He therefore never managed to reach what he humorously described as his 'vice', which was to live to more than fifty-five years.

His death, when it came, was mourned by millions of ordinary workers and peasants, not only in Russia, but throughout the world.

At the time of the October Revolution there were also fair-weather friends attracted to the new 'experiment', which had become quite fashionable. Some even made the pilgrimage to Moscow. One of these was the young philosopher Bertrand Russell, who was part of an official delegation to Russia in 1920. He managed to have an hour-long conversation with Lenin. Russell seemed suitably impressed, so much so that immediately following Lenin's death, he wrote the following:

> The death of Lenin makes the world poorer by the loss of one of the really great men produced by the war. It seems probable that our age will go down in history as that of Lenin and Einstein – the two men who have succeeded in a great work of synthesis in an analytic age, one in thought, the other in action. Lenin appeared to the outraged bourgeoisie of the world as a destroyer, but it was not the work of destruction that made him pre-eminent. Others could have destroyed, but I doubt whether any other living man could have built so well on the new foundations. His mind was orderly and creative: he was a philosophical system-maker in the sphere of practice… Statesmen of his calibre do not appear in the world more than about once in a century, a few of us are likely to live to see his equal.[30]

Russell subsequently wrote a book soon after his trip to Russia, *The Practice and Theory of Bolshevism* (1920), in which he stated:

> The Russian Revolution is one of the great heroic events of the world's history…
> I believe that Communism is necessary to the world, and I believe that the heroism of Russia has fired men's hopes in a way which was essential to the realisation of Communism in the future. Regarded as a splendid attempt, without which ultimate success would have been very improbable, Bolshevism deserves the gratitude and admiration of all the progressive part of mankind.[31]

However, in his autobiography, written much later in life, Bertrand Russell's "gratitude and admiration" had waned, and he was singing a rather different tune. Fifty years on, he found Lenin "rather disappointing", sensing an "impish cruelty" in him and comparing him to "an opinionated professor", which sharply contradicted his earlier assessment.[32] What his later opinion of Einstein was, we do not know. Clearly, it seems to prove the point that, for some, if not all, the older one gets, the more conservative and jaundiced one tends to become. This was certainly the case of Bertrand, 3rd Earl Russell, son of Viscount Amberley and Katherine, daughter of 2nd Baron Stanley of

Alderley. Whatever these former 'radicals' may say, even today, despite all the slanders thrown at him, Lenin's name still resonates with millions, and increasingly with young people.

Rather than an "impish cruelty", Lenin had, on the contrary, a real sense of humour and personal warmth, which Ransome brings out in his writings. "He shook with laughter", wrote Ransome, "laughing over one thing or another."[33] Maxim Gorky also commented about Lenin's chuckling and smiling repeatedly when they talked. "He loved fun, and when he laughed it was with his whole body; he was quite overcome with laughter and would laugh sometimes until he cried."[34] All those who ever met Lenin were struck, not only by his intellect but also by his great sense of humour, an aspect which his detractors wish to eradicate or ignore. They make no mention of this for the simple reason that a sense of humour doesn't quite fit with the 'narrative' of a bloodthirsty dictator.

Lenin considered the rules always applied to him as much as anyone else, a stark contrast to the bourgeois politicians of today. Even as the head of the Soviet Government, on 1 September 1920 he wrote humbly to the librarian of the Rumyantsev Museum, asking if he could have permission to borrow some books on Greek philosophy for one day. "If, according to the rules, reference publications are not issued for home use, could not one get them for an evening, for the night, when the Library is closed. *I will return them by the morning*", he assured.[35]

Balabanoff recalled a time in March 1918 when she and Lenin visited the Moscow Art Theatre to see Chekhov's *Three Sisters*. When they turned up at the theatre, they discovered the place was full and there were no seats left. They were on their way out, when someone called out: "Can't we add two more seats for Lenin and Balabanoff?" They were given seats, but this small incident showed an embarrassed Lenin's aversion to any preferential treatment.

In his life, Lenin showed the greatest simplicity and modesty. He also had a warmth of personality. "When I came to know Lenin better", remarked Lunacharsky, "I appreciated yet another side of him which is not immediately obvious – his astonishing vitality. Life bubbles and sparkles within him."[36]

Lenin was obviously a man of great patience. He was, after all, prepared to give up his precious time to talk to and humour a stream of interested 'well-wishers', the usual philistines, full of their own pretentious opinions of how things should be run. One such encounter was with the English writer and reformist, HG Wells, who wrote an article under the title 'The Dreamer

1. Lenin with HG Wells

in the Kremlin', after an hour's talk with Lenin. It was full of commonplace verbiage such as "Lenin has a pleasant, quick-changing brownish face with a lively smile…"[37] Wells, while he held a sympathetic view towards Russia, was a typical drawing-room socialist, full of advice for the Soviet leader at a time of great difficulties. He was struck by Lenin's plan for electrification, which he dismissed as a "Utopia of the electricians".[38] Following the meeting, Lenin couldn't help repeatedly sighing to Trotsky: "Oh, what a Philistine!"[39] This remark was characteristic of him when he felt inwardly ashamed for another man.

In fact, there is a rather telling photograph of this meeting, featured here, between Lenin and Wells, where Lenin has his hand over his face, trying to hold back a wry smile, which speaks volumes.

He certainly had a broad vision, a world-view, and saw everything in its context and relationship with other things. He would often remark that truth was concrete, and was disparaging of those who engaged in idle speculation and flights of fancy. He always maintained a sense of proportion, even in the most trying of circumstances. In times of great peril, and there were many, Lenin did not try to prettify the situation, but attempted to soberly explain the issues. "Let us not be afraid to call a spade a spade", he would say. In that way, he was not afraid of telling the truth and, above all, he taught his comrades likewise not to be afraid of facing up to difficulties.

These qualities stand out sharply in contrast with today's bourgeois politicians, the Lilliputians and charlatans who brazenly lie through their teeth at every opportunity.

Lenin venerated the truth and had a healthy contempt for 'prestige politics', of false boasting, chest-beating and hollow exaggeration, which serves no purpose but to pull the wool over people's eyes. He was very much down to earth and, above all, a political *realist*. He knew that there were no shortcuts and that you could not reap where you had not sown.

As a leader, the only authority he possessed was a political one, nothing more. There were many occasions in his life where he was in a minority, even of one, within the Bolshevik Party. When he established the newspaper *Vperyod* (*Forward*) in 1905, he sometimes found his articles rejected by the editors. The same was true much later in the newspapers *Proletary*, *Sotsial-Democrat* and *Pravda*. He found himself in a minority in the Bolshevik faction between 1907 and 1909, then in the lead-up to 1912. The same was true in the spring of 1917, and in the autumn of that year; then again after the victory of the Bolshevik Revolution. Despite his undoubted authority, we see how all this is a far cry from his fearsome, 'dictatorial methods' claimed by his bourgeois critics.

In March 1921, he wrote a letter of complaint to Joffe, who had equated Lenin to the Central Committee:

> First, you are wrong in saying (repeatedly) that "I am the CC". This could have been written only in a state of great nervous irritation and overwork. The old CC (1919-1920) defeated me on one of the vastly important questions, as you know from the discussion. I cannot say how many times I have been in a minority on organisational and personal matters. You must have seen this for yourself on many occasions as a member of the CC.
>
> You should not allow yourself to be so nervous as to write *an absolutely impossible, absolutely impossible* thing that I am the CC. This is overwork.[40]

By any measure, Lenin was truly a giant of history. Even a hundred years after his death, his name is synonymous with his life's ambition: revolution and communism. It is for this reason that the defenders of capitalism, consumed by their own fears, are forced to slander him at every opportunity. This is nothing new and comes as no surprise. Lenin himself explained in *State and Revolution*:

During the lifetime of great revolutionaries, the oppressing classes have invariably meted out to them relentless persecution, and received their teaching with the most savage hostility, most furious hatred, and a ruthless campaign of lies and slander.[41]

Their hatred of him has no bounds, and continues right up to the present day. Without doubt, Lenin has become the most denigrated revolutionary leader in history.

There was a similar degree of hatred in the treatment of Oliver Cromwell, following the Restoration of the monarchy in 1660. In revenge for the English Revolution and the killing of Charles I, the Stuart counter-revolution dug up Cromwell's corpse, cut off his head and publicly hung his body in chains, and then later flung it into a pit. His severed head was displayed outside Westminster Hall for some twenty years.

In a similar vein, the bourgeoisie today seeks to disembowel the memory and significance of Lenin. In Russia today, the supporters of the bourgeois counter-revolution have demanded the removal of his body from Red Square, as his corpse is a painful reminder of the overthrow of landlordism and capitalism. Like Banquo's ghost, his image casts a long shadow over them.

Lenin's reputation also stands out in marked contrast to those Labour and trade union leaders – a veritable rogues' gallery of class traitors – who sold out the working class for thirty pieces of silver or some ermine cloth. But the apologists of capitalism knew that the genuine revolutionary Vladimir Ilyich Lenin could never be bought! Lenin stood for uncompromising class war against capitalism, as opposed to the reformist social climbers, self-seekers and careerists.

History has shown the brutal vengeance that the ruling class metes out to those who cannot be bought off and who dare to rise up against them. More than 2,000 years ago, the ruling patrician, General Marcus Licinius Crassus, said that his military campaign to hunt down Spartacus and his slave revolt was not about killing the man, but about killing the *spirit* of Spartacus. For them, Spartacus *personified* the uprising of a hundred thousand slaves. A clear message needed to be sent out, and by way of an example, they showed no mercy and crucified 6,000 captured slaves along the Appian Way from Capua up to the walls of Rome.

The ruling classes of today have the same approach towards Lenin as the patricians had towards Spartacus. He must be ideologically 'crucified' and his name trampled in the dust. The hired bourgeois historians, who dutifully do their masters' bidding, can therefore never be 'objective' where Lenin and the Russian Revolution are concerned. Distortions, lies and slander are all part of their propaganda. For them, it is war to the knife, where there are no prisoners taken. Everything is done to justify and preserve the capitalist system, and nothing must be allowed to get in the way of this. Lenin knew his enemies well. He was not surprised by their reaction and violence, which was dictated by their class interests.

The present work answers this avalanche of falsehoods and distortions of people whose sole function is to vilify him. It puts forward a defence of the real Lenin and the ideas he stood for. In such a defence, it is important, as far as possible, to allow Lenin to speak for himself. We therefore make no apologies for quoting extensively from him throughout the book.

Certainly, Lenin left behind no shortage of material. Even according to Volkogonov, there are 3,724 documents of Lenin that are still unpublished, but these remain within the closed archives in Moscow.*

Nevertheless, even without this missing material, there is already enough to answer the distortions and reveal the real, authentic Lenin, the true standard bearer of orthodox Marxism. His writings constitute a treasure house of the Marxist method and its application.

When reading Lenin, including his personal correspondence, what immediately strikes you is not only his grasp of the subject matter, but his *complete honesty*. Where mistakes are made, he does not attempt to cover them up, but seeks to learn from them and thereby strengthen his and others' understanding.

Some on the 'left' to this day, demoralised and lacking any perspective, are inclined to swallow this anti-Lenin nonsense, which they naively take at face value. Therefore, the centenary of Lenin's death will be another opportunity by the bourgeois commentators to bring out the usual bile of twisted lies and distortions. Their purpose is to show that no one in their right mind could have anything to do with such a toxic individual as Lenin – and should therefore stay clear of him and his ideas.

This campaign has intensified in recent times and the howls have grown louder. There is a very good reason for this. At the present time, as

---

* There have been five editions of *Lenin's Collected Works*, the first of which came out between 1920 and 1926 and numbered twenty volumes in Russian. The second and third (which have the same contents) numbered thirty volumes and were produced between 1930 and 1932. The fourth, which was known as the 'Stalin edition', came out between 1941 and 1957 in thirty-five volumes. The fifth, described as the 'Complete Edition', was published between 1958 and 1965, running to fifty-five volumes in Russian, and forty-five in English, which are used in this work. A sixth was in preparation, when the August 1991 coup stopped production, which was to have been at least seventy volumes in Russian.

is abundantly clear, the capitalist system is in a deep crisis. The growth of anti-capitalist feeling means that the ruling class will again be haunted by the threat of revolution. This was revealed in an article in *The Washington Post* on the centenary of the Russian Revolution, entitled: '100 years later, Bolshevism is back. And we should be worried'.[42]

In these turbulent times, Lenin's ideas of world revolution are becoming more attractive to those seeking a way out of this world of war and suffering. Events are transforming consciousness everywhere. According to a YouGov poll about the popularity of Lenin, only 4 per cent of baby boomers have a positive view of Lenin, but amongst millennials, this figure is 40 per cent. Unfortunately, it did not give the figure for the Generation Z youth, but this would have been certainly much higher, as all they have ever experienced is life under capitalist crisis.

A YouGov poll from 2019, before the pandemic, found that a third of US millennials approved of communism, while the popularity of capitalism has slumped.[43] A year later, it was reported that the number of young Americans who have a favourable view of Marxism had increased five-fold in just one year.[44] Bloomberg is describing it as a "youth quake".[45]

A spectre is once again haunting the world, the spectre of Leninism, to paraphrase *The Communist Manifesto*. And on the centenary of Lenin's death, we believe the time is ripe to publish a book about this extraordinary man, his ideas and his lifelong fight for communism. It is the task of the new generation to absorb the lessons provided by Lenin as they fight for a new world free of misery, hunger, war and exploitation. In the words of *The Communist Manifesto*:

> The Communists disdain to conceal their views and aims. They openly declare that their ends can be attained only by the forcible overthrow of all existing social conditions. Let the ruling classes tremble at a Communistic revolution. The proletarians have nothing to lose but their chains. They have a world to win.
>
> *Workers of all countries, unite!*[46]

1. Lenin's Roots

Vladimir Ilyich Ulyanov (Lenin) was born in the small town of Simbirsk (modern-day Ulyanovsk) on 22 April 1870, according to the New Style Gregorian calendar. In the Old Style calendar it is recorded as 10 April.*

He did not come from the working class. On the contrary, Lenin's social roots were in the middle-class intelligentsia. It might seem strange, at first sight, that the future leader of the revolutionary proletariat came from a relatively privileged background. But this was by no means an exceptional case. The same was true of Trotsky, Plekhanov, Rosa Luxemburg – not to speak of Marx and Engels, for that matter. Marx's wife actually came from an aristocratic Prussian family, while Engels came from a very bourgeois background. His father was the owner of cotton mills in Salford and Barmen.

Nevertheless, they all had one thing in common: they had all broken from their class background and had come over – without reservation – to the standpoint of the working class. In doing so, they provided the working class with their greatest revolutionary leaders and theoreticians.

What drove Lenin to pursue this revolutionary road was not down to any single cause. Different factors in his life coalesced to bring this about. As a young man, he developed a thirst for ideas, which pushed him to read extensively and served to widen his horizons.

The world he was growing up in certainly had an impact on his outlook. One incident clearly stands out: the death of his brother Alexander, hanged for terrorism at the age of twenty-one for the part he had played in an attempted assassination of the tsar.

---

* See Note on Dates, page xviii.

2. Simbirsk – postcard from c. 1900

Lenin's simmering hatred of tsarism, together with his family associations with an executed state criminal, meant he was clearly open to revolutionary feelings and thoughts. Later on, his study of Marx's writings and his discussions with the older generation of revolutionaries gradually provided these early revolutionary stirrings with form and content.

However, this radical outlook was far from unique for a definite layer of young people in Russia. In the heyday of the Narodniks ('Populists'), thousands of individuals, many of them students from the upper class, abandoned everything and went 'to the people' – that is to say, to the village poor. It is possible that the young Vladimir Ilyich may have sympathised with those ideas at first. But over time, his active brain became attracted to the ideas of revolutionary Marxism, which had begun to percolate from Western Europe through the porous borders of the Russian Empire.

Ilyich was born less than a decade after the so-called emancipation of the Russian serfs. The town of Simbirsk, where he was brought up, had a population of around 30,000 and was part of a vast area dominated by the Volga river, the longest river in Europe, which flows through Central and Southern Russia into the Caspian Sea.

The region had experienced two important rebellions: the first was in 1670-71, led by Stepan Razin, who attempted to "wipe out the notables and the boyars", and the second was led by Yemelyan Pugachev in 1773-75. Both of these rebellions were put down in blood. Pugachev was decapitated in Red

3. Stepan Razin   4. Yemelyan Pugachev

Square. "These two Volga rebellions", notes Trotsky, "constitute the authentic peasant-revolutionary tradition of old Russia."[1] This rebellious spirit was born out of the seething discontent in this rural, peasant-based region, ruled for centuries by a privileged landowning nobility. The majority of the peasants, as elsewhere in tsarist Russia, scraped a living from the soil, and led lives little different from pack animals. "What's a poor peasant to a gentleman? Why he's worse than a dog. At least a dog can bite", stated a peasant who was arrested for failing to remove his hat before a captain.[2]

Abolition of serfdom

The period of Vladimir Ilyich's early life – in the decades of the 1870s and 1880s – was one of social and political turmoil within the country. The Great Russian Empire, that 'prison house of nations', was undergoing profound changes under Tsar Alexander II. In 1861, serfdom had been abolished by decree, which was supposed to bring about the liberation of the peasantry from their enslavement.

But despite this proclamation, the serfs still remained shackled to the landlords and markets. Completely bewildered, the mass of peasants wondered why one-half of the land they had previously worked was still in the hands of the landlords. Furthermore, the land they were allowed to buy came with strings attached. To obtain this land, they were forced to pay a hefty tax to the state in instalments for the next forty-nine years, with interest. The landlords did not lose out, as they were immediately compensated by the state. In reality, the 'emancipated' serfs would carry the burden of their own liberation well into the next century.

In practice, the 1861 decree was a bourgeois reform carried out from the top by feudal landowners. It was an attempt to 'reform' Russia 'from above', taking care not to destroy tsarism or the roots of landlordism. The 'emancipated' peasant had simply swapped one oppressor for another; one form of slavery for another. As Lenin explained later:

> It was the landowners themselves, the landowning government of the autocratic tsar and his officials, that 'emancipated' the peasants in Russia. And these 'emancipators' manipulated matters *in such a way* that the peasants entered 'freedom' stripped to the point of pauperism; they were released from slavery to the landowners to fall into bondage to the very same landowners and their flunkeys.
>
> The noble landowners 'emancipated' the Russian peasants in such a way that *more than a fifth* of all the peasant land was cut off and taken away by the landlords. The peasants were compelled to pay *redemption money*, i.e. tribute to the former slaveholders, for their own peasant land drenched with their sweat and blood. The peasants paid hundreds of millions of rubles in such tribute to the feudal lords, thus lapsing into ever greater poverty.[3]

It was to take a further fifty-six years, with the victory of the October Revolution of 1917, before the land would eventually be given over to the peasants.

Land of plough and ox

While in Western Europe the vestiges of feudalism had been largely swept away, Russian society remained mired in semi-feudal backwardness. Some 87 per cent of the population of the Russian territories lived on the land in the most backward, semi-medieval conditions. Tsarist Russia was commonly known as the land of the wooden plough and the ox. The remainder of the population lived in the towns and cities, like St. Petersburg and Moscow. The total population was 74 million in 1861, but this rose to 126 million by the end of the century.

The Russian Empire was ruled by a landowning aristocracy with an absolute ruler, the tsar (a word derived from the Roman title, Caesar), as the absolute monarch at the top of this social pyramid. Beneath them, the sea of peasants were bled dry, while the power and wealth of the landlords and Holy Mother Church was greatly enhanced.

The regime of the Romanovs constituted a form of Asiatic despotism, which became the bulwark of European reaction. Russian despotism was a colossus that spanned one-sixth of the earth's surface and introduced the world to the blessings of tsar, pogroms (the organised massacre of an ethnic group), and the knout, a heavy scourge-like instrument used for flogging. Such was the brutality of the regime that Nicholas I was notoriously known as 'The Knout'.

As a social group, it was the Jews who suffered most at the hands of the Great Russian chauvinists during the years of tsarism. In fact, under Nicholas II, anti-Jewish pogroms were considered an act of patriotism that glorified God, the Tsar, and the Fatherland. The last two tsars of 'All the Russias' openly revelled in their antisemitism, which was rife among the ruling elite. "Bozhe Tsaria Khrani!" ("God Save the Tsar!") was traditionally combined with the cry of "Bey Zhidov!" ("Beat the Jews!"). It became an established ritual of tsarism, which was put into practice by the bloody work of the fascist Black Hundreds.[4]

The brutal life of the peasants, which constituted the vast majority of the population, was dominated by religious superstition, backwardness and violence. It was regarded as a God-given right that a husband should beat his wife. In such a society, adulterous wives and horse-thieves received the harshest of punishments, with women being stripped naked and beaten in public, while horse-thieves were castrated, branded with hot irons or hacked to death with sickles.

Into the factories

Increasingly, landless peasants were driven from the countryside by extreme poverty in search of work in the towns, where factories had been established by foreign capital. This was especially the case with the youth, who were desperate to escape the misery of rural life. They were to become the new Russian proletariat, regarded by the capitalists merely as a source of raw material for exploitation and super profits. The conditions in the factories, such as the huge Putilov metalworks in St. Petersburg, were abysmal. The workers were treated little better than animals and housed in hovels. At the same time, many capitalists were growing fat from government contracts.

The belated shoots of Russian capitalism had produced a feeble bourgeois class, which clung to the coat-tails of the landlords, foreign capitalists and bankers, who in turn clung to the old tsarist autocracy.

This meant the bourgeoisie was incapable of carrying out a bourgeois-democratic revolution that would sweep away the relics of feudalism and so lay the basis for modern capitalist development. Instead, the bourgeois-liberals desperately hoped the tsarist regime would 'self-reform' and Russia would draw closer to Europe, allowing them to play a more leading role. While they yearned for a taste of political power, they were terrified of revolution, as well as giving leadership to the peasant masses who were desperate for the land. In the wise words of Peter Struve, "the further to the East one goes in Europe, the weaker in politics, the more cowardly, and the baser becomes the bourgeoisie."[5]

The Russian intelligentsia, feeling the impasse of society, acted like a social barometer. Choked and suffocated by tsarism, denied the liberties they yearned for, as in the West, they were in a continual state of ferment. This middling stratum became the transmission belt for revolutionary ideas in the youth, especially the students, who were eager for change.

They formed the fertile soil in which Narodnism grew: a broad and diverse revolutionary movement that spanned the ideas of anarchism to its left and bourgeois liberalism to its right. The Narodniks, influenced by utopian socialism, held the idea that the Russian peasantry (the 'people'; *Narod* is the Russian word for people) could bypass capitalism and make the leap to a form of rural 'communism'.

Chernyshevsky

There are many people who can be said to have had an influence on the Narodnik movement. However, Nikolai Chernyshevsky, along with Alexander Herzen, could be considered the founding father of Narodnism. Chernyshevsky was a political writer and socialist, who attacked the so-called 'emancipation' of the serfs as robbery and became a symbol of resistance for a whole generation of radicalised youth.

For his opposition to tsarism, Chernyshevsky was condemned to twenty years of imprisonment and exile, including several years of hard labour. The manuscript of his book, *What Is to Be Done?*, which he smuggled out of prison and got published, made an enormous impact on the youth of Russia, including the young Vladimir Ilyich Ulyanov.

The young Lenin was so enthusiastic about Chernyshevsky's book, which was a novel, that he read it five times during one summer. "It completely reshaped me", he told Nikolai Valentinov, who shared lodgings with Lenin in 1904. "This is a book that changes one for a whole lifetime", he said.[6] Nadezhda Krupskaya, Ilyich's lifelong partner and comrade, confirmed that he had an intimate knowledge of Chernyshevsky. "I was surprised to see how attentively he read that novel, and how he took note of all the very fine nuances that are to be found in it", she explained.[7]

5. Nikolay Chernyshevsky   6. *What Is to Be Done?* (1867)

In fact, during his life, Lenin cited Chernyshevsky more than any other writer, over 300 times in his *Collected Works*. It is therefore no accident that Lenin adopted the title of Chernyshevsky's novel for his own book in 1902. In particular, Lenin shared the author's profound hostility towards liberalism, which remained with him throughout his life. Krupskaya confirmed this view:

> If we review Lenin's subsequent activity, we see that Chernyshevsky infected him with his intransigent attitude to Liberalism. Mistrust in Liberal phrases, in the whole position of Liberalism, runs like a red thread throughout all Lenin's activity.[8]

The Ulyanov family

As with any young man, Lenin's family life had a major impact on his development, but in ways they never contemplated. His father was a person of standing. Ilya Nikolayevich Ulyanov was originally a teacher, who then became a high-ranking official in the Simbirsk region, having been promoted from an inspector of public schools to the post of Director of Schools.

As a result of his work and diligence in establishing schools, Ilyich's father was awarded several decorations, including the Order of Stanislav, First Class. He was then raised to the rank of 'State Councillor', a hereditary title of

7. Ilya Nikolayevich Ulyanov   8. Maria Alexandrovna Ulyanova

nobility. This position provided the family with social status, stability and, above all, a steady income.

Ilya Nikolayevich was a devout member of the Orthodox church and, given his position, was also a firm supporter of the tsarist regime. According to Lenin's elder sister, Anna, her father "had never been a revolutionary and wanted to protect the young from that way of thinking. He much admired Alexander II, whose reign, especially its first phase, was for him 'a bright period'."[9] Nevertheless, given his lifelong promotion of education, he held a certain tolerant outlook towards his children.

Lenin's mother, Maria Alexandrovna, came from a very well-off background, with Jewish roots. Her father, Alexander Dimitrievich Blank, had been a doctor and owner of a large estate, which would later be used by the Ulyanov family for summer holidays. When Anna Ulyanova traced the Jewish lineage on this side of the family in 1932, she approached Stalin about using this fact against antisemitism, which still simmered. But he refused, insisting this fact should remain buried.*

According to his granddaughter, Dimitrievich Blank was a man of advanced views for his time, which mirrored the growing ferment in the intelligentsia. He married a German woman who brought up his children,

---

* Stalin certainly stirred up antisemitism and used it against the leaders of the Left Opposition. In her memoirs, Stalin's daughter Svetlana Alliluyeva attributed her father's antisemitism to his struggle against Trotsky and the Left Opposition. According to her, this became an aggressive, official ideology, "spreading far and wide with the speed of a plague." (Rogovin, Vadim, *1937: Stalin's Year of Terror*, Mehring Books, 1998 p. 160)

9. The Ulyanov family in 1879
Standing children (left to right): Olga, Alexander, Anna
Seated children: Maria, Dmitri, Vladimir Ilyich

including Lenin's mother, in her native ways and traditions. Some years after Dimitrievich's death, his grandchildren moved into his large country house, where they discovered a wide collection of radical literature left behind by an unknown uncle. As avid readers, different radical and revolutionary ideas began to seep through these cracks into the family.

Although Lenin's mother did not attend university, she was well-educated and was widely read in European literature. She also learned music, played the piano and spoke Russian, German and French fluently. As a result of her cultured background, she was inclined to progressive ideas.

Maria Alexandrovna learned the virtues of being neat and orderly, as well as industrious. Krupskaya, who knew Lenin's mother very well, was convinced that her son had inherited his organising ability from her. This view was repeated by Maria, Lenin's younger sister:

10. Vladimir Ilyich and Olga Ilyinichna in 1874

Characteristic of Vladimir Ilyich were his great punctuality and thoroughness and his strict economy in spending money, especially on himself. Vladimir Ilyich probably inherited these qualities from our mother, whom he resembled in many ways. Our mother was of German descent on her mother's side, and these qualities were deeply ingrained in her character.[10]

As husband and wife, Ilya Nikolayevich and Maria Alexandrovna were happily married and had eight children, but two, Olga and Nikolay, born in 1868 and 1873, died young. Their first child, Anna, was born in 1864. The next eldest was Alexander, affectionately called Sasha, born in 1866, and who was regarded as the pride and joy of the whole family.

Vladimir Ilyich, known as Volodya within the family, was the third eldest who survived, born in 1870. The subsequent children in the Ulyanov family were a second Olga, born in 1871; Dmitry, born in 1874; and Maria, or Maniasha, as she was affectionately called, born in 1878. "We were a friendly and closely-knit family", said one of Lenin's sisters.[11] Out of all his brothers and sisters, Lenin was closest to Olga, probably due to the closeness of their ages, and he was deeply affected by her premature death at the age of nineteen.

The third eldest child, the future Lenin, was christened with the imposing Slavonic name Vladimir, which means lord or ruler of the earth. For those of a religious disposition, this fact would have great significance. "The parents and priest hardly suspected that the name contained a prophecy", notes Trotsky:

> This boy born on the Volga was destined to become the leader and ruler of a people. Simbirsk was to become Ulyanovsk. The Simbirsk Assembly Hall of Nobles was to become The Lenin Palace of Books. And the Russia of the tsars was to be transformed into the Union of Soviet Socialist Republics.[12]

Such is the unexpected path of history.

As respectable middle-class parents, the Ulyanovs focused their attention on their children's education and future prospects. At home, Shakespeare, Goethe and Pushkin, among other writers, were read aloud on Sunday afternoons. Volodya's mother taught him French, German and English. There were days when 'German only' or 'French only' were spoken. Maria Alexandrovna acted in reality as a tutor for each of her children.

The young Vladimir Ilyich certainly had all the advantages of a decent education, schooling and settled family life, which provided him with the benefits of a strong intellectual foundation. Volodya was very diligent. For instance, in preparation for an essay he would make extensive notes and was meticulous with references. This was an important basis for his future political development.

Rise of the Narodniks

By Russian standards, the Ulyanovs could be considered a fairly prosperous middle-class family. However, it was precisely this class that was being shaken by the upheavals in Russia, epitomised by the rise of the great Narodnik movement that swept the country. Trotsky writes:

> One cannot understand the destiny of the Ulyanov family without understanding the logic of this earlier independent revolutionary movement of the Russian intelligentsia, and therewith the logic of its collapse.[13]

The Narodnik movement was inspired by a number of radical figures, like Chernyshevsky, Nikolay Dobrolyubov, Bakunin, Pyotr Lavrov and Alexander Herzen, all of whom urged the student youth to dedicate themselves to the liberation of the people ('going to the people').

Herzen had published his anti-tsarist newspapers, *Polar Star* and *Bell*, from exile in London in the fifties and sixties. Even today there is a plaque on a house in Orsett Terrace, Westminster, commemorating his stay in the capital from which he fomented rebellion. His clarion call was taken up

11. Alexander Herzen   12. Vera Zasulich

enthusiastically by a generation of radicalised youth. However, the movement
tended to idealise the peasants and their readiness for revolution, as reflected
in their communes. Bakunin even went as far as to declare that the Russian
peasants were "born socialists".

In April 1866, a failed assassination attempt of the tsar resulted in the
execution of a young student, Dimitri Karakozov. This act of terrorism sent
shock waves through the regime and introduced panic in the ruling circles.
The regime soon regained its nerve and engaged in a campaign of repression
against these young revolutionaries, who had left their mark for the future.
As Lenin remarked, "Nearly all had in their early youth enthusiastically
worshipped the terrorist heroes."[14] But the repression put an end to this wave.

In the early 1870s, a new upsurge arose culminating in the 'summer of
madness' of 1874, when as many as 3,000 students, many of them young
women, abandoned their studies and even their families and went 'to the
people'. They had no definite programme but were gripped by a youthful
idealism. But the peasantry, although discontented, was still immersed in
backwardness and was unmoved by this revolutionary propaganda. Neither
the Volga nor the Don answered the call to revolution.

Contrary to the suppositions of Bakunin, the peasants regarded the
students with suspicion. They reacted to revolutionary propaganda with
indifference and even hostility, often turning these young revolutionaries

over to the authorities. As a result, there were widespread arrests, and the movement 'to the people' once again suffered a defeat.

The Narodnik movement regrouped and in 1876 established an organisation called *Zemlya i Volya* (Land and Freedom), which gave the struggle greater coordination. They likewise believed in the old Narodnik idea that Russia would bypass industrialisation and would not create a working class as in the West, but would somehow leap from peasant small-scale production to a commune-based socialism.

However, the methods of the *Zemlya i Volya* were firmly based on terrorism as the only means of removing tsarism. There had been terrorist acts before, mainly as acts of revenge against landlords and the like. But with the formation of *Zemlya i Volya*, terrorism acquired a greater *political* significance. They targeted hated police chiefs, ministers, tyrants, torturers and suchlike for assassination. They hoped that the example of their heroic deeds would inspire the peasantry to act. In doing so, they called for the formation of fighting units. Given the repressive nature of tsarism, such groupings could only exist as underground organisations.

On 24 January 1878, the courageous young female student Vera Zasulich, one of their members, shot and wounded General Trepov, the St. Petersburg chief of police. Trepov had recently ordered a prisoner, Arkhip Bogolyubov, to be flogged for failing to remove his cap in his presence. A prominent trial took place, presided over by a liberal judge, and Zasulich was eventually acquitted by the jury. She became a populist heroine, and fled to Switzerland, where she later joined the Marxists and established contact with Friedrich Engels in London, eventually helping to found Russian Social-Democracy.*

Narodnaya Volya

There were always tensions in the movement and a division opened up between those who favoured terrorist methods and those, such as Lavrov, who leaned towards propaganda aimed at the masses. Some were moving away from revolution to reformism, doing what they described as 'little things'.

---

* The term 'Social-Democracy' and 'Social-Democrat' had a radically different meaning at this time. In fact, it meant the opposite of what it means today. In this early period, a Social-Democrat was someone who was a committed revolutionary and Marxist, while today, the term describes right-wing reformists within the labour movement who are hardly distinguishable from bourgeois politicians.

After the October Revolution, the Bolsheviks abandoned the term 'Social-Democrat' altogether in favour of 'Communist', which reflected a return to Marx, Engels and *The Communist Manifesto*, and meant the adoption of a clean, unstained banner following the betrayal of August 1914.

This ended in a split between the two tendencies at the Congress of Voronezh in 1879. The pro-terrorist wing took the name of *Narodnaya Volya* (People's Will). Those opposed attempted to establish a group with the name of *Chernyi Peredel* (Black Repartition), which aimed to distribute the land among the 'black' people (the peasants). The leader of this latter group was a man called Georgi Plekhanov.

Although this group failed to develop, most significantly from our point of view, it later became a bridge to Marxism in Russia.

The individual terrorism of the *Narodnaya Volya* was known as the 'propaganda of the deed'. As one of their leaflets explained:

> Just as in the days of yore the peoples' battles were fought out by their leaders in single combat, so now the terrorists will win Russia's freedom in single combat with the autocracy.[15]

This method involved a handful of revolutionaries, where the masses were excluded and regarded merely as passive onlookers. "The warrior replaced the apostle", comments Trotsky.[16] Through such daring examples, they hoped to inspire others. "History is too slow", said one of its leaders, Andrei Zhelyabov. "We must hurry it on."[17]

The mailed fist of tsarism forced the Russian intelligentsia to arm itself with extreme ideas and large quantities of dynamite. It was regarded by both sides as a fight to the finish. However, this was a blind alley, later described by Lenin as "the theory of single combat",[18] which "has the immediate effect of simply creating a short-lived sensation, while indirectly it even leads to apathy and passive waiting for the next *bout*."[19]

Following twelve years of failed assassination attempts, on Sunday 13 March 1881, the young terrorists of the *Narodnaya Volya* finally succeeded in killing Tsar Alexander II. However, this did not result in the destruction of tsarism. Paradoxically, this very success sealed the fate of the *Narodnaya Volya*.

The people did not rise up and the terrorist movement suffered brutal repression from the tsarist state. Five revolutionaries were hanged, while others were sentenced to long prison terms and exile. The new Tsar, Alexander III, issued a manifesto which stated:

> We proclaim this to all Our faithful subjects: God in His ineffable judgement has deemed it proper to culminate the glorious reign of Our beloved father with a martyr's death, and to lay the Holy duty of Autocratic Rule on us.[20]

Disintegration

As the blows of state repression rained down, and arrests and executions intensified, the *Narodnaya Volya*, composed of a dedicated few – less than fifty in total – was completely smashed. Trotsky explains:

> Very likely, there was no shortage of young men and women ready to blow themselves up along with their bombs. But there was now no one to unite and guide them. The party was disintegrating. By its very nature, the terror used up the forces supplied to it during the propaganda period long before it could create new ones. "We are using up our capital", said the leader of the People's Will, Zhelyabov. Furthermore, while individual tyrants could be eliminated, the tyrannical institutions remained. To be sure, the trial of the assassins of the tsar evoked a passionate response in the hearts of the individual young people. Although Petersburg was soon swept all too clean by the police, People's Will groups continued to spring up in various provinces until 1885. However, this did not go to the point of a new wave of terror. Having burned their fingers, the great majority of the intelligentsia recoiled from the revolutionary fire.[21]

Despite all attempts to stay clear of politics, the Ulyanov family was not immune to these upheavals. The young eleven-year-old Lenin was certainly aware of the tsar's assassination, as services were held in schools and churches where priests spitefully denounced the regicide. Having said that, he was generally unaware of the unfolding political drama.

At this point in his life, the young boy was completely absorbed in his studies and literature. The bookcases in the house contained works by Zola, Daudet, Victor Hugo, Heine, Schiller and Goethe, as well as the Russian classics. He liked to read the novels of Turgenev. But Latin was his passion, and he immersed himself in the classics, where Cicero was his favourite. He had become so proficient in Latin that he was able to coach his older sister, Anna. He also developed an enthusiasm for chess.

Ilyich, by all accounts, had been a happy and contented child. He enjoyed his pastimes, which included playing music and chess with his siblings and with his father. He and his brother Sasha played for hours on end. They enjoyed playing the piano and singing together. Volodya looked up to his brother, and whenever asked to make a decision about something, he would answer: "I'd do what Alexander would do." He had a sense of humour and would always tease his younger brothers and sisters. He also developed wider interests, which according to his sister included "sport – shooting, skating, cycling and chess", and he "engaged in these amusements with all the ingenuousness of a youth..."[22]

All this provides a most effective antidote to the sinister picture of his childhood painted by malicious bourgeois historians, whose class hatred and venomous spitefulness compel them to attempt to trace his 'inhuman' characteristics back to his family upbringing.

The 'crowned idiot'

The new tsar, Alexander III, the Emperor of All the Russias, was known by the nobles as the 'crowned idiot' and the 'august imbecile', which was a fair description of his limited abilities. Rather dull-witted, when he ascended the throne he declared that, henceforth, he would not discuss the destiny of his empire with anyone but God Almighty personally. He was the 'Absolute Monarch' personified.

Under this reign, past reforms were eradicated and replaced with far-reaching counter-reforms. The universities, long seen as an arena for intellectual and political dissent, were robbed of their autonomy. Local self-government, the *zemstvos*, also under suspicion, was brought under the heel of the central authorities.

The new laws banned such works as Spinoza's *Ethics*, Hobbes's *Leviathan*, Voltaire's *Philosophy of History* and Lecky's *History of European Morals*. Anti-Jewish pogroms, the traditional hallmark of tsarism, became more common. Alexander's favourite adviser and diehard reactionary, Konstantin Pobedonostsev, believed that the threat of revolution and bloody upheaval was far more preferable than the granting of a constitution. He stated bluntly:

> This may be the *finis Russiae* [the end of Russia]... There are some people who would like us to introduce a constitution... a falsehood which... as Western Europe shows us, is the tool of every untruth... [this would be] our misfortune and our perdition...[23]

The regime's abrupt change in policy, which specifically targeted education, had a direct impact on the Ulyanov family. In 1884, Lenin's father was informed by the Ministry of Education that, given the changes, he was requested to retire from his post four years earlier than was customary.

The new view from the Ministry was that the children of the lower orders were receiving too much education for their own good. As a result, there would be no more elementary schools established and existing ones would be transferred from the control of the *zemstvos* to the parish priests. This

13. Tsar Alexander III

measure, in effect, meant a return to the pre-reform dark period of twenty years earlier.

This was a devastating blow to Lenin's father, who tried to keep his fears for the future away from his children. He was feeling professionally humiliated. Edmund Wilson writes:

> He spent his later years under the oppression of the Statute of 1884 which effected the dismissal of liberal professors and the exclusion of unreliable students, administered by a Minister of Education who forbade the education of 'the children of cooks'.[24]

His daughter, Anna, wrote:

> Only later did I understand how much distress all this gave to father and how it hastened for him the fatal *dénouement*... This meant that the whole work of his life was blotted out.[25]

In January 1886, suffering from acute stress, Ilya Nikolayevich suffered a brain haemorrhage and died. Vladimir Ilyich was fifteen years old at the time. This had a dramatic effect on him and the family. The loss of his income also imposed a heavy financial burden on them, which forced their mother to plead for help from the state, as befitting her husband's status. In doing so, she faced bureaucratic delays and, even then, the sum granted was not sufficient to cover their outgoings and they had to let out part of the family home. Consequently, the Ulyanov family fell on hard times.

Alexander Ulyanov

Lenin's elder brother, Alexander, known as Sasha within the family, had done remarkably well at school, where he was a model student. He was extremely diligent and engrossed in his studies, especially chemistry. As a result, he invariably came first in his class. He graduated with a gold medal, two years or so ahead of other boys his own age. This would secure him a place to further his studies at the University of St. Petersburg.

Alexander's teenage years also coincided with the revolutionary movement of the Russian intelligentsia. It was this generation that was inspired by Pushkin's fiery language against the tsars:

O, despotic villain
I hate you and your line
I will see your ruin and your children's death
With a wicked delight.[26]

Sasha had lost his religious faith, but said nothing to his family. In the first three years of university life, he avoided all contact with revolutionary circles, which certainly existed in St. Petersburg. Instead, his academic interests widened further, and he added zoology and biology to his study of chemistry. As far as Sasha's parents were concerned, learning seemed to be his preoccupation. His letters to them certainly reassured them on this account.

Nevertheless, an early letter of his did describe his interest in Turgenev's funeral: "Today was Turgenev's funeral. We went with Anna and saw the procession: a mass of wreaths and of people and the coffin under a golden canopy covered with flowers and garlands." However, "it was impossible to enter the cemetery", as the police blocked the way.[27]

The event seemed to have little consequence for Alexander, and he diligently continued with his science studies. Even during the holidays, he would lock himself away in his 'laboratory', with his glass pipes and test-tubes, where he conducted his experiments and read his books. These included works by Darwin, Huxley, Spencer and Mill, but he also liked reading the novels of Dostoevsky.

14. Alexander Ulyanov

However, among these books, there was one which he seemed especially interested in, and one which no one in the family had ever heard of: *Das Kapital* by Karl Marx. Alexander even began to read some of Plekhanov's philosophical writings.

Despite such interests, he never informed or involved his younger brother in his newly emerging thoughts about life. Alexander was in his final year of university and his studies had won him a top award in zoology for a paper on annelid worms.

And yet, his attention had begun to shift away from scientific pursuits to social affairs and politics. He began to participate in some radical protests, such as the one commemorating the life of the anti-monarchist writer Nikolai Dobrolyubov, where some of his fellow students were arrested. At this point, he must have started to draw his own conclusions as to what should be done.

Alexander became attracted to the People's Will, and, after due consideration, decided to join them. His decision to join should not be a complete surprise. After all, the links between his student milieu and the Populist movement had long been established. Once convinced, Sasha became dedicated to its revolutionary cause.

In March 1887, a group of young student revolutionaries, including Alexander, plotted to assassinate the new tsar. He was to make use of his knowledge of chemistry to prepare the necessary explosives. He even pawned his gold medal he had won at high school to buy nitric acid. But it was clear that while they were passionate about their cause, they were completely inexperienced in the methods of terrorism.

Execution of Sasha

The day they chose to carry out the assassination also coincided symbolically with the date of the anniversary of the murder of Tsar Alexander II. This gave them two months to make the necessary preparations. However, the plot was foiled when the police intercepted a letter from one of the group's members and widespread arrests followed. This included Alexander, but also his sister Anna, who was visiting him on the day of the arrests.

News travelled slowly, and it took some time before word of the arrests reached Simbirsk. A schoolteacher, who the Ulyanovs knew well, had received a letter from relatives in St. Petersburg containing the news. When Alexander's mother heard what had happened, she dropped everything and headed for St. Petersburg. As there was no railway through Simbirsk, she had to travel by horseback part of the way.

In St. Petersburg, she spent almost a month visiting police headquarters and offices of the Public Prosecutor, pleading with them to be allowed to see her son and daughter. When finally allowed, she spent another month visiting her children in prison. She managed to see Alexander two weeks before the opening of his trial for terrorism. This was only three weeks after his twenty-first birthday. He cried, embraced his mother, and asked for her forgiveness.

In all, fifteen people were brought to trial, accused of attempting to assassinate the tsar. The youngest of the boys was twenty and the eldest was twenty-six. The bulk of the accused faced long prison sentences at best. However, Alexander, who was neither the originator nor the organiser of the plot, took the entire responsibility on himself. As a result, he was found guilty and sentenced to be hanged.

His mother tried desperately to get his sentence commuted, writing a letter to the tsar, asking for clemency and pleading for mercy. But the tsar was intransigent and her son refused to ask for clemency, despite his mother's pleading. He found Sasha's frankness "quite touching", but refused to commute the death sentence.[28]

The last words she shouted to Alexander as she left his cell were: "Take heart! Take courage!"[29]

On 20 May 1887, Sasha was taken from his cell with only two hours' notice and hanged along with four other conspirators in the courtyard of the Shlisselburg Fortress. Defiant to the end, after refusing to appeal for mercy, he made a declaration on behalf of his comrades:

> There is no finer death than death for one's country's sake; such a death holds no terror for sincere and honest men. I had but one aim: to help the unfortunate Russian people.[30]

Alexander's mother learned about her eldest son's fate from a newspaper she had bought on the street when on her way to visit her imprisoned daughter. Anna had been involved in revolutionary activities, but never involved in the assassination plot. A few days after Alexander's death, she was released, but banished to her grandfather's estate, where she remained under police supervision.

His last wish to his mother was that she should bring him a copy of a book by Heine to read. In all, the five defendants who were hanged had a combined age of barely 110 years.

To his family, Sasha was a hero. Cynical bourgeois historians like Helen Rappaport cannot refrain from pouring scorn on the memory of those heroic young people: "As conspirators they were inept", she says from the comfort of her study. She talks of "bungling incompetence". As for the failed assassination, it "might sound like the stuff of tragicomedy", she sneers.[31] No doubt, if it had succeeded, she would wax indignant at the viciousness of the assassins.

But the jaundiced opinions of this breed of bourgeois historians need not bother us unduly. Their lies can never obscure the truth. And this is that Alexander Ulyanov was an incredibly brave young man, only twenty-one years old. He was willing to sacrifice his life for a noble cause. And while his methods were bound to fail, his idealism and heroism cannot fail to arouse a profound sense of sympathy and admiration. Whatever the shortcomings of these young people, they deserve to be remembered as heroes and martyrs of the revolutionary cause.

Alexander had made sure not to tell his younger brother about the conspiracy, refusing to mention even a single word to him. This was no accident. He wanted to protect his younger brother and remained tight-lipped so as not to compromise him.

According to Krupskaya in her *Reminiscences*, while the two boys, Sasha and Volodya, had common tastes, "the difference in their age, though, made itself felt in various ways. There were certain things that Alexander did not tell Vladimir."[32] These secrets included his clandestine revolutionary thoughts and activities. However, Krupskaya states that despite the age difference between them, the "fate of his brother undoubtedly influenced Vladimir Ilyich profoundly."[33]

Much later, Lenin mentioned to Krupskaya the thoughts that went through his mind: "No, my brother won't make a revolutionary, I thought at the time. A revolutionary can't give so much time to the study of worms."[34] But he was clearly wrong.

A life-changing experience

Vladimir Ilyich was seventeen years old and still at school when his brother was hanged by the tsarist state. On a personal level, he would have been devastated by such a tragedy, coming on top of his father's death the previous year. Both deaths in their own way produced deep emotions in the young Lenin, provoking a critical attitude towards religion, and a hatred of the hangman and the regime. "This youthful experience undoubtedly did leave its imprint on Lenin's attitude towards the Liberals", explains Krupskaya. "It was early that he learned the value of all Liberal chatter."[35]

The experience of his brother's death would always remain with him. It provoked tremendous personal feelings of revulsion deep down inside. "His brother's execution, indelibly stamped on his consciousness, helped to determine his later life", writes Trotsky.[36] Anna, his sister, believed that he was "hardened" by the affair. But he certainly kept these feelings to himself.

It is certain that his brother's ultimate sacrifice strengthened the young Lenin's sympathies for the Narodniks and their cherished cause of freedom. He would always express his admiration for the courage of these young heroes, who dared to challenge tsarism, whatever the cost. He even admired their conspiratorial methods of organisation, which he later praised in his own pamphlet, *What Is to Be Done?*

Over the following months, he must have mulled over the meaning of his brother's fate and its significance. But he never expressed these thoughts. At this point, Ilyich began to think in political terms, although he was still feeling his way. In this period, he drew closer to his mother and developed a very strong bond with her. Krupskaya writes:

> The fate of his brother undoubtedly influenced Vladimir Ilyich profoundly. Another important factor was that he had begun to think for himself on many questions and had decided in his own mind the necessity of revolutionary struggle…

> As it was, the fate of his brother gave his mind a keener edge, developed in him an extraordinary sombreness of thought, an ability to face the truth without letting himself for a minute be carried away by a phrase or an illusion. It developed in him a scrupulously honest approach to all questions.[37]

Vladimir Ilyich was not the only member of his family, apart from Sasha, to be involved in revolutionary politics. His younger brother Dmitri was expelled later from Moscow University in 1897 for involvement in revolutionary activities, then arrested and exiled to Tula. His sister Maria was also arrested for her involvement and banished to Nizhny Novgorod. Anna had been arrested with Sasha, while Maria and Dmitri were arrested again in Kiev in 1904. In fact, all five of the Ulyanov children who reached adulthood ended up joining the revolutionary movement.

There is a story, seemingly made up in 1924 by Lenin's sister, Maria, that shortly after his brother's execution, Ilyich was supposed to have cried out: "No, we will not follow that road. That is not the road to take." But this is highly improbable, as Trotsky remarks:

> To whom were these words addressed? The mother was in Petersburg, Anna was still in prison. Evidently Vladimir imparted his tactical discovery to the thirteen-year-old Dimitri and the nine-year-old Maria…[38]

Such a story is one of the many myths that surround the young Lenin. However, what is certain is that he was at one of the many crossroads in his life. The death of his brother definitely marked the end of Volodya's innocent childhood world and adolescence. The hangman had seen to that. Vladimir Ilyich would also break with religion. And his brother's death would cast a shadow over him and his family for a long time to come.

2. The Early Years

Ilyich had excelled at school and was the top of his class in Simbirsk. In June, only one month after his brother's death, he was awarded the gold star for academic excellence. As we have seen, he had developed a passion for Latin and the classics, but he also studied the books he obtained from his grandfather's library. In fact, books became one of the great loves of his life.

By the strangest quirk of history, the headmaster at Ilyich's school was a man called Fyodor Mikhailovich Kerensky. He was the father of the future head of the Provisional government in 1917, Alexander Kerensky, who, as events would have it, was deposed by the victorious October Revolution. Fyodor Mikhailovich soon recognised Ilyich's academic abilities and gave the future Lenin a glowing letter of recommendation for university entrance:

> Quite talented, invariably diligent, prompt and reliable. Ulyanov was first in all his classes, and upon graduation was awarded a gold medal as the most meritorious pupil in achievement, growth and conduct. There is not a single instance on record either in school or outside of it, of Ulyanov's evoking by word or deed any adverse opinion from the authorities and teachers of his school. His parents always watched carefully over the educational and moral progress of Ulyanov, and since 1886, i.e. after the death of his father, the mother alone has devoted all care and labour to the upbringing of her children... The mother of Ulyanov intends to remain with him throughout his stay at the university.[1]

These qualities of diligence in his early years stayed with Lenin for the rest of his life.

The family of a convicted terrorist inevitably was shunned by 'respectable society', and they felt socially isolated in Simbirsk. Worn down by constant worries, Ilyich's mother's hair had turned white. She nevertheless tried to understand her children's revolutionary aspirations and became proud of their views. In one of her numerous visits to the police department, she was one day confronted with the cynical remark: "You can be proud of your offspring – one of them was hanged and another one is asking for the rope." To which Lenin's mother replied with dignity: "Yes, I am proud of my children!"[2]

The family seemed to be constantly on the move. One such move resulted from Ilyich's acceptance as a student at the University of Kazan to study law in the autumn of 1887, the university where his father had studied. Fyodor Mikhailovich had reassured the authorities, who would have been alerted to Alexander's fate about Ilych's perfect conduct and reliability.

The University of Kazan was the only one of its kind in Russia's eastern provinces. It was about 200 kilometres up the Volga from Simbirsk and Lenin was accompanied on his journey by his mother, brothers and sisters. Everything seemed quite bright. However, unrest had spread from Moscow, and students were demanding the restoration of certain rights of which they had been deprived.

It was therefore not long before the young Lenin became involved in these protests. He did not play a prominent role, but he was expelled simply for participating, along with thirty-nine others. In addition, given his personal relationship with a 'state criminal', he was forced to leave Kazan and live on the family estate at Kokushkino, some thirty-five kilometres from the city. This effectively banished him from the state education system.

However, it was not long before the family was allowed to return to Kazan, where Ilyich made contact with a radical circle founded by Nikolai Fedoseyev, a young student who had been won over to Marxism.

Expulsion

Ilyich's expulsion from Kazan university at the age of seventeen was his first taste of direct revolutionary activity. One might be forgiven for thinking that this experience had turned him into a fully fledged revolutionary, but this was not the case.

While harbouring natural sympathies for the Narodniks, he did not choose the same path as his brother. The reason for this was quite simple. This avenue had now been completely blocked. Following the attempted assassination of Alexander III, the oppressive atmosphere throughout the country was such

15. Fyodor Mikhailovich Kerensky   16. Vladimir Ilyich in 1887

that any movement in that direction was ruled out. Everything was shrouded in a cloud of extreme reaction and the movement was, in reality, dead.

Without doubt, Ilyich must have had a strong sentimental attachment to the old Narodniks and the courage they displayed in the face of repression. "He has always inculcated into us the most ardent respect for this cluster of brilliant revolutionary fighters, the first generation of Populist revolutionists", explained Gregory Zinoviev in his lectures on Lenin's life. "And comrade Lenin did not renounce this heritage. He said: This heritage belongs to us, and only to us."[3]

As explained, the breakup of *Zemlya i Volya* in 1879 had led to the formation of *Chernyi Peredel* (Black Repartition) led by Georgi Plekhanov, who stood out as the theoretical giant of the group. But this grouping soon faced disintegration. "The organisation had no luck from the first days of its creation", complained Leo Deutsch, one of its founders.[4] Its main cadres – Georgi Plekhanov, Vera Zasulich, Pavel Axelrod, Vasily Ignatov and Leo Deutsch – were compelled to emigrate abroad. Plekhanov had previously been arrested for his revolutionary activities, but was now forced to live in exile in Switzerland.

Plekhanov and the other members of the group had naturally joined the Narodnik movement, as the working class in Russia was still quite small and only in its formative stage at that time. The peasantry was therefore regarded as the social force destined to overthrow tsarism. However, from the 1870s, a young working class began to emerge and develop with the growth of Russian industry. This altered the perspective of the Plekhanov group, who now looked, not towards individual terrorism, but to the organisation of the working class as the means to overthrow the old order.

Plekhanov and his small group of exiles soon came into contact with the ideas of Marx and the European social-democratic movement. It was not long before they were convinced of Marxism and regarded the new Russian proletariat alone, due to its cohesion and collective consciousness, as the class that could carry through the socialist revolution.

Originally, Plekhanov had the view of winning over the Narodniks and transforming the People's Will into a Marxist party, but that idea proved short-lived. As a result, with the formation of a Russian Marxist group, an ideological battle opened up between them and the Narodniks as to the way forward. At first, the People's Will had a more revolutionary aura about them – after all, they planned to kill the tsar – as opposed to the Marxists who used propaganda and organised workers' circles. But the growth of Russian capitalism, and with it the working class, was beginning to confirm the perspectives of the Marxists.

Russia's rapid growth

Russia's industrial development took off around 1890 and experienced meteoric growth, especially in the main cities. This was a graphic expression of the law of combined and uneven development, where the most advanced industrial techniques emerged in the midst of backward agricultural methods, with Russia's industry advancing rapidly.

Some economists have estimated that, during this decade, industrial productivity in Russia increased by 126 per cent, twice the rate of Germany and triple that of the United States. Between 1890 and 1900, the value of Russian industrial production more than doubled. Pig iron output grew by 216 per cent, iron ore output by 272 per cent, petroleum by 449 per cent and railways by 71 per cent. This development was due to the rapid increase of foreign capital, especially British, French and German, which owned about 40 per cent of all stock capital in Russia. These enterprises, in turn, were dependent on the banks and the western European money market.

The Russian proletariat underwent a massive transformation, as starving peasants were thrown off the land and forced into the giant foreign-owned

17. Georgi Plekhanov

factories. The most advanced industrial techniques were grafted onto the old, semi-feudal conditions. This process was not gradual, but resulted in a rapid and violent break in social relations. While in Britain, the proletariat evolved over more than a hundred years, the Russian proletariat sprang up over a decade or so.

To show the degree of concentration of workers, 44.4 per cent of the workers in Russia were employed by the largest factories (those above 1,000 workers each), while in the United States this proportion was only 17.8 per cent. In the Moscow district, the density was 57.3 per cent. By the end of the 1890s, 5 per cent of industrial enterprises employed 53 per cent of the total number of workers. The Putilov factory in St. Petersburg, for instance, employed tens of thousands of workers. Nevertheless, Russia still remained a relatively under-developed country, with only 13 per cent of the population living in the towns, while the remainder were tied to the land.[5]

It was in this context that Plekhanov, in July 1889, attended the First Congress of the Second International in Paris, and uttered the famous words: "The Russian revolution will either triumph as a revolution of the working class or it will not triumph at all."[6]

He was the first individual to formulate such a courageous statement in view of the fact there was no workers' party as yet in Russia and the working class was only just emerging. However, there was an important element in the equation: precisely because it lacked any real organisations, the young Russian working class also lacked the conservative traditions that characterised the established labour organisations of the more advanced countries of Europe. Subject to the most vicious exploitation, the Russian working class was wide open to revolutionary ideas.

Plekhanov's exiled group understood that their main task was to disseminate propaganda in Russian. Given the tiny size of the group, this was the unavoidable first step for establishing a viable Social-Democratic organisation within Russia. Replying to the advocates of individual terrorism, Plekhanov described the Marxist ideas as "dynamite which no other explosive in the world can replace…"[7]

Emancipation of Labour group

Through Vera Zasulich, Plekhanov's group was in personal contact with Marx and Engels in London. As a result of this influence, in 1883, the year of Marx's death, they constituted themselves as the Emancipation of Labour group. Their initial nucleus, all of whom were in exile, was composed of Plekhanov, Zasulich, Deutsch, Axelrod and Ignatov. In that year, Plekhanov wrote a major work, *Socialism and the Political Struggle*, followed in 1885 by *Our Differences*, which proclaimed the leading role of the working class in the revolution against tsarism.

With this, Plekhanov's small grouping had crossed the bridge from the old Populism to Social-Democracy, that is (in the language of those days) revolutionary Marxism. Nevertheless, the group was numerically very weak for understandable reasons. Its precarious situation was made worse by the arrest of Deutsch, who was sent to Siberia, while Ignatov tragically contracted tuberculosis and died.

Plekhanov's group was in contact with Engels until his death, mostly through correspondence, but also through personal visits from Zasulich.

Engels was delighted by this development and always displayed great enthusiasm about the prospects of revolution in Russia. In February 1895, some months before his death, Engels had written to Plekhanov thanking him for the copy of his *The Development of the Monist View of History*. "Vera has given me your book, for which many thanks. I have begun to read it, but it will take some time", wrote Engels. "However, it is a great success to have managed to have it published in *your country*. That is a step forward, and even if we cannot retain the new position we have just gained, a precedent has been established, the ice is broken."[8]

This contact with Engels provided the Plekhanov group with a lifeline, and enormous encouragement given the former's authority. It placed them in firm contact with the newly formed Socialist (Second) International, together with its world outlook.

It is not an exaggeration to say that within this tiny Emancipation of Labour group, originally composed of five people, are to be found the seeds of Bolshevism. This was practically all that existed of Russian Marxism from 1883 to 1893. It would take the pivotal intervention of Lenin for these seeds to germinate and eventually flourish. For the moment, such a development was far into the future. In fact, it would be another ten years of hard work before the first Social-Democratic organisation would be established on Russian soil.

Lenin later paid tribute to the pioneering work of the Emancipation of Labour group, when he explained that its writings, "printed abroad and uncensored, were the first systematically to expound and draw all the practical conclusions from the ideas of Marxism…"[9]

'Wilderness years'

But for now, despite its best efforts, the Plekhanov group was alone and completely isolated. Looking back, the period can be regarded as its 'wilderness years', in which only the most tenacious of people, with the necessary vision, managed to survive. Gradually, the group began to smuggle small amounts of Marxist literature into Russia from their exile in Switzerland and build up a small circle of contacts.

This tiny handful of dedicated comrades, working against all odds, took up the defence of Marxism against the dominant Narodnik trend, and its view that Russia could somehow bypass capitalism and go straight to peasant socialism. Instead, they advanced the ideas of *The Communist Manifesto*. The pioneering work of Plekhanov, in particular, in whose works the theoretical foundations of Russian Social-Democracy were laid down, rightly earned him the title of 'the father of Russian Marxism'.

Marx and Engels had raised a theoretically bold perspective for the Russian Revolution in the 1882 preface to the second Russian edition of *The Communist Manifesto*, published by Plekhanov's group. In this, they linked the fate of Russia to the world revolution:

> *The Communist Manifesto* had, as its object, the proclamation of the inevitable impending dissolution of modern bourgeois property. But in Russia we find, face-to-face with the rapidly flowering capitalist swindle and bourgeois property, just beginning to develop, more than half the land owned in common by the peasants. Now the question is: can the Russian *obshchina*,* though greatly undermined, yet a form of primaeval common ownership of land, pass directly to the higher form of Communist common ownership? Or, on the contrary, must it first pass through the same process of dissolution such as constitutes the historical evolution of the West?
>
> The only answer to that possible today is this: If the Russian Revolution becomes the signal for a proletarian revolution in the West, so that both complement each other, the present Russian common ownership of land may serve as the starting point for a communist development.[10]

This was a truly remarkable statement, completely free from the mechanical stages that were the hallmark of future Menshevism, where every country must follow the same path as the most advanced – step by step.

The groundwork for the growth of a Social-Democratic organisation was being prepared within Russia with the growth of a fresh working class. As its activities expanded, the revolutionary party would develop a larger and larger audience, and would need to carry out its work on two levels, namely of propaganda and agitation.

With his small group, Plekhanov nevertheless deepened the movement's understanding by clearly defining the distinction between agitation and propaganda. "A sect can be satisfied with propaganda in the narrow sense of the word: a political party never", he wrote in *Tasks of the Socialists in the Fight Against the Famine in Russia*. He then went on to famously define the differences between the two approaches: "A propagandist presents many ideas to one or a few persons; an agitator presents only one or only a few ideas, but he presents them to a mass of people."[11] Lenin was to later repeat this classic definition many times, including in *What Is to Be Done?*

---

* The *obshchina* was an agricultural commune.

18. Karl Marx

First steps

In early May 1889, Lenin's mother sold their property in Simbirsk as well as her father's estate in Kokushkino and used the money to buy a farm near the village of Alakayavka, a suburb of Samara. From there, Vladimir Ilyich made an appeal to the Ministry of Education to be allowed to take his final exams as an outside student, but this was rejected. By the autumn, the family had moved once again into the centre of Samara. Now aged eighteen, Ilyich became the male head of the family and began to take his first steps into adulthood. However, given the reputation that surrounded Alexander's name, the family was under constant police surveillance.

Nevertheless, for Ilyich, Samara opened up new and wider possibilities, where he was able to come into contact with a network of former exiles, revolutionaries, and others 'under surveillance'.

Over the next four or five years, Ilyich involved himself with the local workers' circles, in both Samara and in Kazan, at a time before any workers' party existed.

The most important circle was the one established by Nikolai Fedoseyev, who was a year older than Vladimir Ilyich. He had been expelled from school and had got involved in revolutionary activities, establishing an illegal library and setting up an underground press. Nikolai eventually became a Social-Democrat and attacked the terrorist tactics of the People's Will. However, Nikolai and Ilyich never met in Kazan. Trotsky puts this hesitation down to the fact that Vladimir Ilyich had not long before been expelled from university and his brother had been executed as a terrorist. However, it also may have been to do with security, as everyone only knew the members of their own circle, and Fedoseyev attended others. Trotsky notes:

> In taking up the study of *Das Kapital*, he did not intend at all to break with the traditions of People's Will. At the same time, he could not have felt sufficiently well grounded to defend that tradition from the criticism of a Social-Democrat who rejected terror. If you add to this his distaste for surrendering to other people's arguments, especially people his own age, it became understandable why Vladimir might have preferred not to expose himself prematurely to an opponent's attack. Through the other members of the circle, he found himself sufficiently *au courant* with the thoughts and arguments of Fedoseyev in order to take them into consideration as he studied.[12]

Vladimir Ilyich's grasp of foreign languages allowed him to read far more broadly, especially books that had been smuggled into Russia from abroad. It was here in Samara that he first read Marx. Through different student friends, he had come across the writings of Marx in German, and eventually *Capital*, which had escaped the attention of the censor, which he began to study in great detail. He read Engels' *The Condition of the Working Class in England* the following year.

Lenin's elder brother had read Marx, but these ideas, at that time, had not touched the young Ilyich. It was here, in Samara, that things changed. His thirst for reading had awakened a new consciousness within him and he began to chart a way forward. But it was still only the beginning of his political journey.

He did not, as yet, consider himself a Social-Democrat, or Marxist, as some would later suggest. Such a change would occur a few years later. But Ilyich was nevertheless a quick learner and, whenever he could get hold of them, treated Marx's writings extremely seriously. He developed a reverence for Marx's writings, which he turned to at every important juncture in his life for clarification. According to Krupskaya, Lenin would mentally 'consult' Marx.

At this time, however, while he advanced in his political studies, he still held onto some lingering sympathies towards the Narodniks. Things were, for the moment, still not politically clear in his own mind. For instance, he had not, as yet, read anything by Plekhanov.

The following May, in 1890, his mother again went to St. Petersburg to appeal to the Ministry of Education to allow him to finish his studies. After a long and persistent campaign, she finally managed to persuade the authorities to allow Vladimir Ilyich to take his law exams at St. Petersburg University as an external student. This opportunity allowed him to spend two months in the capital, where he managed with great difficulty to get hold of Engels' *Anti-Dühring*, which he eagerly read.

It was at this time that Lenin suffered another personal blow, when his sister, nineteen-year-old Olga, who was also a student in St. Petersburg, contracted typhoid. They had both discussed and read a lot together, and they had become very close. Ilyich took her to the hospital, but she died there on 8 May, which was also the anniversary of Alexander's death. He was deeply distressed by her tragic death and returned with his mother to Samara.

Samara's famine

In 1891-92, the Samara region suffered from a severe famine, combined with an epidemic of cholera and typhus, resulting in the deaths of some 400,000 people. This was another tragedy that had a tremendous impact on Lenin, which served to reinforce his hatred for an unjust and inhumane social system.

As usual, the bourgeois historians, in an attempt to slander him, claim that he wanted the peasants to suffer and therefore welcomed the famine. Orlando Figes asserts:

> While, of course, it is too easy to impose the Lenin of 1917 on that of the early 1890s [which is precisely what Figes does here – RS and AW], it is clear [!] that many of the characteristics which he would display in power were already visible at this early stage. Witness, for example, Lenin's callous attitude to the suffering

of the peasants during the famine of 1891 – his idea that aid should be denied to them to hasten the revolutionary crisis.[13]

The 'evidence' for this was taken from the memoirs of V Vodovozov, who claims that Lenin had said the following:

> The famine is the direct consequence of a particular social order. So long as that order exists, famines are inevitable. They can be abolished only by the abolition of that order of society … It will cause the peasant to reflect on the fundamental facts of capitalist society. It will destroy his faith in the tsar and in tsarism and will in time speed the victory of the revolution.[14]

The historian Richard Pipes states that this "proved" that Lenin treated human beings as "ore" and sent "people to their death before execution squads with the same lack of emotion…"[15]

Firstly, the above quote is not from "a friend of the Ulyanovs", as Pipes claims, but a Populist opponent. As Edmund Wilson, who is no friend of Lenin, explains: "Our only knowledge of his position at this time is derived from the indictment of a Populist opponent, who declares that Vladimir welcomed the famine as a factor in breaking down the peasantry and creating an industrial proletariat."[16]

However, if we simply take the quote itself, there is nothing wrong with the statement as such:

1. "The famine is the direct consequence of a particular social order" – *correct.*

2. "So long as that order exists, famines are inevitable" – *correct.*

3. "They can be abolished only by the abolition of that order of society" – *correct.*

4. "It will cause the peasant to reflect on the fundamental facts of capitalist society" – *correct.*

5. "It will destroy his faith in the tsar and in tsarism and will in time speed the victory of the revolution" – *correct.*

The attempt by Richard Pipes and Orlando Figes (and many others) to claim Lenin was by nature a callous individual falls flat on its face. There is no mention anywhere of denying aid to the peasantry on the part of Lenin. What Lenin opposed was the attempts of the liberals to reduce the struggle against the famine to a series of petty reforms, that did not tackle the roots of the problem, and offered a harmless alternative to a serious struggle against a cruel and unjust social and political regime.

Following the example of Leo Tolstoy, they set up canteens for famine relief, which closely corresponded to the cowardly 'little steps' of the liberals to reform the infamous tsarist regime. By contrast, Lenin stood for the root-and-branch eradication of the causes of this social calamity.

Plekhanov wrote a pamphlet called *Tasks of the Socialists in the Fight Against the Famine in Russia*, published in Geneva in 1892. This correctly placed the blame for the famine on the tsarist government and the exhaustion of the land due to capitalist farming. This followed the line of the old revolutionary, Pyotr Lavrov, who proclaimed in print: "Yes, the only 'good cause' we can possibly embrace is not philanthropic but the revolutionary cause."[17]

As Trotsky explains in relation to this point: "The Marxists, of course, oppose not aid to the starving, but the illusion that a sea of need could be emptied with the teaspoon of philanthropy."[18]

Not satisfied with falsifying the position of the young Lenin, Orlando Figes cannot resist writing: "Thirty years later he [Lenin] would show the same indifference to their suffering."[19] This is a reference to the famine of 1921-22, which killed an estimated 5 million people. Figes conveniently forgets the little detail that these horrific conditions were not the result of a 'callous' Lenin, but of the imperialist blockade and a savage civil war, when twenty-one foreign armies invaded Russia to overthrow the Soviet Republic.

From lawyer to revolutionary

In the four-year period that Lenin spent in Samara, he came into contact with older revolutionaries of *Narodnaya Volya*, who would have defended the old terrorist methods. Given these acquaintances and his own past sympathies, it took a real internal struggle – an internal revolution – before Lenin could openly break with such traditions and fully commit to the Marxist outlook.

When Lenin finally got hold of Plekhanov's works, he was completely captivated. Throughout his life, Lenin held Plekhanov's writings in the highest esteem. "The services he [Plekhanov] rendered in the past were immense", he wrote. "During the twenty years between 1883 and 1903 he wrote a large number of splendid essays, especially those against the opportunists, Machists* and Narodniks."[20] These writings of Plekhanov helped to clarify his thoughts and convince him of Marxism. Trotsky explains:

---

* The Machists were followers of the theories of the physicist and philosopher Mach, in particular, empirio-criticism.

19. Vladimir Ilyich in 1891

All that was best in the old revolutionary intellectuals of earlier times: their spirit of self-denial, their audacity, their hatred of oppression – all this was concentrated in the figure of this man who, already in his youth, broke irrevocably with the intelligentsia because it was too strongly tied to the bourgeoisie; this man absorbed completely the spirit and just cause of the working class...[21]

Despite the terrible personal blows, Vladimir Ilyich finally passed his law exams in November with a first-class degree. In January 1892, he became a qualified lawyer and in March began to practise in the Samara Regional Court. During 1892-93, he appeared in court for the defence more than twenty times. But it soon became obvious to him that his new profession was incompatible with his recently discovered revolutionary beliefs and aspirations.

The earliest surviving manuscript by Lenin was an article called 'New Economic Developments in Peasant Life', written in Samara in the spring of 1893, which circulated among young activists in the town.

Much later in his life, Lenin would joke about his fleeting career in the legal profession. He was not the kind of person to do things by half measures. If he was to commit to something, it was done in a serious way. "Vladimir Ulyanov despised dilettantism", explains Trotsky.[22] He detested people who simply dabbled in things. It seems clear that it was at this time in Samara that Ilyich finally emerged as a revolutionary Social-Democrat, a fully fledged Marxist.

3. St. Petersburg

At the end of August 1893, at the age of twenty-three, Lenin abandoned the provincial life of Samara for the Russian capital of St. Petersburg. He arrived just before the new upsurge in the Russian working-class movement.

To begin with, Lenin joined a Marxist circle and met with a variety of radical people of a similar age to himself, including such notable figures as Peter Struve and Mikhail Tugan-Baranovsky, who later became Finance Minister in a Ukrainian government. This gave him the opportunity to discuss developments within Russia with like-minded people. In 1894, he also met Nadezhda Konstantinovna Krupskaya, who was to become his wife and lifelong companion. Around this time, she was following in the footsteps of her parents, having become a teacher in an adult Sunday School. After reading volume one of Marx's *Capital*, she became a convinced revolutionary and so became involved in the circle.

The movement attracted many different people who had become interested in Marxism. Struve and Tugan-Baranovsky dabbled with Marxism, but were destined to part company with these ideas and venture into the camp of bourgeois liberalism and beyond. First, however, they passed through the phase of 'Legal Marxism', which was a peculiar attempt to adapt Marxism to the legalities of the regime. As a trend, it represented a distortion of Marxism, which was attractive to the bourgeois intelligentsia, especially its historical justification of capitalism and arguments against the Narodniks.

Marxist circles had been set up in many large towns: in St. Petersburg, Moscow, Kharkov, Kiev, Kazan, Samara, Odessa, Tula, Minsk and elsewhere. It is in St. Petersburg that we see the real beginning of Lenin's *professional*

20. Nevsky Prospekt, Saint Petersburg, c. 1900

revolutionary activity. He began to teach the fundamentals of Marxism to workers in the circles. His prominent role meant that he drew the attention of the police, and between 1893 and 1895, he was forced to change address eight times to evade surveillance.

At this point, Lenin's life merged with the building of the revolutionary party. As his ideas began to crystallise, he advanced from being a pupil of Marxism to become a teacher of Marxism.

Lenin was preparing himself, not simply to become a writer or even a theoretician, but, unconsciously, to become a future leader of the revolutionary movement. His growing authority and political impact were noticed by those around him. Isaak Lalayants, a former Kazan student, states:

> This man of twenty-three was a most remarkable combination of simplicity, sensitivity, love of life, and enthusiasm on the one hand, and of firm and profound knowledge and merciless logical consistency … on the other.[1]

It can be said that between his brother's death and his move to St. Petersburg, the outline of the future Lenin was being formed. However, this development would not stop there. Trotsky explains:

21. Nadezhda Konstantinovna Krupskaya

He was still to make great strides forward, not only externally but internally; several clearly delineated stages can be seen in his later development. But all the fundamental features of his personality, his outlook on life, and his mode of action were already formed during the interval between the seventeenth and twenty-third years of his life.[2]

These changes in Lenin's personal development were no accident. They reflected not only a change in his outlook, but were also a reflection of the changing situation nationally and internationally. World events were having an increasing impact within Russia, especially in revolutionary circles.

In July 1889, the mighty Second International was formed. In contrast to its predecessor, the First International, it represented a *mass* force embracing large working-class parties, the German being the pre-eminent one. This great advance was greeted with jubilation everywhere.

It coincided with the stormy reawakening of the British working class, marked by the dockworkers' strike and the wave of 'New Unionism' that was beginning to sweep Britain. In Germany too, the illegal Social Democratic Party had made a breakthrough, winning almost 1.5 million votes in the

1890 elections, 20 per cent of the popular vote. Within Russia, it was also a time of increasing strikes and the rise of workers' discussion circles. A new generation of young people were awakening to Marx's ideas and becoming politically involved.

Lenin and the Russian Marxists, working under very difficult conditions of illegality, regarded themselves as part of this worldwide army of the working class, from which they drew tremendous inspiration. They naturally looked towards the mass Social-Democratic parties of Western Europe, especially to Germany, its most powerful section.

The German Social Democratic Party (SPD), given its prestige and powerful apparatus, was the envy of the world. This was particularly so following the defeat of the revisionist trend of Eduard Bernstein at the hands of Karl Kautsky, August Bebel and other leaders of the SPD.* However, Kautsky was reluctant to engage in an all-out fight with Bernstein, and when he did so, his response was somewhat reserved.

It was Rosa Luxemburg who undertook a full-frontal attack against Bernstein's revisionism, which irritated Kautsky. However, this conservative side of Kautsky and the German leadership was not visible to Lenin at this time. He still looked up to Kautsky with reverence, and the German SPD was the type of party that Lenin modelled himself on and was determined to build in Russia.

Modest beginnings

Every revolutionary movement has very modest beginnings. In its embryonic stages, the revolutionary organisation is primarily based upon the intelligentsia – especially the students – who tend to form the initial cadre. Such beginnings are primarily the preserve of the youth, who are especially attracted to its revolutionary banner. Such was Lenin's generation.

Although Lenin was still quite young at this time, he took his revolutionary responsibilities very seriously. He developed an extremely attentive attitude to Marxist theory. The more he read, the more he wanted to read. He did everything he could to get his hands on Marxist literature, despite the difficulties. Lenin did not simply intend to *read* Marx, just repeating him by rote, but wanted to *master* these ideas. He made sure to make copious notes to thoroughly absorb its content. Even then, he modestly regarded himself as the pupil, a learner, and did not strive for originality. Nevertheless, he constantly tried to relate the ideas of Marxism to the problems he faced, especially in

---

* For a full account see Sewell, *Germany 1918-1933: Socialism or Barbarism*, pp. 28-39.

22. Eduard Bernstein   23. Karl Kautsky

his polemics with the Narodniks. He benefited enormously from this clash of ideas, which served to sharpen and clarify things in his own mind. Lenin adopted this rigorous approach to study throughout his life, which equipped him for his future role. Trotsky notes:

> In later years, Lenin used to astound people with his ability to read quickly and grasp the essence of what he read at a glance. But he had developed this faculty by learning, when necessary, to read very slowly. Beginning in each new field by laying down a solid foundation, he worked like a conscientious mason. He retained to the end of his life the capacity to re-read a necessary and important book or chapter several times. Indeed, he truly valued only those books which have to be re-read.[3]

The early interest in Marx's ideas in Russia is illustrated by the fact that the first translation of Marx's *Capital* into Russian appeared in 1872, only five years after the original, while the French edition appeared in 1883 and the first English translation only appeared in 1886. In other words, the Russian language edition of *Capital* was the *first* foreign translation of this important book. The tsarist censor had in fact passed the first two volumes of *Capital* without much hesitation. In regard to the first, the censor wrote: "One can with certainty say that in Russia only a few will read the book and still fewer understand [it]." The second volume was allowed through as it was "in content and presentation a serious economic study comprehensible only to the specialist."[4]

This view of the censor was clearly mistaken, as Marx's *Capital* was read and studied in workers' circles throughout Russia. Some copies were physically torn up into separate chapters, which were passed around to read among workers. The censor's opinion was very fortunate indeed.

Even from this young age, the study of theory for Lenin was paramount. He quickly came to the firm conclusion, explained in his pamphlet, *What Is to Be Done?*, that without revolutionary theory there can be no revolutionary movement. He fully endorsed Engels' view that the class struggle is conducted on three levels: the economic struggle, the political struggle and, just as important, the theoretical struggle. It is no accident that he proudly repeated the words of Engels from 1874:

> For the first time since a workers' movement has existed, the struggle is being conducted pursuant to its three sides – the theoretical, the political, and the practical-economic (resistance to the capitalists) – in harmony and in its interconnections, and in a systematic way. It is precisely in this, as it were, concentric attack, that the strength and invincibility of the German movement lies.[5]

Personal concerns

Lenin developed the habit of being frugal and careful with his finances, especially when he was not earning any money and relied mostly on 'philanthropy' from his mother, as he liked to call it. Even then, he could sometimes let things slip.

In a letter to his mother from St. Petersburg in October 1893, Lenin told her about his job prospects: "I have been promised a job in a consulting lawyer's office here, but when that will be arranged (and whether it will be arranged) I do not know." He then asked if she could "please send me some money, mine is nearly at an end." Feeling somewhat guilty, and so as to reassure her, he then explained: "I am now, for the first time in St. Petersburg, keeping a cash-book to see how much I actually spend."

Lenin then went on to outline his finances and money he spent on galoshes, clothes, books, an abacus, etc. He also included expenses for a court case (about 10 rubles), which "I shall probably conduct..." He continued, in a note of self-criticism: "Obviously I have not been living carefully; in one month I have spent a ruble and 36 kopeks on the horse trams, for instance. When I get used to the place I shall probably spend less."[6]

24. Maria Alexandrovna in 1895   25. Maria Ilyinichna Ulyanova

His letters to his family in this period are full of references to how the family is doing, their health, studies and so on. He would often write and comment about the books he was reading. In December 1894, he wrote to his sister, Maria, advising her about health and education, but also inquiring about her personal relationships:

> You ought to force yourself to take a walk for about two hours every day. It is not worthwhile poring over your lessons so industriously – you will ruin your health. What do you do apart from school work? What are you reading? […]
>
> How is your new acquaintanceship proceeding?[7]

Many of Lenin's letters written to his mother deal with a host of family and personal issues. In May 1895, for instance, he wrote to her describing his stay in Switzerland:

> The scenery here is splendid, I am enjoying it all the time. The Alps began immediately after the little German station I wrote to you from; then came the lakes and I could not tear myself away from the window of the railway carriage; if I could find out something about local conditions and prices (one could surely put up cheaply in the country districts) it would perhaps be possible to spend the summer here. The fare is not much and the scenery is splendid.[8]

Lenin's mother dedicated herself to all her children and supported their revolutionary instincts. Maria Alexandrovna became very sympathetic to her son's politics and supported him in his efforts. "Even our mother, who was born in 1835 and who was over sixty at the end of the century, when house searches and arrests became particularly frequent, showed full sympathy for our revolutionary activities", explains Maria Ulyanova.[9]

Lenin's sister also stressed how greatly he was attached to his mother. This can be seen from his letters, which are full of questions about her health and how she was coping.

"I am worried that your apartment is so cold; what will it be like in winter if the temperature is only 12 degrees now? You must not catch cold… Is there nothing you can do? Perhaps you should put in a small stove", he wrote in one letter.[10] His sister Maria related that it was in times of misfortune that Ilyich was especially worried:

> Vladimir Ilyich was particularly attentive to his mother at those times when some misfortune overtook her, and misfortunes were many in her life. First one, then another member of our family was arrested and exiled, sometimes several of us were arrested at the same time and she, though advanced in years, had to go again and again to prisons to visit her family and take things to them, to sit for hours in the waiting rooms of the gendarmerie and the secret police, and was often left completely alone with her heart aching for her children who had been deprived of their liberty. How worried Vladimir Ilyich was at such times, and how heavily the lack of personal contact with his mother weighed upon him.[11]

In 1902, Maria Alexandrovna lived with her son for about a month in the north of France. The last time he saw her was in 1910, in Stockholm, when she was accompanied by her daughter, Maria Ilyinichna. Maria Alexandrovna died in July 1916, not long before the February Revolution, which caused Lenin a great deal of pain.

These personal letters are rarely quoted, if ever, by the bourgeois historians when dealing with Lenin's personality. The reason is simple: they cut across the 'narrative' they wish to promote, which constantly describes Lenin as 'inhuman', 'callous', 'uncaring', etc. But Lenin had none of the monstrous qualities that these people scandalously ascribe to him.

"Vladimir Ilyich inherited his mother's strength of mind as well as her tact and kindness towards people", commented Krupskaya.[12]

Agitation

In the mid-1890s, the young Russian working class was flexing its muscles and had taken to strike action. When Lenin was in St. Petersburg, he was therefore keen for the Marxist circle not simply to discuss theory, but to engage in political agitation among the workers. This change was increasingly reflected in Lenin's writings, with more articles on factory conditions.

At this time, Lenin became the author of the first address to the workers of the Seymyannikov works in St. Petersburg, which was written down on paper, copied out four times by the group, then distributed by hand. Other leaflets were given to the women workers of the Laferm tobacco factory, who had also gone on strike. Later, such handwritten leaflets were duplicated and distributed far more widely. Lenin recalled in *What Is to Be Done?* how they collected material from workers to make their leaflets:

> I vividly recall my 'first experiment', which I would never like to repeat. I spent many weeks 'examining' a worker, who would often visit me, regarding every aspect of the conditions prevailing in the enormous factory at which he was employed. True, after great effort, I managed to obtain material for a description (of the one single factory!), but at the end of the interview the worker would wipe the sweat from his brow, and say to me smilingly: "I find it easier to work overtime than to answer your questions."[13]

Such methods were also employed in other workers' circles. Trotsky relates his own experience in producing leaflets:

> I wrote proclamations and articles, and printed them all out in longhand for the hectograph. At that time we didn't even know of the existence of typewriters. I printed the letters with the utmost care, considering it a point of honour to make them clear enough so that even the less literate could read our proclamations without any trouble. It took me about two hours to a page. Sometimes I didn't even unbend my back for a week, cutting my work short only for meetings and study in the groups. But what a satisfied feeling I had when I received the information from mills and workshops that the workers read voraciously, the mysterious sheets printed in purple ink, passing them about from hand to hand as they discussed them! They pictured the author as a strange and mighty person who in some mysterious way had penetrated into the mills and knew what was going on in the workshops, and twenty-four hours later passed his comments on events in newly printed handbills.[14]

Reflecting an eagerness for ideas, different Marxist texts, such as Engels' book, *The Origin of the Family, Private Property and the State*, were passed around the members. Vladimir Ilyich also took the time to read Marx's *Capital* with groups of workers, who were eager to learn more. This contradicts the false idea that workers are somehow uninterested in theory.

Lenin's first major work was *What the 'Friends of the People' Are and How They Fight the Social-Democrats*. Written in 1894, and subtitled *A Reply to Articles in 'Russkoye Bogatstvo' Opposing the Marxists*, the book was a powerful polemic against the Populist Mikhailovsky, which in reality settled accounts with the Narodniks. In it, he concluded that Narodnism had degenerated into "petty-bourgeois opportunism", which had now merged with liberalism and worked against their interests. They were therefore false "friends of the people", against the interests of the exploited and oppressed. Lenin then went on to expound the tasks of the revolutionary Social-Democrats:

> The political activity of the Social-Democrats lies in promoting the development and organisation of the working class movement in Russia, in transforming this movement from its present state of sporadic attempts at protest, 'riots' and strikes devoid of a guiding idea, into an organised struggle of the WHOLE Russian working CLASS directed against the bourgeois regime and working for the expropriation of the expropriators and the abolition of the social system based on the oppression of the working people. Underlying these activities is the common conviction of Marxists that the Russian worker is the sole and natural representative of Russia's entire working and exploited population.[15]

Lenin's book ended with the conclusion:

> When its advanced representatives have mastered the ideas of scientific socialism, the idea of the historical role of the Russian worker, when these ideas become widespread, and when stable organisations are formed among the workers to transform the workers' present sporadic economic war into conscious class struggle – then the Russian WORKER, rising at the head of all the democratic elements, will overthrow absolutism and lead the RUSSIAN PROLETARIAT (side by side with the proletariat of ALL COUNTRIES) *along the straight road of open political struggle to* THE VICTORIOUS COMMUNIST REVOLUTION.[16]

Lenin's call for the communist revolution echoed the words of the founders of scientific socialism. He followed this work with another devastating critique called *The Economic Content of Narodnism*, which, along with *What the 'Friends of the People' Are*, was of necessity printed and circulated illegally.

What the 'Friends of the People' Are was published in 1894, the same year as the accession to the throne of Nicholas II after his father, Alexander III, died from illness. The new tsar was rather an inept figure, even in comparison to his father. This reflected the growing degeneration of the old regime and its feeble

26. Tsar Nicholas II

representatives. "I understand absolutely nothing about matters of state", Nicholas remarked on the occasion of his own coronation. Unfortunately for him, this was a skill he would never manage to acquire.

His interests centred instead on the most worthwhile of pursuits: horse riding, skating and especially hunting. As regards politics, his sympathies were, unsurprisingly, associated with the most reactionary of organisations, such as the Union of Russian People, which was connected with the fascist Black Hundreds. To augment his autocratic power, like the pharaohs of ancient Egypt, Nicholas constructed a giant statue of himself in the centre of Moscow. It was dismantled in 1918 and is featured in Eisenstein's film *October*, symbolically falling to pieces as the old regime collapses.

In the footsteps of Marx and Engels

As we have seen, at this time, Lenin was deeply impressed with the writings of Plekhanov, especially his book, *The Development of the Monist View of History*, published in 1895.

27. The toppling of Nicolas II's statue as depicted in Eisenstein's *October*

In this text, Plekhanov outlined the materialist conception of history and was very critical of those, such as Struve, who had, by now, abandoned Marxism. He conducted a defence of materialism, while combatting philosophical idealism, historical subjectivism and the utopian views of the Narodniks. Lenin referred to Plekhanov's *Monist View of History* as a work "which had helped to educate a whole generation of Russian Marxists."[17] Even though Plekhanov would later diverge from the path politically, Lenin never forgot Plekhanov's colossal services to the movement.

While Plekhanov's works of this period helped deal a decisive blow to Narodnism, it can be said with justification that within socialist circles, Lenin's efforts put the final nails in its coffin.

In the middle of February 1895, Vladimir Ilyich attended a conference of Social-Democratic groups, where they read and discussed a pamphlet 'On Agitation', written by Arkadi Kremerm, edited with an introduction by Julius Martov, and issued by the Vilna Social-Democrats. This raised the need for the Social Democratic groups to engage in agitation on concrete demands. This would allow them to connect with the working class.

For Lenin, the work at this time was unfortunately cut across by a serious case of pneumonia, which resulted in him seeking permission to go abroad

28. Friedrich Engels

for treatment. This was granted in April, and allowed him to spend the whole summer in Europe. This provided him with a valuable opportunity to meet personally with Plekhanov, Axelrod and Zasulich in Geneva and Zurich for discussions. "He was not only an educated Marxist – of these there were very many", remarked Axelrod later, "but he knew what he wants to do and how it is necessary to do this."[18]

Following a week of these meetings, Lenin travelled to Paris to meet and talk with Paul Lafargue, Marx's son-in-law, and visited the Père Lachaise cemetery and the wall of the Communards. Next, he went to Berlin to speak with Wilhelm Liebknecht, the prominent German Social Democrat, and attended some workers' meetings. While he was in Berlin, he took some time out to visit the theatre, where he saw Hauptmann's *The Weavers*. He wrote to his mother:

> Although I had read the whole play beforehand in order to be able to follow it, I could not catch all the phrases. Still, I am not discouraged and only regret that I have too little time to study the language thoroughly.[19]

Lenin very much wanted to go to London to visit Engels, but this proved too difficult to arrange. Unfortunately, unbeknown to him, Engels was extremely ill and passed away in August of that same year.

Lenin had developed the greatest affection for Marx and Engels and their common lifelong struggle. He was determined to follow in their footsteps. Following Engels' death, Lenin wrote a short obituary, which stated:

> In him the Russian revolutionaries have lost their best friend.

> Let us always honour the memory of Friedrich Engels, a great fighter and teacher of the proletariat![20]

Lenin was to inherit Marx and Engels' iron will. In the later words of Alexander Potresov, one of the early members of the *Iskra* editorial board:

> Lenin alone embodied the phenomenon, rare everywhere but especially in Russia, of a man of iron will, inexhaustible energy, combining a fanatical faith in the movement, in the cause, with an equal faith in himself.[21]

Bourgeois philistines imagine that they detect in these important traits 'fanaticism', 'intolerance', 'narrow-mindedness' and, of course, the seeds of a future dictator. They are utterly incapable of understanding that such qualities are to be found in all truly great revolutionaries, whether it is Marat, Danton or Cromwell. They all possessed enormous determination, an iron will and a tremendous faith in their cause – that is what made them revolutionary leaders and allowed them to play the role they did.

The more these qualities crystallised within Lenin, the more he began to understand his future role. In his meetings with Plekhanov, he certainly regarded himself as very much the student and Plekhanov the teacher, and rightly so. He was still learning and deepening his knowledge of Marxism. However, according to Potresov, Ilyich revealed "a mind of brilliance and power. Every remark showed deep reflection."[22]

The League of Struggle

When Lenin finally returned from Europe to St. Petersburg in September 1895, he was brimming with enthusiasm and ideas. "He came back full of impressions, and brought with him a double-lined suitcase crammed with illegal literature", wrote Krupskaya.[23]

On his return, he met another young comrade in St. Petersburg, Julius Martov, who had also been expelled from university for his revolutionary activities. Martov, who was from a Jewish family, was also deeply attracted to Marxism and had been involved in the Jewish workers' organisations in Vilna. From their first meeting, these two young men were to form a strong

29. Julius Martov

bond. They decided to use their energies to build up the Marxist circles, with the aim of establishing a Social-Democratic party in Russia.

Their group had around a dozen members who organised a further two dozen workers' study circles. These, in turn, gathered around them some 150 contacts. Soon, branches of the organisation sprang up in Odessa and Tula. They fused their group with those of the veterans, like Gleb Krzhizhanovsky, to form the League of Struggle for the Emancipation of the Working Class.

For Lenin, this marked both a personal and political turning point. When filling in a Party questionnaire in 1922, while attending the Eleventh Congress, he wrote that he was a member of the Russian Communist Party "at its foundation" in 1895, the founding of the League. The following year in Nikolayev, a young student, Lev Bronstein (later known as Trotsky) helped to found the Workers' Association of South Russia. Workers' circles were springing up everywhere. As a result of their increased activities, these groups came under constant state surveillance by the Okhrana (The Department for Protecting the Public Security and Order), which had been set up specifically to combat underground left-wing activity.

30. Leading members of the League of Struggle for the Emancipation of the
Working Class in February 1897
Standing (left to right): AL Malchenko, PK Zaporozhets, Anatoly Vaneyev
Seated: Victor V Starkov, Gleb Krzhizhanovsky, Lenin, Martov

Lenin and his comrades were planning to issue a workers' newspaper, called
*Rabocheye Dyelo** (*Workers' Cause*). In doing so, they established an illegal
print shop to bring out the paper. However, just as they were about to get it
printed, Ilyich and four others were arrested. That was in December 1895. The
following year, Martov and Krupskaya were also arrested and imprisoned. As
intended, these arrests served to deplete the active forces of the League, and
undermined its work. As a result, the *Rabocheye Dyelo* never saw the light of day.

While in prison in St. Petersburg, Vladimir Ilyich maintained contact with
his comrades by correspondence and through visits from a 'fiancée', which
facilitated the undercover work. Krupskaya states:

It wasn't very long before we got in touch with Vladimir Ilyich. In those days
people committed for trial were freely permitted to receive books. They were given

---

* The name *Rabocheye Dyelo* eventually also adopted as the name of the Economists' newspaper
(April 1899 – February 1902).

31. Lenin's record card made by tsarist police in 1895

only a perfunctory examination, during which the tiny dots in the middle of the letters and the slightly changed colour of the paper where the milk had been used for ink, escaped notice.[24]

In this secret correspondence, milk rendered the words invisible to the naked eye until exposed to a hot flame. These letters were delivered every Saturday, which was book-receiving day.

In order not to waste time, Ilyich spent his time in prison writing pamphlets. These included the *Explanation of the Law on Fines Imposed on Factory Workers* and *The New Factory Law*. These concrete questions that affected the workers acted as a bridge for them to draw political conclusions. Krupskaya explains:

> At that time Vladimir Ilyich had made a thorough study of factory legislation. He believed that explaining these laws to the workers made it much easier to show them the connection that existed between their position and the political regime.[25]

Lenin began to prepare his first major book, *The Development of Capitalism in Russia*, which was to appear in 1899. He also wrote the *Draft and Explanation of the Programme for the Social Democratic Party*, for the First Congress of the Russian Social-Democratic Labour Party (RSDLP), which was to take place in March 1898.

He became so engrossed in his work that, when he was being released from prison to be deported, he joked with Krupskaya that they were letting him out too soon. "I haven't quite finished the book, and it will be difficult to get books in Siberia", he wrote.[26]

In 1896, an unprecedented strike broke out in the textile mills of St. Petersburg, involving around 35,000 workers. Thanks to the support they gave to the strike, the League made a number of recruits. A further strike occurred in early 1897, which won the eleven-and-a-half hour working day. However, with the League's leadership in prison, leadership of the St. Petersburg group had changed considerably and the new raw recruits, lacking a solid grounding in theory, tended to get carried away by the strike movement. This, according to Krupskaya, "had turned many heads…"[27] She explains:

> True, new comrades joined the group, but these people were not so well up on theory and experience. There was no time for them to learn, as the movement had to be taken care of and demanded a lot of energy. Agitation was the order of the day. We simply had no time to think of propaganda. Our leaflet agitation was a great success.[28]

4. Exile to Siberia

The Okhrana and its agents worked hard to suppress the budding revolutionary movement within Russia. In these years, many revolutionaries were rounded up and imprisoned or exiled by the tsarist regime. The arrest of Lenin along with the leading comrades of his group were part of this general clampdown.

After spending fourteen months in prison, on 10 February 1897, Lenin was finally sentenced for his illegal activities to a three-year internal exile in the village of Shushenskoe in eastern Siberia, which was an isolated settlement of a thousand inhabitants. The official document has been preserved, and runs as follows:

> The Police Department informs Vladimir Ilyich Ulyanov, junior barrister, that, in accordance with His Majesty's order of 29 January 1897 [10 February in the New Style], resulting from his conviction of a crime against the State, he, Ulyanov, is to be exiled to Eastern Siberia, under police surveillance, for a period of three years, until 29 January 1900.[1]

While being transported to Siberia, he wrote to his mother about the journey, the surrounding scenery and the utter isolation of the region:

> The country covered by the West-Siberian Railway that I have just travelled throughout its entire length (1,300 versts* from Chelyabinsk to Krivoshchokovo – three days) is astonishingly monotonous – bare, bleak steppe. No sign of life, no towns, very rarely a village or a patch of forest – and for the rest, all steppe. Snow and sky – and nothing else for the whole three days. [...] The air in the steppe,

---

* A Russian verst, now obsolete, was equivalent to 1.067 km or 0.663 miles.

however, is wonderful; breathing is so easy. There is a hard frost, more than twenty degrees below, but it is easier to bear here than in Russia.[2]

At the height of winter, the temperature in this part of Siberia reached lows of negative 30 degrees.

Krupskaya too was exiled for three years after she finished her prison sentence, but to a different place from Lenin, in Ufa Gubernia. She organised a campaign to be allowed to be with her 'fiancée'. As a result, she managed to get a transfer, on the condition the couple were immediately married. She therefore immediately set off, accompanied by her mother, Yelizaveta Vasilyevna, and finally joined Lenin in May 1898. Once settled in, Lenin wrote again to his mother about his impressions of the reunion with Krupskaya, and the reaction of her mother:

> Nadezhda Konstantinovna [Krupskaya], I find, is not looking at all well – she will have to take more care of her health while she is here. As for me – Yelizaveta Vasilyevna exclaimed, "Oh, how fat you're getting!"; and so, you see, you could not wish for a better report![3]

In June, he wrote again:

> We are now having real summer weather. The heat is exceptional – YV finds it very difficult. Nadya and I have begun bathing and have gone over to a summer system. [...]

> I am quite well (Nadya and YV, too). I am finishing the translation and shall then go back to my work again. I have been informed that the collection of my articles is soon to be printed.[4]

While in exile, Lenin continued to work during the evenings on his book, *The Development of Capitalism in Russia*. Each morning, together with Krupskaya, he spent time translating a new book by the British Fabians, Sidney and Beatrice Webb, called *The History of Trade Unions*. For them, this translation work was important as it brought in badly needed income, and their finances were almost exhausted.

"We shall send Webb off today, at long last; he has made us thoroughly tired of him, I must say", they wrote to Lenin's mother, although they still needed to finish the index.[5]

Apart from working on translations, Lenin spent most evenings reading literature or books on philosophy – Hegel, Kant and the French materialists. He wrote to Potresov:

32. Shushenskoe in Siberia, where Lenin was exiled

... I am only too well aware of my lack of philosophical education and I do not intend to write on these subjects until I have learned more. That is just what I am now doing – I have started with Holbach and Helvetius, and am now taking up Kant. I have got hold of the chief works of the chief classical philosophers, but I do not have the neo-Kantian books (I have only ordered Lange). Tell me, please, whether you or your comrades have them and whether you could not share them with me.[6]

But time seemed to pass slowly in exile. Whenever possible, Lenin and Krupskaya would go for walks and recreation, weather permitting. Lenin had a deep love of nature and the great outdoors. This was where he was able to take a break from his studies. "No people and no work – that is the best thing for me", he wrote at one point.[7] He also wrote to his mother and sister Anna:

Life here is not bad, I go shooting quite a lot; I have got to know the local sportsmen and go shooting with them. I have begun bathing; up to now I have had to go quite a long way, about two and a half versts, but soon I shall be able to go to a place about a verst and a half away. Such distances mean nothing to me because, apart from shooting and bathing, I spend a lot of time walking.[8]

In 1899, Lenin wrote a favourable review of *The Evolution of Modern Capitalism* (1894), by JA Hobson, an English radical thinker. He thought quite highly of Hobson and would use much of his material in a future work on imperialism.

A lot of his time was nevertheless taken up with writing *The Development of Capitalism in Russia*, which was based upon a systematic study of a huge amount of statistics. When completed, it was a substantial work of over 600 pages in the English translation, crammed full of economic facts and figures. It took Lenin more than three years to complete and was eventually published legally in March 1899, under the name of Vladimir Ilyin. It would be a few more years before he would adopt the pseudonym of 'Lenin'. The initial print run of 2,400 copies sold out quite quickly. As he explained in the preface to the first edition:

> In the work here presented, the author has set himself the aim of examining the question of how a home market is being formed for Russian capitalism. As we know, this question was raised long ago by the principal exponents of Narodnik views (chief among them being Messrs VV and N –on),* and it will be our task to criticise these views. We have not considered it possible to limit ourselves in this criticism to examining the mistakes and misconceptions in our opponents' views; in answering the question raised it seemed to us that it was not enough to adduce facts showing the formation and growth of a home market, for the objection might be raised that such facts had been selected arbitrarily and that facts showing the contrary had been omitted. It seemed to us that it was necessary to examine the whole process of the development of capitalism in Russia, to endeavour to depict it in its entirety.[9]

"Generally speaking, exile did not pass by so badly", explained Krupskaya, who tended to look more on the positive side of things. "Those were years of serious study."[10] Study was a key part of prison life for revolutionaries, a way of preparing for the future revolution.

More and more, Lenin looked to his future political work in developing the revolutionary party, which he thought about a great deal. He therefore wrote *The Tasks of the Russian Social-Democrats* at the end of 1897, in preparation for the first Social-Democratic Party Congress. "Russian Social Democracy is still very young", he explained. "It is only just emerging from its embryonic state in which theoretical questions predominated. It is only just beginning to develop its practical activity."[11]

Such activity was a turn towards the working class, which showed enormous promise. "And so, to work, comrades! Let us not lose precious time!"[12] Lenin

---

* 'VV' was the pseudonym of VP Vorontsov and 'N –on' the pseudonym of NF Danielson.

was very eager to write articles for workers and was keen to hear the opinions of Plekhanov and Axelrod about his efforts. "There is nothing I have wanted so much, or dreamed of so much, as an opportunity of writing for workers. But how to do this from here? It is very, very difficult, but not impossible, I think", he wrote to Axelrod.[13] In this letter, we can see his frustrations about exile.

First Congress of the RSDLP

While Lenin was still in Siberia, the first all-Russian Congress of the Russian Social Democratic Labour Party took place in Minsk, in March 1898. This reflected the yearnings within Russia to establish a real workers' party and a section of the mighty Second International.

The driving force behind this Congress was the newly established League of Jewish Workers of Poland and Lithuania, commonly referred to as the 'Bund', the Yiddish word for 'league'. This was the reason why the Congress was held in Minsk, a city of the Jewish Pale, although the Polish and western areas of Russia were also hotbeds of revolutionary agitation.*

The Congress was a very modest affair with a total attendance of nine delegates, representing the Bund, a Kiev group, St. Petersburg, Moscow and Ekaterinoslav Unions for the Liberation of Labour. After their deliberations, they published a manifesto and elected a three-person Central Committee. However, the congress lasted only three days, most of the delegates were arrested soon afterwards, and their illegal press was seized by the police. Its main achievement was to produce a manifesto written by Peter Struve, which contained a statement pregnant with meaning:

> Fifty years ago the life-giving storm of the revolution of 1848 swept over Europe. For the first time the modern working class came onto the stage as a major historical force. By using its efforts the bourgeoisie succeeded in sweeping away many obsolete feudal-monarchic institutions and laws. However, it quickly saw in its new ally its most avowed enemy and betrayed itself, the latter and the cause of freedom into the hands of reaction. But it was already too late: the working class which for a while was pacified, ten to fifteen years later reappeared on the historical scene, but with redoubled force and an adult self-consciousness, as a wholly mature fighter for its own final liberation...[14]

> The farther east one goes in Europe, the weaker, meaner and more cowardly in the political sense becomes the bourgeoisie, and the greater the cultural and political

---

* The Pale covered an area of about 472,590 square miles from the Baltic Sea to the Black Sea. According to the 1897 census, nearly 5 million Jews lived there – 94 per cent of the Jewish population of Russia.

tasks which fall to the lot of the proletariat. This is an essential step, but only the first step, to the realisation of the great historic mission of the proletariat, to the foundation of a social order in which there will be no place for the exploitation of man by man.[15]

However, within days of the end of the Congress, the organisation ceased to function at a national level, shattered by a wave of arrests. This abortive attempt was the last time a congress was held on Russian soil until after the Revolution in 1917.

In Lenin's Siberian exile, the post arrived twice a week, Tuesdays and Thursdays, bringing letters, papers and books. At this time, the tsarist authorities allowed such materials. Lenin also received visits from other Social-Democrats from time to time, depending on the restrictions. He soon became identified as the central figure among the exiles.

While he welcomed these visits from fellow comrades, Lenin longed to meet his main comrade-in-arms Julius Martov, who had been exiled to far-away Turukhansk. This isolated place was just south of the Arctic Circle, where the temperatures plummeted in the winter. This was torture for Martov, who was suffering from tuberculosis which was aggravated by the extreme weather. While they were separated by huge distances, Martov and Lenin nevertheless maintained a lively, if insufficient, correspondence. Martov was desperately hoping for a transfer on health grounds. Lenin expressed his frustrations to Potresov in April 1899:

> I was very glad, AN [Potresov], to receive your letter of 27 March, which at last broke your long and persistent silence. A heap of questions to be discussed has indeed accumulated but there is no opportunity of having any detailed conversation here on subjects that are mainly of a literary nature. And now there is the journal [*Nachalo*]: without talks with one's colleagues one feels too cut off for writing. There is only Julius [Martov], who takes all this quite closely and actively to heart, but the accursed "long distances" prevent sufficiently detailed conversation with him.[16]

This shows Lenin's close affection for Martov, the "only" one, according to him, to take things seriously to heart.

In spite of all this, Lenin kept himself busy, even engaging in his favourite pastime, chess matches, at which he excelled. He wrote to his brother-in-law:

> I received your letter on the 8 February. Your chess game came in very handy. The people from Minusinsk were here at the time as visitors and as they are now

33. Peter Struve   34. Alexander Potresov   35. Pavel Axelrod

enthusiastic chess players we had some exceedingly tough battles. We analysed your game, too. Judging by that, you have begun to play much better.[17]

The main thing that preoccupied Lenin's mind at this time, especially after the demise of the first Congress, was a plan to develop the work of the Party. Given its weaknesses, scattered in isolated circles, the Party needed to be given a professional and centralised character. He discussed his plans with Krupskaya, Martov and Potresov and these were later elaborated in articles, as well as in the pamphlets 'Where to Begin?', *What Is to Be Done?* and 'Letter to a Comrade on Our Organisational Tasks'.

The central element of these plans was the establishment of an all-Russian Social-Democratic newspaper. This paper would be published outside of Russia to ensure its continuity and then smuggled into the country. It would be a central organ that would bind the organisation together and help direct the work in the interior through a network of worker-correspondents. Given the fragmentation of the revolutionary movement into numerous circles, a newspaper would serve to direct the work and overcome their isolation. This is where the idea for *Iskra* (*The Spark*) originated.

In September 1899, Lenin and Krupskaya had received a copy of Eduard Bernstein's book that advocated a revision of the ideas of Marxism. Having read it, Lenin wrote to his mother, expressing his indignation:

> Nadya and I started reading Bernstein's book immediately; we have read more than a half and its contents astonish us more and more as we go on. It is unbelievably weak theoretically – mere repetition of someone else's ideas.
>
> There are phrases about criticism but no attempt at serious, independent criticism. In effect it is opportunism (or rather, Fabianism – the original of many

of Bernstein's assertions and ideas is to be found in the Webbs' recent books), unbounded opportunism and possibilism, and cowardly opportunism at that, since Bernstein does not want to attack the programme directly. There is little doubt but that it will be a fiasco. Bernstein's statement that many Russians agree with him ... (pp. 170 and 173, footnotes) made us very indignant.[18]

'Legal' Marxism

Under tsarism, state censorship of books and newspapers had been quite ruthless. Until 1865, books and papers could not be published without prior state approval. Then, under Alexander II, new 'liberal' rules over censorship were introduced, overseen by tribunals. But little changed as these tribunals were in the pockets of the authorities and simply acted as their agents.

Consequently, it was not possible for revolutionaries to operate openly under such conditions, otherwise they would be liable to imprisonment and exile. Therefore, they tried where possible to get around the censor, as did Lenin, using Aesopian language, such as 'the new theory' instead of 'Marxism' and avoiding the words 'Marxist' and 'socialist' altogether. Such legitimate methods were then combined with illegal publications putting forward the full uncensored programme of Marxism.

In this early period, Peter Struve was considered a promising young Marxist. As explained, he had drafted the Manifesto of the First RSDLP Congress. However, he drifted politically and later in life became a right-wing bourgeois liberal and then a monarchist. However, for the time being, Struve showed a positive interest in Marxism. In 1894, he published his *Critical Notes*, which sharply criticised populism. "Russia is moving forward, factories and plants are going up and the urban industrial proletariat is making its appearance. Capitalism in Russia is inevitable", he wrote.[19] Struve's views at this time were in complete agreement with those of Plekhanov and Lenin.

However, while Plekhanov and Lenin used their efforts to build a revolutionary workers' party to fight for communism, Struve grew increasingly sceptical and eventually lost sight of this aim. This 'little difference' between the bold programme and its watered-down version was to become the basis of 'Legal Marxism', which Struve and Tugan-Baranovsky represented.

The arguments of this emasculated 'Legal Marxism' became very useful for the liberal opposition in its struggle against the autocracy. Given their weakness, the liberals needed to lean for support on the workers. But to do this, they needed to appear 'revolutionary', at least in words. They accomplished this by using 'Marxist' phraseology, but bereft of its revolutionary content. They used edited passages from *The Communist Manifesto* to justify the progressive mission of capitalism, but left out such phrases as the "gravediggers of capitalism", so as not to offend their liberal friends and to get through the censor. This forced Lenin to comment:

> One cannot help remarking in this connection that Marxism is most atrociously narrowed and garbled when our liberals and radicals undertake to expound it in the pages of the legal press. What an exposition it is! Just think how this revolutionary doctrine has to be mutilated to fit into the Procrustean bed of Russian censorship![20]

Struve, Tugan-Baranovsky and their friends were assisted in their endeavours by the state censors, who allowed a number of Marx's economic writings to pass scrutiny, mainly because they did not understand these ideas, but also because they believed they might provide a useful criticism of populist extremism. Of course, any of Marx's work passed by the tsarist censor was welcomed by the Marxists! Lenin later explained how the phenomenon of 'Legal Marxism' came into being:

> Speaking generally, this was an altogether curious phenomenon that no one in the eighties or the beginning of the nineties would have believed possible. In a country ruled by an autocracy, with a completely enslaved press, in a period of desperate political reaction in which even the tiniest outgrowth of political discontent and protest is persecuted, the theory of revolutionary Marxism suddenly forces its way into the *censored* literature and, though expounded in Aesopian language, is understood by all the 'interested'. The government had accustomed itself to regarding only the theory of the (revolutionary) Narodnaya Volya as dangerous, without, as is usual, observing its internal evolution, and rejoicing at *any* criticism levelled against it. Quite a considerable time elapsed (by our Russian standards) before the government realised what had happened and the unwieldy army of censors and gendarmes discovered the new enemy and flung itself upon him. Meanwhile, Marxist books were published one after another, Marxist journals and newspapers were founded, nearly everyone became a Marxist, Marxists were flattered, Marxists were courted, and the book publishers rejoiced at the extraordinary, ready sale of Marxist literature. It was quite natural, therefore, that among the Marxian neophytes who were caught up in this atmosphere, there should be more than one 'author who got a swelled head...'.[21]

'Legal Marxism', which rendered Marxism harmless, was regarded by its advocates as a 'bridge' into the camp of bourgeois liberalism and other establishment careers. These 'critics of Marxism', in reality, reflected the same political tendency as the revisionist Eduard Bernstein in Germany. It is no accident that Lenin described Struve as the 'Russian Bernstein'.

'Economism'

Another trend that began to make headway among the Social-Democrats in Russia was Economism. It was this tendency that had influenced the work of the League for the Emancipation of the Working Class in St. Petersburg. "By this rather slangy term ['Economism'] we meant the childish vulgarisation of Marx's views on historical materialism", Lenin explained.[22] The Economists argued that the Social-Democrats should reduce everything to economic demands and not involve themselves in politics. In other words, the Economists saw the economic struggle as an end in itself and not something organically linked to the fight for a proletarian revolution.

The Economists argued that raising political demands to overthrow tsarism would only frighten workers away – far better that the workers should not bother with politics, but rather, leave such matters to the liberals. After all, as they understood, as the coming revolution was a *bourgeois* revolution, the liberal-bourgeoisie should be left alone to lead *their* revolution. This would then allow the workers to concentrate on matters that were of direct interest to them, namely bread-and-butter economic issues to improve their lot. They laid heavy stress on the need to concentrate on the 'immediate', 'concrete', 'practical' demands that, according to them, were the only things that workers had any interest in.

Of course, Marxists are in favour of taking up economic demands, such as wages and conditions. Lenin himself wrote articles on strikes and workers' fines, which were immediate issues facing the working class. However, Lenin always linked these day-to-day problems to political questions and ultimately to the overthrow of the autocracy. He also explained that the working class must fight for its own class demands, both economic and political, as there was no wall separating the two.

As explained, the 1890s were a period of intense industrial boom. The working class was growing in strength and was making its mark on the life of the country. Strikes were becoming more prevalent. The following figures show the rising number of strikes, which reflected the developing confidence and organisation of the young Russian working class:[23]

	1893	1894	1895	1896	1897	1898	1899
Strikes (1,000s)	35	41	68	118	145	215	189

During this time, the Economists' newspapers, *Rabochaya Mysl* (*Workers' Thought*) and *Rabocheye Dyelo* (*Workers' Cause*), emphasised the virtues of the spontaneous movement of the working class and enjoyed a considerable influence in the circles of St. Petersburg. The industrial ferment provided fertile ground for the success of agitation. However, instead of building on this movement, the whole approach of the Economists in practice subordinated the working class to the liberals. True, they also criticised the 'Legal Marxists', but from their own opportunist viewpoint, which only served to introduce confusion into the newly emerging workers' movement. The task of counteracting these influences became a vital one for Lenin. He stated: "it is not surprising that an open war against Economism became more and more urgent and inevitable."[24]

Lenin's attacks on Economism were coupled with the need to fuse the local Social-Democratic groups into a single centralised party. In contrast to the Economists, Lenin stressed the positive features of the old centralised Narodnik organisation, the *Zemlya i Volya*, "…the magnificent organisation that the revolutionaries had in the seventies…should serve us as a model", he wrote.[25]

From Lenin's perspective, an all-Russian newspaper was vital in developing the Party and he won over Martov and Potresov to this view. They became so enthused about the idea that they engaged in a lively correspondence about the project. From there, they turned their attention to the fine details of who would write for it, how it was to be printed and even how it was to be distributed and smuggled into Russia. Having discussed all the angles and reached absolute agreement, they then made plans to go abroad as soon as possible to meet with Plekhanov and gain his backing.

New turning point

There was great optimism at the dawn of the new century. Lenin looked forward to being released from exile, and on 11 February 1900 he was finally allowed to leave Shushenskoe. Six days later he had settled in Pskov, as a condition of his release was a prohibition from living in St. Petersburg, Moscow, or any industrial city. He soon applied for permission to go abroad on the pretext of needing medical treatment, which was accepted on 4 May. The request was probably granted to Lenin with the idea that the further away such undesirables were from Russia, the better. He wrote to his mother the following day:

> Yesterday I received a certificate from the local Chief of Police to the effect that he has no objection to my making a journey abroad; today I paid the stamp duty (ten rubles) and in two hours' time I shall receive my passport. And so I shall be moving to warmer parts in summer.[26]

Lenin then met with Vera Zasulich illegally in St. Petersburg and used her to sound out support for the new initiative. Things seemed to go well, and he met up with Martov and Potresov to develop the plans further. On behalf of their group, Potresov went to Germany to meet with the Emancipation of Labour Group to confirm their agreement. While he was in Germany, he also sounded out the Social-Democrats about using their printing facilities to publish the new paper. Again, everything seemed entirely possible.

Then, on 16 July, Lenin left Russia and set off for Geneva in order to meet personally with Plekhanov. Expectations were high, but unfortunately, the meeting did not go as planned. In fact, it almost led to an immediate rupture and the abandonment of the entire project.

Lenin had been joined by Potresov in the discussions with Plekhanov. It was evident that Plekhanov, who for years had held things together almost single-handedly, was suspicious of both of these newcomers and their grand ideas. The meeting, as a result, became rather tense. Lenin was deeply shocked and taken aback by Plekhanov's cantankerous and aggressive behaviour.

The whole experience for them was extremely painful. Soon afterwards, Lenin wrote down his personal impressions of the meeting for his closest comrades in a very long report called, 'How the *Spark* Was Nearly Extinguished'.

Plekhanov's nerves had clearly been on edge for some time. He had just gone through a bitter split a few months earlier in April with the Union of Russian Social-Democrats Abroad after they had adopted the ideas of Economism and then denied the struggle for socialism. Things turned into a nasty row and Plekhanov and his group walked out. "Woe to the party that patiently tolerates such confusion!", said Plekhanov.[27]

This split was not only a political clash but also a generational one. The youth in the Union of Russian Social Democrats Abroad had all the contacts with Russia from which Plekhanov's group was excluded. The years in exile had certainly affected Plekhanov and his group had all the hallmarks and defects of a propaganda circle, isolated from the working class and isolated from Russia. This experience certainly coloured Plekhanov's behaviour, and he became very suspicious of such outsiders.

Therefore, in his meeting with Lenin and Potresov, who he must have considered very inexperienced compared to himself, Plekhanov displayed excessive intolerance and even bad temper. The meeting soon became impossible. As Lenin recalled afterwards:

> ... Arsenyev [Potresov] began by declaring that as far as he was concerned his personal relations with Plekhanov were broken off once and for all, never to be restored. He would maintain business relations with him, but as for personal relations – *fertig* [finished]. Plekhanov's behaviour had been insulting to such a degree that one could not help suspecting him of harbouring 'unclean' thoughts about us (i.e. that he regarded us as *Streber* [careerists]). He trampled us underfoot, etc. I fully supported these charges. My 'infatuation' with Plekhanov disappeared as if by magic, and I felt offended and embittered to an unbelievable degree. Never, never in my life, had I regarded any other man with such sincere respect and veneration, never had I stood before any man so 'humbly' and never before had I been so brutally 'kicked'. That's what it was, we had actually been kicked.[28]

Fortunately, with the intervention of Zasulich and Axelrod, they managed to cool tempers and repair relations. Before leaving, in their final interview with Plekhanov, the old man admitted that there had been a sad misunderstanding and his nerves were frayed. All he now wanted was to mend fences and restore comradely relations. "Plekhanov displayed all his dexterity, the brilliance of his examples, smiles, jests, and citations, which compelled us to laugh in spite of ourselves", noted Lenin.[29]

For those who attack Lenin for 'intolerance' and 'ruthlessness', this whole episode again reveals Lenin's real character when dealing with problems and people: a great deal of patience and flexibility. These were important skills he was to retain throughout his life. Even in the sharpest of polemics between comrades, Lenin would always seek to soften the blows at the end of the day and part on friendly terms.

The breakdown had been avoided. Lenin still looked up to Plekhanov, but his original estimation had been marred by the whole experience.

Nevertheless, despite everything, Plekhanov and his group were on board with the *Iskra* project, which was the main thing as far as Lenin was concerned. A new chapter was about to unfold with the birth of *Iskra*, the first all-Russian underground Marxist newspaper.

5. 'Iskra' Launched

In September 1900, Lenin left Geneva to go to Nuremberg, where he met with a leading Social-Democrat to discuss the technicalities of typesetting and printing the new *Iskra*. Soon afterwards, he journeyed to Munich to find a suitable operational base. Despite all the precautions, police agents still retained an interest in him after a circular was issued by the Okhrana to its foreign bureaus to be on the lookout for Ulyanov as a subversive individual.

Fortunately for Lenin, this interest seemed to wane and he took up lodgings at the home of a German Social-Democratic sympathiser. Soon afterwards, Vera Zasulich arrived and met him in Munich. Lenin became quite fond of her and he had a high opinion of her as a revolutionary figure, her courage and self-sacrifice, despite her Bohemian ways and persistent chain-smoking. "Wait till you see Zasulich", he told Krupskaya when she first arrived in Munich, "She is true to the core."[1]

For now, at least, the conflict with Plekhanov had been smoothed over. It was resolved that *Iskra* would have an editorial board made up of six members: Plekhanov, Axelrod and Zasulich from the old veterans; Lenin, Martov and Potresov from the younger generation. Given the even number, and in the eventuality of a tied vote, Plekhanov, as the most authoritative political figure, was given two votes. Relations were thus patched up. However, it would still take a prolonged period of common work to iron everything out and for things to completely settle down.

"Among these six people", notes Zinoviev in passing, "was one future Bolshevik and five future Mensheviks", but this development lay very much in the future.[2]

Lenin was at pains to draw a line under the previous experience. Nevertheless, given the frictions that still existed, he was very mindful of future difficulties. As he explained:

> We had agreed among ourselves not to relate what had passed to anyone except our most intimate friends. [...] Outwardly it was as though nothing had happened [...] but within a cord had broken, and instead of splendid personal relations, dry, business-like relations prevailed, with a constant reckoning according to the principle: *si vis pacem, para bellum* [if you desire peace, prepare for war].[3]

The decisive thing was that the launch of *Iskra* would go ahead as agreed. However, another disagreement soon surfaced, as to where the paper was to be published. For rapid distribution purposes, its production needed to be located on a route with good communications with Russian cities. Germany was clearly best suited for this purpose, being on the border with Russia.

Furthermore, Lenin, Potresov and Zasulich were all now living in Munich, and Martov was soon to arrive there, so the idea of creating the *Iskra* centre in Germany sounded ideal. But Plekhanov remained at home in Geneva and Axelrod remained in Zurich, so they argued that the operation should be based in Switzerland. This was clearly unsatisfactory, and in the end, Munich was chosen. While the editorial board was based in Munich, Plekhanov and Axelrod would maintain contact with the other editors through correspondence and occasional trips to Germany.

With this matter now settled, *Iskra* was to be printed on the presses of the German Social Democratic Party and a network of collaborators was organised to distribute the paper within Russia.

In September it was agreed to issue a public *Declaration* in the name of the *Iskra* editors, which announced the impending launch of the All-Russian Marxist paper. For all intents and purposes, this announcement was a declaration of war on all revisionist tendencies in the movement, especially Economism and 'Legal Marxism'.

In early December, Lenin travelled to Stuttgart to prepare the launch of *Zarya* (*Dawn*), the theoretical magazine of the group, then to Leipzig, where *Iskra* was originally typeset and printed. Things had come together. On Christmas Eve, 1900, the first issue of *Iskra* rolled off the printing press.

It was the first ever such newspaper to be launched and distributed in Russia, and it represented a historic milestone. Several thousand copies were printed in close typeface, with no pictures, on four pages of onionskin – a

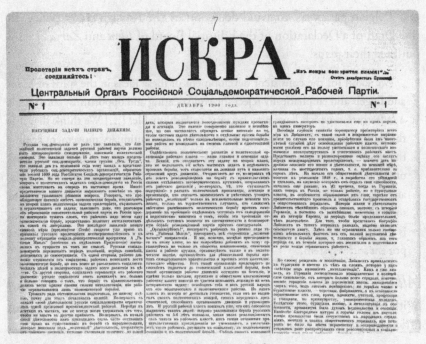

36. The first issue of *Iskra*

thin, translucent paper. The masthead of *Iskra* boldly proclaimed the words of the martyred Decembrists* to Pushkin: *"Out of this spark will come a flame…"* The paper appeared at a decisive time for the Russian movement.

The *Declaration* and the first article were written by Lenin and were a resolute call to action. "We must train people who will devote the whole of their lives, not only their free evenings, to the revolution", wrote Lenin in the first issue of *Iskra*.[4] He began as he meant to continue. In fact, encapsulated within this single line lies the basis of his organisational principles for the party, as expressed later in *What Is to Be Done?*

In addition, the new theoretical magazine *Zarya* was issued in April 1901, which, it must be said, the older members seemed more enthusiastic about. Still weighed down by their small circle mentality, they had not, as yet, fully grasped the real historic significance of *Iskra*.

After the first issue, the remainder were printed in Munich until the paper's move to London in 1902. Krupskaya had joined Lenin from Russia. From now on, the *Iskra* organisation became the centre of their lives. They now both lived under the assumed names of Dr and Mrs Meyer, together with

---

* A group of radical army officers who staged an uprising in December 1825.

fake Belgian passports, to avoid detection by the Russian secret police. In the 'Draft of a Declaration of the Editorial Board of *Iskra* and *Zarya*', Lenin outlined their plans.

> ... we stand for the consistent development of these ideas in the spirit of Marx and Engels and emphatically reject the equivocating and opportunist corrections *à la* Bernstein which have now become so fashionable. [...] We think that it is the duty of Social-Democracy to support every revolutionary movement against the existing political and social system, and we regard its aim to be the conquest of political power by the working class, the expropriation of the expropriators, and the establishment of a socialist society. We strongly repudiate every attempt to weaken or tone down the revolutionary character of Social-Democracy, which is the party of social revolution, ruthlessly hostile to all classes standing for the present social system.[5]

'All wheels stand still...'

With strikes becoming more common in Russia, Lenin wrote an important article explaining their significance:

> ... strikes, which arise out of the very nature of capitalist society, signify the beginning of the working-class struggle against that system of society. [...]
>
> ... when the workers state their demands jointly and refuse to submit to the money-bags, they cease to be slaves, they become human beings, they begin to demand that their labour should not only serve to enrich a handful of idlers, but should also enable those who work to live like human beings. [...]
>
> Strikes, therefore, always instil fear into the capitalists, because they begin to undermine their supremacy. "All wheels stand still, if your mighty arm wills it", a German workers' song says of the working class. [...]
>
> Every strike reminds the capitalists that it is the workers and not they who are the real masters – the workers who are more and more loudly proclaiming their rights. Every strike reminds the workers that their position is not hopeless, that they are not alone. See what a tremendous effect strikes have both on the strikers themselves and on the workers at neighbouring or nearby factories or at factories in the same industry.[6]
>
> A strike, moreover, opens the eyes of the workers to the nature, not only of the capitalists, but of the government and the laws as well.[7]

Lenin went on to explain that behind every strike "lurks the hydra of revolution", and went on:

37. Lenin in 1900

Strikes, therefore, teach the workers to unite; they show them that they can struggle against the capitalists only when they are united; strikes teach the workers to think of the struggle of the whole working class against the whole class of factory owners and against the arbitrary police government. This is the reason that socialists call strikes 'a school of war', a school in which the workers learn to make war on their enemies for the liberation of the whole people, of all who labour, from the yoke of government officials and from the yoke of capital.[8]

While Lenin explained that strikes, representing "a school of war", provided a vital education for the working class, only the war itself would lead to the overthrow of capitalism. The task was to draw these struggles together and unify them politically. Above all, they must be linked to the building of a revolutionary workers' party, the means to overthrow the capitalist system. This was the aim of both Lenin and *Iskra*.

Everything was in place to win the battle of ideas, especially in Russia, where the paper would play a decisive role. The strategy was to defeat the revisionists wherever they arose and make *Iskra* the dominant tendency in the Russian working-class movement.

Throughout its existence, *Iskra* was to carry articles by the outstanding figures of Russian Marxism – Plekhanov, Lenin, Martov, Axelrod, Trotsky – which laid the basis for its success as a tendency. It adopted a polemical style that marked it out from all the rest. Its content would connect with the advanced layers of the young working class, who were beginning to develop a class consciousness.

Eventually, *Iskra* would act as the centre for the unification of the Party forces, with groups in a whole series of Russian cities. While the movement was politically guided by the editorial board, the *Iskra* organisation on the ground was run by the 100 or 150 *Iskra* agents, the leading professional revolutionaries of the time.

When Krupskaya arrived in Munich in 1901, she was appointed the secretary of *Iskra*, and took care of the growing correspondence with Russia, a position she relished. In many ways, she became the centre of the organisation: newly arrived comrades would report to her first; she would brief those who were leaving; she established clandestine contacts and connections; she gave instructions, wrote letters and decoded messages. Her room always had the faint smell of heated paper, which had been warmed over a flame. She observed Lenin at work and discussed the stream of news from Russia with him.

The printed copies of *Iskra* were shipped off to Berlin, to the offices of *Vorwärts*, the paper of the SPD. There, they were folded into small parcels and concealed in packing cases. From there, they were dispatched to towns on the German border with tsarist Russia, where they were picked up and smuggled across by *Iskra* agents. In this way, they were distributed throughout Russia. As can be imagined, the distribution of the paper was a very elaborate, difficult and dangerous operation. *Iskra* agents had to work hard to avoid the Prussian police who, like the Okhrana agents, were on the lookout for Russian revolutionaries.

Papers were smuggled into Russia in various ways, using double-bottomed suitcases, special waistcoats and bodices, as well as being sewn into women's skirts. "With our equipment women would carry about three or four hundred copies of *Iskra*", explained Krupskaya.[9] Not infrequently, batches of newspapers would be confiscated, with agents arrested and exiled. According to Krupskaya, probably no more than 10 per cent of the revolutionary literature ever arrived at its destination. The entire batch of the first issue, which was being smuggled across the Russian border at Memel in East Prussia, was seized. Despite this, a further thousand copies made the crossing in false-bottomed trunks. To increase the circulation, issues would be reprinted within Russia on illegal printing presses, but this was a highly dangerous affair.

French, and sometimes Russian steamers, brought copies of *Iskra* from Marseilles to the Black Sea ports of Batumi and Odessa, or to Baku. From there, they were wrapped in waterproofing and dumped overboard where they were picked up for distribution across the Caucasus and beyond. In the north of Norway, they were dispatched after being wrapped in greaseproof paper and stored inside boxes of salted fish. The whole operation was nothing short of incredible under such conditions.

Despite all the difficulties and hold-ups, the establishment of *Iskra* proved to be a turning point in the history of the Russian revolutionary movement. Within the space of three years, the task of becoming the dominant political tendency in Russia had been accomplished.

Even at this stage, Lenin's status within the *Iskra* organisation was noted. This was revealed by the comment of another editor, Potresov:

> Plekhanov was esteemed, Martov was loved, but only Lenin was followed unquestioningly, as the only undisputed leader. For only Lenin embodied ... a personage of iron will, indomitable energy, combining a fanatical faith in the movement, in the cause, with as great a faith in himself.[10]

'Where to Begin?'

While in Munich, Lenin sought to give guidance to the Party, not only through the pages of *Iskra*, but in other important writings such as his article, 'Where to Begin?' (May 1901) and, in particular, his pamphlet, *What Is to Be Done?* (March 1902), where these ideas were further developed. These writings pointed the way forward for the movement and laid down its organisational principles. It was "an attempt... in the simplest possible style, illustrated by numerous and concrete examples, *systematically to 'clarify' all* our basic points of difference with all the Economists."[11] In criticising the worship of spontaneity, he constantly stressed that without strong organisation, the working class would not be able to succeed in its objectives. "Here we come to the most urgent question of our movement, to its sore point – organisation", he wrote.[12]

Up until this time, the local Social-Democratic circles in Russia were largely uncoordinated and leaderless, and engaged in work that was both inconsistent and haphazard. Lenin was keen to rectify this and establish the

Party on a sound basis. He had given a great deal of thought to the need to professionalise the work and developed a set of clear ideas about how this could be achieved. To overcome the scattered, localised nature of the organisation, there needed to be a greater centralism. This, in turn, would provide a basis for the necessary coordination and leadership. Lenin therefore proposed that the Party be guided by *two* leading bodies: a *Central Organ*, the editorial board of the paper, operating in exile, and a *Central Committee*, responsible for work within Russia.

In this way, the Central Organ would be responsible for the ideological leadership and operate from abroad, out of harm's way of the police. This would provide continuity and stability to the organisation. At the same time, the Central Committee would direct the practical, day-to-day side of the work in the interior. These bodies would then work in tandem. Within this, Lenin believed that there should be room for maximum local initiative and involvement. These two approaches – centralism and local initiative – would dialectically complement one another as the situation demanded.

> We must centralise the leadership of the movement. We must also […] as far as possible *decentralise responsibility to the Party* on the part of its individual members, of every participant in its work, and of every circle belonging to or associated with the party. This decentralisation is an essential prerequisite of revolutionary centralisation and an *essential corrective to it*.[13]

The role of the newspaper in the building of the party was always key in Lenin's thinking. In 'Where to Begin?' (*Iskra*, No. 4), he outlined the classic functions of the party newspaper as educator and organiser:

> The role of a newspaper, however, is not limited solely to the dissemination of ideas, to political education, and to the enlistment of political allies. A newspaper is not only a collective propagandist and a collective agitator, it is also a collective organiser. In this last respect it may be likened to the scaffolding around a building under construction, which marks the contours of the structure and facilitates communication between the builders, enabling them to distribute the work and to view the common results achieved by their organised labour. With the aid of the newspaper, and through it, a permanent organisation will naturally take shape that will emerge, not only in local activities, but in regular general work, and will train its members to follow political events carefully, appraise their significance and their effect on the various strata of the population, and develop effective means for the revolutionary party to influence those events.[14]

In order to achieve these ends, Lenin criticised the arguments of the Economists, especially their stress on working-class spontaneity and their excessive concentration on basic economic demands. Lenin regarded the Economists as a Russian variety of opportunism and Bernsteinism. In fact, Lenin saw the fight against the Economists in the same light as Kautsky's fight in Germany. That is why Lenin included this point in the *Declaration* on behalf of the editorial board:

> ... among wide circles an ideological wavering is to be seen, an infatuation with the fashionable 'criticism of Marxism' and with 'Bernsteinism,' the spread of the views of the so-called 'economist' trend, and what is inseparably connected with it – an effort to keep the movement at its lower level, to push into the background the task of forming a revolutionary party that heads the struggle of the entire people.

Lenin continued:

> *It is a fact* that such an ideological wavering is to be observed among Russian Social-Democrats; that narrow practicalism, detached from the theoretical clarification of the movement as a whole, threatens to divert the movement to a false path. [...]

> We do not desire to exaggerate the gravity of the situation, but it would be immeasurably more harmful to close our eyes to it. For this reason we heartily welcome the decision of the Emancipation of Labour group to resume its literary activity and begin a systematic struggle against the attempts to distort and vulgarise Social-Democracy.[15]

Lenin argued that the prime task was to work for *ideological unity* within the movement, which would be forged through the adoption of a clear Party programme. However, Lenin went on to reiterate a point he would use many times in the future:

> *Before we can unite, and in order that we may unite, we must first of all draw firm and definite lines of demarcation.* Otherwise our unity will be purely fictitious, it will conceal the prevailing confusion and hinder its radical elimination.[16]

He then went on to define the character of the newspaper, not as a free-for-all, but as a strictly Marxist organ, striving for a definite set of ideas:

> It is understandable, therefore, that we do not intend to make our publication a mere store-house of various views. On the contrary, we shall conduct it in the spirit of a strictly defined tendency. This tendency can be expressed by the word Marxism,

and there is hardly need to add that we stand for the consistent development of the ideas of Marx and Engels and emphatically reject the equivocating, vague, and opportunist 'corrections' for which Eduard Bernstein, P Struve, and many others have set the fashion.[17]

Professional revolutionaries

In his book *What Is to Be Done?*, Lenin returned to the theme of organisation and the need for the party to be based upon "professional revolutionaries", who would dedicate their lives to its work and goals. He explained it was their "duty to assist every capable worker to become a *professional* agitator, organiser, propagandist, literature distributor, etc., etc."[18] "Attention, therefore, must be devoted *principally* to *raising* the workers to the level of revolutionaries…"[19]

These professional revolutionaries were to become the backbone of the party and its underground work. Soon, there were hundreds of activists working within Russia, risking life and limb for the cause. Given the tsarist regime, they were forced to work in clandestine conditions, on false papers and many with no fixed address.

These revolutionaries, who worked full time for the movement, would receive no wages, but rely on material assistance from members and sympathisers. They would work to distribute the illegal paper and literature, as well as raise funds to keep the underground work going. Their meeting places would vary between outdoor 'picnics', clubs, studios, and even boat trips, wherever they could meet away from the prying eyes of the Okhrana.

The noble character of these professional revolutionaries was illustrated by Elena Stasova, who, following her arrest, wrote these lines from prison:

> … my life is in this, in this and only in this. No other work can give me the strength to live … without this work of mine I cannot live. This is the flesh of my flesh.[20]

Under her guidance, the St. Petersburg Marxist circle was clandestinely printing and distributing weekly broadsheets, often in runs of 10,000 copies. The revolutionaries in Russia lived for the movement, not only in their daily efforts, but with their very body and soul. Faced with extreme hardships, they were completely dedicated and openly identified with the cause they served. It was from such men and women that the movement created the fighters who would become the many points of support for the future proletarian revolution.

However, the idea of the 'professional revolutionary' has drawn scorn from the apologists of capitalism and drawing-room socialists, who portray them as being some kind of wild fanatics. Trotsky ably defends these revolutionaries against such slanders:

A professional revolutionist is a person who completely dedicates himself to the labour movement under conditions of illegality and forced conspiracy. Not everyone is capable of that, and certainly, in any event, not the worst kind of person. The labour movement of the civilised world knows numerous professional officials and professional politicians; the preponderant majority of that caste is noted for its conservatism, egotism and narrow-mindedness, living not for the movement, but at its expense. By comparison with the average labour bureaucrat of Europe or America, the average professional revolutionist of Russia cut an incomparably more attractive figure.

The youth of the revolutionary generation coincided with the youth of the labour movement. It was the epoch of people between the ages of eighteen and thirty. Revolutionists above that age were few in number and seemed old men. The movement was as yet utterly devoid of careerism, lived on its faith in the future and on its spirit of self-sacrifice. There were as yet no routine, no set formulae, no theatrical gestures, no ready-made oratorical tricks. The struggle was by nature full of pathos, shy and awkward. The very words 'committee', 'party' were as yet new, with an aura of vernal freshness, and rang in young ears as a disquieting and alluring melody. Whoever joined an organisation knew that prison followed by exile awaited him within the next few months. The measure of ambition was to last as long as possible on the job prior to arrest; to hold oneself steadfast when facing the gendarmes; to ease, as far as possible, the plight of one's comrades; to read, while in prison, as many books as possible; to escape as soon as possible from exile abroad; to acquire wisdom there; and then return to revolutionary activity in Russia.

The professional revolutionists believed what they taught. They could have had no other incentive for taking to the road to Calvary. Solidarity under persecution was no empty word, and it was augmented by contempt for cowardice and desertion. [...]

The young men and young women who devoted themselves entirely to the revolutionary movement, without demanding anything in return, were not the worst representatives of their generation. The order of 'professional revolutionists' cannot suffer by comparison with any other social group.[21]

Of course, the role of the professional revolutionary did not invalidate the vital importance of the working class in fighting for its own emancipation, but served to complement it. For Lenin, the task of the party was to take advantage of the spontaneous activity of the working class to direct it towards revolutionary ends. To that end, he very much welcomed the upsurge of the new strike movement as an opportunity for the revolutionary party to fertilise it with its ideas.

As Marx himself explained, the emancipation of the working class is the task of the working class itself. However, the need for a revolutionary party as a vanguard party arises from the fact that the working class is not completely homogeneous.

The working class is made up of different layers, many with separate skills, with their own sectional interests. In the class struggle, different layers often draw different conclusions at different times. The role of the party is precisely to draw these separate strands together and direct them towards the conquest of power. This is the role of the conscious subjective factor in history. If the working class were completely homogeneous, there would be no need for a party. The class would move together as one. But this is not the case.

This was graphically illustrated by Trotsky in his *History of the Russian Revolution*, where he represented the energy of the masses as steam and the revolutionary party as a piston-box. The steam, instead of dissipating into thin air, was channelled through the piston-box and so became a powerful unstoppable force that could be harnessed. The party is the highest expression of working-class consciousness. This, very simply, is the key role of the party.

It was Lenin alone, more than anyone else, who grasped the importance of the revolutionary party, even more than Trotsky or Rosa Luxemburg. He stood far above everyone else on this question. "Give us an organisation of revolutionaries, and we will overturn Russia", stated Lenin, paraphrasing Archimedes.[22]

Early on, using the arguments in *What Is to Be Done?* and other writings, Lenin began to lay down the organisational principles of the party. He fully understood that it was not possible simply to improvise the party when revolution broke out. The party had to be consciously built in advance of the revolution, "since it is too late to form the organisation in times of explosions and outbursts…"[23]

As it was not possible to create such a party overnight, this demonstrated the limits of spontaneity. There were no shortcuts to the hard work of party-building.

The Party needed to be based upon a layer of the most advanced, educated, and developed cadres who fully understood the precise nature of the tasks required to prepare for the overthrow of capitalism. The revolutionary party is, first and foremost, the programme, perspectives and methods, then secondly, an organisation that is equipped to carry these ideas into the working class, beginning with its most advanced stratum.

The kind of organisational structure needed for this must be based on the principles of *democratic centralism*. This corresponds closely to the basic democracy of the working-class movement itself. Its principles were simple: following a thorough, free and democratic debate, where matters would be clarified satisfactorily, a vote would then be taken to decide the outcome. The majority would decide and the minority would abide by, and carry out, the decision of the majority.

The party was not a debating society or a forum in which every individual is free to express any ideas that occur to them. It is a weapon in the fight to change society. Everything was subordinated to this fact.

Lenin wrote to an old friend, Apollinaria Yakubova, who had been involved in the old St. Petersburg group, but had now sided with *Rabochaya Mysl* and the Economists. He explained that there was no reason to be so afraid of a political struggle:

> ... a struggle may cause annoyance to some *individuals*, but it will clear the air, define attitudes in a precise and straight-forward manner, define which differences are important and which unimportant, define where people stand – those who are taking a completely different path and those Party comrades who differ only on minor points.

He continued:

> Without struggle there cannot be a sorting out, and without a sorting out there cannot be any successful advance, nor can there be any *lasting unity*.[24]

At the end of 1901, Lenin again crossed swords with the Economists, who attacked *Iskra*'s "excessive predilection for controversy", which they put down to "its exaggerating the role of 'ideology' (programmes, theories...) in the movement" and the "internecine squabbles" amongst exiles.[25]

Lenin replied to these criticisms in an article in *Iskra* called 'A Talk With Defenders of Economism'. In this, he argued that to refrain from the theoretical struggle was immoral and was "tantamount to a surrender of leadership [of social democracy] to bourgeois democracy..."[26] He went on to quote the letter from Lassalle to Marx in 1852 about the controversies among the exiles in London:

> The publication of your work against the 'big men', Kinkel, Ruge, etc., should hardly meet with any difficulties on the part of the police… For in my opinion, the government is not averse to the publication of such works, because it thinks that 'the revolutionaries will cut one another's throats'. Their bureaucratic logic neither suspects nor fears the fact that it is precisely internal Party struggles that lend a party strength and vitality; that the greatest proof of a party's weakness is its diffuseness and the blurring of clear demarcations; and that a party becomes stronger by purging itself.[27]

He then commented: "Let the numerous complacent opponents of severity, irreconcilability, and fervent polemics, etc., take note!"[28]

'What Is to Be Done?'

Over time, the difficulties of exile and the punishing production schedules of *Iskra* began to take their toll. Lenin wrote to Axelrod:

> The whole paper now rests on me and the administrative end has been complicated by transport hitches and mix-ups in Russia, and my pamphlet [*What Is to Be Done?*] is pressing on me. I am devilishly late![29]

Money was always scarce and there were growing distribution problems, which prompted Lenin to write to Nikolai Bauman in Moscow asking about his work as an agent for the paper and what progress he was making:

> We ask about this because the question is very important. Things with us are going none too well. We are badly off financially, Russia gives almost nothing. Shipping is still unorganised and haphazard.[30]

He therefore asked Bauman to take a more rigorous approach to the finances, and for the money raised to be urgently sent to the cash-strapped editorial board. The following month he wrote to another *Iskra* agent in Baku, LY Galperin, urging him to make "every effort to obtain money." He then asked him if he could explore and find better routes through which to despatch *Iskra*:

> As regards the Eastern shore of the Black Sea, you must look for routes without fail. Devote your efforts especially to the French steamships – we hope to find a means of contact with them from here.[31]

While *Iskra* was making steady progress, political differences began to surface within the organisation. For instance, Lenin had written a politically sharp article against the bourgeois-liberals, which he equated with Economism. This attack outraged Plekhanov, Axelrod and Zasulich, who were shocked at Lenin's tone, which they regarded as aggressively sharp. Plekhanov wrote:

> You must tone down something. There is no call now for abusing the liberals in general. This is not tactful; we must appeal from the bad to the good liberal – even though we have doubts concerning the existence of such a liberal… It should be mentioned repeatedly that those whom you contemptuously certify as liberals, properly speaking, do not deserve to be called liberals, that such liberals are bad ones, but that liberalism in itself deserves great respect. We must regard the liberals as possible allies, but your tone, it must be admitted, is not at all that of an ally. Tone it down, my dear fellow! You are talking like an enemy when you should be talking like an ally (even though only potentially).[32]

In the end, Lenin agreed to "tone it down", but he still believed they were being too soft on the liberals, as it was "our right (and our duty)" to "trounce" them. "We must attack the narrowness of both the one and the other."[33]

What had surfaced was clearly an underlying political difference over their attitude towards the liberals. Lenin, following in the footsteps of Marx, adopted a very hard line towards them. This 'softness' of Plekhanov and the others towards liberalism pointed in the direction of a future Menshevism.

Interestingly, Trotsky recalled an exchange at this time between Lenin and Zasulich, when she also complained that *Iskra* was attacking the liberals too much. To back up her argument she pointed to an article written by Struve, who welcomed the overtly friendly approach of Jean Jaurès towards the French liberals. But Lenin regarded this as far too soft and replied: "One more reason to attack them strongly."

"Well… Well…!" Zasulich exclaimed in despair, "they make a step in our direction, and *we* have to 'attack them strongly'." "That's right", stated Lenin.[34]

Lenin was having none of this softness towards these political enemies. This question would surface again in the future, and would define the political difference between Bolshevism and Menshevism. But for the moment, this was yet the distant music of the future.

Lenin had spent a great deal of time throughout 1901 working on *What Is to Be Done?* He wrote in a letter to the *Iskra* organisations in Russia:

All the disagreements will be analysed there in great detail. We shall show there how *pernicious* the *Rabocheye Dyelo* trend is, and reveal all their disgraceful vacillation and impotence in the face of Bernsteinism and Economism. This pamphlet is nearly ready and is rapidly approaching completion.[35]

Given the impossibility of publishing it inside Russia, it was printed in Stuttgart in March 1902, under the authorship of N Lenin, a name he adopted a few months earlier. It was no accident that he chose as a title *What Is to Be Done?* which – as we have seen in previous chapters – he took from his hero, Chernyshevsky.

This text was a summation of Lenin's views on organisation to answer the "burning questions of our movement", which was the pamphlet's subtitle. It was received with much interest and great approval within the *Iskra* organisation, especially among those within Russia. It was the first time that anyone had dealt with the organisational question in such a comprehensive fashion and put the final nail in the arguments of the Economists.

Bourgeois criticisms

Not for nothing, the notion of a professional centralised revolutionary party always sends the bourgeois historians into a blind frenzy. "The dictatorial implications of *What Is to Be Done?* – that the party's rank and file would be forced to obey, in military fashion, the commands of the leadership – were as yet not fully realised", writes Professor Figes.[36]

It was "not fully realised" for the simple reason that "dictatorial implications" were simply non-existent. According to Figes, the book envisages all-powerful party leaders who "command" a passive, sheep-like rank and file. But anyone who reads Lenin can see that such an idea is nonsense.

Figes actually goes as far as stating that the writing style of *What Is to Be Done?* is greatly suited to dictators! "Lenin's strident prose style, which was imitated by all great dictators and revolutionaries of the twentieth century, emerged for the first time in *What Is to Be Done?*" Finally, breaking into a cold sweat, Figes continues: "It had a barking, military rhythm, a manic violence and decisiveness, with cumulative cadences of action or abuse, and opponents lumped together by synecdoche ('Messrs Bernstein, Martynov, etc')."[37]

There is no denying that the book was written in a polemical style against the Economists, and that the pamphlet robustly takes up their arguments and answers them one by one. But there is not a trace of "barking" or anything of the sort in *What Is to Be Done?*, although it is certainly present in every page of Figes' violent diatribe against Lenin and Bolshevism. As Lenin once quipped, in a preface to *What Is to Be Done?* in 1907, which applies in this case: "Unfortunately, many of those who judge our Party are outsiders, who do not know the subject…"[38]

As always, Lenin was particularly interested in hearing what workers thought of *What Is to Be Done?* He wrote a letter to Ivan Radchenko on 16 July 1902 about his contact with local workers:

> I was ever so glad to read your report about the talk with the workers. We receive such letters much too rarely. They are really tremendously cheering. Be sure and convey this to your workers with our request that they should write to us themselves, not just for the press, but to exchange ideas, so that we do not lose touch with one another and for mutual understanding. Personally I am particularly interested to know what the workers think of *What Is to Be Done?* So far I have received no comments from the workers.[39]

At this time, Lenin was arguing for nothing more than a revolutionary party modelled on German Social-Democracy as applicable to Russian conditions. He specifically rejected the idea that he was creating some new 'Bolshevik' trend, which he underlined at the future Second Congress of the Party in 1903, when he explained he had no "intention of elevating my own formulations, as given in *What Is to Be Done?*, to a programmatic level, constituting of special principles."[40]

However, for Lenin, the party could only succeed if it was built on correct political and organisational foundations. Irrespective of Russian conditions, it needed to be first and foremost a *revolutionary party* to correspond to its *revolutionary programme*, which determined its character. The revolutionary party must be based upon theoretical clarity and vehemently oppose all forms of opportunism. It must provide the necessary shield against alien class ideas and influences. This was summed up by Lenin:

> *Without revolutionary theory there can be no revolutionary movement.* This idea cannot be insisted upon too strongly at a time when the fashionable preaching of opportunism goes hand in hand with an infatuation for the narrowest forms of practical activity.[41]

Lenin went on to stress the words of Engels from 1874 on the need for the theoretical struggle. "The people who cannot pronounce the word 'theoretician' without a sneer", observed Lenin, were precisely those who wallow in their own ignorance:[42]

In our opinion, the absence of theory deprives a revolutionary trend of the right to existence and inevitably condemns it, sooner or later, to political bankruptcy.[43]

This summed up Lenin's real character. He also went on to describe the problems of building the party and, in particular, how the leadership must not be sidetracked by short-cuts and easy solutions:

We are marching in a compact group along a precipitous and difficult path, firmly holding each other by the hand. We are surrounded on all sides by enemies, and we have to advance almost constantly under their fire. We have combined, by a freely adopted decision, for the purpose of fighting the enemy, and not of retreating into the neighbouring marsh, the inhabitants of which, from the very outset, have reproached us with having separated ourselves into an exclusive group and with having chosen the path of struggle instead of the path of conciliation. And now some among us begin to cry out: Let us go into the marsh! And when we begin to shame them, they retort: What backward people you are! Are you not ashamed to deny us the liberty to invite you to take a better road! Oh, yes, gentlemen! You are free not only to invite us, but to go yourselves wherever you will, even into the marsh. In fact, we think that the marsh is your proper place, and we are prepared to render *you* every assistance to get there. Only let go of our hands, don't clutch at us…[44]

'Bending the stick'

In his attack on the Economists and their worship of spontaneity, Lenin, as he himself put it, "bent the stick" in the other direction. In his argument, he uses the words of Kautsky to say that socialist consciousness can only be brought to the workers from outside by the intelligentsia and that the working class was only capable of a "trade union" consciousness.

This idea of the working class being capable only of a trade union consciousness is clearly wrong. While it is true that the highest expression of socialist consciousness, namely the theory of Marxism, was not thrown up by the working class, but arose from a fusion of the most advanced ideas of the time – German philosophy, English classical political economy and French socialism – workers on their own were nevertheless capable of drawing political and revolutionary conclusions. The history of 'physical force' Chartism in England is one example where the workers themselves threw up their own socialist theoreticians, such as Bronterre O'Brien, and drew very revolutionary conclusions.

Lenin soon realised his mistake and a year later, during the Second Congress of the RSDLP, he explained:

> We all know that the 'Economists' bent the stick in one direction. In order to straighten the stick it was necessary to bend it in the other direction, and that is what I did.[45]

In other words, Lenin's error was a polemical exaggeration against spontaneity, nothing more, which he never repeated. On the contrary, throughout his life, Lenin displayed nothing but enormous confidence in the independent initiative of the masses and their ability to draw revolutionary conclusions.

As an aside, today's petty-bourgeois sects constantly repeat the falsehood that socialist consciousness needs to be brought to the workers from outside and highlight this mistake in *What Is to Be Done?* This, presumably, justifies their own 'self-importance' as the missionaries of socialist consciousness.

Despite this "bending of the stick", Lenin's book clearly pointed the way forward on party organisation. It was to become a classic of Marxism in regard to how the revolutionary party was to be built. It was no exaggeration on Krupskaya's part when she said the book should "be studied by everyone who wants to be a Leninist in practice, and not in words alone."[46]

In conclusion, it is worth quoting the wise words of Engels used by Lenin in *What Is to Be Done?*:

> In particular, it will be the duty of the leaders to gain an ever clearer insight into all theoretical questions, to free themselves more and more from the influence of traditional phrases inherited from the old world outlook, and constantly keep in mind that socialism, since it has become a science, demands that it be pursued as a science, i.e. that it be studied.[47]

6. The Work of 'Iskra' Progresses

Krupskaya recalled in her *Reminiscences*:

> Vladimir Ilyich and I were once reminded of a simile used by Lev Tolstoi. He was going along and saw from afar a man squatting and waving his arms about in a ridiculous way; a madman, he thought, but when he drew nearer, he saw it to be a man sharpening a knife on the kerb. The same thing happens in theoretical disputes. From the outside it seems a sheer waste of time, but when you go into the matter more deeply you see that it is a momentous issue. It was like that with the programme.[1]

This sums up very well the view held by those outside of the revolutionary movement, by people who are amazed initially by the frantic debates that seem to endlessly occur within it. On further examination, however, these disputes make perfect sense for those willing to look more closely.

Despite all the pressures and frictions, this was a very fruitful period for *Iskra*. They were, after all, clearly winning the struggle against the Economists and were emerging as the key force within the Party organisations.

The collaboration on the newspaper had involved a highly gifted layer of individuals and intellects, who stood head and shoulders above their contemporaries and saw further into the future than most.

Despite the many problems over the finance and distribution of the newspaper, the editorial board functioned well. The agents working for *Iskra* within the interior made huge sacrifices travelling around Russia, expanding the influence of the paper and working to promote the underground party. Krupskaya wrote:

The collection of forces around *Iskra* was pursued intensely. Everyone felt the growth of the organisation, was conscious that the line for the formation of the Party had been correctly laid down.[2]

As mentioned, there were certain underlying political frictions. But this could be expected in such a responsible undertaking. These differences of opinion arose mostly between Plekhanov and Lenin, who were the leading lights. One such conflict emerged over the drafting of the Party Programme, when Lenin criticised Plekhanov's first draft for being too abstract, and proposed over thirty amendments. More than anything else, this approach reflected Lenin's meticulous attitude to all political questions, and his insistence on precise formulations. Lenin argued:

> The *entire character* of the programme is, in my opinion, the most general and basic defect of this draft, one that makes it unacceptable. Specifically, it is not the programme of a party engaged in a practical struggle, but [...] rather a programme *for students...*[3]

This criticism was certainly felt by Plekhanov. In the end, Lenin submitted his own alternative programme, while Plekhanov resubmitted his own second draft. Eventually, after much discussion, a single draft programme was agreed upon.

The controversy revealed certain underlying political tensions between the younger and older members of the *Iskra* group. By this time, Plekhanov was forty-five; Axelrod, fifty-one; Vera Zasulich, fifty; while Lenin was thirty-one; Potresov, thirty-two and Martov, twenty-eight. Even younger was Trotsky, the newest collaborator, who was twenty-two.

Move to London

By the beginning of 1902, the difficulties of producing *Iskra* in Germany were becoming increasingly problematic. Given the intensifying pressure from the Okhrana on the German authorities and the risks that this involved, it was decided to move the newspaper's operations from Munich to London. Enquiries were made, and it was discovered that the Social Democratic Federation's print shop at its Clerkenwell Green offices could be used to print *Iskra*. As a result, Lenin, Krupskaya, Martov and Zasulich decided to make their way to London, while Plekhanov and Axelrod decided to remain behind in Switzerland.

Lenin and Krupskaya were especially keen to leave Munich and eventually arrived in London, after a brief break in Cologne and Liège, in the middle of April 1902. They had arranged to meet an old comrade, Nikolai Alexeyev, at Charing Cross station. He had been living in London for some time and managed to fix up a temporary furnished room for them in Sidmouth Street, near King's Cross. Within a week they had been helped to move by their old acquaintances, Konstantin and Apollinaria Takhtarev, into a more suitable first-floor two-room house in Holford Square, for a rent of one pound a week.

While Apollinaria had been part of the League for the Emancipation of the Working Class in St. Petersburg, where she had met Lenin, her husband, Konstantin, edited the Economist paper, *Rabochaya Mysl*. Nevertheless, they helped the new arrivals to settle in and later assisted in finding venues for the Party's Second Congress. Since the rooms they rented were unfurnished, they had to buy some cheap furniture and some linoleum for the floors. It was here that they remained until their departure from London the following year.

They were able to blend in without much trouble, as the East End of London had a thriving Russo-Jewish community, swelled by immigrants who had fled after the assassination of Alexander II.

However, this milieu attracted its fair share of dissidents, and in turn also attracted the eyes of Okhrana agents. It was therefore necessary for Lenin and Krupskaya to take precautions. One of these was for them to live under the assumed names of Dr and Mrs Richter. Oddly enough the ruse was so successful that their landlady took them, not for Russians but Germans. Nevertheless, the landlady was worried about the impression Krupskaya was making on the neighbours as she was not wearing a wedding ring. She needed to be reassured by the Takhtarevs that the Richters were, in fact, a lawfully wedded couple. The landlady also insisted that the couple put up curtains on their windows to show that they were 'respectable'.

Max Beer, who worked for many years as the London correspondent of *Vorwärts* and *Die Neue Zeit*, the publications of the German Social-Democrats, wrote in his book that he was the individual who arranged for *Iskra* to be produced in Clerkenwell. He related the time when Lenin visited him:

> One morning in June 1902 – I lived then in Clarence Gardens, Regent's Park – a foreign gentleman, as my landlady announced to me, called with a letter from Karl Kautsky, the foremost Marxist author in Berlin. Kautsky asked me to assist the bearer of the letter, the Russian comrade Lenin, in procuring a printing office for the *Iskra* (*Spark*), the weekly paper of the Russian Social-Democracy. The paper had until lately been published in Munich, but as the Constitutional Democrats (Cadets) started printing there the *Osvobozhdenie*, the Socialists decided to get the *Iskra* printed in London. I paid no special attention to Lenin, who outside Russia

was still an unknown figure, and after a few words of greeting went with him to my friend Harry Quelch, the editor of *Justice*, and manager of the Twentieth Century Press in Clerkenwell Green, and we arranged for the printing of the *Iskra*.

Lenin never mentioned this, but even if it is true, Beer seems to have mixed up the dates. Lenin, after all, arrived in London in April, not June. Also, the arrangements to print *Iskra* in London had been made before Lenin had arrived, which also seems to conflict with Beer's account. Nevertheless, he went on to give his impressions of Lenin, whom, he says, he met regularly:

> Lenin took lodgings in Holford Square, King's Cross, where, at his request, I used to call two or three times a week. There was nothing striking in his appearance. He was a fairly well nourished, middle-aged man of medium height with a round head, fair complexion, friendly grey eyes, and firm mouth. His wife looked younger, a lithe figure and slightly taller than he. She rarely spoke, as I do not understand Russian, and she did not venture to speak German, the language in which Lenin and myself used to discuss socialist and political matters. Once, in the spring of 1903, I met there her mother, who had come from Petersburg, a lively, elderly lady, the only one in the family who smoked cigarettes. She invited me to come to Petersburg, where "we shall soon enjoy greater freedom than in any capital of Europe." She spoke French and German equally well.

He continued by revealing a glimpse of the couple's domestic routine:

> Lenin and his wife lived an austere life, in total abstinence from smoking and alcohol and all those articles of food which in a working-class family would be called luxuries. They did their housework by themselves and alternated weekly in the work; one week he swept the room and kitchen, made the beds, prepared the food, and the next week it was her turn to care for the house.

> They looked a very happy couple, united in love and spiritual comradeship. He had a fine sense of humour, and could roar with laughter at a good joke.[4]

Daily routine

The location of Lenin and Krupskaya's accommodation was very convenient in other ways. A few streets away, in Sidmouth Street, Martov, Zasulich and later Blumenfield, the *Iskra* business manager, set up their lodgings in a three-storey house. Six months later, Trotsky arrived from abroad and joined them in what was to become the centre of *Iskra* editorial board operations. Plekhanov and Axelrod, who remained in Switzerland, made trips to London, to what they described as "the den", for *Iskra* editorial meetings and consultations.

38. The Crown and adjoining buildings, Clerkenwell Green, London, c. 1900

Unfortunately, prior to the move to London, Potresov fell seriously ill and could do little editorial work.

During his time in London, Lenin tended to work by a set daily routine. Every morning, he would spend time studying at the British Museum and then visit the other comrades in the afternoon to discuss editorial work. He had obtained a ticket for the reading room at the Museum under his assumed name of Dr Richter. He also spent time in his editorial office – a tiny room on the first floor of the Twentieth Century Press at Clerkenwell Green – with just enough space for a small table, a few books and a chair. Lenin later recalled that Harry Quelch, the editor of *Justice*, "had to 'squeeze up'":

> A corner was boarded off at the printing-works by a thin partition to serve him as [an] editorial room. The corner contained a very small writing table, a bookshelf above it, and a chair. When the present writer visited Quelch in his 'editorial office' there was no room for another chair…[5]

It was in this tiny room, which is still preserved today, that he read and worked on the proofs of *Iskra*. It was in these premises that the paper was printed on the ground floor using a flat-bed machine, although the proofs had to be sent to an East End printer for the Cyrillic typesetting to be done by *Iskra*'s own compositor, Blumenfield, who had managed to escape from a Kiev prison. Sometimes, after doing some editorial work, Lenin would buy himself some refreshments at The Crown pub on Clerkenwell Green, near the office.

To their astonishment, despite learning English from books and translations, when Lenin and Krupskaya arrived in London, they could not understand a single word spoken with an English accent! Due to their own accents, nobody could understand them either. "It amused Vladimir Ilyich", writes Krupskaya, "but at the same time put him on his mettle. He tackled English in earnest."[6] They eventually picked up the language after studying English at home and by listening to speakers at public meetings and at Speaker's Corner in Hyde Park. They also managed to arrange to take exchange lessons in English with three Londoners keen to learn Russian.

The couple were initially shocked at the high cost of living in London, which put a strain on their finances. "Besides", explained Krupskaya, "we were living at the organisation's expense, and that meant we had to economise every penny."[7] This meant doing their own cooking on the open fire or on a small primus stove in the back room.

The historian Volkogonov, probably out of spite, plays down such difficulties stating that Lenin and Krupskaya, in fact "lived quite well" as "professional revolutionaries". According to him: "Neither in Russia nor abroad did Lenin suffer deprivation."[8] Again, he asserts, "Lenin, whether in Russia or abroad, was never short of money", which contradicts the facts, as can be seen from Lenin's letters.[9] It seems that for the likes of Volkogonov, the life of a revolutionary in exile was a leisurely affair!

The reality, however, was quite different. As Krupskaya explained: "it was very difficult to live 'underground' in those days, and not everybody had the strength to endure it."[10]

The couple soon settled down into a routine, and they began to travel around East London visiting pubs, clubs and reading rooms, a favourite being the Working Men's Institute and Club – better known as the Communist Club. Lenin often enjoyed going on rides on the top of an open-topped bus to observe the sites of the capital. With the gulf between rich and poor so evident in London, he would mutter through gritted teeth and in English: "Two nations!"

They sometimes managed to get some cheap tickets to visit the theatre to hear a music concert. Their first one was at the Queen's Hall on 1 February 1903, and was recorded in a letter to Lenin's mother: "We recently went to our first concert this winter and were very pleased with it – especially with [Tchaikovsky's] latest symphony (*Symphonic pathétique*)."[11]

39. The British Museum reading room, c. 1903

The couple often travelled to Primrose Hill, where Engels had lived, and from there they walked to Marx's grave at Highgate. Above all, Lenin was enthusiastic about the British Museum, which housed the greatest library in the world, where it is estimated he spent half his time researching material. Not long afterwards, they were joined by Krupskaya's mother, as Max Beer recalled, who assisted with the cooking and general upkeep. Lenin wrote regularly to his mother about life in London and what they were up to:

> It is warm here. We recently took YV [Krupskaya's mother] on a long outing too – we took sandwiches with us instead of lunch and spent the whole of one Sunday *ins Grüne* [in the countryside] (quite unintentionally we are taking to foreign ways and arrange our outings on Sundays of all days, though that is the worst time because everywhere is crowded). We had a long walk, the air went to our heads as if we were children and afterwards I had to lie down and rest, as I did after a shooting trip in Siberia. In general, we do not miss a chance to go on outings. We are the only people among the comrades here who are exploring *every bit* of the surrounding country. We discover various 'rural' paths, we know all the places nearby and intend to go further afield.[12]

It was clear they were coping, despite the financial pressures. Above all, politically things seemed to stabilise. "The conflict with Plekhanov was over more or less", remarked Krupskaya.[13] Lenin then managed to take a month off to visit his mother and sister in Brittany and he spent a few weeks with them at the seaside.

Increased responsibility

With Plekhanov and Axelrod living in Switzerland, the main responsibility for producing *Iskra* now fell on Lenin's shoulders. Apart from Lenin, Martov, his closest companion-in-arms, was the main contributor to the paper and was regarded by him as a first-rate journalist, although Lenin's output was even greater.

Up until this point, Lenin regarded himself as a pupil of Plekhanov, especially in regard to theory and philosophical questions. He listened respectfully to Axelrod and exchanged opinions with Martov and Potresov, but he could not help realising he had grown in stature in comparison to his fellow collaborators.

Lenin's frustrations with Plekhanov were becoming more evident, but matters worsened soon after he arrived in London. Lenin felt that Plekhanov's dealings with the other members of the editorial board were far too dismissive, even bordering on contempt. He therefore decided to confront Plekhanov to clear the air. In May 1902, he wrote to Plekhanov with his concerns:

> I have received the article with your comments. You have fine ideas of tact towards editorial colleagues! You do not shrink from choosing the most contemptuous expressions [...] I should like to know what you would say, if I were to answer your article on the programme in a similar manner? If you set yourself the aim of making our common work impossible, you can very quickly attain this aim by the path you have chosen. As far as personal and not business relations are concerned, you have already definitely spoilt them or, rather, you have succeeded in putting an end to them completely.[14]

Lenin's straightforward criticisms forced Plekhanov to retreat, and he wrote to Lenin apologising and offering to arrange a meeting. This response came as a great relief to Lenin, who was also anxious to re-establish good relations with Plekhanov. So much excellent work had been done and nothing should be placed in its way to undermine it. After all, it was clear to Lenin that greater successes for *Iskra* lay in the future.

With relations re-established, Lenin felt a great burden lifted from his shoulders. But Plekhanov used the opportunity to take Lenin up over his sharp criticisms of his draft programme. Lenin defended himself by saying he had no intention of offending him in any way. As an excuse, Lenin admitted he was feeling exhausted and was intending to take a break to see his mother in Germany. "My nerves are worn to shreds and I am feeling quite ill", he wrote to Plekhanov.[15] This episode highlighted the increasing burden that was being placed on Lenin's shoulders, not only in producing the paper, but also in running the organisation.

From time to time, whenever such disputes arose, Zasulich and Martov usually acted as the go-betweens to smooth things over. Zasulich told Trotsky about a very interesting remark she made to Lenin about the two men, and his reaction: "George (Plekhanov) is like a greyhound: he will shake you and shake you and will let you go; you are like a bulldog; you have a deadly grip." Lenin appeared very proud of this. "He was very pleased. 'So I have a deadly grip, have I?', he asked delightedly."[16] This simply highlighted that iron determination that was characteristic of Lenin, and which was to prove vital in the struggles that lay ahead.

Despite such frictions, these dedicated men and women were nevertheless very much bound together in a common cause. They were comrades-in-arms, a true fellowship. The close collaboration between these six individuals, whatever the ups and downs, proved to be an undoubted success. "Lenin did not have the fortune ever again in the future to work in such a milieu", remarked Trotsky, who looked back on those years.[17]

Nevertheless, it was clear that a differentiation was taking place in the editorial board, especially centred around Lenin. "He himself became greater, but his collaborators were of significantly lesser dimensions", Trotsky wrote in a later notebook.[18]

While they tended to avoid contact with the Russian émigrés, Lenin did speak twice at such meetings: in Russian to a workers' club in Whitechapel, and on another occasion to a meeting organised by the East London Jewish branch of the Social Democratic Federation. According to Alexeyev, it was a "brilliant speech, which to my regret was not taken down."[19] Lenin's last speaking engagement in London was at the May Day rally in Alexandra Palace, alongside Keir Hardie and others, although again there is no record of what was said.

Lenin maintained his contact with the members of the Social Democratic Federation, the first Marxist organisation in Britain, and in particular the veteran Harry Quelch. Harry's son, Tom, joined the Communist Party and met Lenin in 1920 in Moscow when he attended the Second Congress of the

Communist International. To show his fondness for the old place, Lenin's first question to Tom Quelch was: "How is everyone at Clerkenwell Green?"[20]

Trotsky's arrival

Soon after Lenin's death, Krupskaya began to write her *Reminiscences of Lenin*, and the first part was published in English in 1930. However, within a few years, the book came under the unwelcome attentions of the Stalinist censorship. By this time, the campaign against 'Trotskyism' was in full swing and the entire section in the book about Trotsky's arrival in London and his meeting with Lenin was expunged from later editions. Even now, all the reprints of Krupskaya's book are simply replicants of the bowdlerised version.

It is therefore worth quoting the missing passages in full from the Martin Lawrence edition of 1930, which casts light on the real relationship between Lenin and Trotsky at this time. The encounter also illustrates Lenin's attentive approach in dealing with young comrades who showed promise for the Party. At the time, Trotsky was only twenty-two years old. The following are the censored passages:

> At about that time we learned from Samara that Bronstein (Trotsky) had arrived there following his escape from Siberia. They said he was a fervent supporter of *Iskra* and produced a very good impression on everybody. "He is a real young eagle", wrote the Samara comrades...
>
> Soon after – I believe in October – Trotsky arrived in London.
>
> One morning there was a violent knocking at the front door. I knew full well that if the knock was unusual it must be for us, and hurried downstairs to open the door. It was Trotsky, and I led him into our room. Vladimir Ilyich had only just awakened and was still in bed. Leaving them together, I went to see to the cabman and prepare coffee. When I returned I found Vladimir Ilyich still seated on the bed in animated conversation with Trotsky on some rather abstract theme. Both the hearty recommendations of the 'young eagle' and this first conversation made Vladimir Ilyich pay particular attention to the new-comer. He talked with him a great deal and went [for] walks with him.
>
> Vladimir Ilyich questioned him as to his visit to the *Yuzhni Rabochy*.* He was pleased with the definite manner in which Trotsky formulated the position. He liked the way Trotsky was able immediately to grasp the very substance of the differences and to perceive through the layer of well-meaning statements their

---

* A Social-Democratic group formed in the south of Russia.

40. Leon Trotsky in 1898

desire, under the guise of a popular paper, to preserve the autonomy of their own little group.

Meanwhile the call came from Russia with increased insistence for Trotsky to be sent back. Vladimir Ilyich wanted him to remain abroad in order to learn and help in the work of *Iskra*.

Plekhanov immediately looked on Trotsky with suspicion: he saw in him a supporter of the younger section of the *Iskra* editorial (Lenin, Martov, Potresov) and a pupil of Lenin. When Vladimir Ilyich sent Plekhanov an article of Trotsky's he replied: "I don't like the pen of your 'Pen'."* "The style is merely a matter of acquisition", replied Vladimir Ilyich, "but the man is capable of learning and will be very useful." In March 1903 Vladimir Ilyich proposed co-opting Trotsky on the *Iskra* editorial board.

Soon after Trotsky went to Paris, where he began to advance with remarkable success.[21]

---

* Trotsky had made a name for himself as a writer and was ascribed the Party name of 'Pero', meaning 'The Pen'.

In his book *My Life*, Trotsky also recalled this first meeting with Lenin and
the long walk they had in London:

> Either the same or the next morning, Vladimir Ilyich and I went for a long
> walk around London. From a bridge, Lenin pointed out Westminster and some
> other famous buildings. I don't remember the exact words he used, but what he
> conveyed was: "This is their famous Westminster", and "their" referred of course
> not to the English but to the ruling classes. This implication, which was not in
> the least emphasised, but coming as it did from the very innermost depths of
> the man, and expressed more by the tone of his voice than by anything else, was
> always present, whether Lenin was speaking of the treasures of culture, of new
> achievements, of the wealth of books in the British Museum, of the information
> of the larger European newspapers, or, years later, of German artillery or French
> aviation. They know this or they have that, they have made this or achieved that
> – but what enemies they are! To his eyes, the invisible shadow of the ruling classes
> always overlay the whole of human culture – a shadow that was as real to him as
> daylight.[22]

At this time, Lenin was clearly on the lookout for new talent that could be
used to strengthen the *Iskra* organisation, including the editorial board. He
also hoped that the inclusion of a promising individual such as the young
Trotsky would change the balance of forces within the editorial board, which
was still evenly divided. This addition, he believed, would provide greater
stability to the work, but as can be seen, he would meet resistance from
Plekhanov.

Lenin was feeling somewhat isolated. Life in exile required a lot of
stamina and sacrifice to see it through successfully. The endless work on the
paper, maintaining contacts with Russia, as well as the preparations for the
forthcoming Second Congress of the RSDLP, took up a colossal amount of
time and kept the editorial board busy. The efforts by the Economists, now a
dwindling force, to delay a new Congress had come to nothing.

As the work for the Congress intensified in the winter of 1902, the job
of assembling the delegates for such a clandestine event, given the arrests,
harassment, and activity of police spies, was no easy task. An organising
committee had been established made up of a majority of *Iskra* supporters, all
of which placed a heavy burden, not only on Lenin, but also on Krupskaya,
who acted as secretary and carried out the correspondence with the interior.
She had become the centre of the organisational work as well as the treasurer,
responsible for the allocation of the finances.

Given the clandestine nature of the work, inevitable delays and dislocations were commonplace, causing a great deal of stress, which in particular affected Lenin's nerves. Added to this, the continuing friction with Plekhanov didn't help matters and, according to Krupskaya, Lenin found it difficult to sleep. "Those sleepless nights remain engraved on my memory", she wrote.[23]

Move to Geneva

Once again, the idea was raised of moving the *Iskra* operations to Geneva to provide a location nearer to Russia. Lenin wanted to remain in London, given his access to the greatest library in the world, but found himself in a minority of one on the editorial board. Having accepted the view of the majority, he and Krupskaya got ready for the move.

They arrived back in Geneva in May and went to live on the outskirts of the city. On the journey, Lenin was suffering from great pain after contracting ringworm in London. Not able to afford a doctor, Krupskaya treated him with iodine, which itself was excruciatingly painful. However, he recovered after a few weeks in bed.

As the Second Congress approached, delegates began to arrive from Russia, including Trotsky. Lenin, who admired Trotsky's talents, again raised the idea of him being brought on to the editorial board to strengthen its work. Lenin therefore wrote to Plekhanov:

> I am submitting to all members of the Editorial Board a proposal to co-opt 'Pero' as a full member of the Board. [...]
>
> 'Pero' has been writing in every issue for several months now. In general he is working for *Iskra* most energetically, delivering lectures (and with tremendous success), etc. [...]
>
> He is unquestionably a man of more than average ability, convinced, energetic, and promising. And he could do a good deal in the sphere of translation and popular literature.
>
> We must draw in young forces...[24]

But Lenin's proposal to "draw in young forces" was stubbornly resisted by Plekhanov, who acted as a veto. Lenin was beside himself with anger at this wilful obstruction. Unfortunately, once again, this episode as dealt with in the 1930 edition of Krupskaya's *Memoirs of Lenin* is completely erased from later editions:

Trotsky arrived. We had to explain [to the delegates who were arriving for the Congress] that under conditions of illegality a popular paper could not be a mass organ, could not count on a mass circulation. The position of Vladimir Ilyich and Martov on this question was defended by Trotsky, but attacked by Plekhanov. A meeting of delegates was held in the Café Landold and a discussion took place between Plekhanov and Trotsky. The delegates, most of whom had come into contact with the *Southern Worker* in Russia, considered Trotsky's position more correct. Plekhanov was beside himself.

All kinds of misunderstandings arose among the *Iskra* editorial board. The position became unbearable. The editorial board was generally divided into two groups: Plekhanov, Axelrod, Zasulich on the one hand, and Lenin, Martov, Potresov on the other. Vladimir Ilyich again put forward the proposal, already mooted by him in March, that a seventh member, Trotsky, be co-opted on to the editorial board. This co-option was not brought about, owing to the categorical protest of Plekhanov. Once Lenin returned from an editorial meeting in a terrific rage. "A damned fine state of affairs", he said. "Nobody has enough courage to reply to Plekhanov. Look at Vera Ivanovna! Plekhanov trounces Trotsky, and Vera just says: 'Just like our George. All he does is to shout.' I can't go on like this."[25]

At this time, along with improving the Party organisation, Lenin began to give serious thought to the future composition of the *Iskra* editorial board. It was now very clear to him that as it stood, it was inadequate to the task. This, however, was a difficult problem for him to deal with, as any serious change would involve the removal of close comrades and friends.

For Lenin, this was simply a recognition of the fact that the bulk of the editorial work was done by himself, Martov and Plekhanov, while the others contributed very little. With the campaign to professionalise the party, such a sloppy, amateurish approach existing at this level could not be allowed to continue. If the organisation was to be tightened, then this should begin at the very top.

Lenin believed that such a change would spread responsibilities and serve to reduce the old frictions. But this posed a serious dilemma. "The fact that the *Iskra* editorial board as then constituted was no longer able to handle the job was too painful a thing to talk about", explained Krupskaya.[26]

However, given the importance of Party leadership, change was essential and the Congress was the correct place to carry through such changes. Krupskaya explained:

He [Lenin] held that the Party Congress to be the highest authority, where all things personal had to be cast aside, where nothing was to be concealed, and everything was to be open and above board.[27]

The systematic work of *Iskra*, especially Lenin's leading role, had laid the basis for the much-needed Congress of the Party. As early as April 1902, there had been an attempt to organise such a Congress at Bialystok, but it turned out to be inadequate. It showed the need for a properly organised one, which, in reality, would be a real founding Congress of the Party. "How Vladimir Ilyich had dreamt for such a Congress!", remarked Krupskaya.[28]

This Congress, building on the success of *Iskra*, would prove a historic milestone. It would mark the end of its prehistory and serve to open up a further chapter of the revolutionary movement in Russia. But, unbeknown and unexpected by either the organisers or delegates, it would also be the Congress in which the first split in the Party would emerge between two mutually exclusive groupings. These were known initially as the 'hards' and the 'softs', and subsequently crystallised into Bolsheviks and Mensheviks.

But how can this be explained? It is necessary to proceed from fundamentals. The revolutionary party is a living organism. It is tested by events and will grow and develop on the basis of collective experience. And as with any organism, the revolutionary organisation goes through different stages in its development. The initial small circle stage played a progressive role, but eventually this form became a barrier to the further development of the party. Some individuals who had played a role in the past will tend to fall by the wayside, while new fresh layers will replenish and fill out its ranks, preparing the way for the emergence of a newer, higher stage.

This was precisely the task that faced the Russian movement at this time. Lenin was obliged to conduct a struggle to overcome the old small circle mentality, with its informality and excessive emphasis on personal ties. He was fighting to professionalise the work and carry it to a higher level. But this inevitably led to friction with those who remained fixed in the past, involving resistance, arguments and clashes.

Sometimes these clashes were heated, but they were inevitable if the party was to advance. Lenin has been accused of being doctrinaire, bureaucratic, or even despotic in his treatment of the old editors, but this was far from the case. In order to take even a single step forward, it was necessary to overcome the obstinate resistance of the old timers.

Lenin was striving to prepare the party for the next stage in its development, to advance from small circles to prepare the organisation for serious mass work.

With the wisdom of hindsight, this could be described as an 'internal revolution'. But at the time, the final outcome of this dispute was not obvious to anybody – including Lenin. He never expected that it could lead to a formal split at the Second Congress in 1903. Nor that the Party would suffer an irreparable split between Bolshevism and Menshevism.

All that Lenin was proposing was a series of elementary measures to ensure the most effective and efficient functioning of the organisation. He was not looking for a split. But he understood the impossibility of continuing with the old methods for a moment longer. For Lenin, differences always had a principled character. And he was never willing to compromise on questions of principle.

7. The Second Congress and its Myths

In the history of Bolshevism, there have been quite a few myths generated, in particular about the Second Congress of the Russian Social Democratic Labour Party, and especially in relation to Lenin's role, who is falsely accused by the bourgeois historians of imposing totalitarian rule within the Party. "He did not care a fig for democracy", wrote Service.[1] The fact that there were speeches, resolutions, amendments and democratic votes that were taken suggests otherwise.

A myth promoted by a combination of Stalinists and sectarians, each for their own reasons, was that Bolshevism emerged fully fledged at this Congress. "The history of the Bolshevik Party as such really begins from the Second Party Congress", stated Popov, in his Stalinist history.[2]

The truth is that the Bolshevik Party was not a monolithic Party, which had a separate existence right from its inception in 1903. In fact, Bolshevism was then a *faction* within the RSDLP, and did not become a separate party until 1912. Even then, there were repeated attempts to unite the Party on a principled basis. At the Second Congress, there were no political differences between Bolsheviks and Mensheviks, as we will see.

According to Lenin, it was not until 1905, two years *after* the Second Congress, that Bolshevism became a real tendency: "Bolshevism as a tendency took definite shape in the spring and summer of 1905…", he explained.[3] In other words, the two tendencies really emerged not over a squabble over the rules, but later over their approach to the liberal bourgeoisie.

41. Delegates at the Second Congress of the RSDLP

Even on the cover of the English-language edition of the book containing the minutes of the Second Congress of the RSDLP,* the falsehood is again repeated that "Lenin and his supporters forged a cast-iron basis for the split with Menshevism." But there was no such "cast-iron basis" for any such split in 1903. Certainly, Lenin never regarded it as such at the time.

The split occurred, not over political fundamentals, but simply over who was to be a member of the *Iskra* editorial board. At best, you can say that the Second Congress was an *anticipation* of future political differences, but nothing more than that. The seeds of Bolshevism and Menshevism were present – but only as seeds, as broad tendencies.

So, in dealing with the Second Congress of the RSDLP, it is important to separate out myths from reality.

The Congress opened on 30 July 1903 in Brussels at the Maison du Peuple, a co-operative society building, amid much excitement. And what was the principal task of the Congress? In the words of Lenin, it was to formally agree to ideas that had been now accepted by the majority: "To create a real party on the basis of the principles and organisational ideas that had been advanced and elaborated by *Iskra*."[4]

* *1903: Second Congress of the Russian Social-democratic Labour Party*, New Park, 1978.

II СЪЕЗД Р.С.-Д.Р.П. 1903г.(II)

ИСКРОВЦЫ МЕНЬШИНСТВА

АНТИ-ИСКРОВЦЫ

ЦЕНТР (БОЛОТО)

42. Delegates at the Second Congress of the RSDLP (continued)

There were forty-two delegates who attended with full voting rights and another fourteen with a consultative vote, which gave the proceedings the feel of a real Congress. This grand total of fifty-six in attendance was a dramatic increase on the handful who attended the First Congress in Minsk five years previously. All who attended clearly recognised that this was the real founding Congress of the Party, the genuine beginnings of a true party of the working class in Russia.

Of course, in these early days, there were still very few workers and many more intellectuals involved in the party. In fact, given this nascent character, only three of those present were workers. Looking back on it, there were quite a few present who were either there by accident or were to play no further role in the Party's future development. But that was the nature of things. The RSDLP was as yet a Party in formation.

As the Second Congress opened, it became very clear that supporters of *Iskra* were in the overwhelming majority. Its united block of thirty-three delegates was an impressive show of strength. This was then followed by a very small grouping of Economists, represented by three supporters from the paper *Rabocheye Dyelo*, the most prominent being Martynov and Akimov. Its small numerical representation was a reflection of its rapid decline. *Rabocheye*

Dyelo ceased publication in February 1902, and *Rabochaya Mysl* soon after in December of that year. For all intents and purposes, they had practically disappeared as a tendency by the time of this founding Congress.

Next was the Jewish Bund, which, although it had the prestige of the First Party Congress behind it, now only had five delegates present at the Second Congress. Its key representative was a man called Mikhail Liber. These tendencies were then joined by those who could be considered as the 'non-aligned' faction, which totalled six delegates. They were described by Lenin and Plekhanov as supporters of 'the swamp', a reference to 'the marsh' in the French National Convention, who sat in the middle between the left and the right.

The success of *Iskra* had outstripped all expectations. The newspaper had served through its work to bind together the local groups and provide them with the political and theoretical clarity needed. This built up *Iskra's* political authority to become the dominant tendency. This outcome was a colossal achievement for Lenin, Martov, Plekhanov and the rest of the editorial board. Given *Iskra's* numbers and political superiority, everything was lined up for a very successful founding Congress.

As expected, the Congress opened amid great anticipation and was reflected in the excitement of the delegates. Plekhanov, as elected chairman of the Congress, as well as the recognised father-figure of the Party, naturally towered over its proceedings. He was at his zenith during this Congress. In a rousing opening speech, he explained:

> … in the words of the humanist knight:* "It is joyous to live at such a time" […] one wants to live, in order to go on fighting. In this lies the whole meaning of our lives.
>
> I said that the situation is now extremely favourable for our Party. These words may seem exaggerated in view of the many disorders, disagreements and differences which have made themselves felt so severely in the last five years. These disorders, disagreements and differences have certainly been very great and very regrettable. But they have not prevented our Party from becoming, both theoretically and practically, the strongest of all the revolutionary and opposition parties in Russia! Despite all our differences and disagreements, we have already won more than one glorious theoretical victory and have had many substantial practical successes. Twenty years ago we were nothing, now we are a great social force…[5]

His speech was met with prolonged applause.

---

* Plekhanov is referring to the German knight and reformer, Ulrich von Hutten (1488-1523).

Trotsky later wrote down his impressions of Plekhanov's presence at the Congress and how he dealt with issues:

> At every question raised and at every quibble he quite effortlessly mobilised his outstanding erudition and made his audience, including his opponents, convinced that the question only started where the authors of the amendment thought it finished. With a scientifically organised conception of the programme in his head, confident in himself, his knowledge and his strength, with a merry twinkle of irony in his eye, his spiky whiskers merry too, his just slightly theatrical but vivid and expressive gestures Plekhanov sat in the chair and illuminated the whole of the numerous sections like a living firework of learning and wit. His brilliance lit up a flush of adoration on every face and on those of his opponents ecstasy struggled with embarrassment.[6]

Against federalism

Firstly, the Congress had to deal with some procedural points and arrangements, including the election of committees and the Congress committee's report. With Plekhanov as chairman, and with Lenin and Pavlovich elected as vice-chairmen, the praesidium were all Iskra-ites.

Once this business was out of the way, the next important item – and one of the most controversial – was the Party's relations with the Jewish Bund. The Bund had become an autonomous component of the Party at the founding Congress in 1898. However, given the arrests, the Party quickly ceased to function after that date, except as a number of localised groups. The real founding Congress now needed to take a position on the Bund's exact status within the Party.

The full name of the Bund was the 'General Jewish Workers' Union of Lithuania, Poland and Russia' and had been founded in 1897. To its credit, it had played an important role in organising Jewish workers and artisans in fighting against widespread Great Russian chauvinism and antisemitism within tsarist Russia. Antisemitism was so rife that in 1881, for instance, Jews were publicly blamed for the assassination of Alexander II.

However, controversy surfaced at the Second Congress over the Bund's insistence that their autonomous status be maintained within the Party. They claimed that they must be regarded as the "sole representative of Jewish proletariat" living in Russia.[7] However, this idea ran counter to the idea of a united party, and so led to sharp disagreements.

The Bund's belief in a separate autonomous organisation arose from their idea that Jews constituted a separate nation and should be treated as such. But there was a problem with this view. Jewish workers were not a separate 'nation', with their own territory, but scattered within the local populations. It therefore made more sense for them to join the local Party organisation where they lived, as with the Finnish, Estonian, or workers of other nationalities.

Furthermore, an autonomous organisation for Jews would only lead to the fragmentation of the Party into its separate national groupings, rather than unite the proletariat into a single party against the class enemy. Logically, if Jews were to be separate, why not all the different nationalities that made up Russia? Clearly, if accepted, this would be a recipe for disintegration.

As a result, the Bund's proposal led to fierce opposition. The supporters of *Iskra*, and Lenin in particular, fought against the idea of separatism within the party. They argued against such a petty-bourgeois and nationalist conception of party building. It was vital that the party based itself firmly on the sacred unity of the working class, without which, the victory of the revolution would be impossible. This, for the supporters of *Iskra*, was of the highest consideration.

The Bund's federalist idea would undermine the unity of the party and serve to reinforce backward nationalist prejudices. Lenin and the *Iskra* comrades instead argued that the working class should aim to stand united at the head of the whole nation, as the sole defender of all the oppressed. They believed a strong unified workers' party was a question of principle.

One *Iskra* delegate, Karsky, explained the dangerous implications of the Bund's proposal:

> To do this it would be necessary to point to the existence of a difference of interests between the two proletariats. One cannot set up two committees without giving prominence to such a difference. Consequently, we create conditions that lead not towards unity but towards separation into a distinct party. On the other hand, we should be weakening the Party by detaching from it such a powerful element as the Jewish proletariat.[8]

Although there must be one party, within it there was certainly room for Jewish workers, and others, to have their subsidiary groups to allow them to publish their own newspapers in their native tongue, take up specific questions, and so on. But the party as a whole needed to speak to workers with one voice, whatever their nationality. The idea of separate autonomous national entities within the party would not work. This view was supported by the overwhelming majority of delegates, apart from those of the Bund.

Outrageously, Robert Service asserts, without any foundation, that the "Bundists for their part sniffed a degree of antisemitism at the Congress."[9] In fact, according to Joshua Rubenstein, nearly half the Congress delegates were Jewish. Martov, Axelrod and Trotsky, also Jewish, spoke against the Bund's position.[10]

Much later in the Congress, at the 27th session, the delegates voted by forty-one votes to five against the Bund's proposal, with five abstentions. As a result, the Bund chose not to participate further in the Congress and walked out.

Party Programme and the Economists

The RSDLP Congress could not be held in tsarist Russia for obvious reasons. Brussels was chosen as it was out of reach from the secret police. However, within one week of the Congress opening, the proceedings had to be abandoned. Firstly, the venue had become overrun with fleas, which made things unbearable. Secondly, the Belgian authorities had become heavy-handed, which led to harassment and even the deportation of some delegates, including Rosa Zemlyachka, an *Iskra* agent. Others were given twenty-four hours' notice to leave the country.

This disruption may have had something to do with the fact that one member of the Congress Organising Committee, Dr Yakov Zhitomirsky, was also a member of the tsarist police, the Okhrana. But this fact only came out later. "It would seem as if tsarism held all the strings", noted Trotsky. "And yet even this did not save it."[11]

Out of necessity, the Congress was moved to London, where other meeting places and accommodation had been found. The first London session, on 11 August, was held not far from the Communist Club in Charlotte Street, in the venue of an anglers' club.

To ensure the security of the delegates, the event was disguised as a meeting of Belgian trade unionists. Furthermore, to avoid the eyes of Russian agents, the venue of the Congress changed several times during its stay in London, most notably in back rooms of pubs. Whether these precautions managed to throw the Okhrana off the scent, we do not know.

As the Congress was now in London, two London-based Social-Democrats asked to participate and were given a consultative vote. These were Konstantin Takhtarov ('Strakhova') and his wife, Apollinaria ('Yuzhin'), who had already helped with the Congress arrangements. As previously explained, Apollinaria had been involved in Lenin's group in St. Petersburg, while her husband was a former editor of an Economist paper. As it turned out, both supported the position of the Bund and later supported the minority, but it appears they never spoke in any of the debates.

Given its real nature as a founding Congress, an important debate took place over the Party Programme, which had been drafted and submitted by *Iskra*. While there was quite a lot of debate over details, there was little in the way of real controversy. Some Economist delegates raised an objection about including the idea of the dictatorship of the proletariat in the programme, which was answered ably by Plekhanov. "The revolutionary proletariat may restrict the political rights of the upper classes in the same way as the upper classes used to restrict its political rights", he stated. "Translated into the language of the revolutionary, this means that the success of the revolution is the highest law."

> And we must take the same attitude where the question of the length of parliaments is concerned. If, in an outburst of revolutionary enthusiasm, the people should elect a very good parliament – a sort of *Chambre Introuvable* – it would suit us to try and make that a *Long Parliament*; but if the elections turned out badly for us, we should have to try to disperse the resulting parliament not after two years but, if possible, after two weeks.[12]

Krupskaya commented that Plekhanov's contribution had made a profound and lasting impression on Lenin. "He recollected it fourteen years later, when the Bolsheviks were faced with the question of dismissing the Constituent Assembly", she explained.[13] This was when Lenin wrote *The Proletarian Revolution and the Renegade Kautsky*:

> And in that year Plekhanov declared at our Party Congress, which was then adopting its programme, that in the revolution the proletariat would, if necessary, disfranchise the capitalists and *disperse any parliament* that was found to be counter-revolutionary. That this is the only view that corresponds to Marxism will be clear to anybody even from the statements of Marx and Engels which I have quoted above; it patently follows from all the fundamental principles of Marxism.[14]

Plekhanov was certainly correct in regards to a reactionary parliament in 1903. However, by early 1918, he had completely changed his tune and came out against the Bolsheviks when they dispersed the reactionary Constituent Assembly.

Martynov and Akimov, the Economists, used the session at the Congress to criticise Lenin's *What Is to Be Done?* This was hardly surprising, as Lenin's book was specifically aimed at the errors of Economism. In the debate, Martov and Plekhanov, the future leaders of Menshevism, immediately came to Lenin's defence. Plekhanov explained:

> Lenin was writing not a treatise on the philosophy of history, but a polemical article against the economists, who said: we must wait for the working class to catch up, without the help of the 'revolutionary bacillus'. The latter was forbidden to tell the workers anything, precisely because it was a 'revolutionary bacillus', that is, because it possessed theoretical consciousness. But if you eliminate the 'bacillus', then you are left with a uniform unconscious mass, into which consciousness has to be injected from without.[15]

Plekhanov, in his usual witty style, continued:

> Comrade Akimov is like Napoleon in this respect – he wants, at any cost, to divorce me from Lenin. But I shall show more character than those Marshals of Napoleon's. I shall not divorce Lenin and I hope he does not intend to divorce me. [*Comrade Lenin laughingly shakes his head.*][16]

Lenin, nevertheless, felt obliged to answer his critics personally, although, as he explained, there was little to add. But he did clarify one point:

> I turn to that passage in my pamphlet *What Is to Be Done?* which has given rise to so much comment here. It would seem that after all these comments the question has been so well clarified that very little is left for me to add. Obviously, an episode in the struggle against Economism has been confused with a principled presentation of a major theoretical question, namely, the formation of an ideology. Furthermore, this episode has been presented in an absolutely false way.

He went on to stress that it "was indeed an episode in the struggle against Economism" in which he 'bent the stick'.[17]

In the end, differences were settled and the programme was adopted with only one abstention. This reflected the crushing political weight of the *Iskra* tendency within the Congress, which remained solidly united, apart from some secondary votes on peripheral questions. Everything proceeded very smoothly – until the 22nd session of the Congress, where this unity suddenly came crashing down.

Membership question

At this session, a debate taking place over the Party rules escalated into an almighty row. It was like a thunderbolt from a clear blue sky. The controversy broke out over Paragraph 1 of the Rules, which dealt specifically with the definition of Party membership. On this issue, two different drafts were put forward, one by Lenin and the other by Martov.

Lenin's draft definition was: "A Party member is one who accepts the Party's programme and supports the party both financially and by personal *participation in one of the Party organisations.*"[18] Whereas Martov's draft argued that a member was someone who accepted the programme and supported the party financially but gives the Party "regular personal assistance *under the direction of one of its organisations.*"[19]

On the surface, there seemed very little difference between the two positions, and hardly a fundamental one. One seemed to stress "participate in the Party", while the other stressed "work under direction" of the Party.

Lenin argued that the concept of a Party member must differentiate between 'those who merely talked' and 'those who worked' for the Party. In contrast, Martov talked about 'broadening' the Party and spoke of the need for a broad class movement. Ironically, in defence of their position, the Martovites cited passages from Lenin's *What Is to Be Done?* Martov, however, was firmly opposed by Plekhanov, believing that his formulation would fling open the door wide to all kinds of opportunists.

To understand what was happening at the Congress, we have to grasp what was behind these two propositions. There was clearly substance behind the wording. It is fashionable to argue, as the bourgeois historians do, that Lenin stood for a small centralised party, whereas Martov was for a broad-based democratic party. In reality, *all* the supporters of *Iskra* – Lenin, Martov, Plekhanov, Axelrod, etc. – stood for a strong centralised party. This was precisely the argument they had used against the federalism of the Bund. Again, this was Marx's conception, who favoured centralism over federalism, and the supporters of *Iskra* all accepted this principle, at least in theory.

Lenin had always argued for the Party to be built on the principle that a member should be someone who participates directly in the work of the organisation, fulfils its obligations, pays members' dues, observes discipline, and so on. Under existing conditions at the time, a member would join an underground cell and would work within the illegal organisation. This obviously entailed all the personal risks that come with underground work. Such firm commitments and responsibilities, especially under tsarism, would attract the best, most self-sacrificing fighters to the ranks of the party.

The revolutionary party, by its very nature, needed to represent the most conscious sections of the proletariat. It would form its vanguard and march at the head of the proletarian army of labour. Its revolutionary tasks defined its character. The party was not a home for sick souls, or a talking shop, or a model of the future socialist society, but a combat organisation. Given its revolutionary tasks, the party could not, therefore, be a loose, broad-based organisation, embracing the entire working class. As Lenin explained:

> It would be Manilovism* and 'tail-ism' to think that the entire class, or almost the entire class, can ever rise, under capitalism, to the level of consciousness and activity of its vanguard, of its Social-Democratic Party.[20]

Martov's proposal was reflecting those who wished for a much looser form of organisation. For Martov, a member was someone who worked under the direction of the party, but would not have the obligation to be involved in the underground work. This was not aimed at the most dedicated elements, but those who desired fewer obligations to the party. The aim of Martov's proposal was to make the party much more attractive to the *sympathiser* and petty-bourgeois *fellow-traveller* rather than the committed revolutionary.

It was Axelrod, in supporting Martov, who blurted out the truth behind the proposal. He referred to certain "professors" who would have difficulty in accepting Lenin's definition.[21] This was the *real* problem, not the recruitment of workers, but the difficulties of attracting the petty-bourgeois intellectuals to the Party. It is clear that Martov's proposal reflected the pressures from this petty-bourgeois milieu, the sympathisers and friends, who were not prepared to fully commit to the party and its obligations.

In contrast, Lenin wanted to restrict the membership of the Party to genuine revolutionaries, prepared to shoulder the pressures and sacrifice of underground work. After all, these were the normal conditions in which the Party operated within Russia. The danger of Martov's proposal, as Lenin saw it, was in strengthening opportunism. Plekhanov shared this view. In effect, Martov's proposal would open the doors to petty-bourgeois sympathisers who would act as a transmission belt for opportunist and alien class pressures into the Party.

It was this dispute that led to a furious argument and split the *Iskra* tendency down the middle. In the course of the debate, Lenin was accused of creating a "state of siege" in the Party, to which he bluntly replied that he was in favour of such a "siege", if it meant keeping out such alien class influences. He explained:

---

* 'Manilovism', from the character Manilov in Gogol's *Dead Souls*, embodying smugness, complacency, empty sentimental daydreaming and unprincipled philistinism.

... all our Party rules, the whole system of centralism which the Congress has now approved, are nothing but a 'state of siege' with regard to the numerous sources of *political diffuseness*.[22]

Lenin was simply upholding the organisational principles that were already contained in *What Is to Be Done?* and 'Where to Begin?', and advanced by *Iskra* over a period of three years. They had been explained in detail in 'A Letter to a Comrade on Our Organisational Tasks', again written by Lenin.

Lenin took the floor to firmly argue his case. But in doing so, he also showed flexibility and recognised that his formulation was not a life and death question. This was a point he repeated again and again:

I do not at all regard our difference so vital as to be a matter of life and death for the party. *We shall certainly not perish because of a bad point in the rules!*[23]

However, having said that, he continued:

But since it has come to a choice between *two* formulations, I simply cannot abandon my firm conviction that Martov's formulation is a *worsening* of the original draft, a worsening which *may*, in certain circumstances, cause no little harm to the party.[24]

He then went on to warn:

... in the period of the Party's life which we are now passing through it is just this 'elasticity' that most certainly opens the door to all the elements of confusion, vacillation and opportunism.[25]

Lenin saw in Martov's proposal a retreat to the confusions of the past period that would only weaken the party. Its acceptance would undo all the progress made over the past three years and he was determined not to throw away these gains.

Of course, according to that supposedly 'unbiased' historian, Professor Robert Service, "Martov wanted a set of Party Rules to restrain the ruthlessness of Lenin and his like."[26] Such are the learned observations of an academic philistine who is only too eager to spread malicious poison to justify his 'narrative' of 'Lenin the dictator'. There is more:

"Martov wanted a party with members who had scope to express themselves independently of the leadership", a claim Service conjures up out of thin air. "For Lenin, the need was for leadership, leadership and more leadership – and everything else, at least for the present, was to be subordinate to this need."[27]

And, spitting poison, Service concludes: "From this time onwards he turned his cantankerous, dishonest methods into a political art."[28]

It is enough to compare this nonsense to the *real* Lenin. When an *Iskra* conference was held in January 1902 in Samara, which set up a Bureau in the interior, Lenin wrote to the organisers, not to condemn or subordinate them to "leadership", but to *praise* their independent initiative:

> Your initiative has heartened us tremendously. Hurrah! That's the right way! Reach out wider! And operate more independently, with greater initiative – you are the first to have begun in such a broad way, and that means the continuation, too, will be successful.[29]

While Martov had the support of two editorial board members, Axelrod and Zasulich, Lenin had the support of Plekhanov. "… the more that was said on the subject and the more attentively I listened to the speeches the more convinced I became that Lenin is right", explained Plekhanov. He went on to forcefully argue Lenin's case:

> The whole question boils down to this: what elements can be included in our Party? According to Lenin's draft, only someone who joins a particular organisation can be regarded as a party member. Those who oppose this draft say that this will cause unnecessary difficulties. But what do these difficulties consist of? They talk of persons who do not want to join, or who can't join, one of our organisations. But why *can't* they? As someone who has himself taken part in Russian revolutionary organisations, I say that I do not admit the existence of objective conditions constituting an insuperable obstacle to anyone's joining. And as for those gentlemen who *do not want* to join, we have no need of them.

Plekhanov continued:

> It has been said here that some professor who sympathises with our views may find it humiliating to join a local organisation. In this connection I remember Engels saying that when it comes your lot to deal with professors, you have to be prepared for the worst. [*Laughter.*] The example is, in fact, an extremely bad one. If some Professor of Egyptology considers, because he has by heart the names of all the Pharaohs, and knows all the prayers that the Egyptians submitted to the bull Apis, that it is beneath his dignity to join our organisation, we have no need of that professor. To talk of control by the Party over persons who are *outside* the organisation means playing with words. In practice such control is impossible.[30]

Nevertheless, despite the firm support of Plekhanov, Lenin lost the vote on Paragraph 1 of the Rules by twenty-eight votes to twenty-two, when the five Bund delegates (who had not yet walked out at this stage) and the two Economists voted with Martov. It was these seven non-*Iskra* votes that gave Martov his majority. From then on, this bloc was to dominate the Congress, until the group of unstable allies walked out.

This clash was an initial warning that two tendencies were beginning to crystallise within the *Iskra* camp, between what became known as the 'hards', around Lenin, and 'softs', around Martov. This was an anticipation of the future split between Bolsheviks and Mensheviks, a revolutionary wing and an opportunist one.

However, at the time, this was far from clear. The lines were not yet clearly marked and nobody could have foreseen the seriousness of the political differences that only emerged after the Congress had concluded, when Plekhanov moved sharply to the right, while Trotsky, who had supported Martov in the Congress, broke with the Mensheviks and moved in the opposite direction.

Of course, for the bourgeois historians, who have no real idea of what is happening, behind these votes lay something deeply sinister. According to Professor Service, although Martov and his supporters had won the vote, "nevertheless the Russian Social Democratic Labour Party had acquired a gangsterish aspect"![31]

After the decision on Paragraph 1, Lenin found himself in a minority in the Congress from the 22nd session until the 27th session. It is worth again quoting from the uncensored *Reminiscences of Lenin* by Krupskaya:

> At the beginning of the Congress, Trotsky spoke very competently. He was then regarded by everyone as an ardent supporter of Lenin, and someone nicknamed him 'Lenin's cudgel'. Indeed, Lenin himself at that time least of all thought that Trotsky would waver.[32]

Krupskaya's remarks about Trotsky, obviously missed by the early Stalinist censor, are remarkable, given that the Left Opposition led by Trotsky had been banned by this time, and Trotsky himself had been expelled and exiled from the Soviet Union by Stalin. As we have seen, they made sure in later versions that these offending sentences were struck out, a classic example of the dishonest school of Stalinist falsification.

But the young twenty-four-year-old Trotsky would later break with Lenin during the Congress and side with Martov. Trotsky, who was still very inexperienced and impulsive, did not grasp the substance of what was happening. He was influenced by the indignant appeals of the old editors, who he had thought were being unfairly treated and took their side. He later admitted unreservedly that Lenin had been right and he had been wrong. "My attitude towards the editors of the *Iskra* was still touched with the sentimentality of youth", he later explained.[33]

Tension

During the Congress, political differences also began to surface over the attitude towards the liberal bourgeoisie, which had surfaced in some of the earlier disputes within *Iskra*. As the liberals tentatively began to organise themselves in opposition to the autocracy, what should the attitude of the workers be towards them?

As far as Lenin was concerned, the workers could make use of the liberals' opposition to tsarism, where possible, but at the same time as class enemies they could not be trusted. In contrast, Martov, Potresov and others – the future Mensheviks – proposed that the workers should support the liberals, but place conditions on them and so hope to win over the better ones. This approach was regarded by Martov as a 'litmus test' for the genuine liberals. However, what lay behind the idea of 'winning over' was not so much using the liberals, but a step towards creating a political bloc with them.

Both Lenin and Plekhanov sharply criticised this approach. They argued that the liberals, as opportunists, would accept all kinds of conditions for their own ends, but would end up betraying the workers at the earliest opportunity. The task of the Party must therefore be not to encourage illusions in the liberals, but, on the contrary, to destroy these illusions and teach the workers to have no trust in them.

However, the differences on this question during the Congress were not as clear cut as they were to become in the future. They were as yet rather undefined and only just beginning to crystallise. As a result, two different resolutions were passed, which papered over the differences and gave the impression there was broad unanimity on this issue.

But the really crucial differences only began to emerge forcibly when the Congress proceeded to hold a debate and vote over the future central organ of the Party – the paper – which ended with the agreement that *Iskra* was to become the official Party organ. This seemed to be a straightforward matter, as the supporters of *Iskra* were in a clear majority. Muravyov had already explained the wide support for *Iskra*:

> ... I want to stress that *Iskra* has been accepted as the guiding organ not only by the delegates at this Congress but also by the majority of committees...[34]

Strangely, Bertram D Wolfe states that "Martov, as a loyal Iskrist, fell into the trap and voted in favour of the motion."[35] Why this should be a "trap" when Martov was an editor of *Iskra* doesn't make any sense. It is clearly thrown in by Wolfe to distort what actually happened and to create more of a 'conspiratorial' atmosphere.

By the close of the 27th session, everything had changed. The Bund delegation walked out when their demand for federal autonomous status was overwhelmingly rejected. They were quickly followed by the Economist delegates, who also felt quite isolated. But this walkout resulted in a change in voting strengths, where Martov now found himself in a minority.

At this point, there began endless procedural wranglings: different organisational questions were raised; amendments put forward and voted on. There was a host of protests and counter-protests. This went on until the 30th session of the Congress held on 19 August. Then came the final showdown.

At this session, the question of the composition of the *Iskra* editorial board was raised for discussion, where Posadovsky, supported by Lenin, proposed an editorial board of three instead of the previous six. This led to a further wrangle over procedure and points of order. Others, such as Popov, proposed keeping the original six members, amid stormy applause and general commotion, according to the minutes. Trotsky put forward a resolution: "The Congress considers it necessary to confirm the former editorial board of *Iskra* as a whole, without any elections."[36]

The whole Congress erupted in a state of tension, where things became extremely polarised. "Why all this pathos, these just-shed tears? After all, nobody wants to murder anyone here!", stated the delegate Lange.[37]

When the session continued the following day, Trotsky's resolution was voted down, as was his proposal of a secret ballot by nineteen votes to seventeen, with three abstentions. It was then decided to elect an editorial board of three.

That is when Martov suddenly intervened to declare the minority's boycott: "I must declare on my own behalf and that of the three other comrades that none of us will sit on this new editorial board."[38] He railed at the delegates:

> What has now taken place is the last act of the struggle which has raged during the second half of the congress. It is no secret to anyone that the issue involved

in this reform is not 'efficiency' but a struggle for influence on the Central Committee [...] I thought that the congress would put an end to the 'state of siege' in the Party and would establish normal conditions. But in fact the state of siege, with its exceptional laws against particular groups, is being continued and even stepped up.[39]

Lenin asked to reply to the allegations. But when he began to speak, he was met with a barrage of interruptions, especially when he said he had raised the composition of the editorial board with Martov personally, who had never raised any objections.

And I am not in the least frightened by the dreadful words about 'a state of siege in the Party', about 'exceptional laws against particular persons and groups', and so on. We not only can but must create a 'state of siege' in relation to unstable and vacillating elements, and all our Party rules, the whole system of centralism which the Congress has now approved, are nothing but a 'state of siege' with regard to the so numerous sources of *political diffuseness*. Against diffuseness special laws are needed, even if they be exceptional laws, and the step taken by the congress has correctly indicated the political direction to be followed, by creating a firm basis for *such* laws and *such* measures.[40]

The Congress then approved the proposal to elect the three-person editorial board by secret ballot. The results announced for the highest votes were: twenty-three votes for Plekhanov, twenty-two for Martov and twenty votes for Lenin.

The elections to the Central Committee, also by secret ballot, took place next. Three members were elected with twenty-four votes cast. This meant that twenty of the forty-four delegates in the hall abstained from voting. Glebov, Clair and Kurz were duly elected. The same voting numbers were recorded for the fifth member of the Party Council.*

The decisions led to enormous rancour, with all sorts of allegations and abuse being thrown about, producing a lot of bruised feelings. This then opened up a long and acrimonious debate and divided the Congress between the 'majority-ites' and 'minority-ites' – in Russian, the 'Bolsheviks' and 'Mensheviks'.

---

* The Second Congress had established a 'Party Council' as the highest body of the Party. It was composed of two representatives each from the editorial board and the Central Committee, with a third member elected by the Congress. Its role was to oversee relations between the bodies. It proved ineffective following the split and was therefore abolished by the Third Congress in 1905.

'One Step Forward, Two Steps Back'

Looking back on these events, Lenin attempted to draw out the lessons of what had happened. Summing up the work of the Congress, Lenin wrote a pamphlet, *One Step Forward, Two Steps Back:*

> Our Party Congress was unique and unprecedented in the entire history of the Russian revolutionary movement. For the first time a secret revolutionary Party succeeded in emerging from the darkness of underground life into broad daylight, showing everyone the whole course and outcome of our internal Party struggle, the whole character of our Party and of each of its more or less noticeable components in matters of programme, tactics, and organisation. For the first time we succeeded in throwing off the traditions of circle looseness and revolutionary philistinism, in bringing together dozens of very different groups, many of which had been fiercely warring among themselves and had been linked solely by the force of an idea, and which were now prepared (in principle, that is) to sacrifice all their group aloofness and group independence for the sake of the great whole which we were for the first time actually creating – the *Party*. But in politics sacrifices are not obtained gratis, they have to be won in battle. The battle over the slaughter of organisations necessarily proved terribly fierce. The fresh breeze of free and open struggle blew into a gale. The gale swept away – and a very good thing that it did! – each and every remnant of all circle interests, sentiments, and traditions without exception, and for the first time created genuinely Party institutions.[41]

When it was raised that the editorial board (the 'central organ') should be subordinate to the Central Committee, Lenin objected.

"This will not work", Lenin replied, "because of the relation of forces... Well, how will they direct us from inside Russia? No, it won't work... We constitute the stable centre and we shall direct affairs from here."

"In that case the 'central organ' will exercise a complete dictatorship?" Trotsky asked. "What's wrong with that?", retorted Lenin, "In our present situation it cannot be otherwise."[42]

And Lenin was absolutely correct. The special circumstances in which the Party was operating required special measures. Working within Russia in illegal conditions made the membership of the Central Committee unstable due to the danger of arrests and persecution. This was a fact. The only stable body, free from the long arm of the law, was the political leadership represented by the editorial board, that was based abroad. The editorial board, therefore, was the central political authority within the Party, and not the other bodies. It was the supreme body, next to the Party Council and the

Congress, and it was in this sense that Lenin likened it to a 'dictatorship' over the rest.

Lenin recalled a discussion he had with one of the centrist delegates who was upset at the tone used during the Second Congress, which he published in *One Step Forward, Two Steps Back*. He wrote:

> I cannot help recalling in this connection a conversation I happened to have at the congress with one of the 'Centre' delegates. "How oppressive the atmosphere is at our Congress!", he had complained. "This bitter fighting, this agitation one against the other, this biting controversy, this uncomradely attitude…" "What a splendid thing our Congress is!" I replied. "A free and open struggle. Opinions have been stated. The shades have been brought out. The groups have taken shape. Hands have been raised. A decision has been taken. A stage has been passed. Forward! That's the stuff for me! That's life! That's not like the endless, tedious word-chopping of intellectuals, which stops not because the question has been settled, but because they are too tired to talk any more…"
>
> The comrade of the 'Centre' stared at me in perplexity and shrugged his shoulders. We were talking different languages.[43]

Krupskaya commented about the quote: "Here, in this quotation we have the whole of Ilyich."[44]

8. Aftermath of the 1903 Split

The bitter row at the Second Congress was clearly overladen with personal conflicts and not a few bruised feelings and egos, where the minority, in particular, hurled insults against Lenin and the majority. "This is a dictatorship!" they claimed. Vera Zasulich compared Lenin to Louis XIV, while Trotsky, who originally supported him, called him "Maximilien [i.e. Robespierre] Lenin".[1]

There was a great war of words. Takhtarev, who supported Martov, complained of "underhand polemical tricks and intolerance".[2] But this, in reality, reflected the fact that the professionalism of Lenin had won the day. Despite the personal animosities, what was being decided was the fate of the Party, although that wasn't immediately obvious to most.

"In 1903, the whole point at issue was nothing more than Lenin's desire to get Axelrod and Zasulich off the editorial board", explained Trotsky later.[3] This was certainly true, but behind this was Lenin's struggle to rid the Party of its circle mentality, a product of the past period, and to put the Party on a more professional footing.

Lenin had first-hand experience of the "old family character" that characterised the relationship of the six editors, "a body based on indulgence and slackness", to quote his words.[4] It was this state of affairs that he tried to end. Lenin followed the important observations of Engels about party building:

> The movement of the proletariat necessarily passes through different stages of development; at every stage part of the people get stuck and do not join in the further advance...[5]

He went on to add:

> It seems that *every* workers' party of a big country can develop only through internal struggle, which accords with the laws of dialectical development in general.[6]

Of course, any proposal, from Lenin or whoever, to remove long-established comrades from their positions was always going to ruffle a few feathers. With the best will in the world, the problem of personal feelings always tends to enter into such matters, no matter how things are presented. But rather than accept the decision and move on, all hell was let loose.

Trotsky, who had originally supported Lenin, took the removal of the old-timers very badly and was indignant at Lenin's ruthlessness. "How will the editors who are not re-elected feel about the fact that the Congress does not want to see them on the board any more?", asked Trotsky.[7]

Yet Lenin correctly replied that "such arguments simply put the whole question on the plane of *pity and injured feelings*, and were a direct admission of bankruptcy as regards the real arguments of principle, real political arguments."[8] Lenin went on to quote approvingly comrade Rusov:

> If we adopt this standpoint, which is a *philistine* and not a Party standpoint, we shall at every election have to consider: will not Petrov be offended if Ivanov is elected and not he, will not some member of the Organising Committee be offended if another member, and not he, is elected to the Central Committee? Where is this going to land us, comrades? If we have gathered here for the purpose of creating a Party, and *not of indulging in mutual compliments and philistine sentimentality*, then we can never agree to such a view. We are about to *elect officials*, and there can be no talk of lack of confidence in any person not elected; *our only consideration should be the interests of the work and a person's suitability for the post to which he is being elected*.[9]

Lenin was certainly correct, as was Rusov. Many were hurt by feelings of personal sentiment, and some by personal prestige, but not politics, which Trotsky later confirmed:

> My attitude towards them [Axelrod and Zasulich] was full of respect, and there was an element of personal affection as well. Lenin also thought highly of them for what they had done in the past. But he believed that they were becoming an impediment for the future. This led him to conclude that they must be removed from their position of leadership. I could not agree. My whole being seemed to protest against this merciless cutting off of the older

ones when they were at last on the threshold of an organised Party. It was my indignation at his attitude that really led to my parting with him at the Second Congress. His behaviour seemed unpardonable to me, both horrible and outrageous. And yet, politically, it was right and necessary, from the point of view of organisation.[10]

Krupskaya admitted that Lenin was so on edge that he hardly ate anything during the Congress. "In London he worried so much that he stopped sleeping altogether."[11]

In the end, Plekhanov, Lenin and Martov were elected to the Central Organ, or the editorial board. But Martov refused to take up the position, which meant a rupture. "The split was obvious", noted Krupskaya.[12]

When the Congress came to an end, the following day, the delegates took a trip to Highgate Cemetery to visit Marx's grave, where speeches were made, then on to the British Museum. But, given what had happened, the mood was still fractious. After a few days, delegates began to disperse back home to ponder over the recent events. Lenin and Krupskaya returned once again to Geneva. However, it wasn't long before serious problems began to surface within the Party.

Immediately following the Congress, Martov and his supporters refused to recognise the decisions and engaged in a campaign of sabotage. Martov's policy of an open boycott succeeded in paralysing the whole Party. "We are not serfs!", Martov exclaimed indignantly. Plekhanov, however, expressed the minority's rebellion as a "general strike of generals".[13] As a result, *Iskra* was left to Lenin and Plekhanov alone to edit.

'Have they gone mad?'

The split came as a massive shock to everyone, including Lenin. He had taken it very badly and Krupskaya revealed how the conflict had undermined his health. On his return to Geneva, completely exhausted, Lenin suffered what appeared to be a nervous breakdown. He was physically and mentally shattered. He felt depressed and unable to eat or work. It took him a great deal of time to recover his strength, pick himself up, and digest the significance of what had happened.

At one point, Lenin felt so disheartened by everything that he even thought of emigrating to America. This brings to mind Oliver Cromwell, the leader of the English Revolution, who considered leaving England if the Parliament failed to pass the Grand Remonstrance. But Lenin gave up on the idea, as did Cromwell, and he remained to carry on the struggle.

Lenin is always falsely portrayed as 'ruthless' and 'rigid' by bourgeois historians. However, the truth is that he originally tried to seek a compromise with Martov. Lenin was able to engage in sharp polemics, but afterwards, when the dust had settled, he was prepared to make organisational concessions to preserve the unity of the Party. But his efforts at a compromise this time were rebuffed by Martov.

"… to cause a split because someone has been excluded *from a central body* seems to me a piece of inconceivable folly", stated Lenin.[14] He wrote to Alexandra Kalmykova: "Someone or other was merely removed from the *central body* – is that a matter for offence? Should the Party be torn apart for that?" "And to make such a finale a reason for resentment, offence, a split in the Party! It is madness."[15] It was "senseless", he repeated.[16]

Lenin again explained that the split boiled down to nothing more than dissatisfaction with the composition of the leading bodies. In other words, there were no differences of principle, and nothing that would warrant such a rupture:

I already said at the Congress, and have since repeated it time and again, that "I by no means consider our difference [over Paragraph 1] so vital as to be a matter of life or death to the Party. We shall certainly not perish because of an unfortunate clause in the Rules!"[17]

Furthermore, he explained:

Examining the behaviour of the Martovites since the Congress, their refusal to collaborate on the Central Organ (*although officially invited by the editorial board to do so*), their refusal to work on the Central Committee, and their propaganda of a boycott – all I can say is that this is an insensate attempt, unworthy of Party members, to disrupt the Party – and why? *Only* because they are dissatisfied with the composition of the central bodies; for, speaking *objectively*, it was *only* over this that our ways parted, while their subjective verdicts (insult, affront, slurs, ousting, shutting out, etc., etc.) *are nothing but the fruits of offended vanity and a morbid imagination.*[18]

Nevertheless, Lenin made repeated requests to the minority to heal the rift. He even praised Plekhanov's attempt to broker a peace. He wrote in a letter:

"…it is essential to safeguard the unity of the Party and avoid new splits – *especially over differences which cannot be considered important.* To appeal for peaceableness, mildness, and readiness to make concessions is highly praiseworthy in a leader at all times, and at the present moment in particular.[19]

Lenin wrote to Potresov saying that while he may have overreacted to the provocations during the Congress, he felt he had done nothing wrong and was not intentionally insulting to anyone:

> And so I ask myself: over what, in point of fact, would we be parting company as enemies for life? I go over all the events and impressions of the Congress, *I realise that I often behaved and acted in a state of frightful irritation, 'frenziedly'; I am quite willing to admit this fault of mine to anyone, if that can be called a fault which was a natural product of the atmosphere, the reactions, the interjections, the struggle, etc.* But examining now, quite unfrenziedly, the results attained, the outcome achieved by frenzied struggle, I can detect nothing, absolutely nothing in these results that is injurious to the Party, and absolutely nothing that is an affront or insult to the Minority.[20]

But Martov and the minority would have none of it and pushed on with their boycott. This only caused the rift in the Party to widen even further.

The split in the Party clearly affected Lenin, as to part with his closest comrades, some of whom were also close friends, on this basis was difficult to swallow. Months passed by, but the impasse remained. It was becoming clearer that while it was "a piece of inconceivable folly", there seemed to be no going back.[21] While Lenin was in favour of making a last appeal to Martov, as time went on, and with no positive reply, he soon faced up to the cold reality of a split.

Despite all this evidence, Helen Rappaport, the historian, reveals her complete ignorance of the facts when she states: "As in everything, Lenin had made it impossible to find a middle ground."[22]

As Lenin tried to focus more on the work, he began to plan a way forward. He realised that a critical juncture had been reached in the Party. The storm at the Congress had revealed serious fault lines and there was no point in hiding this fact. He and his supporters had no alternative but to face up to the situation and draw the necessary conclusions.

"Friendship is at an end here", he wrote. "Down with all softness! Prepare for the most vigorous resistance…"[23]

This view showed Lenin's firm qualities. When he became convinced of something, he was determined to carry it through to the end. He could be accommodating when he wanted, but also very firm when necessary. This was one of his great strengths. Nevertheless, breaking with Martov was exceptionally difficult. He had the highest regard for Martov, to whom he had developed a close personal and political attachment. Lenin knew Martov's weaknesses, but he also appreciated and valued his strengths. Although 'soft', Martov was a dedicated and very intelligent comrade and journalist whom Lenin wanted to retain on the *Iskra* editorial board. His loss was a blow. Krupskaya wrote:

> It was very hard for him to have to break with Martov. Their work together in St. Petersburg and on the old *Iskra* had drawn them close together. Extremely sensitive, Martov in those days had been very quick at grasping Ilyich's thoughts and developing them in a talented manner. Afterwards Vladimir Ilyich had fiercely fought the Mensheviks, but whenever Martov's line showed a tendency to right itself, his old attitude towards him revived. Such was the case, for example, in Paris in 1910, when Vladimir Ilyich and Martov worked together on the editorial board of *Sotsial-Demokrat* (*Social-Democrat*). Coming home from the office, Vladimir Ilyich often used to tell me in a pleased tone that Martov was taking a correct line and even coming out against Dan. Afterward, in Russia, Vladimir Ilyich was very pleased with Martov's stand during the July days, not because it was any good to the Bolsheviks, but because Martov bore himself as behoves a revolutionary.
>
> Vladimir Ilyich was already seriously ill when he said to me once sadly: "They say Martov is dying too."[24]

According to Maxim Gorky:

> The only regret he ever expressed in my presence was: "I am sorry, deeply sorry, that Martov is not with us. What a splendid comrade he was, what an absolutely sincere man!"[25]

Lenin's appreciation and his tender feelings for Martov completely cuts across the 'inhuman' Lenin continually broadcast by bourgeois commentators.

In Russia, the news of the split within the Second Congress was met with complete astonishment. Many were bewildered and angered by something that seemed to make no sense whatsoever. To split the Party over one rule and the composition of the editorial board seemed to many as completely light-minded. Very few understood the real reasons behind it. Lunacharsky explained the feelings in *Revolutionary Silhouettes*:

> At all events the news of the split at the Second Congress hit us like a bolt from the blue. We knew that the Second Congress was to witness the concluding moves in the struggle with *The Workers' Cause*, but that the schism should take a course which was to put Martov and Lenin in opposing camps and that Plekhanov was to 'split off' midway between the two – none of this so much as entered our heads.

The first clause of the Party statute – was this really something which justified a split? A reshuffle of jobs on the editorial board – what's the matter with those people abroad, have they gone mad?[26]

Plekhanov surrenders

Plekhanov, who had remained firm up until this point, began to grow ever more alarmed at the paralysis. He began to waver and then sought accommodation with Martov, but on Martov's terms. In reality, it represented a capitulation. Martov had demanded that all the old members be brought back onto the editorial board, and two others brought onto the Central Committee, while a further minority supporter became a member of the Party Council. Eventually, Plekhanov, in the hope of buying peace, accepted the proposals. Lenin, however, regarded it as total surrender and a complete violation of the Congress decisions. He referred to them as simply "peace terms put by victors to the vanquished".[27] Lenin could not stomach it any longer. "Plekhanov has betrayed us", he wrote, "there is terrible bitterness in our camp; all are indignant…"[28]

In November 1903, weary of the intrigues and sabotage, Lenin felt he had no alternative – having been placed in an impossible position by Plekhanov's capitulation – but to resign from the *Iskra* editorial board. Even following this, he made an offer of peace a month later in his 'Letter to the Editors of *Iskra* (Why I Resigned from the Editorial Board)' and again in the Party Council in January 1904. The minority, whom Plekhanov had co-opted onto the editorial board, rejected Lenin's proposals out of hand and took the road of open war against the majority. This was Lenin's final gesture. He had now no alternative but to reply in kind. It became war to the finish. Beginning with issue No. 52, with Lenin's resignation, *Iskra* now became the organ of the Menshevik faction.

"*Iskra* may come to a stop", concluded Lenin. "The crisis is complete and terrible."[29] Given this impasse, Lenin believed that the only way out was to call a new Third Party Congress, with the authority to democratically decide on all matters. However, unless both the minority and majority agreed to this proposal, it was not going to happen – and the minority, fearing that they would be a minority again, were refusing to endorse it.

But Lenin, sensing the stalemate, was not prepared to accept this arrangement. To get around this blockage, Lenin established a body known as the Southern Bureau of the Central Committee, under the guidance of Vorovsky. He hoped to use this body as the mechanism for calling a new

Congress, but the Central Committee stepped in and dissolved the Southern Bureau before it had time to meet. Furthermore, to add insult to injury, the Central Committee also replaced Lenin's foreign representative on the body, and then prevented the publication of Lenin's writings without their prior permission. This put Lenin in an impossible position.

He therefore took the step of establishing his own, separate, Bolshevik committees within Russia. To this end, local conferences were organised in December 1904, which elected a Bureau of Majority Committees with the aim of preparing the Third Congress of the Party.

Following months of wavering, Lenin realised that the break with Plekhanov was an established fact. However, as Krupskaya explained, "it was the hardest of all to break with [him]."[30] It was not easy, but Lenin believed there was no point in capitulating to the Martovites and he had grown tired of all the bickering. He nevertheless made an effort to see Plekhanov, only to convince himself that a reconciliation was absolutely impossible. He returned from the meeting in a depressed mood. "Vladimir Ilyich was gloomier than ever", noted Krupskaya.[31]

A chasm had opened up between the old and the new *Iskra*, noted Trotsky. Despite the difficulties, Lenin was determined to make the most of it and to strike out in a new direction. The minority, in the meantime, stepped up their campaign of resistance. So great were the obstacles placed in his way that he was finally compelled to convene the Third Congress, based solely on the Bolshevik faction. That took more than a year – it did not take place until May 1905. The Mensheviks, as expected, refused to attend and instead held their own separate conference elsewhere. The split had become an obvious reality as the two groupings, minority and majority, now operated independently under the banner of the Russian Social Democratic Labour Party.

Prior to the holding of the Third Congress, Lenin tried to build up his support within the Party inside Russia. However, there was still a lot of confusion about the split in the membership, which Lenin complained about. He realised that the only way to cut across this was to launch a new separate Bolshevik newspaper. And so he single-mindedly put all his energies into this, writing:

> The whole crux now lies in this organ, without it we shall be heading for certain, inglorious death. We must get some money at all costs, come what may, if only a couple of thousand, and start immediately, otherwise we are cutting our own throats.[32]

'Vperyod' launched

Remarkably, within only a month, Lenin's efforts had paid off and the new paper, *Vperyod* (Forward), was established. This immediately served to rally support for the Bolshevik cause. However, this was only the start. The split within Russia was far from uniform and many districts still had a mixed character, representing both majority and minority. Some layers had dropped out of activity, having lost heart after the split.

A year after the Second Congress, Trotsky wrote a pamphlet, *Our Political Tasks*, which was a litany of attacks on Lenin and his supporters. In its pages, Trotsky tried to answer Lenin's book, *One Step Forward, Two Steps Back*. Trotsky accused Lenin of creating a bureaucratic dictatorship and creating a "barracks discipline" within the Party. Many of the allegations – and much of the language – contained in the pamphlet were a reflection of the antagonisms produced by the split. Trotsky would later admit that the allegations he made were wrong and he rejected them. The pamphlet, he wrote later, contained "not a little that is immature and erroneous in my criticisms of Lenin", although there were certainly pages that were criticisms of the Bolshevik 'committee-men', who Lenin also clashed with.[33] We will meet this problem of the 'committee-men' during the Third Congress.

Trotsky's pamphlet predicted that Lenin's methods would eventually "lead to the Party organisation 'substituting' itself for the Party, and finally the Central Committee substituting itself for the Party organisation, and finally the dictator substituting himself for the Central Committee."[34] Trotsky's description has an uncanny resemblance to the Party as it was to become under Stalin, where the position of the general secretary became omnipotent. However, that was never the case during Lenin's lifetime, and it had nothing whatsoever to do with Lenin's principles of party organisation. The rise of Stalin was due to the bureaucratisation of the Soviet Union in conditions of national isolation and the extremely backward economic conditions in Russia. Trotsky himself later categorically repudiated the mistakes he had made on this question in his youth, which were the typical product of polemical exaggerations.

Centralism, in fact, was common to both Bolsheviks and Mensheviks. It was simply the application of the organisational methods previously supported by the old *Iskra* under Lenin, Plekhanov and Martov. In any case, despite all the talk of centralism, the Party was still organisationally quite loose.

Lenin wrote *One Step Forward, Two Steps Back* in order to put the record straight. He concluded that the split between 'majority' and 'minority' was a division between the revolutionary 'majority' and the opportunist 'minority'. This was reflected, not in a disagreement over tactics or policy, but "opportunism in matters of organisation."[35]

Lenin pointed to their "hostility to the idea (the 'bureaucratic' idea) of building the Party from the top downwards, starting from the Party Congress and the bodies set up by it." In this, he said, they were expressing "their leaning towards the mentality of the bourgeois intellectual, who is only prepared to 'accept organisational relations platonically'; their penchant for opportunist profundity and for anarchistic phrases; their tendency towards autonomism as against centralism…"[36]

Bolsheviks lose control

"The year 1904 was perhaps the most difficult in Lenin's life, barring the last years of his illness", wrote Trotsky.[37] With the loss of the editorial board, followed by Plekhanov, and coupled with arrests in Russia, the Bolsheviks lost control of the Party's Central Committee in the summer of 1904. Plekhanov's defection to the Mensheviks also gave Martov control of the Party Council. Thus, within a short space of time, the Bolsheviks had lost control of all the central positions within the Party. All of which added to their difficulties.

Then, to add to this, the leaders of the Second International came out in support of Martov and his faction. These included the authoritative figures such as Karl Kautsky, August Bebel and Rosa Luxemburg, who had relied on the one-sided information supplied to them by the Mensheviks. Echoing the Martovites, they condemned Lenin's 'extreme centralism'. Luxemburg's attacks were published in *Die Neue Zeit* and in the Menshevik-controlled *Iskra* (No. 69). In reply, Lenin wrote to Kautsky in October 1904:

> I am sending you by post my article which should serve as a reply to Comrade Rosa Luxemburg's attacks. I am aware that the sympathies of the editors of *Neue Zeit* are with my opponents, but it would be only fair to grant me the right to correct some of the inaccuracies in Rosa Luxemburg's articles.[38]

Lenin made it perfectly clear that the split was not about the degree of centralisation, but about organisational opportunism, namely between the "circle spirit against the party spirit".[39] In doing so, he answered Rosa Luxemburg by denying he was advocating a different system of organisation:

> Comrade Luxemburg says, for example, that my book is a clear and detailed expression of the point of view of "intransigent centralism". Comrade Luxemburg thus supposes that I defend one system of organisation against another. But

43. Rosa Luxemburg   44. Alexander Bogdanov

actually that is not so. From the first to the last page of my book, I defend the elementary principles of any conceivable system of party organisation. My book is not concerned with the difference between one system of organisation and another, but with how any system is to be maintained, criticised, and rectified in a manner consistent with the party idea.[40]

Kautsky, who sided with the Mensheviks, spitefully refused to publish Lenin's reply.

It is clear, when reading what Rosa Luxemburg wrote at this time, that she was equating the views advocated by Lenin with the growing centralisation within the German Social Democratic Party, describing it as the "ultra-centralist wing of the party."

But to desire, as Lenin does, to deck out a party leadership with such absolute powers of a negative character would be only to multiply artificially and in the most dangerous measure the conservatism which is a necessary outgrowth of every such leadership... The ultra-centralism advocated by Lenin, however, appears to us as something which, in its whole essence, is not informed with the positive and creative spirit, but with the sterile spirit of the night-watchman.[41]

It was precisely the German Social-Democracy under Kautsky that was becoming the "sterile spirit of the night-watchman", whose "ultra-centralism"

45. Anatoly Lunacharsky c. 1923   46. Leonid Krassin in 1903

Luxemburg was fighting against. But it was false to equate this regime with Lenin's attempts to professionalise the Russian Party.

At the end of the day, out of sheer necessity, the Bolsheviks were now forced to operate as an independent faction within the Party. The whole episode around the Second Congress was an *anticipation* of future political divisions, which only began to surface during 1904 and 1905, but did not lead to a final break until 1912. In fact, within that time, there would be many attempts to achieve a reunification. At this point, there were only the outlines of a future Bolshevism and Menshevism, and nothing more than that.

Once the dust began to settle, while the Martovites had gained many of the 'big names', especially with Plekhanov's authority, Lenin had won over the ordinary delegates who had come from Russia, the provincial Party members and professionals, such as Alexander Bogdanov and Anatoly Lunacharsky. Bogdanov in particular was one of the most important of Lenin's gains at this time, who from now on carried the brunt of the work in building up the Bolshevik faction. Another asset was Leonid Krassin, an engineer who was a brilliant organiser of illegal operations. With these key people and others, Lenin sought to tap into the new reserves within the party in order to rebuild their support.

9. The Revolution Begins

At the end of the nineteenth century, an inter-imperialist struggle had broken out over control of the Pacific and the division of China. Russia also participated in this venture, seizing northern Manchuria.

This brought the tsarist regime into conflict with Japan, which had its own ambitions in the region, and in early 1904 war broke out between the two contending powers. It proved an unpopular war.

The Russian forces suffered defeats, which only added to the already existing hatred for the regime. The discontent over the war found its expression in the assassination of Vyacheslav von Plehve, the Minister of the Interior. The liberal bourgeoisie, hoping to squeeze some concessions from the old order, welcomed the Russian setbacks, as did the intelligentsia.

The Bolsheviks, however, sought to bring out the class questions and therefore raised the idea of turning the imperialist war into a civil war. The Mensheviks, in turn, also adopted an anti-war, defeatist position towards the regime.

In the same year, at the International Socialist Congress in Amsterdam, Plekhanov put forward this class position on the war:

> I said that in the event of a victory of the tsarist government over Japan, the vanquished would turn out to be none other than the Russian people itself. The triumphant tsarist government would take advantage of the aura of victory to draw the chains with which it had fettered the Russian people even more tightly.

He continued:

I reminded the Congress of that unfortunate indisputable historical truth that the foreign policy of the tsarist government had for long been a policy of plunder and conquest; that this government had invariably striven to dominate all those nations surrounding it which had not been strong enough to give it a firm rebuff and that it had enclosed strictly Russian land with a solid ring of defeated nationalities which repaid it in hatred what they received from it in oppression. And I added that from such a policy the Russian population itself suffered not less but most of all, because not a single nation can be free if it serves as the instrument for the oppression of its neighbours...

And in saying all this I acknowledged that I was expressing the thoughts and feelings of the vast mass of the Russian people. Never before had the voice of Russian Social-Democracy been in such strong measure the voice of the Russian people.[1]

In January 1905, the Japanese finally took Port Arthur in Manchuria. Lenin wrote an article, 'The Fall of Port Arthur', in which he quotes from a European bourgeois newspaper describing it as "one of the greatest events in modern history." He drew out the implication of the defeat, which caused a "profound political crisis" and quoted the letter from Prince Trubetskoy to the Minister of the Interior stating: "there is evidently real ground for the fear of a revolution in Russia." Lenin concluded:

> Yes, the autocracy is weakened. The most sceptical of the sceptics are beginning to believe in the revolution. General belief in revolution is already the beginning of revolution.*[2]

The humiliating military defeat served to expose the inner rottenness of tsarism. On 16 January 1905, a strike broke out at the Putilov works and began to spread. The next day, they were joined by workers at the Franco-Russian Factory, then by workers at the Neva Shipbuilding Factory. By 20 January, a general strike was under way involving 456 enterprises with up to 150,000 workers.

Father Gapon, a priest who was involved with the workers, suggested a demonstration be organised to present a petition to the tsar. He had built up an organisation of 8,000 workers called the Petersburg Society of Russian

---

* Compare this to the extreme chauvinist position of Stalin, published in the *Daily Worker* in 1945:

> But the defeat of the Russian troops in 1904 in the period of the Russo-Japanese war left a grave imprint on the mind of the people. It was a black stain in the history of our country. Our people were confident and awaited the day when Japan would be routed and this dark spot wiped out. (*Daily Worker*, 3 September 1945)

47. Father Gapon in 1904 (centre-left)

Factory and Workshop Workers, which had been tolerated by the police. On Sunday 22 January (9 January, Old Style), some 200,000 workers and their families peacefully marched to the Winter Palace, with icons, a large portrait of the tsar, and a priest at their head, to present a humble petition outlining their grievances to the 'Little Father', the *tsar-batiushka*, and Ruler of All the Russias.

> Sire – We working men and inhabitants of St. Petersburg... our wives, our children and aged and helpless parents, are come to Thee, Sire, to seek for truth and protection. We are become beggars; we have been oppressed; we are breathless... There has arrived for us that great moment when death is better than the continuation of our intolerable tortures... We are seeking here the last salvation...[3]

But instead of sympathy, the peaceful procession of workers and their families was ruthlessly cut down in cold blood by the tsar's soldiers who opened fire on the mass crowd. Over 1,000 were killed and over 2,000 wounded on that day. The worker-priest, Father Gapon, who led the procession, was so horrified that he responded to the outrage by saying: "There is no God any longer. There is no Tsar."[4] Bloody Sunday, as it became known, shook the very foundations of Russian society and the illusions in tsarism were shattered. Barricades went up and firearms stores were raided. It marked a fundamental turning point in Russia and the beginning of what was to become the Revolution of 1905. "People were awakened to political consciousness for the first time", explained Lenin.[5]

This revolution – the first of its kind in Russia – was famously described by him as a "dress rehearsal", the preparation for the victorious October Revolution of 1917.[6] It transformed the political landscape of Russia and had an impact internationally. It propelled the young working class into an all-out struggle with tsarism that swept the liberals aside in the process. These stormy events put all the main parties and tendencies to the test, including the Bolsheviks. As news filtered through about the events in St. Petersburg, it was apparent that the revolution had taken the socialist organisations by surprise. Looking back at these events, Lenin explained:

> Two months before January 1905 [...] no revolutionary, whatever his experience and knowledge, however familiar he was with the life of the people, could have foreseen that Russia would be shaken by such explosions.[7]

Revolution finally arrives

Even the Bolsheviks, who had predicted a forthcoming revolution, were taken aback by the sudden turn of events. Given the split and the subsequent difficulties, their organisation was not in a good shape for what was to come. "I now think that the 1905-6 revolution caught us somewhat unprepared", remarked Lunacharsky.[8] In fact, they were a bit more than "somewhat" unprepared.

The split at the Second Congress of 1903 had cast a long shadow over the Bolsheviks, a number of whom were still suffering from disorientation, and even demoralisation. Lenin openly recognised the situation. "That our Party is seriously ill and has lost a good half of its influence during the past year is known to the whole world", he wrote at the beginning of January 1905.[9] They were so wrong-footed by events that they even questioned whether they should participate in the demonstration led by Gapon. In the end, they gathered as a separate block at the back of the demonstration, a decision that would fortuitously save many of their lives.

48. Cavalry at the Pevchesky Bridge protect the Winter Palace, 9 January 1905

Lenin, from exile, fully understood that the events unfolding in Russia were unprecedented:

> Russia has never yet witnessed such a gigantic outbreak of the class struggle. [...]
> Throughout these past days mass meetings of workers are daily taking place in all city districts at the headquarters of the 'Association of Russian Workers'. The surrounding streets are filled with thousands of workers.[10]

In Switzerland, he was only able to scour the newspapers for scraps of information. "... in Geneva, so damnably far away, we find it exceedingly difficult to keep pace with events", wrote a frustrated Lenin.[11] Despite this, it was from there that he issued a call to arms. If the Russian revolution was to succeed in overthrowing tsarism, he explained, it would need to be armed.

Lenin drew parallels with the Chartists in Britain who had called on the workers to arm themselves in face of the state repression. He quoted the words of Gapon, the priest, who had also spoken of the need for an armed uprising. In fact, street fighting had already broken out and barricades were being thrown up in St. Petersburg and elsewhere. "Events are developing with astonishing rapidity", explained Lenin.[12] This speed was characteristic of a revolution and everything was heading in the direction of a national uprising. Later, Lenin went further in his estimation:

In its extent and acuteness, the strike struggle had no parallel anywhere in the world. The economic strike developed into a political strike, and the latter into insurrection. The relations between the proletariat, as the leader, and the vacillating and unstable peasantry, as the led, were tested in practice.[13]

The masses were rapidly learning from their experience of struggle. They chanted anti-government slogans, and "Down with the Autocracy!" became the battle-cry of the 1905 Revolution.

When news reached Lenin of strikes, street fighting and barricades in St. Petersburg, he was elated. Mass meetings of workers were taking place and committees were being thrown up everywhere as the revolution spread to the countryside. In the villages, the peasants withheld their rents, looted the estates, and attacked the landlords. "Finally, the revolution had arrived!", Lenin must have thought, after predicting such events for many years.

Trotsky had independently reached similar conclusions to Lenin. On 20 January he wrote:

The *forms* taken by the uprising of 9 January could not have been foreseen. A revolutionary priest, in perplexing manner placed by history at the head of the working masses for several days, lent the events the stamp of his personality, his conceptions, his rank. This form may mislead many an observer as to the real substance of the events. The actual meaning of the events, however, is just that which Social-Democracy foresaw. The central figure is the Proletariat. The workingmen start a strike, they unite, they formulate political demands, they walk out into the streets, they win the enthusiastic sympathy of the entire population, they engage in battles with the army... The hero, Gapon, has not created the revolutionary energy of the Petersburg workingmen, he only unloosed it. He found thousands of thinking workingmen and tens of thousands of others in a state of political agitation. He formed a plan which united all those masses – for the period of one day. The masses went to speak to the Tzar. They were faced by Ulans, Cossacks, guards. Gapon's plan had not prepared the workingmen for that. What was the result? They seized arms wherever they could, they built barricades... They fought, though, apparently, they went to beg for mercy. This shows that they went *not to beg, but to demand*.[14]

When Gapon declared that "a river of blood divides the tsar from the people", this was not simply the voice of a priest, but it personified the voice of millions of workers and peasants.[15] The floodgates had truly opened and the masses poured through. Lenin wrote: "Events of the greatest historical importance are developing in Russia. The proletariat has risen against tsarism."[16]

49. Barricades in St. Petersburg, 1905

In the days before Bloody Sunday, Lenin had drawn the conclusion that the split in the Party had become permanent and all the efforts to reach a compromise with the 'minority' had come to nothing. The Bolsheviks had therefore no alternative but to set out on a separate path. This was an audacious move, but was also the thinking behind the calling of the Third Congress. Lenin explained:

> The *split is now complete*; for we have exhausted all means. It is the *Third Congress* against the will of the Central Committee and the Council and *without them*. Complete rupture with the Central Committee. An open statement that we have our own Bureau. The complete removal of the Mensheviks and the new-Iskrists everywhere. We did everything we could to get on together, and should now declare openly and bluntly that we are obliged to work separately.[17]

The 1905 Revolution had now introduced a note of urgency to the proceedings. Lenin was nevertheless very frustrated by his isolation in Switzerland. Richard Pipes, a professional cynic who pretends to be a historian, once again twists the facts, slyly insinuating that Lenin's Swiss exile was proof that he "preferred to observe them [events in Russia] from the safety of Switzerland".[18]

Nothing could be further from the truth. All the evidence shows that Lenin was like a caged tiger. Deeply frustrated by his enforced exile, he yearned with every fibre of his being to be back in Russia, in the heat of action, instead of commenting on events from afar.

Lenin, observing the sweep of the Revolution, was amazed at the way Gapon, who had increasingly shifted to the left, guided the movement. Lenin was so impressed that he was even keen, if possible, to meet Gapon, in contrast to Plekhanov, who stated that no good can come from a priest. As it turned out, Gapon also wanted to meet Lenin in Geneva, and so a meeting was arranged at a late-night cafe. Lenin found Gapon sincere, but more importantly, he viewed him as part of the unfolding revolution. Krupskaya related what happened:

> Gapon was a living part of the growing revolution in Russia, a man closely bound up with the working-class masses who implicitly believed in him. Ilyich was excited at the prospect of meeting that man.
>
> One comrade was recently shocked to learn that Vladimir Ilyich had had to do with Gapon.
>
> Of course, one could simply have dismissed Gapon by deciding beforehand that nothing good could ever be expected of a priest. That is what Plekhanov did. He gave Gapon a very cool reception. But Lenin's strength lay in the fact that to him the revolution was a living thing, like a face that one could study in all its varied features, because he knew and understood what the masses wanted. And a knowledge of the masses can only be obtained by contact with them. Ilyich was curious to know what influence Gapon could have had upon the masses.[19]

Some time later, Gapon, although he was gunrunning for the revolution, was accused of being a police informant. He was subsequently murdered by members of the Socialist-Revolutionaries,* and his body was found hanging from the rafters of a cottage in April 1906. However, independently of his personal intentions, the priest had – at least for a time – played the role of the lightning rod and expression for the anger of the masses.

The 'committee-men'

Despite all their preparations for the coming revolution, the Bolsheviks were nevertheless lagging behind, weighed down by internal troubles. It is true that even the most revolutionary parties are not always free from tendencies

---

* The Socialist-Revolutionary Party was established in 1902 and were the ideological heirs of the Narodniks. They were agrarian socialists, and based themselves on the peasantry. In 1917, they entered the Provisional Government and then split between Right and Left SRs. The Left SRs briefly entered the Soviet Government, but resigned over the Brest-Litovsk Treaty.

50. A demonstration in Moscow, 1905
The first banner reads: 'Proletarians of all countries, unite!'

towards conservatism and routinism. Such tendencies can be even more exaggerated when the party is working in illegal and underground conditions, when the centralising principle becomes paramount.

But when conditions change and a sharp turn is required, a layer of comrades who had become accustomed to the old methods of work often find it difficult to adapt to the new environment. This was the case of those who Lenin called the 'committee-men' – party functionaries for whom clandestine methods had become a way of life. These people caused problems that would sharply surface at the coming Third Congress in London.

Lenin laid heavy stress on the revolutionary movement of the masses and was highly critical of the Party's seeming inability to intervene effectively. He did not mince his words when he wrote of the failings of the Party to the Bolshevik paper, *Vperyod*: "9 January 1905 fully revealed the vast reserve of revolutionary energy possessed by the proletariat, as well as the utter inadequacy of Social-Democratic organisation."[20]

The revolutionary mass movement caught the regime off-balance. The tsarist state was temporarily suspended in mid-air. Although not yet defeated, the regime had been badly shaken by the events and was attempting to get a grip of the situation. "The government is veering from the policy of the bloody knout to a policy of promises", noted Lenin.[21]

As the working class battled for its freedoms, it created tremendous new openings for the Party. "The first wave of the revolutionary storm is receding. We are on the eve of an inescapable, inevitable second wave", wrote Lenin.[22] The Bolsheviks needed to advance the slogans that corresponded with the needs of the Revolution, in particular the call for an armed mass uprising to topple the regime.

Unfortunately, such an approach was not adopted by the Bolsheviks on the ground. Rather than audaciously engaging with the mass movement, they routinely tried to impose their own abstract conceptions on the working class. This was a classic case of sectarianism, reflected in an inability to connect with the real movement. Lenin laid the blame for this routinism on the Bolshevik centre in Russia, which was failing to provide leadership. In February, a month into the revolution, Lenin showed his growing frustration in a sharply written letter to the leading comrades, Bogdanov and Sergei Gusev:

> … I am so sick of this procrastination […] A nice business: we talk of organisation, of centralism, while actually there is such disunity, such amateurism among even the closest comrades in the centre, that one feels like chucking it all in disgust. […]
>
> … from our own people not a word. We refuse to believe that Bolsheviks could have taken such an imbecilic, suicidal step. […]
>
> But people, it seems, have gone soft now that we have a 'revolution'![23]

"Really, I sometimes think that nine-tenths of the Bolsheviks are actually formalists", he complained.[24] He then went on to compare the intervention of the Mensheviks, who had adapted much better to the situation than the Bolsheviks:

> The Mensheviks have more money, more literature, more transportation facilities, more agents, more 'names', and a larger staff of contributors. It would be unpardonable childishness not to see that. And if we do not wish to present to the world the repulsive spectacle of a dried-up and anaemic old maid, proud of her barren moral purity, then we must understand that we need war and a battle organisation. Only after a long battle, and only with the aid of an excellent organisation can we turn moral strength into material strength.[25]

Lenin attempted to bring home the gravity of the situation, while pointing to the enormous potential that the revolution had thrown up. The language he used could not have been more forceful:

We need young forces. I am for shooting on the spot anyone who presumes to say that there are no people to be had. The people in Russia are legion; all we have to do is to recruit young people more widely and boldly, more boldly and widely, and again more widely and again more boldly, *without fearing them*. This is a time of war. The youth – the students, and still more so the young workers. Get rid of all the old habits of immobility, of respect for rank, and so on. Form *hundreds* of circles of *Vperyod*-ists from among the youth and encourage them to work at full blast.[26]

These criticisms were clearly aimed against the 'committee-men', who were clinging onto their old tried and tested methods, which were now out of date. Lenin demanded that the Bolshevik leaders break from this routinism and place the organisation on a war-footing. Once again Lenin called for action:

Only you must be sure to organise, organise, and organise *hundreds* of circles, completely pushing into the background the customary, well-meant committee (hierarchic) stupidities. This is a time of war. Either you create *new*, young, fresh, energetic battle organisations everywhere for revolutionary Social-Democratic work of all varieties among all strata, or you will go under, wearing the aureole of 'committee' bureaucrats.[27]

But the 'committee-men' resisted these methods, which held back the progress of the Bolsheviks at this time.

In the midst of the revolution, Lenin's confidence in the working class shone through as he described the features of a revolution and the awakening of the masses – which was now playing out in front of their very eyes:

In the history of revolutions there come to light contradictions that have ripened for decades and centuries. Life becomes unusually eventful. The masses, which have always stood in the shade and have therefore often been ignored and even despised by superficial observers, enter the political area as active combatants. These masses are learning in practice, and before the eyes of the world are taking their first tentative steps, feeling their way, defining their objectives, testing themselves and the theories of all their ideologists. These masses are making heroic efforts to rise to the occasion and cope with the gigantic tasks of world significance imposed upon them by history; and however great individual defeats may be, however shattering to us the rivers of blood and the thousands of victims, nothing will ever compare in importance with this direct training that the masses and the classes receive in the course of the revolutionary struggle itself. The history of this struggle is measured in days.[28]

This echoed the point made by Marx that in revolutionary times there were days in which twenty years were concentrated. And in Russia events were unfolding at a lightning speed. The energy of the masses enthused and inspired Lenin, and it was precisely this energy that represented the very powerhouse of the revolution.

Third Congress opens

Accompanying the first shocks of the revolution, preparations for the Third Congress were announced in early February 1905, as reports arrived of growing support for the initiative. Lenin was proud to announce that towards the end of the month: "We have just received the news that St. Petersburg, Tula, Moscow, the North, Nizhni-Novgorod, the Caucasus, and Odessa have declared for the Congress, and other places will, of course, follow suit."[29]

The Third Congress, as with all the Party Congresses, was organised in secret outside of Russia, this time returning to London in April 1905. It was exclusively a Bolshevik affair, as the Mensheviks deliberately stayed away. It lasted approximately two weeks and was attended by thirty-four delegates, fourteen of whom were consultative.

As soon as the delegates from twenty regional organisations arrived, they were taken straight away to Alexeyev's two attic rooms near Kings Cross. It was here that Krupskaya took down their details and Lenin mingled among them and listened to reports given from their organisations.

The agenda of the Third Congress included items dealing with the Party crisis, the attitude to an armed insurrection, the attitude to other parties, to the liberals, work amongst the peasants and finally organisational questions. As a purely Bolshevik Congress, the gathering served to put its stamp on the split.

It therefore took the bold step of declaring the Bolshevik faction as the only legitimate heirs of the RSDLP and described the Mensheviks as a "seceded portion of the Party".[30] Krupskaya noted:

> The Third Congress was of quite a different character. The organisations in Russia
> definitely existed already in the shape of illegal local committees, which were
> obliged to work under extremely difficult conditions of secrecy. As a result, these
> committees everywhere practically had no workers among their membership,
> although they had a great influence on the workers' movement.[31]

Consequently, Krupskaya wrote: "There were no workers at the Third Congress at least, none of any mark."[32]

This situation reflected the rise of the professional revolutionary who, as an individual, was extremely dedicated and made great sacrifices in the period prior to 1905. Lenin had a very high regard for their work. But he also recognised their weak sides, which tended to give too much importance to the party machine. Amongst them, there grew up a tendency to look down on the workers and the *living* movement and instead to build up the importance of the Party committees. At the Congress, this tendency expressed itself by its distrustful and unhealthy attitude towards workers. Krupskaya wrote:

> The 'committeemen' had done a tremendous job during the period 1904-1905, but many of them found it extremely difficult to adjust themselves to the conditions of increasing legal facilities and methods of open struggle."[33]

Lenin was very alarmed by this development. He strenuously opposed such bureaucratic and sectarian traits and demanded that the Party be opened up to the workers, especially the youth. Compare this approach to the caricature of Lenin as an all-controlling bureaucrat presented by the bourgeois historians!

It was a time to open the doors and not be frightened by the mass movement. This message sounded like heresy to those stuck in the past. He explained:

> A revolutionary epoch is to the Social-Democrats what war-time is to an army. We must broaden the cadres of our army, we must advance them from peace strength to war strength, we must mobilise the reservists, recall the furloughed, and form new auxiliary corps, units, and services. We must not forget that in war we necessarily and inevitably have to put up with less trained replacements, very often to replace officers with rank-and-file soldiers, and to speed up and simplify the promotion of soldiers to officers' rank.

> To drop metaphor, we must considerably increase the membership of all Party and Party-connected organisations in order to be able to keep up to some extent with the stream of popular revolutionary energy which has been a hundred-fold strengthened. This, it goes without saying, does not mean that consistent training and systematic instruction in the Marxist truths are to be left in the shade. We must, however, remember that at the present time far greater significance in the matter of training and education attaches to the military operations, which *teach* the untrained precisely and entirely in *our* sense. We must remember that our 'doctrinaire' faithfulness to Marxism is now being reinforced by the march of

revolutionary events, which is everywhere furnishing *object lessons to the masses* and that all these lessons confirm precisely our dogma. Hence, we do not speak about abandoning the dogma, or relaxing our distrustful and suspicious attitude towards the woolly intellectuals and the arid-minded revolutionaries. Quite the contrary. [...]

Thus, it is not a question of relaxing our Social-Democratic exactingness and our orthodox intransigence, but of strengthening both in *new* ways, by new methods of training. In war-time, recruits should get their training lessons directly from military operations. So tackle the new methods of training more boldly, comrades! Forward, and organise more and more squads, send them into battle, recruit more young workers, extend the normal framework of all Party organisations, from committees to factory groups, craft unions, and student circles! Remember that every moment of delay in this task will play into the hands of the enemies of Social-Democracy; for the new streams are seeking an immediate outlet, and if they do not find a Social-Democratic channel they will rush into a non-Social-Democratic channel. Remember that every practical step in the revolutionary movement will decidedly, inevitably give the young recruits a lesson in Social-Democratic science; for this science is based on an objectively correct estimation of the forces and tendencies of the various classes, while the revolution itself is nothing but the break-up of old superstructures and the independent action of the various classes, each striving to erect the new superstructure in its own way. But do not debase our revolutionary science to the level of mere book dogma, do not vulgarise it with wretched phrases about tactics-as-process and organisation-as-process, with phrases that seek to justify confusion, vacillation, and lack of initiative. Give more scope to all the diverse kinds of enterprise on the part of the most varied groups and circles, bearing in mind that, apart from our counsel and regardless of it, the relentless exigencies of the march of revolutionary events will keep them upon the correct course. It is an old maxim that in politics one often has to learn from the enemy. And at revolutionary moments the enemy always forces correct conclusions upon us in a particularly instructive and speedy manner. [...]

Hundreds of new organisations should be set up for the purpose without a moment's delay. Yes, hundreds; this is no hyperbole...[34]

In conclusion, Lenin underlined the point:

There is no dearth of people; never has revolutionary Russia had such a multitude of people as now.[35]

Extreme flexibility

Again, how different this is from the Lenin of 1903 who wanted to create a "state of siege"! Once again, this clearly revealed Lenin's extreme flexibility on organisational and tactical questions, depending on the concrete needs of the situation. This is the essence of tactics, in politics as in war. It means to concentrate the full force at the point of attack, in that sector of the battlefield where the state of fight most favours victory. Therefore Lenin fully understood a new turn in the work was essential.

The old legacy was most graphically reflected in the disturbing fact that the Petrograd Committee of the Party did not have a single worker on its body, while in the Northern Party Committee only one out of eight members consisted of workers. According to the historian Marcel Liebman, "in most of the committees of the Caucasian towns, with the exception of Tiflis, the number of worker members was either very small or else zero."[36]

Lenin had made his views known in writing to the Odessa Party Committee, when he bitterly complained about the lack of workers:

> Are you taking workers into the Committees? This is essential, absolutely essential! Why don't you put us in direct contact with workers? Not a single worker writes to *Vperyod*. This is a scandal. We need at all costs *dozens* of worker correspondents.[37]

The resistance of the committee-men surfaced at the Third Congress in the debate over the committees. Lenin vigorously intervened in the Congress on this question and, given the degree of opposition from the 'old guard', his speech was accompanied by a lot of interruptions:

> It will be the task of the future centre to reorganise a considerable number of committees; the inertness of the committee-men has to be overcome. (*Applause and booing.*)

> I can hear Comrade Sergeyev booing while the non-committee-men applaud. I think we should look at the matter more broadly. To place workers on committees is a political, not a pedagogical, task. Workers have the class instinct, and, given some political experience, they pretty soon become staunch Social-Democrats. I should be strongly in favour of having eight workers to every two intellectuals on our committees. Should the advice given in our Party literature – to place as many workers as possible on the committees – be insufficient, it would be advisable for this recommendation to be given in the name of the Congress. A clear and definite directive from the Congress will give you a radical means of fighting demagogy; this is the express will of the Congress.[38]

According to Krupskaya, the debate became very heated. At one point, Lenin reacted angrily, saying:

> I could hardly keep my seat when it was said here that there were no workers fit to sit on the committees. The question is being dragged out; obviously there is something the matter with the Party. Workers must be given places on the committees[39].

Together with Bogdanov, a key ally, he put forward an amendment to the Party rules, making it obligatory to place workers on the committees. But Lenin found himself in a minority and, such was the backlash from the committee-men, the amendment was rejected.

However, Lenin was not too perturbed by the Congress vote as he believed that the developing revolution itself would cure this problem, and events were to show that his position was correct.

Nevertheless, Lenin hammered home the idea about recruiting workers whenever he could. Ironically, he had to answer those in the Congress who again invoked the principles of *What Is to Be Done?* against him. His opponents were more interested in texts than the real movement taking place under their very noses. It was always possible to find contradictory quotes in Lenin's writings when he was dealing with different circumstances at different times.

What his opponents failed to understand was Lenin's method and that truth is always concrete. They needed to deal with realities – the real movement of the working class – and not abstractions.

As the Third Congress was taking place in the throes of a revolution, they held a long discussion about the need for armed insurrection and a general strike. However, it was clear that there was not complete agreement among the delegates. Lenin took a firm position as he regarded armed insurrection as the central question.

As far as he was concerned, it was utopian to think that the tsarist regime could be overthrown without such an insurrection. No ruling class in history, no tsar, ever gave up their power and privileges without a struggle, with no holds barred. To quote Trotsky, "No devil had ever voluntarily cut off its own claws."[40]

Finally, a resolution supporting an insurrection was agreed, while also assuaging the concerns of the waverers by placing stress on propaganda and agitation.

As a humorous aside, one of the sessions of the Third Congress was held in the upstairs room of the Crown and Woolpack public house on St. John Street in Islington. Prior to the meeting, a detective from Scotland Yard, Constable Herbert Fitch, hid himself away in a small cupboard to spy on the proceedings. Apparently, Fitch claimed he could understand Russian, but clearly had no idea what these Russians were talking about, given his lack of political knowledge and his police mindset. He later reported he heard Lenin – "Oulyanoff" – speaking of "bloodshed" in Russia and elsewhere, which, according to him, was greeted with fierce cheering. The experience in the cupboard must have left him none the wiser.

For three weeks, a Russian police agent and his team would follow the delegates from place to place across London, reporting their every move, in the hope of gleaning important information. But the Congress proceedings were not affected by this unwanted intrusion.

The Congress elected a new Central Committee that included Lenin, Krassin, Bogdanov, and Alexei Rykov. Lenin remained abroad in Geneva to edit the official organ, *Proletary*, while Bogdanov coordinated work within the interior. Two secretaries were also appointed, Krupskaya for the exile centre and Stasova for the Russian. These individuals made up the working body and leadership of the Bolsheviks in 1905.

Following the Third Congress, the delegates were taken to see various places, including the British Museum and Highgate Cemetery to visit Marx's grave, where revolutionary speeches were delivered.

According to the historian Robert Henderson, by the end of the Congress, Lenin "had succeeded in consolidating his position of power."[41] He even hints at "other forces at play", and points to Vladimir Burtsev's book entitled *Lenin Under the Patronage of the Department of Police and of the Germans*, published in 1927, which places Lenin in the pay of the Okhrana.[42] Henderson, after writing a whole chapter called 'Lenin: Master conspirator or police patsy', then says: "in his view, the catastrophe which erupted in 1917 had already been in preparation from as far back as 1900 thanks, in large part, to the support they [the Bolsheviks] received from the Okhrana."[43] It is quite remarkable how such fairy-tales continue to be spread around after so long.

On their way back home, the delegates, together with Lenin, stopped in Paris where they visited the Wall of the Communards at the Père Lachaise Cemetery. They paid their respects to the fallen, and speeches were made commemorating their bravery and the example of the Paris Commune.

The flames of revolution

Lenin and Krupskaya returned to Geneva, where Lenin kept up the pressure for the Party to break from routinism, and turn outwards towards the workers. He wrote to Bogdanov and Gusev, urging them to act decisively and organise hundreds of circles involving fresh new layers, especially from the youth.

In another letter, Lenin wrote that they intended to bring out the Bolshevik paper, *Vperyod*, on a weekly basis. As part of this, he urged his comrades to take bold initiatives:

> In view of this I would consider it simply necessary and positively essential to hand out a *Vperyod* address (a foreign address, of which we have many now and shall have more) to *every* student circle and to *every* workers' group. I assure you that there is an idiotic prejudice among our committee-men against handing out addresses on a broad scale to the periphery youth. Combat this prejudice with all your might...[44]

This powerful call to open up the Party and recruit new layers into its ranks exposes the stupid allegation churned out by yet another bourgeois historian, Anthony Read, who writes the following:

> Lenin had no time for democracy, no confidence in the masses and no scruples about using violence. He wanted a small, tightly organised and strictly disciplined party of hard-line professional revolutionaries, who would do exactly as they were told.[45]

Quite clearly, the Lenin described in these lines has nothing in common with the real Lenin, or, indeed, any other living person. He is a pure invention – the figment of a brain so poisoned against Bolshevism and the Russian Revolution that no falsehood is too absurd, and no slander too gross to utter.

Lenin used his May Day appeal in the paper to call once again for an insurrection in Russia:

> Comrades! We stand now in Russia on the eve of great events. We are engaged in the last desperate fight with the autocratic tsarist government, we must carry this fight on to its victorious end. To arms, workers and peasants! [...]

> Hold secret meetings, form fighting squads, get whatever weapons you can [...] Let this year's First of May be for us the celebration of the people's uprising, let us prepare for it and await the signal for the decisive attack on the tyrant. Down with the tsarist government![46]

51. Poster for Sergei Eisenstein's 1925 film, *Battleship Potemkin*, which portrays the 1905 mutiny

Trotsky, keenly feeling the need to directly participate in the events, crossed the frontier to Russia to join the revolution, which would continue to unfold for a whole year. Influenced by the general strike in Odessa, the flames of revolution had infected the navy and the sailors aboard the *Potemkin*, who carried out the famous mutiny in June. Strikes spread throughout the industrial areas, and during the spring and summer they took on a far more political character. As the revolution unfolded, it involved different layers at different times, spreading from the towns to the countryside. The agricultural districts, which tended to lag behind, were also drawn into the general struggle. This continual wave of struggle revealed the colossal revolutionary reserves within the masses. These were soon to result in concessions from a frightened regime.

In July, armed clashes were becoming more frequent and Lenin anticipated that they could soon lead to an all-out confrontation:

> The new armed clashes demonstrate more and more strikingly that the decisive armed struggle of the people against the armed forces of tsarism is inevitable. All these separate outbreaks form more and more distinctly the picture of a widespread all-Russian conflagration. [...]

> Away, then, with all doubts and vacillations. Let it be realised by one and all, now without delay, how absurd and discreditable are all pretexts today for evading this urgent task of the most energetic preparation of the armed uprising – how perilous it is to delay...[47]

The underground work of the Party had clearly revealed its limits. "Our Party has stagnated while working underground [...] The 'underground' is breaking up", explained Lenin. "Let us strike out on the new path at once."[48]

> The conditions in which our Party is functioning are changing rapidly. Freedom of assembly, of association and of the press has been captured. Of course, these rights are extremely precarious, and it would be folly, if not a crime, to pin our faith to the present liberties.[49]

The new bold approach of opening the doors bore fruit. However, the flood of new recruits raised fears among the 'old guard' about weakening the Party's ideology, but these arguments were unceremoniously dismissed by Lenin. With a correct approach, he explained, this could be overcome. "Don't invent bugaboos, comrades!", he said:

> Don't forget that in every live and growing party there will always be elements of instability, vacillation, wavering. But these elements can be influenced, and they will submit to the influence of the steadfast and solid core of Social-Democrats.[50]

Lenin stated that "The working class is *instinctively, spontaneously* Social-Democratic..."[51] Gone was the mistaken idea of the workers simply developing trade union consciousness contained in *What Is to Be Done?* On the basis of events, the working class was clearly capable of developing a socialist consciousness, the premise of a conscious working-class socialist revolution.

A few years later, when he wrote an article about the 1905 Revolution, Lenin further underlined this point about consciousness:

The very conditions of their lives make the workers capable of struggle and impel them to struggle. Capital collects the workers in great masses in the big cities, uniting them, teaching them to act in unison. At every step the workers come face to face with their main enemy – the capitalist class. In combat with this enemy the worker becomes a *socialist*, comes to realise the necessity of a complete reconstruction of the whole society, the complete abolition of all poverty and all oppression. Becoming socialists, the workers fight with self-abnegating courage against everything that stands in their path, first and foremost the tsarist regime and the feudal landlords.[52]

Lenin based himself on the initiative of the masses, which is the motive force of any revolution. He was very fond of saying that life teaches. "… needless to say", he explained, "the masses learn from life and not from books…"[53] In looking back at these events, he underlined the point:

When the bourgeois gentry and their uncritical echoers, the social-reformists, talk priggishly about the 'education' of the masses, they usually mean something schoolmasterly, pedantic, something that demoralises the masses and instils in them bourgeois prejudices.

The real education of the masses can never be separated from their independent political, and especially revolutionary, struggle. Only struggle educates the exploited class. Only struggle discloses to it the magnitude of its own power, widens its horizon, enhances its abilities, clarifies its mind, forges its will. That is why even reactionaries had to admit that the year 1905, the year of struggle, the 'mad year', definitely buried patriarchal Russia.[54]

A changed party

Throughout this time, Lenin took the opportunity to emphasise the changing character of the Party, evolving from a propaganda group to a party involved in mass work and agitation. Given the revolutionary events, both the Bolsheviks and the Mensheviks began to grow in membership and influence, with new branches and district committees springing up everywhere.

The Bolsheviks now began to connect with the masses. *Vperyod* not only called for the arming of the working class but also published technical advice for the construction of barricades. This advice on barricades was also given by the Mensheviks, who were moving left under the pressure of events.

By the summer of 1905, such was the pressure of the revolution, that many of the Bolshevik and Menshevik committees within Russia merged. As the year went on, this became more pronounced. In September, a southern regional conference of fifteen Bolshevik and Menshevik organisations decided to merge. In November, the St. Petersburg Bolshevik Committee and Menshevik Group decided to unite, without any reference to the leading bodies. This propelled the two factions together. From small isolated groups, the Party developed a mass audience with mass influence. As Lenin explained:

> The hundreds of revolutionary Social-Democrats 'suddenly' grew into thousands; the thousands became the leaders of between two and three million proletarians.[55]

The irresistible impulse of the revolution unified the struggle. This would eventually lead to a temporary fusion of the factions towards the end of the year and a 'Unity' Congress in 1906. As Lenin observed:

> Old controversies of the pre-revolutionary period gave way to unanimity on practical questions. The upsurge of the revolutionary tide pushed aside disagreements, compelling Social-Democrats to adopt militant tactics; it swept the question of the Duma* into the background and put the question of insurrection on the order of the day; and it brought closer together the Social-Democrats and revolutionary bourgeois democrats in carrying out immediate tasks. In *Severny Golos* the Mensheviks, jointly with the Bolsheviks, called for a general strike and insurrection; and they called upon the workers to continue this struggle until they had captured power.[56]

At the beginning of the revolution in January 1905, the Bolsheviks numbered 8,400 members. This grew steadily until the spring of 1906 when they recorded 34,000 members, a four-fold increase. At the same time, the Mensheviks claimed a figure of 14,000 members.

This explosive growth, in turn, shattered the Party's old underground structures, pushed aside the committee-men and introduced greater flexibility into its work and methods. Under such circumstances, and for the first time, the RSDLP took on all the features of a mass party.

The RSDLP, as with all the parties of the Second International, based itself on the principle of democratic centralism, which combined freedom of discussion with unity of action. The formula of democratic centralism was never a rigid one, and the balance between centralism and democracy could not be worked out in advance, but depended upon the concrete conditions, inside and outside of the party.

---

* The Duma was the Russian parliament or assembly.

Under the new freer conditions in Russia, greater emphasis was placed naturally on internal democracy, where the right of minority groups to freedom of expression was safeguarded.

The norms of democratic centralism were only formally introduced into the Party rules in 1906, on a proposal by Lenin, at a Congress where the Mensheviks were in a majority. This fact demonstrates their general acceptance of the organisational forms needed within the Party. Lenin explained:

> The St. Petersburg worker Social-Democrats know that the whole Party organisation is now built on a *democratic* basis. This means that *all* the Party members take part in the election of officials, committee members, and so forth, that *all* the Party members discuss and *decide* questions concerning the political campaigns of the proletariat, and that *all* the Party members *determine* the line of tactics of the Party organisations.[57]

This democratic regime stands in complete contradiction to the crude fabrication presented by Richard Pipes, who cynically quotes the anti-Leninist views of Axelrod that Leninism was not only a kind of Jacobinism but "a very simple copy or caricature of the bureaucratic-autocratic system of our Minister of the Interior".[58] Not to be left behind, Figes writes that the Bolsheviks "under Lenin's guidance became increasingly intransigent in their opposition to democracy".[59]

These slanders completely ignore the fact that, as a result of the new conditions created by the revolution, great changes were introduced into the Party in 1905. A worker-Bolshevik who had left Moscow in the early months of 1905 said that such were the changes that when he returned he "did not recognise" the new political set-up in his district.[60] These new conditions now prevailed everywhere within the Party. Lenin stood not only for party democracy, but for the widest involvement and initiative possible, especially of the new layers joining the Party. Bolshevism skilfully adapted itself to the new environment. And this great flexibility on all organisational and tactical issues was always an essential feature of Leninism.

10. Perspectives for the Russian Revolution

During 1905, while the Bolsheviks held their own Congress in London, the Mensheviks, who had the support of only a small minority of the thirty-four regional organisations in Russia, held a separate Conference in Geneva.

As we have seen, at the time of the Second Congress in 1903 the political differences between the 'minority' and 'majority' were not at all clear. They were as yet only present in an embryonic form, disguised as organisational differences on essentially secondary matters. But, by the time of the Third Congress in 1905, fundamental political divergences between these two tendencies had become apparent.

Lenin, above all else, demanded political clarity. While he clearly saw the opportunist tendencies of the Mensheviks as in *organisational* matters, he quickly came to understand that there were also underlying *political* differences at issue and was determined to bring them out into the open.

By thoroughly analysing the Mensheviks' tactics and the resolutions passed by their conference, he was able to expose the existence of two mutually exclusive and antagonistic trends in Russian Social Democracy. He summed up the differences in a lengthy article called *Two Tactics of Social Democracy in the Democratic Revolution*.

He pointed out that both tendencies, Bolsheviks and Mensheviks, agreed on the bourgeois character and tasks of the coming Russian revolution, which included the overthrow of tsarism, land reform, and the sweeping away of all the feudal rubbish as preparation for the development of capitalism. The fundamental political difference centred around the question: which class would actually *lead* this bourgeois revolution?

In late 1904, the Mensheviks had increasingly shown illusions in the Russian liberals and enthusiastically supported their campaign of conferences and banquets for constitutional change. The Mensheviks laid heavy stress on the leading role of the bourgeoisie in the pages of the new *Iskra*, as the following extract shows very clearly:

> If we take a look at the area of struggle in Russia then what do we see? Only two forces: the tsarist autocracy and the liberal bourgeoisie, which is now organised and possesses a huge specific weight. The working mass, however, is atomised and can do nothing; as an independent force we do not exist; and thus our task consists in supporting the second force, the liberal bourgeoisie, and encouraging it and in no case intimidating it by presenting our own independent proletarian demands.[1]

This slavish accommodation with the liberals was later to lead them to seek a parliamentary alliance with the bourgeois-liberals, the Constitutional Democrats (the Cadets) within the semi-parliament (the Duma). It was, in plain language, the policy of blatant class collaboration.

Lenin was emphatic that the working class should have no confidence in the liberal bourgeoisie and must march under its own independent banner:

> No, the proletariat will not be drawn into this game of slogans, declarations, and agreements. The proletariat will never forget that bourgeois democrats never make reliable democrats.[2]

It was this fundamental *political* difference that separated Bolshevism from Menshevism – not the organisational questions, but the difference between class independence and class collaboration, between revolutionary politics and reformism.

Counter-revolutionary bourgeoisie

The weak Russian bourgeoisie was a latecomer onto the scene of history. It had arrived too late in the day to play any progressive role. It was tied by a thousand threads to the landlords and dependent upon foreign capital. Above all, it feared the threat posed by the newly-emerging working class. Consequently, as a class it was too weak and cowardly to sweep away the tsarist regime. It would always end up betraying the revolutionary democratic movement.

"Mistrust in Liberal phrases, in the whole position of Liberalism, runs like a red thread throughout all Lenin's activity", noted Krupskaya.[3] This attitude was inherited from Marx and Engels. Lenin quoted Marx's words from 1848:

> The upper bourgeoisie, ever anti-revolutionary, concluded a defensive and offensive alliance with the reactionaries for fear of the people, that is to say, the workers and the democratic bourgeoisie.[4]

On the basis of the experience of 1905, he later added:

> The Russian liberal bourgeoisie, which behaved in just as vile, cowardly, stupid and treacherous a manner as the German bourgeoisie in 1848, hates the Russian proletariat *for the very reason* that in 1905 it proved *sufficiently mature politically* to wrest the *leadership* of the movement from this bourgeoisie and ruthlessly to expose the treachery of the liberals.[5]

The counter-revolutionary instincts of the bourgeoisie were graphically confirmed by the events of the 1905 Revolution. As always, Lenin explained things honestly and in the clearest terms:

> We must be perfectly certain in our minds as to what real forces are opposed to 'tsarism' (which is a real force perfectly intelligible to all) and are capable of gaining a 'decisive victory' over it.
>
> The big bourgeoisie, the landlords, the factory owners, and 'society', which follows the *Osvobozhdenie**lead, cannot be such a force. We see that they do not even want a decisive victory. We know that owing to their class position they are incapable of waging a decisive struggle against tsarism; they are too heavily fettered by private property, by capital and land to enter into a decisive struggle. They stand in too great a need of tsarism, with its bureaucratic, police, and military forces for use against the proletariat and the peasantry, to want it to be destroyed.[6]

Role of the working class

Lenin looked instead to the Russian proletariat as the only class that could ally itself with the peasantry and provide real revolutionary leadership. "No, the only force capable of gaining 'a decisive victory over tsarism', is the *people*, i.e. the proletariat and peasantry", he explained. "No other force is capable of gaining a decisive victory over tsarism."[7]

Given that the mass of the population was made up of peasants, the agrarian revolution was at the centre of the bourgeois-democratic revolution.

---

* *Emancipation*, the organ of the liberals.

The failure of the 'emancipation' of the serfs, which resulted in the worsening of conditions for the peasantry, was a festering legacy of landlordism. The peasantry, as a petty-bourgeois class, would fight for an agrarian programme that would expropriate the landed gentry and distribute the land amongst the toilers. The proletariat would therefore ally itself with the peasants and act as the vanguard of the revolution.

But once the overthrow of tsarism had been achieved by this alliance of proletariat and peasantry, what would the new regime look like? Lenin tentatively proposed the definition of a "revolutionary-democratic dictatorship of the proletariat and the peasantry", a two-class form of rule. This became the policy of the Bolsheviks.

Lenin explained further that a democratic dictatorship needs to rely on the armed masses to break the inevitable resistance of the landlords, the big bourgeoisie, and tsarism. Without this it would be impossible to break down resistance and repel the counter-revolution. "But of course it will be a democratic, not a socialist dictatorship", explained Lenin. "It will be unable (without a series of intermediary stages of revolutionary development) to affect the foundations of capitalism."[8]

According to him, the "democratic" dictatorship would use revolutionary means "in a plebeian way" to sweep away the old feudal order and "the oppressive features of Asiatic bondage" in the villages, by giving peasants the land. It would also improve the position of the working class with the introduction of the eight-hour day and other democratic freedoms.[9] In doing so, it would create favourable conditions for the development of the proletariat and its future struggle for socialism.

Lenin was also aware that the peasantry was a heterogeneous class composed of different layers, ranging from rich kulaks on the one end to the village poor on the other. Throughout history, the peasantry had never been able to play an independent role, but supported one or other of the main classes. If the working class played the leading role, it could draw the peasantry behind it, starting with the poor landless peasants.

More importantly, as far as Lenin was concerned, this agrarian revolution, under the leadership of the working class, and in alliance with the peasantry, would in practice be a bourgeois revolution *against* the bourgeoisie.

This suggests that Lenin went even further than the confines of the classical bourgeois revolution. But he had not yet put forward the idea that there could be a socialist revolution in Russia before it triumphed in the more advanced countries of Europe. He made that a prior condition for the success of a socialist revolution in Russia.

Lenin was a convinced internationalist. He predicted that the achievement of a revolutionary 'democratic' transformation would not simply be a Russian event. It would have profound international repercussions and serve to carry the revolutionary conflagration into Europe. This would lead to the socialist revolution in Europe. Thus, Lenin and the Bolsheviks consistently saw the fate of the Russian revolution as directly linked to the world revolution.

> The significance of such a victory for the future development of Russia and of the whole world will be immense. Nothing will raise the revolutionary energy of the world proletariat so much, nothing will shorten the path leading to its complete victory to such an extent, as this decisive victory of the revolution that has now started in Russia.[10]

The complete victory of the democratic revolution and the establishment of the revolutionary-democratic dictatorship of the proletariat and the peasantry would, explained Lenin, "enable us to rouse Europe; after throwing off the yoke of the bourgeoisie, the socialist proletariat of Europe will in turn help us to accomplish the socialist revolution."[11]

In other words, Lenin regarded the Russian bourgeois-democratic revolution as the *beginning of the world proletarian revolution*. This internationalism was the core of Leninism. This bold perspective was in complete contrast to the Menshevik position, which subordinated everything to not frightening the bourgeoisie.

Lenin repeated this perspective again and again throughout his writings and speeches. He envisaged everything in class terms and linked to the fight for socialism internationally:

> The struggle would have been almost hopeless for the Russian proletariat alone and its defeat would have been as inevitable as the defeat of the German revolutionary party in 1849-50, or of the French proletariat in 1871, *had the European socialist proletariat* not come to the assistance of the Russian proletariat.

> Thus, at this stage, the liberal bourgeoisie and the well-to-do peasantry (plus partly the middle peasantry) organise counter-revolution. The Russian proletariat *plus* the European proletariat organise revolution.

> In such conditions the Russian proletariat can win a second victory. The cause is no longer hopeless. The second victory will be the *socialist revolution in Europe*.

The European workers will show us 'how to do it', and then together with them we shall bring about the socialist revolution.[12]

Two-stage theory

The Menshevik theory was really a mechanical caricature of the Marxist view of history. It was a completely lifeless and abstract perspective in which the revolution was destined to pass through a whole number of stages that eventually would create a democratic capitalist regime. This would allow capitalism to develop to the point where the working class would become sufficiently educated for socialism – sometime in the far-distant future...

The Menshevik 'two-stage' theory was subsequently adopted by Stalinism and would result in disasters for the working class in a whole series of countries, where the interests of the proletariat were subordinated to the so-called 'progressive' bourgeoisie.

The Mensheviks were utterly incapable of understanding the real class dynamics and simply imposed their own schema on reality. They did not understand the decisive difference between the bourgeois revolutions of the past and the problems facing the Russian Revolution.

In fact, even in the bourgeois revolutions of the past, whether in England or France, the leading revolutionary role was not played by the big bourgeoisie but by the revolutionary petty bourgeoisie. This was the Jacobins in the French Revolution, and Cromwell and his New Model Army in England. In order to succeed, the revolutionary petty bourgeoisie had to overthrow the bourgeois elements and base themselves on the semi-proletarian and plebian masses.

In the case of Russia, the situation was still clearer. The feeble bourgeois liberals were tied hand and foot to the landlords and imperialists, and terrified of the workers. They could never present a serious challenge to the tsarist autocracy – let alone overthrow it. The eruption of a combative Russian working class onto the scene had altered the class balance of forces. This was precisely what determined the counter-revolutionary nature of the bourgeoisie.

The Russian proletarians did not wish to play the role of second fiddle to the bourgeoisie. Once mobilised for the struggle, the proletariat was determined to put its own stamp on events, to pursue its own class interests. This was what Lenin based himself on.

The Mensheviks regarded the Bolshevik view as madness. They were completely obsessed with the idea that nothing should be done to frighten the bourgeoisie. Any suggestion that the workers should play an independent

Группа членов III с'езда Росс. Соц.-Демокр. Раб.партии (б.) Лондон, 1905 г.

52. Delegates for the Third Congress of the RSDLP

revolutionary role was anathema to them. The logic of this meant the proletariat should become "an appendage to the monarchist bourgeoisie", to use Lenin's phrase.[13]

Algebraic formula

While the Mensheviks had capitulated completely to the liberal bourgeoisie, Lenin placed all his hopes on the instinctive revolutionary aspirations of the workers and poor peasants, the genuine masses. He quoted with approval the words of Marx:

> Revolutions are the locomotives of history, said Marx. Revolutions are festivals of the oppressed and the exploited. At no other time are the mass of the people in a position to come forward so actively as creators of a new social order, as at a time of revolution. At such times the people are capable of performing miracles, if judged by the limited, philistine yardstick of gradual progress.[14]

These lines clearly demonstrate Lenin's unshakable faith in the working class, something that shines throughout every page of his writings.

In the struggle against Menshevism, the slogan of the revolutionary dictatorship of the workers and peasants undoubtedly played a progressive role. But there was, however, a weakness in Lenin's formula. The concept of the "democratic dictatorship of the proletariat and the peasantry" was ambiguous. It did not define the exact relationship between these two classes – proletariat and peasantry – and in particular which class would predominate in a revolutionary dictatorship.

This ambiguity was not accidental. Lenin's slogan had a largely algebraic character, as it was not as yet clear what form the government would take – for example, it was not clear whether or not the peasantry would emerge as an independent force with its own party.

This ambiguity was to cause a fatal confusion among the Bolsheviks in February 1917 when the revolution was no longer an abstract perspective but a living fact. The question was then posed, not theoretically, but concretely: could the bourgeois Provisional Government, backed by the 'Conciliators' in the Soviet, represent the realisation of the 'democratic' dictatorship of the proletariat and peasantry for which Lenin had argued?

It was this confusion which later led Lenin to abandon the old slogan, which had outlived its usefulness and became filled with a reactionary content. In doing so, he was met with furious opposition from the 'old Bolsheviks'. But we will deal with this question later.

The theory of permanent revolution

We have outlined the differences between the Mensheviks and the Bolsheviks, but there was a third position held by Trotsky, which became known as the theory of 'permanent revolution'.

During 1904, Trotsky had broken with Martov and the Mensheviks over their craven attitude to the bourgeois parties, as well as their stubborn refusal to campaign to reunite the Party. Although Trotsky's position was independent of both factions, it was much closer to Lenin's position and in complete contradiction to that of the Mensheviks.

Trotsky's theory of permanent revolution was based on the idea expressed in 1850 by Marx, who also argued for a "revolution in permanence".[15] The theory was fully outlined in Trotsky's work, *Results and Prospects*, published in 1906, soon after the defeat of the revolution, although he had worked out its essentials as early as 1904. These ideas had been initially formulated in collaboration with Alexander Parvus, a German revolutionary. But Trotsky broke with Parvus when he shifted to the right.

Trotsky, in common with everyone else, recognised the coming Russian revolution as a bourgeois revolution. He agreed, however, with Lenin against the Mensheviks that the Russian bourgeoisie could never play a revolutionary role. But he went much further than Lenin. Rather than a "democratic dictatorship", as advocated by Lenin, he put forward the idea of a *workers' government*, in alliance with the poor peasants, but where the working class played the leading role. The year 1917 showed that he was right.

Trotsky later explained the reasons why the peasantry was incapable of playing an independent role and would either side with the bourgeoisie or the proletariat:

> And as a matter of fact, in the endeavours to create a peasant party, or a workers' and peasants' party – as distinct from a liberal or a proletarian party – every possible political variant was attempted in Russia, illegal and parliamentary as well as a combination of the two: *Zemlya i Volya* (Land and Freedom), *Narodnaya Volya* (People's Will), *Cherny Peredel* (Black Repartition), the legal *Narodnichestvo* (Populists), 'Socialist-Revolutionaries', 'People's Socialists', 'Trudoviks', 'Left Socialist-Revolutionaries', etc., etc. For half a century we had, as it were, a huge laboratory for the creation of an 'anti-capitalist' peasant party with an independent position toward the proletarian party. The largest scope was attained, as is well known, by the experiment of the SR [Socialist-Revolutionary] Party which, for a time in 1917, actually constituted the party of the overwhelming majority of the peasantry. But what happened? This party used its position only to betray the peasants completely to the liberal bourgeoisie. The SRs entered into a coalition with the imperialists of the Entente and together with them conducted an armed struggle against the Russian proletariat.[16]

The working class should in that case win over the peasantry, carry through the revolution, and establish a workers' government. The aim of this government would be to carry out the tasks of the bourgeois democratic revolution – land reform, resolving the national question, establishing a republic, a constituent assembly, an eight-hour day, etc. However, once accomplished, it would not stop, but would immediately proceed to the socialist tasks – nationalisation, workers' control, national planning, etc.

Trotsky regarded counter-revolution as a danger if the peasantry turned its back on such a government. The only solution to this would be to link the fate of the Russian Revolution, as Lenin had done, to that of the socialist revolution in Europe. But, Trotsky went further, and, in contrast to Lenin, viewed the bourgeois revolution in Russia as not ending in a bourgeois republic, but as "growing over" into a socialist revolution.

However, Trotsky fully understood that a socialist revolution could not succeed in isolation in backward Russia, or in any single country, since the material basis for the final triumph of socialism did not exist in individual countries, but only on a world scale.

This argument applied a thousand times more to Russia, where the level of development of the productive forces was on a very low level. He thus envisaged the socialist revolution in Russia as the beginning of the world socialist revolution. Without a world revolution, the revolution in Russia would be isolated and doomed to defeat. This, therefore, demonstrated the importance of the 'permanence' of the revolution.

The Stalinists attempted to accuse Trotsky of "underestimating the peasantry". This is entirely false. In 1905 Trotsky advanced the slogan: 'Neither Tsar nor Zemtsi (the liberals), but the People!' This word "people" included both workers and peasants. Trotsky had no disagreement with Lenin's policy after 1905 that the peasants should take over the land. Only in this way could the alliance between workers and peasants be cemented. However, such a policy could only be carried out once the proletariat had conquered political power.

Trotsky was the first person ever to suggest that the Russian workers could come to power *in advance of the workers of the West*. The idea was so startling that nobody at this time accepted it, including Lenin. Nevertheless, the hypothesis was graphically confirmed in the actual experience of the October Revolution of 1917, when the working class came to power and initiated the movement towards world socialist revolution.

It can be said that while the perspective of the Bolsheviks was not yet complete, its line was generally correct, but the formula of the dictatorship of the proletariat and peasantry was inadequate. The perspective of Menshevism, on the other hand, was false to the core. Trotsky was radically opposed to the Menshevik theory of stages and was always far closer to Lenin on this question.

Although Lenin stated that he rejected the theory of 'permanent revolution', it is pretty certain that he never actually read Trotsky's views first hand. His scattered criticisms are based almost entirely on the foreword written by Parvus to Trotsky's *Before the Ninth of January* or from disputes with other authors. This can be seen in his criticism of Trotsky's ideas in an article entitled 'The Aim of Proletarian Struggle in Our Revolution', written in March 1908, where all the quotes of Trotsky he uses are taken from an article written by Martov.[17]

In fact, under the impact of the 1905 Revolution, Lenin came very near to expressing a view close to 'permanent revolution'. In an article about the revolutionary attitude towards the peasant movement, written in September 1905, Lenin uses an expression, also used by Trotsky, of the "uninterrupted revolution" to describe his views. Lenin wrote:

> … from the democratic revolution we shall at once, and precisely in accordance with the measure of our strength, the strength of the class-conscious and organised proletariat, begin to pass to the socialist revolution. We stand for uninterrupted revolution. We shall not stop half-way.[18]

These views are certainly similar to Trotsky's. Lenin repeated this phrase again in late 1915, and he returned to it more decisively in early 1917 when he began to reassess the perspectives for the Russian revolution in the light of the February experience. As always, Lenin's thoughts on this and other questions tended to evolve on the basis of living experience.

In November 1915, Lenin again defended the idea of the 'revolutionary dicatorship of proletariat and peasantry' as opposed to the permanent revolution. Yet, paradoxically, he actually came very close to Trotsky's position. Lenin wrote:

> From the Bolsheviks, Trotsky's original theory has *borrowed* their call for a decisive proletarian revolutionary struggle and for the conquest of power by the proletariat…[19]

This represented an important shift in Lenin's thinking. Lenin then went on to add that after the conquest of power:

> The proletariat will at once utilise this ridding of bourgeois Russia of tsarism and the rule of the landowners, *not to aid the rich peasants in their struggle against the rural workers, but to bring about the socialist revolution in alliance with the proletarians of Europe.*[20]

Again, this is almost the same idea as Trotsky's theory of permanent revolution. In less than two years, in 1917 Lenin was to abandon completely the slogan of the "democratic dictatorship of the proletariat and the peasantry" and adopt a new perspective that explicitly stated: "Our aim is the dictatorship of the proletariat".[21]

11. The St. Petersburg Soviet

Under pressure from the revolutionary wave sweeping Russia, Alexander Bulygin, the Interior Minister, timidly suggested to the tsar that maybe concessions should be made to calm the country. Nicholas was visibly shocked by what Bulygin was proposing and said: "One would think you are afraid a revolution will break out". Bulygin replied in a respectful tone of voice: "Your Majesty, the revolution has already begun."[1]

Unbeknown to the tsar, cocooned in his palace, revolution had been raging throughout the country for most of 1905. By August, with the situation deteriorating, Nicholas was compelled to announce an 'August Manifesto' in an attempt to placate the movement and also conclude peace with Japan.

The 'Manifesto' contained proposals for constitutional reform with the creation of a new Duma, which took the name of the Bulygin Duma. This proposed parliament was a toothless, consultative body, which was only allowed to deal with minor legislation and budgetary matters, that in turn had to be ratified by the tsar.

To reduce the Duma's effectiveness even further, its functions were divided between the lower and upper chambers, while the franchise was restricted and divided into electoral colleges in favour of the upper classes. Furthermore, the tsar held the power to rule by decree – his favourite option.

As it turned out, this concession was clearly a case of too little, too late. The regime was therefore forced to go further and promise a new constitution. However, these changes were not due to come into force until May 1906. They were clearly an attempt by Bulygin to derail the ongoing revolution. "For a bad government", wrote the shrewd French conservative,

Alexis de Tocqueville, "the most dangerous moment is usually the one when it begins to change."[2] This was a lesson the regime dreaded. However, they had little choice.

In response, given the ongoing revolution, the Bolsheviks came out for an active boycott of the elections to this sham Duma. The Menshevik leaders, however, were ambiguous, somehow hoping that these 'reforms' were the beginning of genuine parliamentarianism in Russia. But most of the rank and file were instinctively against participation. This mood even pushed the Socialist-Revolutionaries to support a boycott.

As a result of the revolution, the masses were feeling their strength and this experience was reflected in the new strike wave. They had little faith, if any, in the proposed so-called parliament. Therefore, the boycott policy connected with the general revolutionary mood of the masses. According to Count Sergei Witte, chairman of the Council of Ministers, "the vast majority of people seemed to go mad."[3] Not surprisingly, to the conservative mind, a revolution that seeks to turn everything upside down can only reflect a bout of insanity.

The government 'reforms' were answered with a new strike wave that hit Moscow and St. Petersburg in September. The capital of the tsars had now become the storm centre of the revolution as a general strike developed. On their own initiative, the workers organised strike committees to help direct the growing number of disputes. To give credit where it is due, it was the Mensheviks who first proposed the establishment of a central strike committee, which on 26 October led to the formation of the St. Petersburg Soviet.

The influence of the Soviet soon spread. Workers elected delegates, one for every 500 workers, to the central body and it quickly drew support from the surrounding factories and workshops, eventually representing some 250,000 workers in the capital. In the middle of November, the Soviet had 562 elected delegates representing 147 industrial factories, thirty-four workshops and sixteen trade unions. The authority of the Soviet increased dramatically, and it began to play a leading role in the revolution, not least in publishing its own newspaper, *Izvestiya*, which spread its influence even further afield.

Meetings called by the Soviet were made up of tens of thousands of people. This central authority rapidly became a beacon for workers everywhere, and soon fifty more Soviets were created in industrial cities around the country. In reality, the Petersburg Soviet was the most influential body in Russia, an organ of workers' power that had the embryonic features of a workers' government.

The twenty-six-year-old Trotsky had returned from hiding in Finland, where he had fled during the summer months. As a result of his diligent work and great ability, he was elected as a member of the Soviet's three-person ruling body and vice-chairman. Following the arrest of Khrustalev-Nosar, its president, Trotsky became the new president and his authority reached new heights. Lunacharsky noted:

> I remember someone saying in Lenin's presence: "Khrustalev's star is waning and now the strong man in the Soviet is Trotsky." Lenin's face darkened for a moment, then he said: "Well, Trotsky has earned it by his brilliant and unflagging work."[4]

Lenin was never one to allow personal resentment and past quarrels to stand in the way of recognising positive achievement in others. In a letter to Pyotr Krasikov, dated 27 September 1905, he chastises him for needlessly complaining about Trotsky:

> … you err and drift into the old, pre-party point of view when you write: "They are printing Trotsky's leaflets" (there is nothing wrong in that if the leaflets are fairly good and vetted. I advise the St. Petersburg Committee, too, to print his leaflets vetted, say, by you)…[5]

The fact that Lenin recommended that the leading St. Petersburg Party Committee republish Trotsky's leaflets says a great deal about Lenin, who was able to stand above scoring petty points in the wider interests of the Party and the working class.

"The Soviet organised the working masses, directed the political strikes and demonstrations, armed the workers, and protected the population against pogroms", wrote Trotsky.[6] The Soviet immediately rose to the occasion and, after calling mass meetings, on 31 October led the struggle for a general strike for the eight-hour day and in solidarity with the rebellion of sailors in Kronstadt and workers of Poland. A national general strike had no parallel in Russia and was a rare occurrence elsewhere. It was called on the same day as the tsar issued his new 'October Manifesto', promising further constitutional change and charging Witte with its implementation. Trotsky explained:

> By the pressure of strikes, the Soviet won the freedom of the press. It organised regular street patrols to ensure the safety of citizens. To a greater or lesser extent, it took the postal and telegraph services and the railways into its hands. It intervened authoritatively in economic disputes between workers and capitalists. It made an attempt to introduce the eight-hour working day by direct revolutionary pressure. Paralysing the activity of the autocratic state by means of the insurrectionary

strike, it introduced its own free democratic order into the life of the labouring urban population.[7]

Faced with certain concessions and a wavering mood nationally, the Soviet was forced to make an orderly retreat. Having gained a moral victory, a vote to call off the strike was held on 20 November. Posters were placed around the city explaining what was happening and on 25 November, the strike ended in the same unified manner as it had begun. The political work of the Soviet was to leave an indelible mark on the consciousness of the masses, which would be revived in 1917.

The Soviet then issued its own 'Financial Manifesto', calling for the non-payment of taxes to bring down the government. But, as Trotsky explained, this "was nothing other than an overture to the December rising".[8] A further strike broke out in December, but this proved to be the very last gasps of the Petersburg working class after months of exhausting struggle. On 16 December, gauging the mood, the government stepped in and arrested the entire executive committee of the St. Petersburg Soviet, including its chairman, Trotsky. Those arrested spent most of the following year in the Peter and Paul Fortress. Afterwards, Trotsky and fourteen others were sentenced to exile in Siberia for life.

Lenin's view of the Soviet

Lenin was deeply excited by the emergence of the Petersburg Soviet and immediately recognised its revolutionary significance:

> I may be wrong, but I believe (on the strength of the incomplete and only 'paper' information at my disposal) that politically the Soviet of Workers' Deputies should be regarded as the embryo of a *provisional revolutionary government*. I think the Soviet should proclaim itself the provisional revolutionary government of the whole of Russia as early as possible, or should *set up* a provisional revolutionary government (which would amount to the same thing, only in another form).[9]

Trotsky, who was at the centre of things, had arrived independently at the same conclusion as Lenin. He also defined the Soviet as "a workers' government in embryo".[10]

Unfortunately, Lenin's correct appraisal of the Soviet was not replicated by the Bolsheviks on the ground, who, under the influence of the committee-men, had adopted a sectarian position. While Bolsheviks were elected as delegates to the Soviet, they completely misread the situation. To begin with, when the Soviet of Workers' Deputies was first established, they

53. The trial of the St. Petersburg Soviet, September 1906
Trotsky is in the center of the second row holding papers

regarded it as a competitor and even organised a campaign against it. The Bolshevik organisation in St. Petersburg went as far as to issue an ultimatum to the Soviet, essentially demanding that they place themselves under the leadership of the Social-Democratic Party, and, if not, to simply disband. This ultimatum clearly did not go down well. When their request was turned down, the Bolsheviks delegates simply walked out.

This adventurous policy was dreamed up by Bogdanov, who was in charge of the Bureau of the Bolshevik organisation within Russia. He nurtured fears that the Soviet would become the basis of a new party that would be a competitor and an obstacle to the Social-Democrats. While other Bolsheviks did not go this far, they instead favoured "exploding [it] from within", an approach that was hardly a great improvement.[11]

This sectarian policy could only be explained as a leftover from the circle mentality of the past, an attitude fostered by the 'committee-men' who displayed hostility towards anyone or anything that seemed to represent a rival to the Party. Instead of trying to connect with the movement, they tried to impose their own preconceived reality upon it.

While the Soviet was a new organisation, it expressed the independent self-organisation of the working class. In the current context, this extended strike council had all the potential to become an alternative power to tsarism. Apart from Lenin, the other leading Bolsheviks were blind to such a reality.

The sectarian approach displayed by his comrades was to persist until Lenin's arrival in Russia in November. This once again served to illustrate the fact that without the guidance of Lenin, the Bolshevik leaders were prone to mistakes, even serious blunders.

By contrast, the Mensheviks actively participated in the Soviet. They, however, regarded it more as a bridge to a broad-based labour party similar to Axelrod's idea of a 'Labour Congress', and on the lines of the labour organisations in Western Europe. The Menshevik view of the Soviets was also linked to the reformist notion of a "broad democratic organisation" of the people. This, in turn, was linked to local autonomy and local self-government, which was in marked contrast to Lenin's idea of the Soviet being an alternative revolutionary government.

The Mensheviks' keenness to participate within the Soviet served to raise the hackles of the Bolsheviks and only pushed them further in a sectarian direction. Krasikov, a leading Bolshevik, sneered that "the Mensheviks have started a new intrigue: they're electing a non-Party Zubatovite committee."[12] This reference to a Zubatov* committee was intended to dismiss the Soviet as some kind of fake trade union body, established by the state. This only served to further isolate the Bolsheviks from the real movement of the working class.

Lenin intervenes

Lenin, on hearing the stand taken by the Bolsheviks, must have clutched his head in dismay. He immediately wrote an article to the Bolshevik paper, *Novaya Zhizn*, urging the Bolsheviks to reappraise their position and adopt a more realistic approach:

> It seems to me that Comrade Radin is wrong in raising the question in No. 5 of *Novaya Zhizn* (I have seen only five issues of the virtual Central Organ of our RSDLP): the Soviet of Workers' Deputies or the Party? I think that it is wrong to put the question in this way and that the decision must *certainly* be: *both* the Soviet of Workers' Deputies *and* the Party.[13]

Significantly, the editors of the Bolshevik paper refused to publish Lenin's criticisms. Nevertheless, he continued to direct his opposition to the stand

---

* Sergey Vasilyevich Zubatov was the deputy chief of the Moscow police in 1889, who tried to cut across the growth of the trade unions by establishing police-sponsored unions, dealing strictly with economic matters. However, the Zubatov union organised by Gapon showed how these organisations could get out of control, and led directly to the 1905 Revolution.

taken by the Party in St. Petersburg, declaring that it was wrong to demand the Soviet support the Party programme and join the Party. He added for good measure that instead the Soviet "should be regarded as the embryo of a *provisional revolutionary government*."[14]

Once again, Richard Pipes, intent on vilifying Bolshevism, states: "Lenin viewed with scepticism the emergence of the Soviets, because they were conceived as 'non-partisan' workers' organisations and, as such, outside the control of political parties."[15] This is the exact opposite of what Lenin believed. But why let the facts spoil a good story?

Lenin argued that the Soviet needed to *extend* its activities to embrace the ranks of the soldiers and sailors, so as to prepare a revolutionary alliance between workers and peasants, given that many peasants had been drawn into the armed forces. This would mean the Soviet becoming a *Council of Workers' and Soldiers' Deputies*. In fact, the Soviet did turn its attention towards the revolutionary soldiers and sailors, but there was little time to fully develop this work before its leaders were arrested. This idea did eventually come to fruition in the events of 1917.

This attempt by Lenin to correct the sectarian line of the Bolsheviks completely undermines the Stalinist myth that the Bolsheviks under Lenin were always united and marching forward in lock-step towards the October Revolution. This was the line promoted by the notorious *History of the Communist Party of the Soviet Union (Short Course)*, which was edited personally by Stalin. According to this falsified 'history':

> The Mensheviks took advantage of Lenin's absence to make their way into the St. Petersburg Soviet and to seize hold of its leadership. It was not surprising under such circumstances that the Mensheviks Khrustalev, Trotsky, Parvus and others managed to turn the St. Petersburg Soviet against the policy of an uprising.[16]

This book, which was made mandatory reading in the curriculum of all university students and attendants of party schools, is full of outlandish myths and legends – and blatant lies – about Lenin and the Bolsheviks. It was later withdrawn under Khrushchev, but in its place appeared another book that peddled the same old anti-'Trotskyist' line.

Lenin's paper, *Novaya Zhizn*, had, in fact, congratulated Trotsky's paper *Nachalo* (*The Beginning*) when it first appeared:

> The first number of the *Nachalo* has come out. We welcome a comrade in the struggle. The first issue is notable for the brilliant description of the October strike written by Comrade Trotsky.[17]

Moreover, Lenin described the differences between *Nachalo* and *Novaya Zhizn* as only "over matters of detail", despite the paper promoting the ideas of the 'permanent revolution'. But this did not worry Lenin:

> *Nachalo* inclined towards the dictatorship of the proletariat. *Novaya Zhizn* advocated the democratic dictatorship of the proletariat and the peasantry. But have not disagreements of this kind been observed at every stage of development of every socialist party in Europe?[18]

Lenin's writings from this period show that he, on more than one occasion, encountered strong resistance to any change among the 'old Bolsheviks'. This is the real picture of Bolshevism, not the idealised view presented elsewhere.

The art of insurrection

From the beginning of 1905, Lenin had developed a great interest in military matters, which formed part of his understanding about insurrection. In particular, he went out of his way to study the military writings of Engels and the great military theoretician Carl von Clausewitz. This gave him a grounding in their approach to tactics and strategy. Lenin took to heart Marx and Engels' comments that "insurrection is an art", which requires serious study.[19] He wrote:

> No Social-Democrat at all familiar with history, who has studied Engels, the great expert on the subject, has ever doubted the tremendous importance of military knowledge, of military technique, and of military organisation as an instrument which the masses of the people, and classes of people, use in resolving great historical conflicts. [...] they [the Social-Democrats] are putting great stress on studying these questions and bringing them to the knowledge of the masses.[20]

Before engaging in war, as Lenin understood, it was necessary to prepare the army and muster the troops. He was very fond of quoting Napoleon: "*On s'engage et puis... on voit*", which means, "First engage and then let us see". The important point for Lenin was to engage, to enter into the struggle, and test things out in practice. The worst thing was to hesitate and procrastinate. You will never learn or act from sitting on the sidelines.

As late as October 1905, Lenin was concerned by the lack of urgency being displayed by the Bolsheviks. It was clear they had been dragging their feet. Lenin had called on the Petersburg Bolsheviks to turn their attention towards the youth and treat the work with greater urgency. He did not mince his words and warned that "judging by the documents, the whole thing threatens to degenerate into office routine." He urged:

> What is needed is furious energy, and again energy. It horrifies me – I give you my word – it horrifies me to find that there has been talk about bombs for *over six months*, yet not one has been made! And it is the most learned of people who are doing the talking... Go to the youth, gentlemen! That is the only remedy! Otherwise – I give you my word for it – you will be too late (everything tells me that), and will be left with 'learned' memoranda, plans, charts, schemes, and magnificent recipes, but without organisation, without a living cause.[21]

This reference about making bombs was an attempt to push the Party leaders into a serious reflection of the most urgent tasks now looming before them. Insurrection was a serious business and needed to be properly prepared. Thousands of men, women and children had been shot down in cold blood in January by tsarist troops.

The Black Hundreds had organised lethal pogroms against the Jews and others. To organise a serious armed defence was the first step to going over to a revolutionary offence – an insurrection. But for this, urgent practical steps had to be taken. The working class needed to be armed, not only with ideas, but with weapons. Armed units would need to be formed if the workers were to succeed in overthrowing the murderous tsarist regime.

Consequently, the Party had established a 'Fighting Technical Group', responsible for the manufacture of explosives, as well as arranging the smuggling and purchase of arms from Finland. The Group was also responsible for the establishment of fighting squads.

The Party also possessed specialists who had knowledge of explosives. However, finding the right materials to manufacture them was not easy, and the devices needed to be tested. This Technical Group obtained explosives from, among others, the Macedonian partisans – the Chetniks – who had been engaged for a long time in guerrilla warfare against their Ottoman oppressors. This work was carried out clandestinely and these comrades were kept at arm's length from the political work of the Party.

Leonid Krassin, as a qualified electrical engineer, was skilled in this field and was therefore placed in charge of this work. He was also made responsible for Bolshevik finances. All these 'technical' details were, of course, necessary for a successful insurrection, but needed to be firmly under the control of the Party. Later, as the revolution ebbed, they would need to be curtailed and wound up altogether.

With the government's political amnesty, Lenin was easily able to return to Russia. On 4 November, still using a forged passport, he crossed the border. Lenin had been away from Russia for five long years.

His presence immediately began to engender a sense of urgency, including his proposal to turn the *Novaya Zhizn*, founded in October, into a legal Party daily newspaper, which soon reached an impressive daily circulation of 80,000 copies. Its editorial offices on Nevsky Prospekt were also used as premises for the Central Committee and St. Petersburg Committee. The celebrated Russian writer, Maxim Gorky, became an active contributor to the paper and helped finance the venture. The foreign contributors included an array of figures, including Rosa Luxemburg, Karl Liebknecht and Paul Lafargue.

It was in these offices that Lenin first met Gorky. Maria Andreyeva, Gorky's wife, recalled the occasion:

> I remember Lenin coming towards us out of some back rooms and quickly going up to Alexei Maximovich [Gorky]. They shook each other's hand for a long time, Lenin laughing joyfully, while Gorky, exquisitely shy, and assuming, as he always did in such cases, a deep solid bass, kept repeating: "Aha, so this is what you're like… Fine, fine! I'm very glad, very glad!"[22]

The Moscow uprising

On 15 December the Rostov regiment mutinied in Moscow. The mutiny was forcibly put down and in response a general strike broke out. Barricades were thrown up as workers and students engaged in street battles with the police. The strike reached insurrectionary proportions, which involved mass demonstrations, barricades, and clashes with the armed forces. The Bolsheviks, however, were unprepared for these events and were taken by surprise.

Under pressure from below, the strike quickly turned into an armed uprising, embracing workers from a whole host of factories. The Moscow Soviet, which had sprung up, attempted to widen the conflict and appealed to the soldiers, but the troops failed to mutiny. The Moscow insurgents looked to the workers of St. Petersburg for assistance, but unfortunately by this time these workers were exhausted and were unable to join in the battle.

With the movement isolated in Moscow, the government went on the offensive and many workers were either arrested or killed in the street battles. Resistance was put up by the armed squads, which had been organised in advance and moved into action. They had been supplied with guns and ammunition smuggled in from Finland and involved Bolshevik,

54. Barricades during the Moscow uprising, 25 December 1905

Menshevik and SR fighters. However, while they drew on the support of the general population, they were severely outnumbered and outgunned. The government's heavy artillery laid waste much of the Presnya district, where the insurgency was centred.

By 31 December, completely isolated, the resistance was eventually put down by the crack troops of the Semenovsky Guards. They had been brought in from St. Petersburg as the troops of the Moscow garrison had proved unreliable. When the fighting came to an end, the general strike was called off. The death toll in Moscow ran into thousands and was then followed by mass arrests, reprisals and deportations.

Uprisings broke out in other parts of Russia, but were soon isolated and crushed. The heroic Moscow workers held out for eleven days, but without mutiny in the army or successful risings in other areas, they were finally defeated and subjected to the brutality of the regime.

Inspired by the revolution, the *émigré* leaders returned to Petersburg, with the notable exceptions of Plekhanov and Axelrod. This was quite telling. Plekhanov, whose reputation was already fading, now declared that the workers "should not have taken up arms".[23] From a man who argued in the past for an armed insurrection against tsarism, this represented a low point. Whatever the rights or wrongs of the insurrection, these remarks from Plekhanov in Geneva contained a cowardly act of betrayal.

We can contrast Plekhanov's remarks to those of Marx in September 1870, six months *before* the Commune, who warned the insurgents about a premature insurrection. However, when they did rise up, Marx gave them enthusiastic support and defended their "heroic" actions internationally, against the howls of the bourgeoisie.

Plekhanov, who denounced the insurrectionists *after* the event, had the effrontery to compare himself to Marx! Lenin issued an indignant rebuff:

> Yes, Marx *also* put the brakes on the revolution. But see what a gulf lies between Plekhanov and Marx, in Plekhanov's own comparison!
>
> In November 1905, a month before the first revolutionary wave in Russia had reached its climax, Plekhanov, far from emphatically warning the proletariat, spoke directly of the necessity to learn *to use arms and to arm*. Yet, when the struggle flared up a month later, Plekhanov, without making the slightest attempt to analyse its significance, its role in the general course of events and its connection with previous forms of struggle, hastened to play the part of a penitent intellectual and exclaimed: "They should not have taken up arms."[24]

Lenin continued:

> Kugelmann apparently replied to Marx expressing certain doubts, referring to the hopelessness of the struggle and to realism as opposed to romanticism – at any rate, he compared the Commune, an *insurrection*, to the peaceful demonstration in Paris on 13 June 1849.
>
> Marx immediately (17 April 1871) and severely rebuked Kugelmann.
>
> "*World history*", he wrote, "*would indeed be very easy to make, if the struggle were taken up only on condition of infallibly favourable chances.*"[25]

In regard to the December events, Lenin took the side of the insurgents:

> The revolution of 1905 was defeated not because it had gone 'too far', or because the December uprising was 'artificial', as renegades among the liberals, and their like imagine. On the contrary, the cause of the defeat was that the uprising *did not go far enough*, that the realisation of its necessity was not sufficiently widespread and firmly assimilated among the revolutionary classes, that the uprising was not concerted, resolute, organised, simultaneous, aggressive.[26]

Plekhanov's jaundiced view of the insurrection was coloured by his isolation abroad. The ferment of the revolution seemed to pass him by. He would never again set foot in Russia. Krupskaya wrote:

55. Tiflis workers overturn a locomotive during the Transcaucasian rail strike
– one of the great events of the 1905 Revolution

Plekhanov's was a tragic fate. In the theoretical field his services to the workers'
movement are almost inestimable. Long years of life as a political emigrant,
however, tolled on him – they isolated him from Russian realities. The broad
mass movement of the workers started after he had gone abroad. He saw the
representatives of different parties, writers, students, even individual workers,
but he had not seen the Russian working-class mass, had not worked with it,
nor felt it.[27]

In contrast, this period of revolutionary upheaval and counter-revolution
certainly had a decisive impact on the fortunes of many individuals, to one
degree or another. It was a testing time. Lunacharsky gave his appraisal about
those he knew:

> I must say that of all the social-democratic leaders of 1905-6 Trotsky undoubtedly
> showed himself, despite his youth, to be the best prepared. Less than any of them
> did he bear the stamp of a certain kind of émigré narrowness of outlook which,
> as I have said, even affected Lenin at that time. Trotsky understood better than
> all the others what it meant to conduct the political struggle on a broad, national
> scale. He emerged from the revolution having acquired an enormous degree of
> popularity, whereas neither Lenin nor Martov had effectively gained any at all.

Plekhanov had lost a great deal, thanks to his display of quasi-Cadet tendencies. Trotsky stood then in the very front rank.[28]

As regards to Lenin, Lunacharsky wrote:

> He worked chiefly behind the scenes, almost exclusively with his pen and at various committee meetings of local Party branches. In short, Lenin, I felt, was still carrying on the fight rather on the old émigré scale, without expanding the work to the more grandiose proportions which the revolution was assuming.[29]

But while Trotsky was acting in the revolution as an individual and leader of the Soviet, Lenin was attempting to guide the Bolsheviks and work through individuals within the Party.

At the same time as this, Peter Struve appeared back on the scene, encouraged by the tsar's constitutional reforms. By this time, he had completely moved over to liberalism and became one of the co-founders of the Constitutional Democrats (Cadets), the party of the liberal bourgeoisie. "Socialism, to tell the truth, never aroused the slightest emotion in me, still less attraction", he wrote.[30] After the October Revolution of 1917, Struve joined the counter-revolutionary White army in the civil war and later became the foreign minister in General Wrangel's military government.

Another bourgeois party created at the same time was the League of October Seventeenth ('Octobrists'), led by the industrialist Alexander Guchkov and the bourgeois proprietor Mikhail Rodzianko, which represented the big merchants, landowners and industrialists. They supported the tsar's 'October Manifesto' and gave full backing to the government's domestic and foreign policy.

Lenin's intervention was crucial in steering the cadres of Bolshevism along the correct path. "We must *learn* to recruit", he explained:[31]

> We suffer from routine, we must fight against it. We must learn to form, where necessary, *lose Organisationen** – looser, broader and more accessible *proletarian* organisations. Our slogan is: *for a larger Social-Democratic Labour* Party, against a non-party labour congress and a non-party party![32]

Organisational and tactical flexibility was on the order of the day. Narrow formalism and routinism within the Party needed to be driven out with sticks and stones. This was the only way the Party could face up to the tasks of the revolution.

As a result of these experiences, Lenin grew in stature, absorbing the fresh lessons from the revolution and preparing himself for the events that were

---

* German for 'loose organisations'

to unfold later. Under his guidance, in 1905 he managed to transform the outlook of the Bolsheviks and turn them towards the mass movement.

Reunification

As we have seen, an important consequence of the events of 1905 was a powerful urge for unity among the Bolshevik and Menshevik workers. In these revolutionary events, the old differences seemed to lose their importance, and the desire to reunite the Party was naturally very strong.

A clear proof of Lenin's great flexibility in organisational and tactical questions is the fact that he supported the reunification of the RSDLP, although maintaining the independence of Bolshevism as a *clearly delineated political tendency*. This point is developed further in *Bolshevism: The Road to Revolution* by Alan Woods:

> Lenin was in favour of organisational unity, but did not for a moment abandon the ideological struggle, maintaining a firm position on all the basic questions of tactics and perspectives. This was entirely characteristic of Lenin's whole approach – extreme flexibility on all organisational and tactical questions combined with an absolutely implacable attitude on all questions of principle and theory. However, we must be careful not to read into the history of Bolshevism intentions and ideas derived from our knowledge of subsequent events. For many years, the official Soviet histories presented the role of Lenin as that of an all-seeing, all-knowing Leader who foresaw everything in advance and guided the party with a sure hand towards the goal of ultimate victory. From this kind of hagiography, no understanding of the real Lenin can be gained. The whole history of Bolshevism remains shrouded in mystery, like a fairy story or a religious myth. It was neither. In fact, far from having an absolutely clear idea of where he was going at this time, Lenin was still very unsure as to how things were going to turn out. Of course, he was very clear on the need to stand firm on the basic ideas and revolutionary principles of Marxism, and also on the need to maintain the Bolsheviks as the consistently revolutionary wing of the RSDLP. But his support for reunification was neither a sham nor a manoeuvre. On the basis of the revolution, the Mensheviks had moved far to the left, and it was not at all clear how this would end up. Lenin was not yet clear in his own mind that it would be necessary to make a complete break, and did not finally come to this conclusion until 1912. It is entirely false to present the picture in any other way.

Again, it is clear that Lenin was certainly in *favour* of the reunification of the Party, but only on a principled basis. At this stage, it was correct to take practical steps to bring this about. "Hence it is now possible not only to *urge* unity, not only to obtain *promises* to unite, but actually to *unite*", he explained.[33]

As a gesture in this direction, in October Lenin wrote again to Plekhanov on behalf of the Bolsheviks, asking him to join the editorial board of *Novaya Zhizn*. He explained:

> ... all this will provide *new ground*, on which it will be so much easier to forget the past and work together in a real live job. [...]
>
> ... the revolution itself will sweep away our tactical differences with astonishing speed...[34]

Lenin was quite prepared to reach out to former comrades, a characteristic that the bourgeois historians completely ignore. However, despite these appeals, Plekhanov kept his distance, preferring to comment from the sidelines from far away Geneva. The real reason for his reticence was that he was moving to the right – a fact that was made clear by his statement that the workers should not have taken arms.

Lenin arrived back in St. Petersburg in early November. Under the new conditions conquered by the revolution, he was able to operate quite openly and freely and even addressed a meeting of the Soviet. However, as the government repression increased, he began to move to different locations so as to avoid the prying eyes of the Okhrana.

Krupskaya explained that all this shifting from one place to another certainly placed a strain on Lenin's nerves: "Sleeping at people's places tired Ilyich out and besides, he found it very irksome. Being a shy man, he felt embarrassed by the attentions of the kind hosts."[35] Eventually, Lenin went to Finland, which allowed him greater peace of mind and a more stable environment in which to plan the work.

By December, under the pressure from below, the Bolshevik and Menshevik leaderships had effectively united. A United Central Committee was created for the first time since 1903. When the *Novaya Zhizn* and the *Nachalo* were closed down for printing the appeal of the Soviet, only one paper remained in operation in St. Petersburg, *Severny Golos* (*Voice of the North*), which served as the joint organ of both Bolsheviks and Mensheviks. Lenin summed up these developments thus:

> Former disagreements gave way to unity of opinion on the question of armed uprising. Social Democrats of both factions were active in the Soviet of

Workers' Deputies, these peculiar instruments of embryonic revolutionary authority [...] Old controversies of the pre-revolutionary period gave way to unanimity on the practical questions. The upsurge of the revolutionary tide pushed aside disagreements, compelling Social Democrats to adopt militant tactics; it swept the question of the Duma into the background and put the question of the insurrection on the order of the day [...] In *Severny Golos*, the Mensheviks, jointly with the Bolsheviks, called for a general strike and insurrection; and they called upon the workers to continue this struggle until they had captured power. The revolutionary situation itself suggested practical slogans. There were arguments only over matters of detail in the appraisal of events: for example, *Nachalo* regarded the Soviets of Workers' Deputies as organs of revolutionary local self-government, while *Novaya Zhizn* regarded them as embryonic organs of revolutionary state power that united the proletariat with the revolutionary democrats.[36]

Tammerfors Conference

From a joint Central Committee, the next step was the calling of a joint conference. But as preparation for this, including the dissolution of the factions, the Bolsheviks and Mensheviks needed to hold separate conferences. The Bolsheviks therefore organised a conference in Tammerfors, southern Finland, at the end of December. Given the changed situation, delegates were elected not by committees, but by the membership.

It was a very serious gathering that reflected the impact of the revolution, as well as the recent defeats in St. Petersburg and Moscow. The conference opened on 23 December and the agenda consisted of the proposed unification, the armed uprising, and the forthcoming elections to the Duma.

Of all the questions under consideration, the Duma elections proved to be one of the most controversial points that centred on the issue of whether or not to boycott the elections. The tactic of boycott was normally employed by a Party when the revolutionary movement was strong enough to sweep away any parliamentary forum. The boycott tactic was certainly correct in the autumn of 1905.

However, with the ebb in the revolutionary movement, the boycott tactic became ineffective and even counterproductive. Where the masses were unresponsive to such a boycott, the party would be isolated and, in effect, end up only talking to itself. Under such conditions, rather than boycott, it was important for revolutionaries to use every legal avenue available for propaganda purposes to widen its periphery.

With the arrest of the leaders of the St. Petersburg Soviet and the crushing of the Moscow uprising, the regime began to regain its nerve. The tide of the revolution was clearly beginning to ebb. The workers of St. Petersburg were exhausted, and harsh government reprisals followed. However, it was difficult for the Bolsheviks to recognise the change and they believed that the revolution was still advancing. The conference therefore came out overwhelmingly for the boycott of the Duma.

Lenin thought the revolution was simply experiencing a temporary lull, hoping that the peasantry would soon rise up. But this turned out not to be the case. Nevertheless, Lenin was against the boycott. In fact, at the conference there were only two votes against – Lenin and Boris Gorev.

Given the strong feelings to boycott the Duma, Lenin refused to push things to an open breach. He instead decided to retreat and accepted the decision, hoping that events would correct this error. Fifteen years later, Lenin wrote, "The Bolshevik's boycott of the Duma in 1906 was a mistake, although a minor and easily remediable one."[37]

Significantly, the Tammerfors Conference also introduced changes to the Party constitution, where Lenin's original definition of a member from 1903 was adopted and new democratic principles were introduced under the freer conditions. These included an increase in the number of elected positions in the Party as well as increased rights of the membership. For instance, with the support of one-sixth of the members, any section could demand that the Party's propaganda machine be placed at its disposal.

It was at this conference that the Georgian delegate, Joseph Dzhugashvili – later known as Joseph Stalin – first set eyes on Lenin. In a speech soon after Lenin's death, in 1924, Stalin mentioned this special occasion. However, his calculated remarks clearly attempted to slyly demean Lenin's standing. With Lenin dead, Stalin had one eye on the leadership and was seeking to enhance his own image, which, up until this point, was very much in the shade, so much so that Nikolai Sukhanov described him as a "grey blur".[38] Stalin wrote:

> I was hoping to see the mountain eagle of our Party, the great man, great not only politically, but, if you will, physically, because in my imagination I had pictured Lenin as a giant, stately and imposing. What, then, was my disappointment to see a most ordinary-looking man, below average height, in no way, literally in no way, distinguishable from ordinary mortals…
>
> It is accepted as the usual thing for a 'great man' to come late to meetings so that the assembly may await his appearance with bated breath… What, then,

was my disappointment to learn that Lenin had arrived at the conference before the delegates, had settled himself somewhere in a corner, and was unassumingly carrying on a conversation, a most ordinary conversation with the most ordinary delegates at the conference. I will not conceal from you that at that time this seemed to me to be something of a violation of certain essential rules.[39]

Lenin did not need showmanship, prestige, or anything of that kind – especially the image of a "mountain eagle", the thought of which would have repelled him. His authority was a political and moral one based on his leadership qualities and grasp of Marxism, nothing more. Personally, Lenin was very approachable in his dealings with comrades, and it was perfectly natural for him to freely discuss with delegates. Above all, he was very interested in hearing the opinion of others. It was these things which endeared comrades towards him. These were characteristics that Stalin, consumed with jealousy, never possessed.

After attending the Tammerfors Conference, Lenin stayed in Finland until the new Party Congress in April, held in Stockholm, which became known as the 'Unity' Congress.

12. The 'Unity' Congress

The Fourth Congress of the RSDLP, known as the 'Unity' Congress, was held in Stockholm from 23 April to 8 May 1906. It was attended by 112 delegates, representing fifty-seven local Party organisations. The attendance was boosted by a further twenty-two consultative delegates, who could speak but not vote. Trotsky did not attend the Congress as he was still in prison awaiting trial on charges of armed rebellion. This Congress was, significantly, the first time that the Bolsheviks and Mensheviks had met together since the split of 1903.

As a result of the revolution, by the spring of 1906, the membership of the Russian Social-Democratic Labour Party had risen to 48,000, of which 34,000 were Bolsheviks and 14,000 were Mensheviks. This was a huge advance compared to the numbers of the past and the highest point reached to date by the Party. In addition, the Congress decided to fuse with the Polish and Latvian Social-Democrats, as well as the Jewish Bund,* which further added to its numerical strength.

Despite the greater number of Bolsheviks within the Party, the representation at the Congress was skewed to the advantage of the Mensheviks. This was due in large measure to the growing repression following the Moscow defeat, which bore down especially on the Bolsheviks. As a result, the Mensheviks ended up with a majority in the 'Unity' Congress.

Krupskaya wrote that Lenin was hopeful the revolutionary events would fuse the Party together, which seemed to be the case. He believed that the

---

* By this time, the Bund decided to accept the centralised character of the Party, although each nationality could hold their special conferences and have representation on local and central bodies of the Party. See *LCW*, Vol. 10, pp. 159-60.

revolution had the effect of propelling the Mensheviks to the left and away from their opportunism. In the words of Krupskaya:

> Ilyich still hoped that the new wave of revolution, of whose rise he had no doubt, would sweep them along with it and reconcile them to the Bolshevik line.[1]

However, having said that, Lenin was also a realist. Given what had occurred over the previous period, he had not come to any final conclusions about the future. Given the political differences that remained, the ground would need to be tested, one step at a time. As it turned out, sharp political differences did emerge during the Congress on a number of questions.

Given its vital importance, the agrarian question became the central theme of debate. The Mensheviks – who, as discussed, feared alienating the bourgeoisie – opposed the call for the peasants to seize the land, but instead talked of 'municipalisation'. This meant the transfer of the land to local government or municipal control.

Lenin, on the other hand, called for the boldest revolutionary measures based on an alliance of workers and poor peasants to completely clear out the feudal landlords. These measures expressly called for the confiscation or nationalisation of the land held by the landowners and Church leaders, which prompted Plekhanov to accuse Lenin and his policy of seizures of 'Blanquism'.*

Plekhanov, who had already said that the workers should not have taken up arms, expressed the traditional Menshevik view that the revolution was bourgeois and therefore had to be led by the bourgeoisie. The role of the workers was to support them, as anything more was deemed as pure adventurism and counterproductive. In reply, Lenin firmly answered Plekhanov by constantly linking the fate of the Russian revolution to the socialist revolution in the West. He explained this bold perspective in the following manner:

> I would formulate this proposition as follows: the Russian Revolution can achieve victory by its own efforts, but it cannot possibly hold and consolidate its gains by its own strength. It cannot do this unless there is a socialist revolution in the West. Without this condition restoration is inevitable, whether we have municipalisation, or nationalisation, or division of the land: for under each and every form of possession and property the small proprietor will always be a

---

* Louis Auguste Blanqui (1805-1881) was a French revolutionary who emphasised the need to organise small conspiratorial groups. In contrast to Lenin and the Bolsheviks, who sought to win a majority to their side, Blanqui believed a small revolutionary minority should seek to seize power, while leaving the workers as onlookers.

bulwark of restoration. After the complete victory of the democratic revolution the small proprietor will inevitably turn against the proletariat; and the sooner the common enemies of the proletariat and of the small proprietors, such as the capitalists, the landlords, the financial bourgeoisie, and so forth are overthrown, the sooner will this happen. Our democratic republic has no other reserve than the socialist proletariat of the West.[2]

In response, Plekhanov accused Lenin of being a utopian dreamer. The political divisions between the two factions at this 'Unity' Congress could not have been greater.

Added to the disagreement over the agrarian question was the question of whether to boycott the Duma elections, which were soon due. While the Mensheviks placed their cherished hopes in the Duma – a reflection of their "parliamentary cretinism", to use Lenin's expression – the majority of Bolsheviks, following the Tammerfors Conference decision, were against participation. But the Bolsheviks were in a minority and the Menshevik position prevailed. Nevertheless, the decision came too late for the Party to participate officially in the elections to the First Duma, but it did take part in the Second the following year.

As the Bolsheviks were in a minority, when it came to the internal elections, the Mensheviks took all five seats on the editorial board, while the Central Committee was made up of three Bolsheviks and seven Mensheviks. The Bolsheviks had no alternative but to accept the result. Lenin made a declaration: "We stand for submission to the decisions of the Congress", which stood out in marked contrast to the sabotage of the Mensheviks following the 1903 Congress.[3]

On Lenin's initiative, the Congress agreed to incorporate democratic centralism formally into the Party Statutes, as well as guaranteeing the rights of all minorities, including the autonomy of every Party organisation. Lenin stressed that this meant the Party accepted the principle of "freedom of discussion, unity of action".[4] He went on to stress:

> But in the united Party this ideological struggle must not split the organisations, must not hinder the unity of action of the proletariat. This is a new principle as yet in our Party life, and considerable effort will be needed to implement it properly. [...]

> But beyond the bounds of unity of action there must be the broadest and freest discussion and condemnation of all steps, decisions and tendencies that we regard as harmful.[5]

Such internal Party democracy would allow the Bolsheviks to continue their opposition to any wrong decisions, as they saw them, taken by the Congress, as long as it did not hinder the struggle of the Party.

At this time, the problem of finance was a continual battle, given the heavy demands on the resources of the Party. This pressure had multiplied during the revolution, where a great deal of money was needed not only for the publication of newspapers and propaganda, but also to buy and smuggle arms. The financing of the Party came from many sources: members' dues, paper sales, small and large donations, as well as loans from sympathisers.

It was during these revolutionary upheavals that the Party was engaged in occasional 'expropriations' to replenish its finances. In such a critical moment, taking money from the bourgeoisie by bank robberies under Bolshevik control was regarded as a legitimate way to help the revolution. However, this usually came with a price, as these 'expropriations' could be dangerous endeavours, which claimed victims on both sides.

With the ebb of the revolution, these 'expropriations' became less and less under the control of the Party, and had a dangerous tendency to degenerate into banditry led by declassed elements. As a result, a special resolution was passed at the Unity Congress condemning the 'expropriations' with the aim of ending them. Under Lenin's pressure, the Congress did allow the expropriation of state funds, but only under the strict direction of the Party. However, by the end of the year, he had come out firmly against such measures.

The vital thing for Lenin was that the events of 1905 demonstrated the ripeness of Russia for revolution. The month following the Congress, Lenin summed up his feelings with the words: "It is good to be alive at a time when the masses begin to stir with political life."[6]

Bloody repression

From July 1906, the brutality of the tsarist regime was undertaken by the new reactionary government of Pyotr Stolypin, who was determined to crush the rebellion and wipe out any vestiges of revolution. He introduced a series of emergency decrees against the mass insurgency, including court martials, the closure of newspapers and the banning of trade unions. Harsh measures were also introduced to quell the peasants' unrest and to teach them a lesson they would not forget. These lessons included mass floggings and the 'Stolypin necktie', as the government's noose was nicknamed. As a result, some 883 state executions were carried out in the nine months between August 1906 and May 1907.

56. Pyotr Stolypin

The First Duma had resulted in the victory of the bourgeois Cadets, who won a sizeable majority of seats. Within the Duma, the Menshevik deputies, numbering eighteen, along with those from the Caucasus, formed their own 'fraction'. There were no Bolshevik deputies. The Cadet parliamentary victory greatly influenced the Menshevik-led Central Committee, which, in turn, began to push for an electoral bloc with the bourgeois parties with the aim of establishing a 'responsible government'. This position underlined their support for the 'progressive' bourgeois liberals and was a further move in the direction of liquidating the underground Party.

Lenin and the Bolsheviks rebutted the class-collaborationist arguments of the Mensheviks with the slogan: "Down with all blocs! Above all, down with blocs with the Cadets!"[7]

In the Duma, the Cadets were under pressure from the peasant masses to raise the question of land reform. However, when these bourgeois representatives urged the government to tentatively consider such reforms, they were ceremoniously dismissed. This was then quickly followed by the tsar's dissolution of the Duma on 21 July, after only forty-two days.

The division over tactics between the Bolsheviks and Mensheviks widened as elections for the Second Duma approached. Lenin was very much in favour of participating in the elections, as the Duma would provide a valuable platform for agitation. The Tammerfors Conference had also agreed that participation was possible if agreement could be reached locally between the revolutionary parties.

Black Hundreds

During 1905, a series of new parties had been set up. Not only were the Cadets formed, but others emerged, such as the Russian Monarchist Party and the Russian Assembly. The most notorious, however, was the Union of the Russian People, a monarchist quasi-fascist party, which was extremely antisemitic and ultra-patriotic.

Not surprisingly, the Ministry of the Interior financed its newspapers and channelled arms into the notorious Black Hundred gangs. At the same time, the court clique also patronised the party, while Nicholas wore the Union's badge and wished them "total success".[8] According to some calculations, this reactionary party could have numbered up to 300,000 supporters, who openly paraded with their tsarist portraits, religious icons and crosses.

Under the protection of the state, the Union's Black Hundreds were engaged in violence in the streets with knives and knuckle-dusters, attacking suspected revolutionaries and beating up anyone seen as having democratic sympathies, much in the same way as the future Nazis in Germany. Above all, they were used to persecute the Jews, with the full support and involvement of the tsarist police. There had been 690 documented pogroms – with over 3,000 reported murders – during the two week period following the 'October Manifesto' of 1905. Nicholas wrote to his mother on 10 November justifying the violence:

> The impertinence of the socialists and revolutionaries had angered the people once more; and because nine-tenths of the trouble-makers are Jews, the people's whole anger turned against them. That's how the pogrom happened. It is amazing how they took place simultaneously in all the towns of Russia and Siberia... Cases as far apart as in Tomsk, Simferopol, Tver and Odessa show clearly what an infuriated mob can do: they surrounded the houses where revolutionaries had taken refuge, set fire to them and killed everybody trying to escape.[9]

These savage pogroms were an accurate reflection of the blood-soaked barbarism of tsarism. The simultaneous nature of the attacks was not at all "amazing", but well prepared and orchestrated by the regime itself.

Liquidationism

Towards the end of 1906, Lenin was fully convinced that the energies of the revolution were now completely exhausted. Even then, in his December 1906 article, 'The Crisis of Menshevism', Lenin wrote that while the revolutionaries were "the *first* to take the path of direct revolutionary struggle", they were to be "the *last* to leave" the arena of struggle.[10] They would leave "only when all possibilities have been exhausted, when there is not a *shadow* of hope for a shorter way, when the basis for an appeal to prepare for mass strikes, an uprising, etc., is obviously disappearing."[11]

Given the increasing repression, by the summer of 1906 Lenin was forced to go into 'semi-exile' in Finland. Under these new harsh conditions, the Bolsheviks began the illegal publication of their newspaper, *Proletary*, which was allowed under Party rules, and took the necessary measures to work underground.

The Mensheviks, on the other hand, began to retreat under these blows. Their activity now became largely confined to writing for the bourgeois press and arguing for a congress of non-party workers.

'The Crisis of Menshevism' was Lenin's reply to a pamphlet by the Menshevik Yuri Larin called *A Broad Labour Party and a Labour Congress* (1906). Larin's pamphlet reflected the retreat of the Mensheviks. The author argued, not for an underground party to carry out illegal work, but for the creation of "a party of the European type", along the lines of the Belgian Labour Party.[12]

Larin, following in the footsteps of Axelrod, championed the idea of a broad 'Labour Congress', which aimed to merge the RSDLP with the Socialist-Revolutionaries and the trade unions to produce a wide 'non-partisan party'. In the context of Russia, this was an argument for nothing less than the liquidation of the revolutionary party.

In response, Lenin thanked Larin for being so frank and honest! This opportunist line of dissolving the Party into the broad mass, which had first raised its head in a tentative way at the Second Congress, was condemned by Lenin as the abandonment of revolutionary politics and the revolutionary party.

In his article, Lenin went on to define the Mensheviks as an opportunist wing of the RSDLP, but he nevertheless rejected the idea that Bolshevism was a separate trend, outside the Party and alien to it, but the revolutionary wing of the Party, conducting an irreconcilable struggle against the opportunism and liquidationism of the Menshevik right wing:

The fact is that right from the very beginning we declared (see *One Step Forward, Two Steps Back*): we are not creating a special 'Bolshevik' trend, always and everywhere we merely uphold the point of view of *revolutionary Social-Democracy*. And right up to the social revolution there will inevitably be an opportunist wing and a revolutionary wing of Social-Democracy.

A cursory glance at the history of 'Bolshevism' is sufficient to convince anyone of that.[13]

In the same article, Lenin once again returned to the importance of the youth in building the revolutionary party. In doing so, he criticised Larin for clinging to the remains of an older, tired, worn-out generation, with its family responsibilities and commitments:

Larin complains, for example, that young workers predominate in our Party, that we have few married workers, and that they leave the Party. This complaint of a Russian opportunist reminds me of a passage in one of Engels' works [...] Retorting to some fatuous bourgeois professor, a German Cadet, Engels wrote: is it not natural that youth should predominate in our Party, the revolutionary party? We are the party of the future, and the future belongs to the youth. We are a party of innovators, and it is always the youth that most eagerly follows the innovators. We are a party that is waging a self-sacrificing struggle against the old rottenness, the youth is always the first to undertake a self-sacrificing struggle.

No, let us leave it to the Cadets to collect the 'tired' old men of thirty, revolutionaries who have 'grown wise', and renegades from Social-Democracy. We shall always be a party of the youth of the advanced class!

Larin himself blurts out a frank admission why he regrets the loss of the married men who are tired of the struggle. If we were to collect a good number of these tired men into the Party, that would make it "somewhat sluggish, putting a brake on political adventures..."

Now, that's better, good Larin! Why dissemble and deceive yourself. What you want is not a vanguard-party, but a *rearguard-party*, so that it will be rather more sluggish. You should have said so frankly.[14]

At this time, Larin was a leading figure of a group of Liquidators within the Party, which Lenin dubbed the "Stolypin Workers' Party", given their capitulation to tsarism. Much later, in 1917, Larin broke from the Mensheviks and joined the Bolsheviks. However, Lenin never fully trusted him and spoke about him in the most disparaging way. Paradoxically, this former right wing Menshevik liquidator ended up joining the 'Left' Communists, led by

57. Yuri Larin 58. Stalin in 1906

Bukharin (who was his son-in-law). He was later given some responsibilities by the government due to his knowledge of the German war economy, but his schemes were generally widely impractical. Lenin commented on Larin with his characteristic irony at the Eleventh Party Congress in March 1922:

> ... he is a very capable man and has a vivid imagination. [...] Imagination is a very valuable asset; but Comrade Larin has a little too much of it. I would say, for example, that if Comrade Larin's stock of imagination were divided equally among all the members of the RCP, there would be very good results. (*Laughter. Applause.*) But until we can perform this operation, Comrade Larin must be kept away from state, administrative, planning, and economic affairs.[15]

The fact that the Bolsheviks were attracting the youth, especially young workers, caused the Mensheviks to sneer: "Lenin is only capable of attracting boys and girls!" But the youth was the key to the future, as Lenin was fond of repeating. These young revolutionary workers, trained in the school of Bolshevism, were to become primarily the forces that would carry through the revolution of 1917.

Pierre Broué gathered some striking information about the youthful nature of the Bolshevik Party, which is worth mentioning. Mikhail Tomsky, a lithographer, joined the revolutionary party at twenty-five years of age. The student Piatakov, son of a large bourgeois family in the Ukraine, became a Bolshevik at twenty, previously having been an anarchist. The student Rosenfeld, whose party name was Kamenev, was nineteen when he joined, as was the metalworker Schmidt and the skilled mechanic Smirnov.

There are those who entered the party at the age of eighteen, namely the metal worker Bakaiev, the students Bukharin and Krestinski, and the shoemaker Kaganovitch. The clerk Zinoviev, the metalworkers Serebriakov and Lutovinov became Bolsheviks at seventeen. Sverdlov was working in a pharmacy when he entered the movement at sixteen, as did the student Kuibyshev. The shoemaker Drobnis and the student Smilga became members of the party at fifteen and Piatnitski at fourteen.

It was not long after leaving adolescence when they were considered experienced militants and leading party cadres. Sverdlov, at seventeen, led the Social Democratic organisation in Sormovo and was twenty when he attended the Tammerfors Conference in 1906. Sokolnikov was eighteen when he became secretary of one of the Moscow party districts. Rykov was twenty-four when he became a member of the Central Committee at the Third Congress in 1905. Zinoviev was already well-known as a leading Bolshevik in St. Petersburg and at the age of twenty-four, he joined the Central Committee. Kamenev was twenty-two when he was chosen as a delegate to the 1905 Congress, and Serebriakov was twenty when he became a party organiser and one of the delegates of the Russian underground to the Prague conference in 1912.

The London Congress

By the time of the Fifth (London) Congress, held between 13 May and 1 June 1907, the Party's membership had risen to 84,000, of which 46,000 were Bolsheviks and 38,000 Mensheviks. Added to this were the Latvian and Polish Social-Democrats, plus the Jewish Bund, which took the total membership of the Party to around 150,000.

Despite the Party's growth, given the retreat of the revolution, its influence in the masses was steadily declining, which would soon make itself felt within the Party.

The Congress was supposed to have been held in Copenhagen, but just before it was due to open, the police informed the organisers that they had twelve hours to leave the country or face deportation back to Russia. Through their contacts in London, notably John Burns MP, a former member of the Social-Democratic Federation who had now become a member of the Liberal government, they secured permission to hold the event at the socialist Brotherhood Church hall in Islington. While the additional travel costs to London had put many, as well as the Party itself, in financial difficulties, there was no alternative but to go ahead.

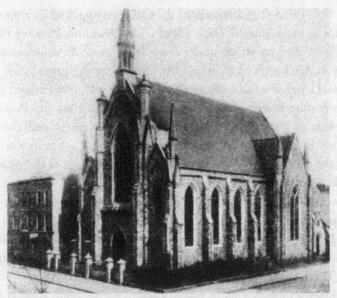

59. Brotherhood Church, Islington, location of the London Conference

The Menshevik Central Committee refused to recognise the Congress as the 'Fifth' as they did not recognise the Bolshevik 'Third' Congress, so simply referred to it as the 'London' Congress.

The London Congress was a much bigger affair than ever before and the Bolsheviks were now in a majority. The Congress proved to be a high point for the Party, with 336 delegates in attendance, including all the most well-known Party figures: Lenin, Plekhanov, Martov, Trotsky, Zinoviev, Maxim Gorky, Rosa Luxemburg, Irakli Tsereteli and others. Trotsky had made his way to London from Finland, having spent weeks on the run after escaping from his second exile in Siberia. Stalin, then an unknown figure, was also present, but did not speak.

The political affiliation of the delegates was made up of 105 Bolsheviks, ninety-seven Mensheviks, forty-four Polish Social-Democrats, twenty-nine Latvians and fifty-seven Bundists. The Bolshevik majority was due to the support from the Polish Social-Democrats, while the Bund tended to support the Mensheviks and the Latvian Social-Democrats wavered between the two.

Although an impressive Congress, it would be the last time all these groups would ever meet under one roof.

Unlike previous Congresses, given its size, it could not meet in secret. All its affairs were conducted in the full glare of publicity, as the delegates had to run a gauntlet of newspaper reporters when they streamed into the church hall. Pictures and reports of the Congress appeared in a number of newspapers, including the *Daily Mirror, The Times* and *Morning Post.* The *Mirror* published an article under the title, 'Russian Revolutionists Meet Secretly in A Church Hall', which obviously gave the game away.[16] Their report said there was not a single man over forty years old who was present, and many were nearer twenty. In fact, Lenin at this time was thirty-seven and Plekhanov was fifty-one. It claimed that the delegates "drill themselves constantly in front of mirrors by which they become adept in aiming and pulling the trigger." *The Times* stated that the real purpose of the visitors was to "make extensive purchase of arms".[17]

Government files from the time reveal how the authorities kept a close watch over the proceedings, in cooperation, of course, with the tsarist police. In fact, there was a police officer on duty outside the entrance. The surveillance also included Herbert Fitch, our detective from the cupboard of the Third Congress, who again managed to worm his way into the proceedings, although what he made of them, is once again another matter.

The 18 May edition of the *Morning Post* printed a protest from the organisers of the Congress, issued through Reuters, about the way certain newspapers were publishing photographs of the delegates. "In Russia", stated the communiqué, "merely for belonging to a Socialist organisation one is liable to penal servitude; and therefore we hope that the English press will not play the part of allies of the Russian police spies." Despite this, the newspapers did not refrain from their coverage.

During this Congress, political differences were still very much in evidence from the very beginning. Plekhanov opened the occasion by repeating the old points that the revolution was bourgeois and the revolutionaries needed to attract allies from the bourgeoisie. As expected, Lenin came out forcefully against this line of argument and attacked the liberals.

> In them [the Soviets] the bourgeoisie saw a revolution that had gone too far ahead. The liberal bourgeoisie wanted to divert the energy of the popular revolutionary struggle into the narrow channel of police-controlled constitutional reaction.[18]

The Second Duma elections held in 1907 saw a more politically polarised Duma, where the number of Cadets was halved and the numbers of Social-Democrats had swollen to sixty-four deputies. The Mensheviks held thirty-six seats, and the Bolsheviks held eighteen, out of a Duma of 512 participants.

As a result, at the London Congress, the debate came to centre around parliamentary tactics, with Tsereteli, a newly elected member of the Second

60. Irakli Tsereteli   61. Maxim Gorky

Duma, speaking for the Mensheviks. In the debate, Lenin was supported in his attack on the bourgeois liberals by Rosa Luxemburg, who was a delegate from the Polish section.

Lenin directed some of his remarks towards Trotsky, who, along with the Bolsheviks, supported the use of a Left Bloc with the Trudoviks (a break-away 'Labour Group' from the SRs) or even the SRs against the liberals:

> A few words about Trotsky. I have no time to dwell here on our differences with him. [...] Trotsky acknowledged the permissibility and usefulness of a Left Bloc against the liberal bourgeoisie. These facts are sufficient for me to acknowledge that Trotsky has come closer to our views. Quite apart from the question of 'uninterrupted revolution', we have here solidarity on fundamental points in the question of the attitude towards bourgeois parties.[19]

As explained, Lenin had not read Trotsky's theory of permanent revolution and it took another ten years for Lenin to fully accept the idea of "uninterrupted revolution" at the time of the October Revolution of 1917. But on the "fundamental points" of their approach to the bourgeois liberals, they were both united.

In fact, when *Proletary* was launched, Lenin, through the editorial board, wrote to Trotsky inviting him to participate, but he turned down the offer. Lenin wrote to Maxim Gorky eight months after the London Congress, saying he did not know the reasons for the refusal but "Trotsky wants to stand 'above the contending factions'…" Given this, he added: "I don't know really whether he will go with the Bolsheviks…"[20]

Lenin opposed Martov's amendment at the Congress that advocated support for liberalism, and he thought that Trotsky's proposed amendment was "Bolshevik", although simply "redundant":

> It must be agreed that Trotsky's amendment is not Menshevik, that it expresses the 'very same', that is, Bolshevik, idea. But Trotsky has expressed this idea in a way that is scarcely better. […] Trotsky's insertion is redundant, for we are not fishing for unique cases in the resolution, but are laying down the *basic* line of Social-Democracy in the bourgeois Russian revolution.[21]

In the end, the Bolsheviks, supported by the Poles and sometimes the Latvians, had a majority at the London Congress and carried the day. Lenin explained:

> The London Congress's adoption of the Bolshevik resolution on non-proletarian parties means that the workers' party decisively rejects all deviations from the class struggle, and recognises, in point of fact, the socialist criticism of non-proletarian parties and the independent revolutionary tasks of the proletariat in the present revolution.
>
> The rejection of the Menshevik amendments to the resolution adds further weight to this.[22]

The Congress again took the decision to condemn the expropriations as "disorganising and demoralising" on Party members by 170 votes to thirty-five, with fifty-two abstentions. Furthermore, it decided, given the new conditions, that all fighting squads connected to the Party would be stood down and disbanded. Some six weeks after the London Congress, the Tiflis expropriation took place – a product of not a little adventurism – which netted some 341,000 roubles. However, the money was of little use as the notes were too large to circulate and those who tried to use them were arrested. Lenin realised that these expropriations had clearly outlived their purpose.

The Congress proceeded to elect a Central Committee composed of five Bolsheviks, four Mensheviks, two Polish and one Latvian Social-Democrat. Nevertheless, some of those elected were politically confused and largely unreliable. As a result, although it was highly successful from a political point of view in endorsing the Bolshevik position, the system of separate factions continued and the Bolsheviks had to elect their own independent Bolshevik Centre.

By the end of the Congress, the funds of those attending were completely exhausted. The extra trip from Denmark at the start, where the Congress was originally supposed to be held, had made a hefty dent in everyone's finances. There were various attempts to raise funds, but none were too successful. Finally, contact was made with a wealthy English soap manufacturer, Joseph Fels, who agreed to a substantial loan, provided he could attend part of the Congress and that all the delegates sign a bond acknowledging the debt. The amount was supposed to be paid off within six months, but unfortunately the reaction in Russia had adverse effects on the Party's finances.

Joseph Fels died in 1914, without the debt being recovered. Nevertheless, in 1922, the amount was finally repaid in full by the Soviet Trade Delegation in Britain. After a certain delay, the pledge of the delegates of 1907 had thus been honoured.

'Stolypin the Hangman'

While the year 1907 marked a new low point in the wave of repression within Russia, 1908 marked the complete victory of reaction. The figures for strikes collapsed. According to the figures supplied by Lenin in his article 'Strike Statistics in Russia', the number of strike days lost were:[23]

	1894-1904	1905	1906	1907	1908
Strike days lost	2,079,408	23,609,387	5,515,749	2,433,123	864,666

The full force of the state's mailed fist was used to crush all resistance, and thousands of militants were sentenced to imprisonment by tsarist tribunals. Many of them were hanged. In fact, between 1906 and 1909, over 5,000 political prisoners were sentenced to death, while a further 38,000 were imprisoned or sent to penal servitude. The prime minister earned the nickname of 'Stolypin the Hangman', who, of course, had the full support of the tsar.

The dissolution of the Second 'Red' Duma was announced in June 1907 by the Tsar, and the fifty-four elected Social-Democrat deputies were imprisoned and deported on charges of high treason. Those who escaped the hangman were sentenced to long prison terms with hard labour. Newspapers were suppressed and printing facilities were closed in a crackdown by the authorities.

This coup d'état in June can be regarded as the end of the revolution and the beginning of intense black reaction. Consequently, the Bolsheviks were forced to operate underground and the Party leaders were forced into exile.

As expected, the bourgeois liberals simply sulked away, making the occasional speech against Stolypin. But for all intents and purposes, the bourgeoisie had accepted Stolypin's constitution. Following the dissolution of the Second Duma, the tsarist government raised the prospect of a new Duma, this time with an even more restricted franchise. This meant that in future elections, the workers' representation would be all but wiped out. This stirred up feelings for a boycott.

Boycott question

Following the London Congress, Lenin therefore ran into opposition at the Party's Kokta conference in Finland, which took place in July, over the issue of a future boycott. While the Mensheviks moved in an opportunist direction, a layer of Bolsheviks moved in the opposite direction to ultra-leftism. In doing so, the 'Lefts' came out forcefully for a boycott. Lenin opposed this on the grounds that, given the objective difficulties, any small legal opening should be used to the maximum extent possible.

While Lenin admitted that the new Duma would be nothing more than an "accursed pigsty", he believed that if it was necessary in the interests of the workers to participate in this pigsty Duma, then they should do so. "We shall work there too for the benefit of the revolution, without whining, but also without boasting", explained Lenin.[24]

Under conditions of counter-revolution, it was essential that the Party members made use of every legal opening. When it came to the vote, Lenin was the only member of the Bolshevik delegation to vote with the Mensheviks against the boycott and in favour of participation. After the October Revolution, Lenin looked back on that controversy in the summer of 1907, when:

> St. Petersburg and Moscow, nearly all the Bolsheviks were in favour of boycotting the Third Duma; they were guided by 'sentiment' instead of an objective analysis and walked into a trap.[25]

Between 1906 and 1908, in a moment when the tide of reaction was raging, Lenin repeatedly warned about the dangers of 'phrase-mongering' and ultra-left gestures. The ultra-left Bolsheviks tried to turn the question of a boycott of elections from a tactical issue into a question of principle. Using the same bad method, they tried to extend the boycott 'principle' to cover work in the trade unions and workers' clubs. Lenin regarded them as a mirror image of the Menshevik liquidators. But he was in a minority. In fact, according to Kamenev, he was completely isolated in his own group.

In August 1907, Lenin attended the Congress of the Second International in Stuttgart. There were 886 delegates from five continents – the largest congress ever held. It was there that he formed a bloc with Rosa Luxemburg to defend the Marxist viewpoint on the question of war and imperialism, and against the growing pressures of opportunism, especially in the German Party.

There were heated debates over war and militarism, and the tactics to be adopted in relation to the war question. This increasingly drew a line between the revolutionaries and the opportunists. Lenin explained:

> The remarkable and sad feature in this connection was that German Social-Democracy, which hitherto had always upheld the revolutionary standpoint in Marxism, proved to be unstable, or took an opportunist stand.[26]
>
> … the trade union half of the German delegation were the most adamant supporters of opportunist views.[27]

Lenin and Luxemburg moved an amendment, drafted by Luxemburg and supported by Martov, to the main German resolution. The conclusion stated:

> In case war should break out anyway, it is their duty to intervene for its speedy termination and to strive with all their power to utilise the economic and political crisis created by the war to rouse the masses and thereby hasten the downfall of capitalist class rule.[28]

When they showed the original to August Bebel, one of the leaders of the German Party, he refused to endorse it, as he believed it would threaten the legal basis of the SPD. Only after consultation with lawyers, did he finally agree on a formula. The amended resolution was then adopted unanimously. But, as we will see, when the war broke out in 1914 the resolution would be totally ignored by the leadership.

Given the extreme restrictions imposed by Stolypin, the Third 'Black' Duma that assembled in November 1907 included only fifteen Social-Democrats, mostly Mensheviks. The reactionary parties made the most gains, especially the 'Octobrists', who dominated the Duma.

As a result, the boycottist tendencies within Bolshevism began to mushroom. A group formed known as the Otzovists (from 'otzvat' – 'recall'), which extended its influence over the next few years. Their chief spokesmen were Bogdanov and Lunacharsky, who demanded complete withdrawal from the Duma as well as from the trade unions. They were joined by the Ultimatumists, who demanded that the deputies throw all caution to the wind and the legal work abandoned.

The Ultimatumists believed that no revolutionary had a place in this rotten Duma, and those who did were liquidators. The growth of these ultra-left tendencies among the Bolsheviks deeply alarmed Lenin. He explained later:

> The Bolsheviks' boycott of the Duma in 1906 was a mistake, although a minor and easily remediable one. The boycott of the Duma in 1907, 1908 and subsequent years was a most serious error and difficult to remedy, because, on the one hand, a very rapid rise of the revolutionary tide and its conversion into an uprising was not to be expected, and, on the other hand, the entire historical situation attendant upon the renovation of the bourgeois monarchy called for legal and illegal activities being combined.[29]

In a period of ebb, Lenin explained, boycottism loses all its revolutionary essence and turns into its opposite. He believed that parliamentary propaganda, where possible, should be used to the maximum effect to develop the Party and widen its support. Nevertheless, the support for the boycott tactic within the Bolshevik faction remained very strong.

The most serious problem for Lenin was the open clash with Bogdanov and Krassin, who championed this ultra-left position. Both men played a key role within the Bolshevik faction, forming part of the secret Bolshevik Centre, along with Lenin, known as the 'Little Trinity'.

The row over boycottism marked a serious rift within Bolshevism, exacerbated by the rising tide of reaction. Following elections to the Third Duma, the boycottist tendency had become solidified into a firm faction, which plagued the Bolsheviks and created a real headache for Lenin.

In times when the objective conditions force an army to retreat, the importance of good generals is even greater than in an offensive. With effective generals, the army can retreat in good order, losses are minimised, and the troops can regroup and prepare for a new advance when conditions permit. But bad generals will turn a retreat into a rout.

The adventurist policies advocated by the ultra-left Bolsheviks would have led to the complete decimation of the Party. Lenin saw this clearly and put up a stiff resistance. This inevitably led the conflict to become increasingly bitter, ending in an inevitable split.

The situation with the Bolsheviks was bad, but the position of the Mensheviks was no better. In fact, it was decidedly worse. Their majority, led by Larin and Potresov, demanded the liquidation of the underground party and the setting up of a legal one. In Moscow, the Mensheviks began to disband their underground organisation, as they believed the existence of illegal organisations only led to further police raids and repression. They instead wanted to work exclusively within the framework of the tsarist laws, which in practice meant the dissolution of the Party. Others held a position that wavered between the two extremes.

Looking back on the history of Bolshevism, Lenin wrote in *'Left-Wing' Communism: An Infantile Disorder* that:

> Little is known in other countries of the fact that Bolshevism took shape, developed and became steeled in the long years of struggle against *petty-bourgeois revolutionism*, which smacks of anarchism, or borrows something from the latter and, in all essential matters, does not measure up to the conditions and requirements of a consistently proletarian class struggle. [...] A petty bourgeois driven to frenzy by the horrors of capitalism is a social phenomenon which, like anarchism, is characteristic of all capitalist countries. The instability of such revolutionism, its barrenness, and its tendency to turn rapidly into submission, apathy, phantasms, and even a frenzied infatuation with one bourgeois fad or another – all this is common knowledge.[30]

Lenin argued that the Party needed to avoid "petty-bourgeois revolutionism" – pseudo-revolutionary phrases – and instead skilfully combine illegal and legal methods of work where possible. This meant making use of the Duma as a tribune that tsarism had been forced to establish. If only a single Bolshevik could gain entry into the reactionary Duma, it would be a gain, as the Party could then print their speeches as leaflets and circulate them to the workers.

Likewise, if the workers are involved in the trade unions, the Bolsheviks must be there to influence them. It was vital for the Bolsheviks to avoid becoming a sect that simply stood on the sidelines of the movement. In fact, it was a weakness of the Bolsheviks that they did not work systematically in the trade unions, which allowed the Mensheviks to fill the vacuum and assume a leading role, which later caused serious difficulties for the Soviet government after the October Revolution.

After the London Congress, no party congress was held for a long time, mainly due to the parlous state of the organisation. This whole period was coloured by reaction, retreat and demoralisation. Towards the end of December

1907, Lenin left Finland and embarked on his second exile, which proved to be an even more difficult one than his first. Lenin wrote in April 1908:

> ... this first half-year has been marked by a considerable decline and weakening of all revolutionary organisations, including that of the Social-Democrats. Wavering, disunity and disintegration – such have been the general features of this half-year.[31]

He went on to quote some reports: "Our ideological forces are melting away like snow", wrote one. "The intellectuals, as is well known, have been deserting in masses in recent months", wrote another.[32] The Mensheviks, likewise, were also experiencing a complete disintegration.

Lenin quoted a weaver from a trade union journal: "The factory owners have taken away what we won, the foremen are once again bullying us, *just wait, 1905 will come again.*"[33] He repeated these words:

> Just wait, 1905 will come again. That is how the workers look at things. For them that year of struggle provided a model of *what has to be done*. For the intellectuals and the renegading petty bourgeois it was the 'insane year', a model of *what should not be done*.[34]

In addition to this boycottist problem, the oppressive atmosphere in exile weighed down on all the comrades, including Lenin. Krupskaya wrote: "We were beginning our second period of emigration, a much harder one than the first."[35]

They arrived in Geneva in January 1908. It would last nine long years and Lenin would not return to Russia until 1917. With his closest collaborators, Bogdanov, Lyadov and Lunacharsky, now in the boycottist camp, and others going over to the side of the conciliators, Lenin found himself quite isolated inside the Bolshevik faction. The mood was quite depressed. Walking in the desolate streets of Geneva, Lenin expressed his inner thoughts to Krupskaya, "I feel just as if I'd come here to be buried."[36]

13. Years of Disintegration

These were years of retreat and disintegration for the revolutionary movement that were clearly taking their toll on those still involved. The Social Democratic Party, which had experienced a period of explosive growth, had now entered into a sharp decline, being reduced in many places to handfuls here and there. That included the Bolsheviks. Instead of tens of thousands, they were reduced to maybe hundreds, or even dozens. Lenin complained of being stuck in "this damned Geneva", as bad news came through of more arrests and imprisonment of Party workers within Russia.

> 'During the years of reaction', Krupskaya explained, 'the number of political emigrants from Russia increased tremendously. People fled abroad to escape the savage persecutions of the tsarist regime, people with frayed and shattered nerves, without prospects for the future, without a penny to their name, and without any help from Russia… We had more than enough of squabbling and bickering.' [1]

Life in exile was difficult at the best of times, but now, with the blanket of reaction, it was deeply oppressive. However, there was little they could do about it and they simply had to hold on until there was a break in the situation.

> 'It was difficult for us, after the revolution, to get used to life in emigration again', continued Krupskaya, 'Vladimir Ilyich spent all his days in the library, and in the evenings we did not know what to do with ourselves. We had no desire to sit in the cold cheerless room we had rented and longed to be among people. Every evening we went to the cinema or the theatre, although we seldom stayed to the

end, and usually left in the middle of a show to wander about the streets, most often around the lake.'[2]

But the period of reaction was to be a long one, with all the difficulties and hardships that went with it. This situation was inevitably reflected within the ranks of the Party, which seemed to be plagued with a host of internal conflicts. The pressure of the period was accompanied by political backsliding, especially expressed in those searching for shortcuts.

Lenin recognised the dangers, and called for a campaign to politically stiffen up the members and cleanse the Party of those who had become disillusioned and had lost their heads. In such a period, the most urgent task was to hold the line theoretically: to defend the principles of Marxism and the integrity of the revolutionary party. Lenin said:

> We certainly need not fear this sorting out. We should welcome it, we should help it. Let there be snivelling from the flabby-minded, who here and there will begin shouting: Again struggle! Again internal friction! Again polemics! Our reply is that without unremitting struggle no genuinely proletarian revolutionary Social-Democracy has ever built up anywhere. [...]
>
> In the interests of this new sorting-out a strengthening of theoretical work is essential.[3]

Krupskaya underlined this point in her reminiscences:

> The years 1908 to 1911 were not merely years of living abroad – they were years of intense struggle on the most important front – the ideological front.[4]

Lenin was merciless against those who were mired in confusion, searching for miracles and shortcuts that did not exist. These tendencies existed on both the right and the left of the Party. Hardened factions had emerged, from opportunists to ultra-lefts, that, under the circumstances of retreat, threatened to derail the Party and destroy it utterly.

Looking back on the challenges that faced the Bolsheviks in early 1909, in an article entitled 'On the Road', Lenin wrote:

> The membership of all our Party organisations has dropped. Some of them – namely, those whose membership was least proletarian – have fallen to pieces. The Party's semi-legal institutions created by the revolution have been broken up time after time. Things reached a point when some elements within the Party, under the impact of the general break-up, began to ask whether it was necessary to preserve the old Social-Democratic Party, whether it was necessary to continue *its*

work, whether it was necessary to go 'underground' once more, and how this was to be done. And the extreme Right (the liquidationist trend, so-called) answered this question in the sense that it was necessary to legalise ourselves at all costs, even at the price of an open renunciation of the Party programme, tactics and organisation.[5]

He concluded by underlining its seriousness: "This was undoubtedly an ideological and political crisis as well as an organisational one."[6]

Lenin believed it was the task of the class-conscious workers in the Party to combat these tendencies of pessimism and despondency. Only by standing firm was it possible to eradicate the disease. In doing so, Lenin was always able to rise above these conflicts and look to the future. He explained:

The Russian proletariat can be proud of the fact that in 1905, under its leadership, a nation of slaves for the first time became a million-strong host, an army of the revolution, striking at tsarism. And now the same proletariat will know how to do persistently, staunchly and patiently the work of educating and training the new cadres of a still mightier revolutionary force.[7]

Lenin explained the reasons for the crisis as overwhelmingly the pressures of the period, which were bearing down on the Party, especially on its intellectual and petty-bourgeois elements. These were largely people who had joined the movement in the hope of an early success of the revolution, but who were now disoriented and incapable of adapting and standing up to a period of retreat. The reaction caused many of them to waver and desert the cause. Lenin explained:

Their instability was revealed both in theory ('retreat from revolutionary Marxism': the resolution on the present situation) and in tactics (the 'whittling down of slogans'), as well as in Party organisation.[8]

On the right wing, the Menshevik opportunists were advocating the liquidation of the 'underground' party – hence they became known as the 'liquidators'. However, Lenin launched an equally ferocious battle against the ultra-left Bolsheviks who, given their destructive role, he described as 'liquidators of the Left'.

Lenin was determined to 'liquidate the liquidators' of both kinds. This struggle was ultimately to lead to a complete rupture with the Bolshevik 'Left', and he ended up losing many who had previously played a prominent role, such as Bogdanov, Krassin, Vladimir Bazarov, Mikhail Pokrovsky, Lunacharsky and others.

But Lenin preferred to break completely with even his closest collaborators, rather than make the slightest concession to their political and theoretical deviations. He launched a merciless attack on the boycottist 'Lefts', who, he said, had nothing in common with genuine Bolshevism:

> Otzovism is *not* Bolshevism, but the worst political travesty of Bolshevism [that] its worst political enemy could invent. There must be *absolute clarity* on this point.[9]

'Wield the razor'

Under such circumstances, Lenin believed that the many desertions from the Party were a positive thing, which meant the removal of the least stable elements, its unreliable fair-weather friends and 'fellow travellers'. For Lenin, the Party could not be built on such weak foundations. Their loss of faith in the working class, and in the revolution, was only serving to corrode and undermine the Party. In facing up to the crisis, Lenin rallied his allies to meet the challenge head on:

> Our supporters should not be afraid of an internal ideological struggle, once it is necessary. They will be all the stronger for it. It is our *duty* to bring our disagreements out into the open, the more so since, in point of fact, the whole Party is beginning to line up more and more with our trend. We call on our Bolshevik comrades for *ideological* clarity and for the sweeping away of all backstairs gossip, from whatever source it may come. There are no end of people who would like to see the ideological struggle on momentous cardinal issues sidetracked into petty squabbles, like those conducted by the Mensheviks after the Second Congress. Such people must not be tolerated in the ranks of the Bolsheviks. The Bolshevik working men should strongly discourage such attempts and insist on one thing, and one thing alone: *ideological clarity, definite opinions, a line based on principle.*[10]

Lenin understood that this challenge signalled a drastic change of direction in their work. The period of revolutionary advance was well behind them. The Party now needed to retrench and take small, steady, incremental steps forward.

> During the revolution we learned to 'speak French', i.e. to introduce into the movement the greatest number of rousing slogans, to raise the energy of the direct struggle of the masses and extend its scope. Now, in this time of stagnation, reaction and disintegration, we must learn to 'speak German', i.e. to work slowly (there is nothing else for it, until things revive), systematically, steadily, advancing step by step, winning inch by inch.[11]

This need for political clarification was present throughout Lenin's life. The discussions, debates and even splits were an inevitable and essential part of revolutionary life, a necessary precursor to building a real revolutionary party.

His call to strengthen the Party ideologically was a direct challenge to all those who wanted to smooth over differences and sweep things under the carpet. But this was not Lenin's method. This was not the time for dithering, backsliding or ultra-left gestures.

But everything has its limits, including internal discussion. Internal controversy was not an excuse for a discussion club of endless debate. Opportunist gestures or ultra-left impatience, if not corrected in time, would lead the Party into a disastrous blind alley. Trotsky explained:

> All his life Lenin fought against sectarian deviations that will have cut revolutionaries off from mass movements and from a clear understanding of the situation.[12]

Much later, Trotsky commented that Lenin, who could be very tolerant in dealing with political opponents within the Party, would act for the most part with tact and patience. But there came a time when he would act with ruthless determination if the situation demanded it.

Lenin is portrayed by the craven bourgeois historians as simply a single-minded, ruthless character, but this is a complete travesty. In his public polemics, it is true that Lenin could be extremely sharp when necessary. But this is only one side of Lenin. His private correspondence shows a man of great patience in dealing with his comrades, who he valued and sought to convince by the logic of this argument. As explained in *Bolshevism: The Road to Revolution*:

> Many people get the idea that Lenin was a very hard man who took perverse delight in 'hammering' his opponents in polemics. This impression – very far from the truth – is derived from a one-sided acquaintance with Lenin's writings. If one merely reads the public articles, many of which were naturally of a polemical character, then it does seem that Lenin treats his opponents none too gently. But this gives only one side of the picture. If one reads Lenin's correspondence, an entirely different picture emerges. Lenin was always extraordinarily patient and loyal in his dealings with comrades. He would go to great lengths to convince and carry his colleagues with him. Only in the last analysis, when the disputed issues passed over into the public domain, especially where issues of principles were at stake, Lenin would come out fighting.[13]

This accurately sums up Lenin's approach. "Friendship is friendship", as he said to Maxim Gorky, "but duty is duty."[14] He would not allow personal feelings to get in the way of what he considered right and believed that such an approach was politically immoral.

Philosophical mysticism

The years of reaction generated the greatest ideological confusion within the movement. It produced a wave of alien ideas that threatened its very foundations, especially among the petty-bourgeois intellectuals who were acting as a transmission belt for such views. They were frantically searching for 'new' ideas to redefine Marxism – namely, to revise it.

At this time, there were efforts to fuse Marxism with a redefined religion, an attempt to reconcile materialism and idealism. This led to the rather fanciful trend known as the 'God-seekers' and 'God-builders'. The name 'God-seekers' tells you everything you need to know about its views, which were pure mysticism, based on the view that the material world is determined by something spiritual.

At bottom, idealism is religion, theology, a belief in the supernatural, the mysterious and the unknowable. "Idealism is clerical obscurantism", wrote Lenin in his *Philosophical Notebooks*.[15] At the head of these 'God-seekers' were the prominent Bolsheviks, Bogdanov and Lunacharsky. These 'seekers' were also supported by the politically muddled Maxim Gorky, who, for health reasons, was now living on the isle of Capri.

Bogdanov had been trying to establish a reputation as a philosopher for some years with the publication of a number of articles and even books on the subject. However, such ideas represented, not an advance but a return towards the philosophical agnosticism of Immanuel Kant. This philosophy took an agnostic, half-way house position between materialism and idealism, saying that the objective world does exist outside of human experience but cannot be understood as it is a 'thing-in-itself'.

"All the philistine trends in Social-Democracy are most of all at war with philosophical materialism, they lean towards Kant, neo-Kantianism, the critical philosophy", wrote Lenin to Gorky.[16] In other words, they leaned towards idealism.

These ideas were made fashionable at this time by Ernst Mach, the Austrian physicist and philosopher, as well as the subjective idealism of Richard Avenarius, a German-Swiss philosopher. They independently promoted Empirio-criticism, a theory intending to develop a 'natural

62. Ernst Mach   63. Richard Avenarius

concept of the world' based on 'pure experience' and constituted a form of subjective idealism.

"They were difficult times", commented Krupskaya, summing up the mood at the time.[17] This search for 'new ideas', this soul-searching, was a reflection of the despondency within the intelligentsia. It was an attempt to quench their thirst with salt water and was a reflection of the dispirited moods amongst the petty bourgeoisie. This social layer, squeezed between the proletariat and the bourgeoisie, is organically prone to instability.

Under the influence of the working class, the intelligentsia can be drawn to the ideas of revolutionary socialism. This is the case in periods of revolutionary advance. But in periods of retreat, the organic instability of the petty-bourgeois intellectuals, always open to alien class pressures, renders them an unreliable ally of the proletariat. Their initial unbounded enthusiasm for the revolution soon gives way to an equally unbounded disillusionment, pessimism and surrender to reaction.

This is precisely what happened in Russia following the defeat of the 1905 Revolution, when psychological reaction found its expression even in the rarefied atmosphere of philosophy. The mood of mysticism that became prevalent among a layer of the intelligentsia was echoed in the philosophical revisionism of Bogdanov, Lunacharsky and others, who attempted to smuggle in the fashionable notions of subjective idealism into Marxism through the back door.

This philosophical backsliding was expressed in a revisionist symposium called *Studies in the Philosophy of Marxism*. "Perhaps we have gone astray, but we are seeking", stated Lunacharsky, reflecting this ideological confusion.[18] This declaration was a direct challenge to Marxism and Lenin had no alternative but to take up the struggle against them. He stated:

> ... some Vperyodists long with all their heart and soul to drag the proletariat *back*, to the ideas of bourgeois philosophy (Machism), while others are indifferent to philosophy and merely demand 'complete freedom'... for Machism.[19]

Lenin wrote to Gorky in February 1908 that while he did not wish to rush into print, he strenuously objected to the compilation of articles put out by Bogdanov, Lunacharsky and others:

> Now the *Studies in the Philosophy of Marxism* have appeared. I have read all the articles except Suvorov's (I am reading it now), and every article made me furiously indignant. No, no, this is not Marxism! Our empirio-critics, empirio-monists, and empirio-symbolists are floundering in a bog. To try to persuade the reader that 'belief' in the reality of the external world is 'mysticism' (Bazarov); to confuse in the most disgraceful manner materialism with Kantianism (Bazarov and Bogdanov); to preach a variety of agnosticism (empirio-criticism) and idealism (empirio-monism); to teach the workers 'religious atheism' and 'worship' of the higher human potentialities (Lunacharsky); to declare Engels's teaching on dialectics to be mysticism (Berman); to draw from the stinking well of some French 'positivists' or other, of agnostics or metaphysicians, the devil take them, with their 'symbolic theory of cognition' (Yushkevich)! No, really, it's too much. To be sure, we ordinary Marxists are not well up in philosophy, but why insult us by serving this stuff up to us as the philosophy of Marxism! I would rather let myself be drawn and quartered than consent to collaborate in an organ or body that preaches such things.[20]

Lenin had differences with Bogdanov on the question of philosophy over a number of years, but he tended to hold back. When Bogdanov joined the Bolsheviks in 1904, he sent Lenin a copy of the first volume of his work on philosophy, *Empiriomonism*, which leaned towards neo-Kantism.

Lenin strongly disagreed with Bogdanov's approach, but, given the recent split, he felt that this was not the time to engage in a battle over philosophy. That would have to wait until later. Of much greater importance to the Party was to arm and consolidate the cadres against opportunism. At the time, Bogdanov played a key role in this fight. Lenin was keen to harness his skills and not provoke a clash.

But as soon as Bogdanov tried to promote his philosophical ideas within the Party, especially in this period of retreat and ideological confusion, Lenin had little choice but to declare war on subjective idealism. He understood that philosophical questions could not be separated, in the final analysis, from political ones. The challenge to dialectical materialism would inevitably become a challenge to the whole of Marxism.

Although Lenin was always modest about the extent of his knowledge of philosophy, he was certainly equipped to deal with these questions. He had studied philosophy when he was first in exile, especially the writings by Marx, Engels and Plekhanov. After that, he went on to study GWF Hegel, Ludwig Feuerbach and Kant. However, before engaging with Bogdanov and the others, he wanted to properly prepare the ground.

In order to write a comprehensive reply, he travelled to London to carry out extensive research in the library of the British Museum, where he found a wealth of material. "Ilyich was pleased with his trip to London", wrote Krupskaya, "where he had succeeded in collecting the necessary material and working it up."[21]

'Materialism and Empirio-criticism'

Lenin completed writing his reply to Bogdanov and the Machians in the autumn of 1908, but it did not appear until May 1909, under the title of *Materialism and Empirio-criticism*. Its subtitle was 'Critical Comments on a Reactionary Philosophy'.

To give an idea of the extent of his research, the list of sources quoted or mentioned by Lenin in his book exceeds 200 titles. The book, composed of over 350 pages, turned out to be a classic of Marxism, although, as expected, it was disparaged and dismissed by its petty-bourgeois critics, who knew nothing of Marxism.

Lenin explained that the ideas of Mach and Avenarius represented a continuation of the same idealism of Bishop Berkeley, writing in the early eighteenth century.

Lenin analyses Berkeley's ideas and early on defined the two great schools of philosophy of materialism and idealism, explaining that materialism is the recognition of the primacy of matter. It accepts the existence of 'objects in themselves', or outside the mind and independent of it. Ideas and sensations are copies or images of those material objects. The opposite doctrine (idealism) asserts, on the contrary, that the material world is only a crude reflection of the Idea, which exists eternally (this is, of course, just another name for God).

These two great schools of thought have constituted the predominant trends in philosophy for two millennia. But, in addition, there is a third tendency – a confused set of ideas that we can describe as subjective idealism, which asserts that the material world does not exist except as objects of perception; nothing exists outside the mind and what we think of as material objects are merely 'combinations of sensations', or, to use the expression of the English logical positivist AJ Ayer, "sense contents".

This was the standpoint of Mach and Avenarius, which influenced the philosophical revisionism of Bogdanov, Lunacharsky and the others who Lenin subjected to a detailed criticism in *Materialism and Empirio-criticism*, where he uses Engels' description of their confusion as "a pauper's broth of eclecticism".[22]

For the supporters of Empirio-criticism, the world consists only of our sensations. But the very existence of sensations presupposes a material brain and a nervous system, that is, the existence of human beings. And Lenin asks the obvious question: did the natural world exist prior to humans? If one accepts the arguments of the subjective idealists, if there was nobody to see, hear, smell or touch it, logically, the world could not have existed. This simple question is a particularly annoying one for the philosophy of Mach and Avenarius:

> Natural science positively asserts that the earth once existed in such a state that no man or any other creature existed or could have existed on it. Organic matter is a later phenomenon, the fruit of a long evolution. It follows that there was no sentient matter, no 'complexes of sensations', no *self* that was supposedly 'indissolubly' connected with the environment in accordance with Avenarius' doctrine. Matter is primary, and thought, consciousness, sensation are products of a very high development. Such is the materialist theory of knowledge, to which natural science instinctively subscribes.[23]

Lenin goes on to quote Plekhanov on materialism:

> Idealism says that without subject there is no object. The history of the earth shows that the object existed long before the subject appeared, i.e. long before the appearance of organisms possessing a perceptible degree of consciousness... The history of development reveals the truth of materialism.[24]

All of human knowledge comes from sensual experience. I interpret the world through my senses. This is an elementary fact. But, our senses are not separate from our material body, which in turn exists in a material world. Objective

64. Immanuel Kant   65. Bishop George Berkeley

reality is the source of this perception and not the other way around. And the final proof of all sense perception is human practice.

Lenin comments with brilliance and profundity on a host of philosophical questions in *Materialism and Empirio-criticism*, including causality, the relationship between accident and necessity, and the nature of time and space. The idea of beings outside of time and space is pure idealistic nonsense, and is the basis of the subjective idealism of Bishop Berkeley, who, in the eighteenth century, attempted to disprove materialism by asserting the non-existence of the physical world. Nature, explained Lenin, can only exist in time and space.

> The teachings of science on the structure of matter, on the chemical composition of food, on the atom and the electron, may and constantly do become obsolete, but the truth that man is unable to subsist on ideas and to beget children by Platonic love alone never becomes obsolete. And a philosophy that denies the objective reality of time and space is as absurd, as intrinsically rotten and false as is the denial of these latter truths.[25]

Lenin concluded his book by emphasising that philosophy was not merely an abstract question with no relevance to politics, but a manifestation of the ideological struggle between antagonistic classes. He writes:

… behind the epistemological scholasticism of empirio-criticism one must not fail to see the struggle of parties in philosophy, a struggle which in the last analysis reflects the tendencies and ideology of the antagonistic classes in modern society.[26]

The struggle against these alien class ideas was at bottom a struggle to maintain a firm proletarian revolutionary line. It was a battle for the very soul of the Party. As Trotsky explains:

Thus Lenin's constant revolutionary struggle, in which he never lost sight of the smallest practical details, went hand in hand with his equally constant theoretical controversies, in which he attained to the greatest heights of comprehensive generalisations.[27]

In December 1908, Lenin, together with Krupskaya, left Geneva for Paris, where he stayed and worked until April 1909 on correcting the proofs of *Materialism and Empirio-criticism*. In this work, he was assisted by his sister Anna in Moscow, who read the proofs and then sent them back to him to check. He had to agree to tone down some passages of the work so as not to give the tsarist censorship an excuse for prohibiting its publication. It was finally published in Russia in May with a print-run of 2,000 copies.

Split with ultra-lefts

In December 1908, a Party Conference was held that brought together both Bolsheviks and Mensheviks under one roof. However, given the objective difficulties, only two delegates were able to attend from within Russia. Following a heated debate, it was finally agreed to establish a common paper for the Party, with an editorial board composed of Lenin, Zinoviev, Lev Kamenev, Martov and Julian Marchlewski.

Lenin always wanted to renew relations with Martov whenever possible. However, this didn't last long as the pressure from the opportunist Fyodor Dan – who was a different type of Menshevik altogether – undermined this collaboration.

Furthermore, within the Bolshevik faction, the troubles with the ultra-lefts still persisted. As Krupskaya explained:

They were difficult times. In Russia the organisations were going to pieces. The police, with the aid of agent provocateurs, had arrested the leading Party workers. Big meetings and conferences became impossible… The masses withdrew into themselves.

She added: "These moods provided a favourable soil for otzovism."[28]

Finally, by February 1909, relations had completely broken down between the Mensheviks and Bolsheviks, and the Bolsheviks were also openly split.

The Liquidators, Ultimatumists, Otzovists and now the 'God-builders', headed by Bogdanov and Lunacharsky, had coalesced as a united grouping around the journal *Vperyod*. They openly accused Lenin of being an opportunist who represented 'right-wing' Bolshevism. Their factional activities stepped up, which severely disrupted the practical work within Russia. In fact, the Party was plagued with endless faction fights, not only involving Liquidators and Boycottists, but also Conciliators within both factions.

The Bolsheviks had maintained their own paper, *Proletary*, which had been established in August 1906. Under Lenin's guidance, an extended editorial board was established which had also included Bogdanov and others. He, after all, had been one of Lenin's closest collaborators in the Bolshevik faction.

Now, however, Bogdanov was promoting his revisionist ideas in *Vperyod*, under the guise of Bolshevism. This deception angered Lenin, who believed a red line should be drawn between *Proletary* and *Vperyod*. His experience soon convinced him that a split was inevitable. However, this view was not shared by a significant wing of the Bolshevik faction, which stubbornly clung to the illusion that unity was possible, at least with the left wing of Menshevism.

The Conciliators were what one might describe as 'unity' mongers – those who stood for unity at almost any price. In practice, they were attempting to reconcile the irreconcilable. Trotsky, who at this time still had illusions in unity, was the main spokesman for this trend.

This inevitably brought him into sharp conflict with Lenin, who was alarmed by the increasingly close links between Trotsky and the Bolshevik Conciliators. In reality, much of the bitter invective of Lenin against Trotsky at this time was directed against Bogdanov and other leading members of the Bolshevik faction, who he did not wish to attack publicly. But no amount of diplomacy could disguise the fact that relations between Bogdanov and Lenin became very strained. Krupskaya wrote:

> The conflict within the group was a nerve-wracking business. I remember Ilyich once coming home after having had words with the otzovists. He looked awful, and even his tongue seemed to have turned grey.[29]

Lenin wrote to Vorovsky, a close collaborator:

> A split with Bogdanov is imminent. The true cause is offence at the sharp criticism of his philosophical views at lectures (not at all in the newspaper). Now Bogdanov is hunting out every kind of difference of opinion...

The storm will burst very soon. A fight at the coming conference is inevitable. A split is highly probable.[30]

Lenin was not sure whether he would win a majority against Bogdanov and the boycottists. For him, it was balanced on a knife's edge. If he lost and was in a minority, he even said he would leave the Bolshevik faction. This was how dangerous the situation had become. "I shall leave the faction as soon as the policy of the 'Left' and of true 'boycottism' gets the upper hand", he wrote to Vorovsky.[31]

But that was the worst-case scenario. The immediate task was to pursue the struggle with vigour. As Lenin explained: "One cannot skip over or avoid this crisis, one can only survive it by means of persistent struggle…"[32]

However, given eighteen months of fruitlessly trying to convince the ultra-lefts, a meeting of the enlarged editorial board, which constituted the Bolshevik Centre, was called for June. This vital meeting lasted nearly ten days and resolutions were passed against the Boycotters and 'God-builders', which represented "a distortion of scientific socialism", a harmful mixture of extreme right and extreme 'left' positions.

The meeting went on to condemn the grouping established by Bogdanov and called for Party unity. But Bogdanov refused to submit to the resolutions. It was then that Bogdanov was removed from the editorial board and expelled from the Bolshevik faction.

It is important to remember that, right up to 1912, the Bolsheviks did not constitute a separate party in Russia. They always saw themselves as a faction of the Russian Social Democratic Labour Party, although they operated under their own factional discipline, with complete political and organisational independence.

To promote their activities, Bogdanov and Lunacharsky organised their own faction and established a separate Party school in Capri, where the writer Maxim Gorky was living, then a school in Bologna. These were not 'Party' schools on Marxism, as claimed, but ones that promoted their factional views. These schools were condemned by the Bolsheviks. When worker-students invited Lenin to attend them, he refused, explaining their factional and idealistic nature. He replied to Gorky: "It is useless and harmful for me to come: I *cannot* and will not talk to people who are preaching the union of scientific socialism and religion."[33]

In response, Lenin established his own school in Longjumeau, just outside Paris, to promote genuine Marxism. A number of the Capri students left the Bogdanov school, repelled by its 'God-building' views, and travelled to Paris to join Lenin's school. After this, they went back to Russia as representatives of Lenin's Bolsheviks.

But the situation within the RSDLP was becoming extremely difficult. Those who remained in the camp of Bolshevism numbered only a few dozen and the number Lenin could reach by correspondence or by agent numbered about thirty or forty at most.

Lenin increasingly felt the pressures of this situation. In a letter to Gorky, he admitted: "Life in exile is now a hundred times harder than it was before the revolution. Life in exile and squabbling are inseparable."[34] Nevertheless, despite all the difficulties, Lenin was more hopeful than before:

> But the squabbling will pass away; nine-tenths of it remains abroad; it is an accessory feature. The development of the Party, the development of the Social-Democratic movement goes forward despite all the devilish difficulties of the present situation.

He concluded:

> The purging of the Social-Democratic Party from *its* dangerous 'deviations', from liquidationism and otzovism *goes forward* steadfastly; within the framework of unity it *has progressed considerably farther* than before. [...]
>
> ... the Social-Democratic movement *as a whole* is coping with them openly and will overcome them honestly.[35]

A Central Committee Plenum of the Party was held in January 1910 and lasted three weeks. This was more in the character of a conference. Given the poor state of affairs, there was again an overwhelming pressure to unite the factions. In the negotiations, Lenin was firm but tactful. "Ilyich believed that the utmost concession should be made on organisational issues without yielding an inch of ground on fundamental issues", explained Krupskaya.[36]

An agreement was finally reached to unite the factions on condition that the factions were to dissolve. In doing so, the Bolsheviks agreed to close their newspaper, *Proletary*. More reluctantly, the Bolsheviks agreed that their funds – obtained by 'expropriations' and other means – were to be handed over temporarily to a committee of 'trustees' set up by the International, which included Kautsky, Clara Zetkin and Franz Mehring. This, however, would present difficulties for the Bolsheviks, as events would soon prove.

14. Factions Disbanded

The concessions to bring about Party unity, including the dissolution of factions, made Lenin very uneasy. However, he felt he had no alternative but to accept them. He was under pressure from the large number of 'conciliators' within Bolshevik ranks, including within the Central Committee. This tendency was led by Iosif Dubrovinsky, who pressed for unity at all costs. They, in turn, linked up with Plekhanov's Menshevik pro-Party faction.

As a result, once again, Lenin found himself in a minority. Soon after the Central Committee plenum, he wrote to his sister Anna, briefly outlining his views:

> We have been having 'stormy' times lately, but they have ended with an attempt at peace with the Mensheviks – yes, yes, strange as it may seem; we have closed down the factional newspaper and are trying harder to promote *unity*. We shall see whether it can be done…[1]

Trotsky, who was the 'arch-conciliator' in calling for unity, had established his own widely read paper with the iconic name *Pravda* (*Truth*), published in Vienna. The Central Committee decided to make Trotsky's paper the official Party organ, which would receive Party funding. Kamenev, Lenin's close collaborator, was then chosen to become a member of its editorial board. Lenin's view about the whole affair was expressed in a letter to Gorky:

> At the Central Committee plenum (the 'long plenum' – three weeks of agony, all nerves were on edge, the devil to pay!) to these serious and deep-lying factors, which were by no means generally recognised, were added minor, petty factors – a mood of 'conciliation in general' (without any clear idea with whom, for what,

and how); hatred of the Bolshevik Centre for its implacable ideological struggle; squabbling on the part of the Mensheviks, who were spoiling for a fight, and as a result – an infant covered with blisters.

And so we have to suffer.[2]

A resolution was passed by the plenum condemning liquidationism and otzovism, but the unity of the Party was very fragile. The responsibility for this lay squarely with the Mensheviks. The Bolsheviks had already expelled the Otzovists from their faction. But the Mensheviks, given the support for liquidationism in their ranks, proved incapable of eliminating this problem. While, as agreed, the Bolsheviks disbanded their faction, the Mensheviks continued to operate theirs and even maintained their paper.

Lenin's scepticism towards the proposed unity – and the difficulties that went with it – became more pronounced. He was nevertheless still prepared to adopt a wait-and-see approach and willing for events to take their course.

Since the Mensheviks had ignored the agreements, the Bolsheviks reinstated their faction. As long as the Menshevik liquidators were still prevalent within its ranks, real unity within the Party would always prove impossible.

Under such conditions, the faction fight, rather than abating, began to intensify. "The unity of all groups, achieved with such difficulty in January 1910, swiftly began to break up", commented Krupskaya.[3] Kamenev, who had now clashed with Trotsky, ended up resigning from the *Pravda* editorial board.

It was around this time that Lenin firmly drew the conclusion that unity was a complete waste of time and a split with the Mensheviks was inevitable – and desirable. There had been a whole string of attempts at fruitless unity, but without success. However, it took a further two years to carry through the split to a final conclusion, mainly due to the resistance within the Bolshevik faction itself. Lenin looked back over these years much later:

> The years of reaction (1907-10). Tsarism was victorious. All the revolutionary and opposition parties were smashed. Depression, demoralisation, splits, discord, defection, and pornography took the place of politics. There was an ever greater drift towards philosophical idealism; mysticism became the garb of counter-revolutionary sentiments. At the same time, however, it was this great defeat that taught the revolutionary parties and the revolutionary class a real and very useful lesson, a lesson in historical dialectics, a lesson in an understanding of the political struggle, and in the art and science of waging that struggle. It is at moments of need that one learns who one's friends are. Defeated armies learn their lesson.[4]

Difficulties

The severe weaknesses and chronic difficulties facing the Party were a constant feature throughout this period. Just to hold things together was a continuous uphill battle.

Towards the end of February or beginning of March, Lenin drafted a letter to the 'trustees', to whom the funds of the Bolsheviks had been handed over in accordance with the January agreement, explaining the breakdown of unity within the Party. He also wrote a letter to Nikifor Vilonov, which stated that "the fog of conciliatory unity among us is beginning to disperse."[5]

At the same time, the objective situation was changing. This could be seen from the increasing number of strikes. In the month of January 1905 alone, the number of strikes was 400,000. In the three years of revolution, the number of strikes, although declining, was historically very high. There were 3 million in 1905, 1 million in 1906 and 750,000 in 1907. But in 1908 there was a drastic fall to 176,000 and in 1909, 64,000. But then the figures began to climb and, by the end of 1910, there were the beginnings of a new upsurge in the class struggle. Lenin followed these developments closely and wrote a long article on strike statistics in Russia:

> And now, after three years of the most wanton riot of counter-revolution, we see that the *mass of the people*, those most oppressed, downtrodden, benighted, intimidated by persecutions in every form, are beginning to raise their heads again, to reawaken and resume the struggle. Three years of executions, persecutions and savage reprisals have destroyed tens of thousands of the 'enemies' of the autocracy, hundreds of thousands have been imprisoned or exiled, many hundreds of thousands more have been intimidated. But millions and tens of millions of people are no longer what they were before the revolution. *Never* yet in the history of Russia have these millions experienced such instructive and vivid lessons, such open class struggle. That a new and profound underlying ferment has set in among these millions and tens of millions is evident from this summer's strikes and the recent demonstrations.[6]

In this period, the Mensheviks were plagued by their own internal difficulties, especially with liquidationism. As a result, a 'pro-Party' faction emerged within their ranks – headed by Plekhanov – that was against liquidationism and defended the need for the underground illegal party. "Why are you offended by the charge of liquidationism when in fact you are very much guilty of this sin?", asked Plekhanov of the Mensheviks.[7] Liquidationism, Plekhanov stated, leads to the "slough of the most disgraceful opportunism".[8]

In reply, the Menshevik leaders ridiculed Plekhanov, saying he had become the "bard of the underground".[9]

This development of a 'pro-Party' faction among the Mensheviks was highly significant and heartily welcomed by Lenin. To carry the work forward, Lenin favoured a rapprochement with Plekhanov. This, he hoped, would become an alliance of all the pro-Party forces that would help to re-establish the Russian Party on firmer foundations. His correspondence in this period showed how tactful he was in attempting to reach an agreement with the pro-Party Mensheviks and with the temperamental Plekhanov in particular. Lenin felt they needed to take one step at a time.

"We managed to smooth things over and *for the time being* we can and must work with Plekhanov", explained Lenin in relation to one incident, "but *formal* unions and meetings are premature and could spoil everything."[10] Regarding a bloc with Plekhanov, I think you are quite right that we should be in favour of it", he wrote. "Since 1909 I have been *wholly* in favour of a *rapprochement* with the Plekhanovites. We can and should build the Party only with the Plekhanovites…"[11]

Given the dire state of things within the Party, it was natural that this development should be seized upon by Lenin. Weakened by demoralisation and arrests, the Party had been split up into tiny groupings and factions as people had begun to lose hope in the cause. The Mensheviks' capitulation to liquidationism meant the open pronouncement of the death of the Party. Therefore, Plekhanov's voice in defending a pro-Party line, although a Menshevik one, was greatly welcomed by Lenin. It was as if Plekhanov was reverting to the good old days, when he had some revolutionary vision. As Lenin explained:

> Plekhanov and I differed sharply, and we still differ on questions of what steps *that* organisation of yesterday, working on the basis of *that* movement of yesterday, should have taken at one juncture or another; but we are drawn together by the struggle against those who *today* deny the very *principles* of yesterday's movement (this includes also the question of hegemony, of which more later), deny the very *foundations* of yesterday's organisation.[12]

Conciliationism

Arising from the January Central Committee decision, Lenin had previously established ties with Trotsky's paper, *Pravda*, but these had floundered before the end of the year due to Trotsky's continued conciliationism. As a result, there were many bitter words at this time between Lenin and Trotsky. For

Lenin, when clarity was vital, Trotsky's conciliationism was seen as the worst of all worlds. He therefore attacked Trotsky in the strongest language, accusing him of being the "match-maker" and "unity-monger".

In these rows, Lenin never held anything back, and neither did Trotsky. "I personally, for example, had a big fight with Trotsky, a regular fierce battle in 1903-05 when he was a Menshevik", wrote Lenin to Gorky.[13] In fact, Trotsky had broken with the Mensheviks by 1904 over their attitude to the liberals. Nevertheless, it was due to his conciliationism, *and this alone*, that Trotsky refused to join the Bolshevik faction.

Trotsky was hoping that events would unify the Party by bringing together the best elements within Bolshevism and Menshevism. Such a unification would, he believed, eliminate the extremes of liquidationism and ultra-leftism. In the end, despite the many attempts, Trotsky's efforts proved completely fruitless. The differences between the factions were much too great.

On the other hand, Lenin's aim was to forge Bolshevism into a weapon that would completely cleanse the Party and eliminate all its defects. Given the trajectory of the Mensheviks, this approach to building the revolutionary party was the only viable one, which, later, Trotsky fully accepted.

Lenin nevertheless fully understood Trotsky's conciliationism. While it was wrong, it was at least consistent. As Lenin himself explained:

Conciliationism is the totality of moods, strivings and views that are *indissolubly* bound up with the very *essence* of the historical task confronting the RSDLP during the period of the counter-revolution of 1908-11. That is why, during this period, a number of Social-Democrats, proceeding from essentially different premises, 'lapsed' into conciliationism. Trotsky expressed conciliationism more consistently than anyone else. He was probably the only one who attempted to give the trend a theoretical foundation [...] For a long time now, Trotsky – who at one moment has wavered more to the side of the Bolsheviks and at another more to that of the Mensheviks – has been persistently carrying on propaganda for an agreement (or compromise) between *all* and sundry factions.[14]

At this time, this struggle over conciliationism could be a very bitter conflict. "Ilyich simply could not stand this diffuse, unprincipled conciliationism", explained Krupskaya. "Conciliationism with anyone and everyone, which was tantamount to surrendering one's positions at the height of the struggle."[15]

Later, Trotsky honestly admitted his mistake. He frankly admitted that Lenin had been right all along in his attitude to these questions. In the end,

66. Lenin in Paris, 1910

he agreed there could be no unity between Bolsheviks and Mensheviks. But there is nothing completely black and white in life or in politics.

As we have seen, Lenin also tried to establish a bloc with Plekhanov's 'pro-Party' faction. And when he returned to Russia in 1917, Lenin made a final effort to reach agreement with the Menshevik-Internationalists, led by Martov. That attempt proved fruitless, as a result of Martov's organic tendency towards vacillation.

Nevertheless, Lenin stated that in 1917 Bolshevism drew towards itself the best elements of the working class, by which he meant the Inter-District Group (Mezhraiontsy), a non-Party organisation including, not only Trotsky, but many of the others with whom Lenin had clashed before 1914. But we will deal with that later.

The end of 1910 was a turning point. It represented the beginning of a new revolutionary upsurge. The Bolshevik newspaper *Mysl* (*Thought*) began to appear in Moscow, as did *Zvezda* (*The Star*), the paper of the Duma's Social-Democratic faction. Lenin outlined an optimistic perspective: "Now they have begun to rise. This upsurge may be rapid, or it may be slow and fitful, but in any case it is leading to a revolution."[16]

Despite this, the Liquidators were still making ground in Russia and "sprang up right and left like mushrooms", according to Krupskaya.[17] The Liquidators had certain advantages; they had developed a strong legal centre in the interior and had acquired greater resources – as compared to the Bolsheviks, who had to fight for every inch of ground. The work of *agent provocateurs*, which was a constant problem, made life even more difficult for the Party. For instance, in April 1911, the newspaper *Mysl* was closed down and later *Zvezda* stopped publishing.

From 1907 to 1910, Bolshevism had experienced a whole series of departures, desertions, splits, as well as individual and group capitulations. But Lenin viewed this as far from completely negative. Lenin often quoted Lassalle's letter to Marx, stating that the party is strengthened by purging itself. Above all, Lenin taught the Bolsheviks not to be frightened by such splits and withdrawals, even when it involved the most 'respected' names. Under his leadership, they remained steadfast in the face of these adversities.

Prague Conference

Not long after the agreement of the plenum in 1910 had collapsed, the international 'trustees' of Bolshevik funds had resigned. Consequently, the Bolsheviks demanded the return of their printing plant, money, and other assets. Lenin devoted all his energies to establishing an Organising Committee within Russia in order to rally all pro-Party workers, with a view to convening a Party conference. The time had come to part company with the Mensheviks, who were holding back the Party's development.

The Sixth Party Conference was eventually called in January 1912 in Prague and marked a decisive stage in the Party's development. It was the first real Party gathering held with workers from the interior since 1908.

Lenin believed the Party had to face up to coming events, with its eyes firmly fixed on the future. There was only one way forward: a radical break with conciliationism. A decisive break with Menshevism was now inevitable.

All of his experiences, right from the founding of *Iskra*, had prepared Lenin for this moment. He *alone* had the foresight and determination to carry things through to the logical conclusion. Even so, this was not at all straightforward.

The Prague Conference of 1912 was the moment of truth. Although attended by only about twenty delegates in number, under Lenin's direction, it took the decisive step of establishing Bolshevism as an independent Party.

The conference declared itself as a Party Congress and expelled the Liquidators, the *Nasha Zarya* and *Dyelo Zhizni* groups, who had, by their actions, "placed themselves outside the Party".[18] Apart from two pro-Party Mensheviks who had arrived from Russia, the rest of the delegates were staunch Bolsheviks, largely steeled during the period of reaction. They took the step of condemning the anti-Party groups abroad, including the Mensheviks, which, from now on, had no right to claim the name of the Party. Instead, the conference decided that the Bolsheviks alone were the genuine Russian Social-Democratic Labour Party.

This decision marked the end of Bolshevism's existence as a faction within the Party. The Bolsheviks became the Party, and the Party *was* now the RSDLP. Given their largely independent existence within the Party since the 1903 Congress, the Bolshevik faction now possessed all the traits of a party. The Prague decision, in reality, simply put a formal stamp on this reality. All further talk of unity with the Menshevik Liquidators was now at an end. This final split was a forerunner of the future split two years later throughout the Second International between the revolutionaries and the reformists.

The delegates debated key questions about immediate tasks, the elections to the Fourth Duma, organisational forms and structures, and other questions. In the absence of the boycottists, the debate on participation in the Duma elections was carried out without the previous rancour and animosity. The Party unanimously agreed to take advantage of every legal opening, including elections to the Duma. This was to result, despite the heavy restrictions, in the Bolsheviks successfully winning the workers' curias in the elections in all six provinces.

The Prague conference also took the decision to raise the funds to launch a legal daily newspaper, *Pravda*, which was launched on 5 May 1912. The newspaper was mainly paid for by the kopecks and half-kopecks collected by the workers in the factories. This step, however, served to further embitter relations with Trotsky, who was angered at the 'theft' of the name of his 'non-factional' paper, published in Vienna.

The launch of the Bolshevik *Pravda* in Russia at this time was very opportune. In particular, it coincided with the earth-shattering news in April of the massacre of 270 strikers at the Lena goldfields in Siberia. This had sparked widespread protests and strikes throughout the country, events not witnessed since the days of 1905. This marked a turning point in the movement and, once again, opened a new chapter in the class struggle.

"Ilyich became another man", commented Krupskaya. "His nerves were steadier, he became more concentrated, and gave more thought to the tasks that now confronted the Russian working-class movement." She explained:

> Only a few months before this Vladimir Ilyich had said with a touch of sadness to Anna Ilyinichna, who had arrived in Paris: "I don't know whether I'll live to see the next rise of the tide", and now he felt the gathering storm, the movement of the masses themselves, with all his being.[19]

The support for *Pravda* within Russia grew by leaps and bounds. The paper was inundated with hundreds of letters and reports sent by workers that gave life to *Pravda*. The Mensheviks steadily lost ground as the '*Pravda* epidemic', as it became known, began to spread far and wide.

As expected, the Mensheviks attacked and ridiculed the Bolshevik conference, saying it was impotent and would play no role in the events. In March, the German Social-Democratic paper, *Vorwärts*, also published a malicious article against the conference. But they had misjudged the mood.

In response to the Bolshevik Prague conference, Trotsky, 'the conciliator', tried to convene a conference of all Social-Democrats in Vienna in August, in the vain hope this initiative would reunite the different factions. But, as the Bolsheviks refused to attend, the initiative was stillborn. The so-called 'August bloc', as it was known, soon collapsed. True to form, Lenin mercilessly attacked this initiative and, above all, Trotsky, the organiser of the 'bloc'. Trotsky explained later:

> I participated actively in this bloc. In a certain sense I created it. Politically I differed with the Mensheviks on all fundamental questions. I also differed with the ultra-left Bolsheviks, the *Vperyodists*. In the general tendency of politics I stood far more closely to the Bolsheviks. But I was against the Leninist 'regime' because I had not yet learned to understand that in order to realise the revolutionary goal a firmly welded centralised party is indispensable. And so I formed this episodic bloc consisting of heterogeneous elements which was directed against the proletarian wing of the party.

In the August bloc the liquidators had their own faction, the *Vperyodists* also had something resembling a faction. I stood isolated, having co-thinkers but no faction. Most of the documents were written by me and through avoiding principled differences had as their aim the creation of a semblance of unanimity upon 'concrete political questions.' Not a word about the past! Lenin subjected the August bloc to merciless criticism and the harshest blows fell to my lot. Lenin proved that inasmuch as I did not agree politically with either the Mensheviks or the *Vperyodists* my policy was adventurism. This was severe but it was true.

As 'mitigating circumstances' let me mention the fact that I had set as my task not to support the right or ultra-left factions against the Bolsheviks but to unite the party as a whole. The Bolsheviks too were invited to the August conference. But since Lenin flatly refused to unite with the Mensheviks (in which he was completely correct) I was left in an unnatural bloc with the Mensheviks and the *Vperyodists*. The second mitigating circumstance is this, that the very phenomenon of Bolshevism as the genuine revolutionary party was then developing for the first time – in the practice of the Second International there were no precedents. But I do not thereby seek in the least to absolve myself from guilt. Notwithstanding the conception of permanent revolution which undoubtedly disclosed the correct perspective, I had not freed myself at that period especially in the organisational sphere from the traits of a petty-bourgeois revolutionist. I was sick with the disease of conciliationism toward Menshevism and with a distrustful attitude toward Leninist centralism. Immediately after the August conference the bloc began to disintegrate into its component parts. Within a few months I was not only in principle but organisationally outside the bloc.[20]

The split, leading to the Bolsheviks and Mensheviks becoming two separate parties, was irrevocable. However, there were still complaints from inside Russia, mainly from the committee-men, about 'squabbles' abroad that were alienating workers. One such Bolshevik from the Caucasus wrote to Moscow about "the 'storm in a teacup' abroad".[21] His name was Dzhugashvili, alias Stalin. This revealed his contemptuous attitude towards what was happening among the 'practicos', who displayed little interest in the broader political questions. Lenin complained to Sergo Ordzhonikidze and others about this light-minded approach:

> Don't be light-hearted about the campaign of the Liquidators abroad. It is a great mistake when people simply dismiss what goes on abroad with a wave of the hand and 'send it to hell'.[22]

Problems with 'Pravda'

However, the influence of Liquidationism was far from over, and, in fact, made itself felt even within the editorial board of *Pravda*. The derogatory word 'Liquidator' disappeared from the pages of *Pravda*. Lenin was furious when he discovered that his articles were being censored and references to Liquidationism were themselves 'liquidated' by the editors. He wrote an indignant letter to Molotov, the secretary of the *Pravda* editorial board, in August 1912:

> You write, and as secretary, evidently, on behalf of the editorial board; that "the editorial board in principle considers my article fully acceptable *including the attitude to the Liquidators*". If that is so, why then does *Pravda* stubbornly and systematically cut out any mention of the Liquidators, both in my articles and in the articles of other colleagues??[23]

After further protests, Lenin wrote a letter to the editors (which at that time included Stalin) in October 1912, complaining about its political softness:

> Meanwhile *Pravda* is carrying on now, at an election time, like a sleepy old maid. *Pravda* doesn't know how to fight. It does not attack, it does not persecute either the Cadet or the liquidator.[24]

The editors of *Pravda*, in spite of all of Lenin's criticisms, went as far as publishing a front-page advert welcoming the appearance of the Liquidators' paper, *Zeit*. Lenin could hardly believe his eyes when he saw it. On 7 February 1913, he wrote another letter expressing his outrage and demanding the expulsion of the editors:

> We have received a stupid and insolent letter from the editors [of *Pravda*]. We are not replying. They should be kicked out. [...]

> Reorganisation, or better still the complete expulsion of all the old ones, is absolutely essential. Absurdly conducted. They lavish praise on the Bund and *Zeit*: it's simply disgusting. They can't take the right line against *Luch*. Disgraceful the way they handle articles. Sheer stupidity about *Rabochy Golos*. Simply exasperating...[25]

He later wrote:

> For God's sake avoid such carelessness: in this way you are giving the *very devil* of assistance to all our enemies.[26]

Lenin once again had to reiterate the reactionary nature of Liquidationism, in which he explained that such views were incompatible with Party membership. Despite the protests from *Luch*, the paper of the Menshevik Liquidationists, he explained:

Liquidationism is "an attempt on the part of a group of Party intellectuals to *liquidate* [i.e. dissolve, destroy, abolish, close down] the existing organisation of the Party and replace it at all costs, even at the price of *downright* renunciation of the programme, tactics, and traditions of the Party [i.e. past experience], by a loose association functioning legally [i.e. in conformity with the law, existing 'openly']".

Such was the Party's decision on liquidationism, adopted more than four years ago. [...]

The Party cannot exist unless it defends its existence, unless it unreservedly fights those who want to liquidate it, destroy it, who do not recognise it, who renounce it. This is self-evident.

Anyone who renounces the existing Party in the name of some new party must be told: try, build up a new party, but you cannot remain a member of the old, the present, the existing Party.[27]

Faced with Lenin's intransigence, the new Central Committee carried out a reorganisation of *Pravda* and dispatched Sverdlov to St. Petersburg to take charge with the expressed right to censor articles. But having been cured of liquidationism, the editors soon veered towards the Otzovists! *Pravda* now published a letter, a reply to Lenin, from its leading representative, Bogdanov!

Lenin was understandably furious. He again wrote protesting to the editorial board and threatened to sever all his connections with the paper:

The action of the editors in respect of Mr Bogdanov's distortion of Party history is so scandalous that, to tell the truth, one does not know whether it is possible after this to remain a contributor. [...]

I demand categorically that the enclosed article be printed *in full*. I have always permitted the editors to make changes in a comradely manner, but after Mr Bogdanov's letter, *I do not grant* any right to alter or do anything else of that kind with this article. If you do not print it, pass it on to *Prosveshcheniye*; I insist on having *complete freedom* to fight against the distortion of Party history. We are struggling against liquidationism and *concealing* otzovism – this is such a despicable position that I can only assume that the blunder was due to *lack of knowledge in the matter*.

The editorial board must state that it has convinced itself that Mr Bogdanov expounded the *Vperyod* platform *incorrectly* and gave the *facts* incorrectly.

I insist on an immediate reply. I cannot continue to contribute articles in face of Mr Bogdanov's despicable lying.[28]

This, in effect, was a declaration of war by Lenin on the editors of *Pravda*. The row was only resolved when Kamenev was sent to take over the editorship of the paper, which he edited until it was closed down by the tsarist state in July 1914.

Conciliationist tendencies have always tended to be strongest within the parliamentary field and this was certainly the case within the Bolshevik deputies in the Duma. Elected in December 1912, this group of six deputies was under the pressure of the opportunist environment in the Duma. As a result, their first act was to come to an agreement with the seven Menshevik deputies to write for both *Pravda* and *Luch*, a Menshevik liquidationist paper. The Mensheviks were also using their majority of one in the Social-Democratic Group to impede and dominate the Bolshevik deputies, despite the fact that the latter represented the working-class districts and a far higher proportion of workers than the Mensheviks. Lenin indignantly explained:

> *Over two-thirds* of the workers of Russia support the views and line of the *six* deputies from the worker curia in the Fourth Duma – Badayev, Malinovsky, Muranov, Petrovsky, Samoilov and Shagov. These deputies are backed by the *overwhelming majority* of class-conscious workers who take an active part in politics.[29]

Lenin therefore demanded equal rights for the Bolsheviks within the united Social Democratic Group in the Duma. When the Mensheviks refused, the Bolsheviks had no alternative but to declare themselves a separate political group and act independently. Even then, this separation took almost a year to accomplish owing to resistance from the Bolshevik side.

'Pravda' advances

Despite all the difficulties, the launch of the Bolshevik *Pravda* had been a major step forward for Lenin, who worked to turn it into a real worker's paper. Not only did workers write for it and discuss its articles, but they financed it through regular collections made in the workplaces. Lenin, in particular, closely followed these contributions and statistics as a gauge of the paper's health and a real indication of the deep roots the Bolsheviks were

67. Bolshevik faction of the Fourth Duma
Middle: Petrovsky; top (left to right): Samoilov, Muranov;
bottom: Badayev, Shagov

establishing among the workers. These financial contributions provided an
accurate barometer of its support in the advanced sections of the working
class. Over a period, *Pravda* reached a circulation of between 40,000 and
60,000 daily sales. Lenin was keen to have a campaign to push the figure up
to 100,000 – a real mass workers' paper.

As a legal paper, given the tsarist censorship, it had to tread a thin line
to avoid closure. As a result, it was forced to use round-about terms, for
example, referring to the Social-Democrats as 'Consistent Democrats'. This
was not a problem, as the advanced workers in the factories knew how to
read between the lines and appreciate its content – although some petty-
bourgeois radicals were attracted to the paper as they actually believed they
were 'consistent democrats'! But this ambiguity was a small price to pay under
the circumstances.

A joint conference of the Central Committee and Party officials took place
in the summer of 1913, which reaffirmed the decisions taken at the Prague
Conference. It also pointed "to the huge importance of the legal press for
Social-Democratic agitation and organisation, and therefore calls upon Party
bodies and upon all class-conscious workers to increase their assistance to the
legal press by securing for it the widest possible circulation, and by organising
mass collective subscriptions and regular collections of contributions."[30]

68. Editorial board and staff of *Zvezda* and *Pravda*

Interestingly, the Conference "reaffirms that such contributions are counted as Party membership dues."[31] In other words, workers who gave regular financial support to the paper were regarded as Party members. This showed how far the Party was once again becoming a mass party. It also showed its organisational flexibility in contrast to the membership statutes of 1903. It showed that the Party statutes served to reflect the different stages of the Party's development. In other words, the statutes were viewed not as something static and unchangeable, but flexibly and dynamically, in the spirit of dialectics.

The revival in the class struggle meant that the immediate task confronting the Bolsheviks was to build the Party and sink deep roots in the working class. It would nevertheless remain a vanguard party, embracing the most advanced layers. "The party is the politically conscious, advanced section of the class, it is its vanguard", explained Lenin.[32] The formal membership of the party in 1913 is not known, but according to Lenin it was somewhere between 30,000 and 50,000. Party sympathisers, indicated by those voting for Social-Democratic candidates, were around 300,000 to 500,000. In Russian conditions, these figures show that the Bolshevik Party was developing into a mass party in these years.

This growth was in complete contrast to the Mensheviks, who were floundering and losing ground to the Bolsheviks. By 1914, Lenin estimated

69. Kamenev in 1923   70. Zinoviev's mugshot from 1908

that four-fifths of the advanced workers were following *Pravda*, the vast bulk of these being young workers. These militant layers were to provide the worker cadres of Bolshevism.

It is ironic that the Mensheviks always accused the Bolsheviks of creating a 'sect', while they were supposedly building a 'mass movement'. But while the Mensheviks adapted to every twist and turn of the workers' movement, the Bolsheviks selected and educated cadres for the period ahead. In this, Lenin provided the theoretical leadership that bound the Party together.

With the departure of Krassin, Bogdanov and Lunacharsky, Lenin was forced to rest on a new layer of cadres, such as Kamenev and Zinoviev, to help shape the Party. Unlike Lenin's earlier collaborators, Kamenev and Zinoviev could not be described as Party theoreticians. Nevertheless, under Lenin's guidance they were able to play an important role.

Despite the progress of the Bolsheviks during these years, many weaknesses and difficulties remained. The tsarist authorities repeatedly suspended, banned, fined and closed down *Pravda*, which often reappeared under different names: *Pravda Truda*, *Za Pravdu*, *Proletarskaya Pravda*, *Severnaya Pravda* and *Put Pravdy*. Its editors, collaborators and staff were arrested so frequently that they weren't able to find a proofreader at one point.

However, with each attack, workers collected the money needed to pay the fines and appoint new editors in place of those arrested. Sometimes the police, increasingly vigilant, would stand guard over the printing facilities to

71. Roman Malinovsky

confiscate the first issues of *Pravda* as soon as they came off the press. Despite this, the paper not only survived, but expanded its appeal. Nevertheless, things remained precarious, with regions dislocated and district and local Party committees unable to function. But such difficulties must be put in the context of genuine qualitative advances.

The tsarist secret police, through their spies, knew very well the advances being made by Bolshevism. One of their *agent provocateurs* was the former metal worker, Roman Malinovsky. This tsarist police spy was not only a member of the Bolshevik Central Committee. He was also the leader of the Bolshevik parliamentary faction in the Duma. The information he provided to the Okhrana led to the arrest of a hundred Bolsheviks. The Director of the Police Department in 1913 wrote:

> During the past ten years, the most energetic, courageous element, capable of tireless struggle, resistance and constant organisation, have been ... the organisations and persons concentrating around Lenin...

> The permanent organisational heart and soul of all Party undertakings of any importance is Lenin... The faction of Leninists is always better organised than the others, stronger in its singleness of purpose, more resourceful in propagating its ideas among the workers ... When during the last two years the labour movement

72. Lenin on a walk with Zinoviev and Sergey Bagotsky in Zakopane,
Poland, 1914

began to grow stronger, Lenin and his followers came closer to the workers than others, and he was the first to proclaim purely revolutionary slogans… The Bolshevik circles, nuclei and organisations are now scattered through all the cities. Permanent correspondence and contacts have been established with almost all the factory centres. The Central Committee functions almost regularly and is entirely in the hands of Lenin… In view of the aforesaid, there is nothing surprising in the fact that at the present time the assembling of the entire underground Party is proceeding around the Bolshevik organisations and that indeed the latter really are the Russian Social-Democratic Labour Party.[33]

This report is quoted by Trotsky in his book *Stalin*. Trotsky simply comments: "There is almost nothing to add to this."[34]

Prior to the war, the renewed upsurge in the class struggle was clearly heralding the opening of a new revolutionary period in Russia. Strikes were widespread and barricades were appearing in the capital.

On 22 January 1914, the ninth anniversary of Bloody Sunday, almost a quarter of a million workers went on strike in St. Petersburg, and more throughout the country. *Pravda* was closed down in July 1914 and arrests followed. This, in turn, provoked a massive protest strike in the capital and barricades were again erected. There were repeated armed clashes with the police. Bolshevik headquarters functioned legally and illegally both in Moscow and St. Petersburg, and were in close touch with Lenin, who was now living in Kraków, Poland.

With four-fifths of the advanced working class supporting the Bolsheviks, the Party was in a prime position to lead the movement, on a far higher level than in 1905. Lenin wrote:

> The years 1912-14 marked the beginning of a great new revolutionary upswing in Russia. We again witnessed a great strike movement, the likes of which the world has never known. The number involved in the mass revolutionary strike in 1913 was, at the very lowest estimate, one and a half million, and in 1914 it rose to over two million, approaching the 1905 level. The first barricade battles took place in St. Petersburg, on the eve of the war.
>
> The underground Russian Social-Democratic Labour Party has performed its duty to the International. The banner of internationalism has not wavered in its hands.[35]

However, this prospect of revolution was dramatically cut across by the news of the outbreak of war in early August 1914. According to Martov and Dan:

> The day after the declaration of war the whole political situation had changed at one stroke. Streets, which yesterday were crammed with the ebb and flow of the striking masses, were now full of patriots. Wave after wave of people made their way to the Winter Palace and sank on their knees before the Tsar, who was standing on the balcony...[36]

Overnight, the objective situation dramatically changed and the work of the Party was once again driven deep underground, swamped by the irresistible patriotic wave.

15. War and the Collapse of the Second International

When the First World War broke out, Lenin was living in the provincial town of Poronin, near Kraków. The war had been expected for a long time. The talk of conflict had become ever more belligerent. The increased antagonisms between the imperialist powers, together with the creation of military blocs and alliances, had all pointed towards an almighty conflagration. "For the first time the world is completely divided up, so that in the future *only* redivision is possible", explained Lenin in his book, *Imperialism, the Highest Stage of Capitalism.*[1]

All that was missing from this conflict was a pretext, which was furnished by the assassination of Archduke Franz Ferdinand in Sarajevo, on 28 June. This was followed by the murder of Jean Jaurès, the French Socialist leader, at the hands of a pro-war fanatic.

The assassination of the Archduke detonated a chain-reaction across Europe, as countries began to line up in the opposing warring camps. In early August, Germany formally declared war against Russia, France and Belgium. In response, as part of the Triple Entente, Britain declared hostilities against Germany. In reaction, Austria-Hungary, as part of the Triple Alliance, declared war on Russia, while France and Britain mobilised against Austria-Hungary.

Their intentions were disguised as a 'just war', 'war against aggression', and so on, but the real purpose of the First World War was to redivide the world among the dominant imperialist powers, as Lenin had explained. The events confirmed the words of Clausewitz, that war was "merely the continuation

73. Lenin in Poronin, Poland, August 1914

of politics by other means."[2] A terrible calamity faced the working class. "Although war had been in the air for a long time it came as a shock to all of us", confirmed Krupskaya.[3] This feeling was widespread.

Collapse of the Second International

The question of war had dominated a series of Socialist International congresses. In Stuttgart (1907), Copenhagen (1910), and Basel (1912), resolutions opposed to war were unanimously passed. Not only this, but the International agreed to use the crisis provoked by war to turn the imperialist conflict into a revolutionary struggle against the capitalist order.

So, surely now with the declaration of war, the leaders of the International would respond and call on the working class to resist. However, to everyone's surprise, the exact opposite took place.

On 4 August, the German Social-Democratic Party, the leading body and authority of the Second International, capitulated to the pro-war hysteria and its deputies voted for the Kaiser's war budget. The trade union leaders, in turn, made an agreement with the employers that there would be no strikes or lockouts "for the duration of the hostilities".

This was followed by the leaders of other sections of the International, the French, British, Belgian, and so on, who, instead of standing by their anti-war commitments, slavishly sided with their own ruling classes. This betrayal of working-class internationalism sounded the death knell of the Second International as a revolutionary force. At the decisive hour, when workers' solidarity was essential, the International simply collapsed.

The 'Left' Kautsky had tried to excuse the betrayal, saying that the purpose of the International was for peacetime and not suitable for war. As a result, when they most needed leadership, the workers were left rudderless. They were left to their own fate as the old International disintegrated into warring parties. Europe descended into the bloody abyss of war. Workers now fought and died on the battlefields for the benefit of their own ruling classes.

Some, it seemed, hoped it would be a short war that would be all over by Christmas. But these were forlorn hopes. The 'Great War' would last more than four long years and result in the death of twenty million people and twenty-one million wounded, many crippled and scarred for life. The world, up until that point, had experienced nothing like the scale of such horror, with its modern techniques and the latest weapons of mass destruction.

The betrayal of the leaders of the Second International came as a terrible shock. Lenin had expected the leaders of the Second International to stand by their anti-war declarations, at least in words. So, when he read that the German Social Democracy had voted for the Kaiser's war credits, he was so shocked that he simply refused to believe it. When he received a copy of the German Party newspaper *Vorwärts* confirming the news, he was convinced it was a forgery of the German General Staff.

"It cannot be", he protested. "It must be a forged number. The scoundrels, the German bourgeoisie, have specially published a number of the *Vorwärts* to compel us to go against the International."[4]

Lenin was mistaken. But this small episode graphically encapsulated the widespread shock and disorientation in the ranks of the workers' movement at that time. August 1914 was to go down as one of the greatest of betrayals in the annals of the workers' movement.

The blow was even more shocking because of the colossal authority of the German Social-Democracy internationally. Their betrayal was hardest of all to bear.

"We honestly admit: the possibility of anything even remotely resembling what we witnessed on 4 August 1914 occurred to none of us", Zinoviev recalled.[5] Trotsky reacted in exactly the same way: "I could not even admit the idea that the Social Democracy would simply cower on its belly before a nationalist militarism".[6] Axelrod, the Menshevik leader, said "the news was a terrible, stunning blow".[7]

Bombarded by government propaganda and under the pressure of nationalist hysteria, millions of honest workers were confused and disoriented. They were dragged into supporting the war. The betrayal of their leaders – including 'Lefts' like Kautsky – played a fatal role. Having carried out their betrayal, they then attempted cynically to cover it up with quotes from Marx and Engels, torn out of context and twisted beyond all recognition to suit their purposes.

Opportunism

The German Social-Democracy, originally guided by Marx and Engels, had been at the centre of the international working-class movement. It had pride of place in the Socialist International. Up until August 1914, Lenin had paid homage to the German SPD as the party that had "upheld the revolutionary standpoint in Marxism".[8] At that time, Zinoviev was with Lenin and relates the conversation that passed between them:

> When the war broke out we were living in a god-forsaken little mountain village in Galicia. I remember having a bet with him. I said: "You will see, the German Social Democrats will not dare vote against the war, but will *abstain* in the vote on the war credits." Comrade Lenin replied: "No, they are not such scoundrels as all that. They will not, of course, fight the war, but they will, to ease their conscience, vote against the credits lest the working class rise up against them." In this case Lenin was wrong, and so was I. Neither of us had taken the full measure of the flunkeyism of the social patriots.[9]

Ruth Fischer, with no exaggeration, stated: "The German Social Democratic Party became a way of life. It was more than a political machine; it gave the German worker dignity and status in a world of his own."[10]

So, when the German Party leadership declared that Germany's war was a 'defensive war' against tsarist aggression and then voted for the Kaiser's war aims, it came like a mighty hammer blow. While the masses were being totally misled and dragooned into war, the leaders of the International acted as willing accomplices of the General Staff of the warring parties.

Of course, there were voices of opposition to the war, most notably Rosa Luxemburg, the well-known German Marxist, who proclaimed that the betrayal had reduced the Second International to a "stinking corpse".[11] Lenin went a step further and called for the abandonment of the old International altogether and the creation of a new Third International.

The old leaders, by their deeds, had completely destroyed the International. It had collapsed and could not be pieced back together. "The International is dead, overcome by opportunism", wrote Lenin.[12] Once he had recognised this fact, he did not hesitate to draw the necessary conclusions. Lenin boldly proclaimed: "Down with opportunism, and long live the Third International, purged not only of 'turncoats' (as *Golos* wishes), but of opportunism as well."[13]

The capitulation of Karl Kautsky was particularly hard to swallow. He was regarded as the heir to the traditions of Marx and Engels. Up until 1914, Lenin held Kautsky in the highest esteem. He referred regularly to Kautsky as a Marxist authority, and often quoted him, including in *What Is to Be Done?*

During Rosa Luxemburg's debate with Kautsky in 1910, Lenin had sided with Kautsky. But Rosa had the advantage of working closely with Kautsky for years, and was able to detect things that were as yet invisible, or unclear, to Lenin.

It is true that Lenin had recognised certain opportunist traits in the German Party, but these did not seem to be fundamental. Luxemburg, being much closer to the workings of the German party, as well as to Kautsky, had a clearer view of their limitations.

For Lenin, the war had ripped away all illusions. Now, Kautsky became a determined foe, a 'renegade', to use Lenin's phrase. He wrote to Alexander Shlyapnikov:

> ... Kautsky, who now is *more harmful than anyone else*. How dangerous and scoundrelly his sophistry is, covering up the dirty tricks of the opportunists with the most smooth and facile phrases (in *Neue Zeit*). The opportunists are an obvious evil. The German 'Centre' headed by Kautsky is a concealed evil, diplomatically coloured over, contaminating the eyes, the mind and the conscience of the workers, and more dangerous than anything else. Our task now is the

unconditional and open struggle against international opportunism and those who screen it (Kautsky).[14]

Again, in another letter to Shlyapnikov:

> I hate and despise Kautsky now more than anyone, with his vile, dirty self-satisfied hypocrisy. [...]

> Rosa Luxemburg was right when she wrote, long ago, that Kautsky has the "subservience of a theoretician" – servility, in plainer language, servility to the majority of the Party, to opportunism.[15]

Lenin attacked so-called 'socialist' leaders of France and Belgium for simply exposing the role of German imperialism while remaining silent about British, French and "particularly the barbarous Russian imperialism."[16] He went on to say:

> It was not socialism that has collapsed, in the shape of the present-day European International, but an insufficient socialism, i.e. *opportunism and reformism*.[17]

He continued:

> Even with their total impotence, they should have voted *against*, should *not have joined* their governments and uttered chauvinistic infamies; should *not* have shown solidarity with their 'nation', and should *not* have defended their 'own' bourgeoisie, they should have unmasked its vileness.[18]

Steeped in their opportunism, the cowardly Social-Democratic leaders ignored the decisions of the International Congresses at Stuttgart, Copenhagen and Basel and corralled the working class into supporting the imperialist war. To have accepted this nationalist poison would have meant a betrayal of the socialist movement and the death of internationalism.

Even then, the previous struggle of the old International against militarism, with all their anti-war rhetoric, was filled with a sentimental and pacifist colouration. Kautsky's advocacy of 'disarmament' was an example of this vulgar opportunism, namely bourgeois pacifism. Rather than a policy of disarmament, Lenin proposed that the proletariat should arm itself to defeat, expropriate and then disarm the bourgeoisie. "We must say: Capitalist society is and has always been *horror without end*", explained Lenin.[19]

Throughout Lenin's writings is a recurring explanation for the collapse of the Second International, which had deep material roots in society. The International, he explained, had grown up in a period of 'peaceful' capitalist upswing, between 1871 and 1914. In that period, capitalism was able to grant certain reforms under the pressure of the workers' organisations. However, over time, the leaders of the mass organisations became accustomed to these reforms and began to adapt themselves to capitalism.

Marx explained that social being determines social consciousness. Over time, these leaders abandoned the perspective of socialist revolution, which in reality they increasingly came to regard as 'utopian'. Talk of socialism became suitable only for May Day and holiday speeches. In practice, they downplayed the class struggle and embraced class collaboration. They also made a fetish of bourgeois parliamentarianism and bourgeois democracy. In other words, they had accepted the capitalist system as permanent and chose to work within it.

This constituted the basis of their reformism and opportunism, which became a stepping stone to patriotism. As a result, these Social-Democratic leaders, with very few exceptions, experienced a political and personal degeneration, as they adapted to capitalism. The only consistent exception, apart from handfuls in different countries, was the Bolshevik Party under Lenin, who kept on the path of internationalism and social revolution.

Against chauvinism

As at the beginning of all wars, under the remorseless pressure of ruling-class propaganda, the overwhelming mass of the population was gripped with a patriotic fervour. Amidst the thunder of shell-fire, the slaughter in the trenches and the lines of barbed wire that reduced all Europe to a monstrous killing ground, all opposition to the war was effectively silenced. The orgy of patriotic flag-waving, the drumbeat of war and the trumpets calling for action drowned out every other voice – at least at the beginning.

The leaders of the Socialist International – complicit in this crime – never met again during the war. In practice, the International had effectively ceased to exist. The International had abandoned the masses to the mercy of their respective ruling classes. Worse still, they actively participated in the imperialist slaughter, joining so-called governments of national unity and throwing their weight behind campaigns for recruitment, and drives for increased production to aid the war effort.

The millions who pledged allegiance to the International were thus handed over by their leaders to the tender mercies of the capitalist war machine. They were to meet in rival uniforms on the blood-soaked battlefields of Europe, slaughtering one another on behalf of the bankers and capitalists of 'their' nation.

74. A Shlyapnikov   75. Eugene V Debs   76. Christian Rakovsky

At this darkest moment, the slogan "workers of all countries unite" must have seemed like an empty phrase. Those few revolutionary internationalists who dared to speak out against the war were like distant voices crying in the wilderness. Apart from a handful of parties, like the Serbs and Russians – and the Italians who at least adopted a neutral stance – there were scattered groups and individuals who also opposed the war. These were practically all that was left of the old International.

Among their ranks stood some outstanding figures, such as Lenin, Trotsky and Martov in Russia, Rosa Luxemburg and Karl Liebknecht in Germany, the Balkan socialist Christian Rakovsky, as well as Eugene V Debs in the USA, John Maclean in Britain and James Connolly in Ireland.

But these anti-war individuals and groupings only made up a small fraction of those parties that formed the Second International. Others opposed the war, but mainly from a muddled pacifist perspective, such as the Independent Labour Party in Britain.

One month after the start of the war, the red banner of opposition was raised in the ranks of German Social Democracy by Liebknecht, Luxemburg, Franz Mehring and Clara Zetkin. They would become the founders of the Spartacus group, the embryo of the future German Communist Party.

Under pressure from the German Social-Democratic party, Karl Liebknecht had originally accepted party discipline and voted for the war credits in August 1914. When he realised his mistake, he voted against renewing the war credits in December.

He was the only deputy out of the 110 SPD deputies to do so and became instantly a national – and international – symbol against the imperialist war,

78. Franz Mehring

77. Clara Zetkin and Rosa Luxemburg in 1910   79. John Maclean

famous for his courageous stand, 'one against 110'. It was not long before he was imprisoned for his anti-war activities, along with Rosa Luxemburg.

The wave of patriotism that swept all of Europe at the outbreak of war inevitably affected Russia, where it was effectively utilised by the tsarist regime to silence the growing revolutionary movement.

Patriotic processions marched to the tsar's palace amid the pealing of bells, while students kneeled in the streets, singing "God Save the Tsar!" The name of St. Petersburg was changed to Petrograd, as it sounded less German and more Russian.

This orgy of chauvinism put the workers' organisations under intense pressure. The workers' parties were crushed by the patriotic steamroller. The voice of the revolutionaries was completely drowned out by the deafening patriotic chorus. Many of the revolutionary workers and youth

80. Karl Liebknecht

were drafted into the army, where they were swamped by the mass of backward peasant recruits.

Despite some initial wavering, the Bolsheviks, guided by Lenin's firm hand, held out against the war hysteria. But it split the Mensheviks from top to bottom. Plekhanov and Potresov supported the war as a means of 'national defence'. Potresov went so far as to join the Moscow Military Industrial Committee. A similar split took place within the ranks of the Socialist-Revolutionaries.

Martov, on the other hand, stood on the left flank of Menshevism and held an 'internationalist' position close to the Bolsheviks. Martov wrote to Axelrod on 27 October 1914: "More readily than with Plekhanov, we could probably come to an understanding with Lenin who, it seems, is preparing to appear in the role of a fighter against opportunism in the International."[20]

Martov edited a newspaper, *Golos*, in Paris, which consistently opposed the war and its internationalism won the support of Lenin, who stated that it was "the best socialist newspaper in Europe."[21] This was certainly high praise from Lenin.

81. Russian troops marching to the front

This gave Lenin some hope that he and Martov might be reconciled after so many years, but Martov's centrism always got the better of him and prevented such a reunion. Although very talented, Martov lacked the necessary will-power to maintain a consistent position.

The question of who fires the first shot is irrelevant, as wars can be easily provoked by one side or the other, according to its interests at a given moment. But the war still created a lot of confusion, even within the revolutionary camp. Some went as far as to enlist in the army. As Krupskaya observed:

> People were not clear on the question, and spoke mostly about which side was the attacking side.

> In Paris, in the long run, the majority of the group expressed themselves against the war and volunteered, but some comrades – Sapozhkov (Kuznetsov), Kazakov (Britman, Zviagin), Misha Edisherov (Davydov), Moiseyev (Illya, Zefir) and others – joined the French army as volunteers. The Mensheviks, Bolsheviks and Socialist-Revolutionary volunteers (about eighty men in all) adopted a declaration in the name of the 'Russian Republicans', which was printed in the French press. Plekhanov made a farewell speech in honour of the volunteers before they left Paris.

> The majority of our group condemned volunteering. But in the other groups, too, there was no definite clarity on the question.

Vladimir Ilyich realised how important it was at such a serious moment for every Bolshevik to have a clear understanding of the significance of events. A comradely exchange of opinions was necessary: it was advisable to fix all shades right away until the matter had been threshed out.[22]

Lenin, on hearing Plekhanov's support for 'defencism', was completely taken aback. "I just can't believe it", he said, adding thoughtfully, "it must be the effect of his military past."[23]

The crisis posed the greatest challenge in the history of the International as the historic consequences began to sink in. Lenin quickly realised what was at stake and the need to rescue the Marxist tradition and the banner of internationalism.

Lenin sent urgent word to Kamenev in Petrograd to instruct the Bolshevik deputies in the Duma to issue an anti-war statement. It was vital that the voice of genuine internationalism be heard at this time. The Bolshevik Central Committee within Russia had already issued a leaflet with the slogans: "Down with the war! War against war!" While the liberal bourgeois deputies sided with the tsarist government, the Social-Democratic deputies, Menshevik and Bolshevik alike, refused to vote for the war credits. Their statement proclaimed that they would neither support the tsarist regime nor the imperialist war. They then walked out of the Duma in protest. This honourable stand was in marked contrast to the capitulation of the German Social Democrats.

Lenin at this time was living in the part of Poland under Austrian rule. Within days of the outbreak of war, he was arrested and imprisoned for suspected espionage, which under war conditions could have ended extremely badly for a Russian citizen. Sensing the danger, Lenin's comrades rushed to his aid by exerting pressure on the Austrian authorities. Victor Adler, the veteran Socialist leader, despite his political differences with Lenin, was urged to intervene to help him. He therefore vouched for his revolutionary integrity and his credentials as the sworn enemy of tsarism. Following this intervention, Lenin was released by the authorities after twelve days of captivity.

Since Austria was now at war with Russia, Lenin and Krupskaya felt it wiser to move to Bern in neutral Switzerland to continue their revolutionary work. But even there, they were always worried that the Swiss police would bring them before the military authorities and expel them for breach of neutrality. They therefore adopted clandestine methods and asked for letters to be written with chemicals to avoid detection.

16. Lenin's Revolutionary Position

Lenin had quickly grasped the seriousness of the situation. It was clear to him that an international struggle needed to be conducted against the war chauvinism, together with the opportunism that dominated the Second International, especially its leaders. Within weeks of the outbreak of war, Lenin drafted a manifesto that was put to the leaders of the Bolshevik Party, entitled *The War and Russian Social Democracy*. He now regarded it essential to salvage the banner of socialist internationalism and the cause of world revolution. The manifesto answered the bourgeois propaganda about the world war being a 'defensive' war and, in unambiguous language, labelled the conflict an imperialist war that the working class could never support.

> The European and world war has the clearly defined character of a bourgeois, imperialist and dynastic war. A struggle for markets and for freedom to loot foreign countries, a striving to suppress the revolutionary movement of the proletariat and democracy in the individual countries, a desire to deceive, disunite, and slaughter the proletarians of all countries by setting the wage slaves of one nation against those of another so as to benefit the bourgeoisie – these are the only real content and significance of the war.[1]

Lenin pointed out that the declared war aims of the imperialists for 'democracy', 'defence of freedom', and so forth were nothing but a smokescreen to cover up their war of conquest and domination. The manifesto clearly described the actions of the leaders of German Social Democracy, the leading light of

82. Lenin in 1915

the Second International, as a "sheer betrayal of socialism".[2] Lenin then went on to condemn the leaders of the Belgian and French Social Democrats for declaring 'social peace' and for entering their bourgeois governments, which he described as "reprehensible".[3]

The manifesto stated that the prime task of the Russian Social Democrats was to "wage a ruthless and all-out struggle against Greater-Russian and tsarist-monarchist chauvinism, and against the sophism used by the Russian liberals, Cadets, a section of the Narodniks, and other bourgeois parties, in defence of that chauvinism."[4]

It then called for a struggle against the bankrupt leaders of the Second International and appealed "to the revolutionary consciousness of the working masses, who bear the entire burden of the war and are in most cases hostile to opportunism and chauvinism."[5]

Lenin came out very sharply, not only against the old reformist leaders, but especially the 'left' centrists, who were complicit in the betrayal. He directed his fire against the social-chauvinists, as well as the liberal-bourgeois pacifists and their supporters who opposed the war. He explained that social-chauvinism (or social-patriotism) meant lining up the workers behind their own ruling class in defending the capitalist fatherland at a time of imperialist war.

He attacked the views of pacifism, which permeated the left wing of the movement. "Pacifism, the preaching of peace in the abstract, is one of the means of duping the working class", wrote Lenin.[6] As opposed to the reformists and pacifists, Lenin's answer to imperialist war was the overthrow of capitalism.

Revolutionary defeatism

Lenin advocated a policy of 'revolutionary defeatism', meaning no support whatsoever for one's own ruling class or government. For the working class, the *main* enemy was not overseas but at home. Therefore, what was needed was to turn the imperialist war into a civil war, or class war, to carry out a socialist revolution. "The conversion of the present imperialist war into a civil war is the only correct proletarian slogan, one that follows from the experience of the Commune and is outlined in the Basel resolution (1912)", read the statement from the Central Committee of the Russian Social-Democratic Labour Party (1914).[7]

Lenin's use of the term 'revolutionary defeatism' has created a great deal of confusion. Lenin did not mean, as some ultra-lefts asserted, that the working class should welcome with open arms the military victory of their country's enemies. Such a position would simply make them inverted chauvinists, and stooges of the enemy power.

What Lenin was saying was that a military defeat resulting from the growth of a revolutionary movement is infinitely more beneficial to the working class than that assured by 'civil peace'. Furthermore, Lenin called for the defeat of *all* imperialist governments, starting with those at home. Lenin did not say, nor did he wish to say, anything more than this.

While revolutionaries should not support their own capitalist government, neither should they support the aims of the capitalists of another country. In any conflict, they must stand for the independent interests of the working class of all sides. War, above all, is a class question. This, in essence, was the Leninist policy towards the imperialist war.

In order to hammer home these points against the waverers, Lenin used some very sharp language. This created some confusion and even opposition to some of the things Lenin was advocating, including in Russia.

Shlyapnikov recalled the perplexity when he and his comrades read Lenin's theses on the war in *Sotsial-Demokrat*. "Comrades did not want to link their tactics to the army's strategic situation, but at the same time nobody wished Nicholas II the smallest victory, as it was clear that a victory would strengthen the vilest reaction", he wrote.[8]

Lenin underlined his points in a further article, 'The Position and Tasks of the Socialist International', written a few months after the start of the war in November 1914, in which he stated:

> Refusal to serve with the forces, anti-war strikes, etc., are sheer nonsense, the miserable and cowardly dream of an unarmed struggle against the armed bourgeoisie, vain yearning for the destruction of capitalism without a desperate civil war or a series of wars. It is the duty of every socialist to conduct propaganda of the class struggle, in the army as well; work directed towards turning a war of the nations into civil war is the only socialist activity in the era of an imperialist armed conflict of the bourgeoisie of all nations. Down with mawkishly sanctimonious and fatuous appeals for 'peace at any price'![9]

This position was in marked contrast to the support for 'conscientious objectors', who refused to join the army on pacifist grounds – a position that was common on the left internationally. But such protests, despite their heroism, would simply cut the revolutionaries off from the workers in uniform. In contrast, Lenin posed things very much in class terms and the need to overthrow capitalism as the only way out. He went on:

> Let us raise high the banner of civil war! Imperialism sets at hazard the fate of European culture: this war will soon be followed by others, unless there are a series of successful revolutions. The story about this being the 'last war' is a hollow and dangerous fabrication, a piece of philistine 'mythology' (as *Golos* aptly puts it). The proletarian banner of civil war will rally together, not only hundreds of thousands of class-conscious workers but millions of semi-proletarians and petty bourgeois, now deceived by chauvinism, but whom the horrors of war will not only intimidate and depress, but also enlighten, teach, arouse, organise, steel and prepare for the war against the bourgeoisie of their 'own' country and 'foreign' countries. And this will take place, if not today, then tomorrow, if not during the war, then after it, if not in this war then in the next one.[10]

Lenin also expressed his gratitude to the preparatory work of the old International, but that era was now over:

> The Second International did its share of useful preparatory work in preliminarily organising the proletarian masses during the long, 'peaceful' period of the most brutal capitalist slavery and most rapid capitalist progress in the last third of the nineteenth and the beginning of the twentieth centuries. To the Third International falls the task of organising the proletarian forces for a revolutionary

onslaught against the capitalist governments, for civil war against the bourgeoisie of all countries for the capture of political power, for the triumph of socialism![11]

Lenin's clarion call went straight to the heart of the matter, within which there was no room for cries of 'peace' when there was no peace, but raging imperialist war between the powers. Pacifism, he stressed, was completely empty in such a situation and he criticised Kautsky's 'peace programme'. This consisted of hypocritical lip service to some democratic pious wishes: democratisation of foreign policy, arbitration courts to settle conflicts between states, disarmament, etc.

> The socialists' 'peace programme', and their programme of 'struggle to end the war', must proceed from the exposure of the lie of the 'democratic peace', the pacifistic intentions of the belligerents, etc., now being spread among the people by demagogic ministers, pacifist bourgeois, social-chauvinists, and Kautskyites in all countries. Any 'peace programme' will deceive the people and be a piece of hypocrisy, unless its principal object is to explain to the masses the need for a revolution [...]
>
> It is the duty of socialists to support, extend and intensify every popular movement to end the war. But it is actually being fulfilled only by those socialists who, like Liebknecht, in their parliamentary speeches, call upon the soldiers to lay down their arms, and preach revolution and transformation of the imperialist war into a civil war for socialism.[12]

Krupskaya quotes Lenin, explaining:

> The peace slogan is in my judgement incorrect at the present moment. This is a philistine's, a preacher's slogan. The proletarian slogan must be civil war.[13]

As imperialist war was a product of the contradictions of capitalism, Lenin understood that war could only be eliminated with the overthrow of capitalism.

Reactionary and progressive wars

All wars are barbaric, since they involve killing people. But merely to react to war with moralistic condemnation of its barbarity does absolutely nothing to prevent this barbarity from happening on a regular basis.

What is necessary, first of all, is to arrive at a scientific understanding of war. What is its real meaning and significance? To this question, the great Prussian military thinker Carl von Clausewitz provided a very simple answer:

"War therefore is an act of violence intended to compel our opponent to fulfil our will"[14]. That goes to the essence of the matter. And it applies just as much to war between the classes as war between nations. As a Marxist, Lenin did not oppose wars in general and his attitude to war had nothing in common with that of pacifists and anarchists. He believed it was necessary to analyse each war historically and separately.

Some wars, despite the horror they may evoke in sensitive souls, can indeed be considered as progressive and necessary. Lenin cites the examples of the fight against colonialism, medievalism and serfdom. But the imperialist war, which sought to redivide the world among the capitalist gangsters, he considered to be reactionary from any point of view. The imperialist character of the conflict was an expression of the highest stage of capitalism, the domination of finance capital and of state-monopoly capitalism. Lenin had precisely deduced the policy of defeatism from the imperialist character of the First World War, the class character of society and the states involved.

The imperialist world war was entirely different from those predominantly national wars from the Great French Revolution to the Franco-Prussian War of 1870-71. During these years, the wars were predominantly aimed at the creation of nation states. The revolutionary wars waged by France, although they contained an element of plunder and conquest, at the same time destroyed feudalism and absolutism across old serf-owning Europe. This was historically progressive. The plunder of France by Germany during the Franco-Prussian War did not alter the fundamental significance of its liberating tens of millions of Germans from feudal disunity and the oppression of two despots, Napoleon III and the Russian tsar. Again, this was progressive, which allowed the further development of the productive forces and culture.

However, from 1871 to 1914, European capitalism developed into monopoly capitalism and imperialism, which in its dash for conquest, sought to divide and redivide the world. In the place of national wars emerged imperialist wars, reflecting the reactionary character of capitalism.

The imperialist subjugation of the world also gave rise to wars of national liberation on behalf of the oppressed peoples. Such wars are progressive in that they create conditions for their own country's development and they also constitute a blow against imperialism, as with the later example of the struggle of the Vietnamese people against French, then American imperialism. These wars are progressive wars.

Lenin emphasised this difference between 'progressive' and 'reactionary' wars in his review of the anti-war pamphlet *The Crisis of Social Democracy*, known as the *Junius Pamphlet*. Unbeknown to him, it was written by Rosa Luxemburg, under the pseudonym of 'Junius', probably taken from a legendary Roman patriot.

While Lenin criticised its weakness in failing to recognise progressive wars, namely national movements of the colonial peoples against imperialism, and the reasons for the collapse of the international, he nevertheless wholeheartedly welcomed the pamphlet, saying "on the whole, the *Junius Pamphlet* is a splendid Marxist work."[15]

The imperialist wars for the seizure of colonies, markets, sources of raw materials, and spheres of influence were always camouflaged under the flags of 'defence of democracy', 'freedom' and 'justice'. For Lenin, it was important to cut through the fog of bourgeois diplomacy, and to see what class was conducting the war and for what aims. The working class must not be fooled by the ruses of bourgeois diplomacy, which always seek to represent the enemy as the 'aggressor' in any conflict. The blame for any conflict is always placed on a country's enemy. Lenin wrote in March 1915:

> The question of which group dealt the first military blow or first declared war is immaterial in any determination of the tactics of socialists. Both sides' phrases about 'defence of the fatherland', about resisting the invasion of the enemy, about a war of defence, and the like, are an utter deception of the people.[16]

Lenin clearly exposed the reactionary aims of this war of modern slave owners bent on preserving capitalist slavery. He explained:

> Britain and France are lying when they assert that they are warring for Belgium's freedom. In reality, they have long been preparing the war, and are waging it with the purpose of robbing Germany and stripping her of her colonies; they have signed a treaty with Italy and Russia on the pillage and carving up of Turkey and Austria. The tsarist monarchy in Russia is waging a predatory war aimed at seizing Galicia, taking territory away from Turkey, enslaving Persia, Mongolia, etc. Germany is waging war with the purpose of grabbing British, Belgian, and French colonies. Whether Germany or Russia wins, or whether there is a 'draw', the war will bring humanity fresh oppression of hundreds and hundreds of millions of people in the colonies, in Persia, Turkey and China, a fresh enslavement of nations, and new chains for the working class of all countries.[17]

Educating the cadres

The betrayal of August 1914 meant that the Rubicon had been crossed. With this debacle and the collapse of the Second International, Lenin saw his prime task as to cut through the hypocrisy and educate the Bolshevik cadres, starting with the imperialist nature of the war. Lenin saw the need for absolute clarity to combat the political confusion that was being spread everywhere.

In this period, Lenin tended to 'bend the stick' in one direction in order to counter the relentless pressures of nationalism and class collaboration. Instead of imperialist war, he proposed the programme of civil war, or class war. In his writings, Lenin could not have presented things more sharply, to the point of being even somewhat ultra-left. He admitted as much at the time of the Third Congress of the Comintern in 1921 when, in a letter to Zinoviev, he said: "when I was an émigré myself (for more than fifteen years), I took 'too Leftist' a stand several times (as I now realise)."[18]

Many, even those on the left within the movement, were horrified by Lenin's strong language, which they believed bordered on madness. Zinoviev explained:

> We approached Robert Grimm, one of the leftest of the lefts in the Second International, with a request that he print short extracts from our manifesto, but he looked at us with bitter compassion as if we were mentally defective, saying that he could not print documents which resembled political deliria.[19]

We must understand that Lenin was not aiming his writings at the broad masses. That was ruled out by the complete isolation of the Bolsheviks at this stage. "During 1915 and 1916 we were an insignificant minority, which was attempting to establish these first international links", explains Zinoviev.[20] Trotsky states: "In the deep recesses of the masses, in the trenches and so on, there was a new mood, but it was so deep and terrorised that we could not reach it and give it an expression."[21]

Lenin was confined to neutral Switzerland throughout this period. Even corresponding with Russia was a Herculean task. His work was therefore mainly limited to educating the cadres of Bolshevism within his greatly reduced periphery, to hammer home the fundamental ideas. That was Lenin's overriding purpose.

This found its most graphic expression in the question of the defence of the fatherland. As an answer to the betrayal of the leaders of the Second International, this was entirely correct. And absolutely necessary. In view of the prevailing confusion, which infected even a layer of the Bolshevik cadres, Lenin laid heavy stress on this point. That was entirely characteristic of his method. He was trying to lay down a solid basis for creating a new revolutionary International. The first step was to advocate a radical break with the old, and the training of the cadres in a spirit of absolute intransigence.

However, it is important to see Lenin's ideas in their proper context. Lenin was no utopian. This supreme political realist knew very well that under the given conditions, slogans of anti-militarism or revolutionary defeatism could not win the broad masses, who did not want a foreign conqueror to rule over them. Any suggestion that the Bolsheviks were actively promoting the cause of the enemy would have ruined the prospect of reaching the mass of workers and peasants. This is shown very clearly when Lenin was later falsely accused of being a German agent.

Some years later, Trotsky explained the position that Lenin faced at the beginning of the First World War:

> During the last war not only the proletariat as a whole but also its vanguard and, in a certain sense, the vanguard of this vanguard was caught unaware. The elaboration of the principles of revolutionary policy toward the war began at a time when the war was already in full blaze and the military machine exercised unlimited rule. One year after the outbreak of the war, the small revolutionary minority was still compelled to accommodate itself to a centrist majority at the Zimmerwald Conference. Prior to the February revolution and even afterwards, the revolutionary elements felt themselves to be not contenders for power but the extreme left opposition. Even Lenin relegated the socialist revolution to a more or less distant future [...]

> In Russia prior to the war the Bolsheviks constituted four-fifths of the proletarian vanguard, that is, of the workers participating in political life (newspapers, elections, etc.). Following the February revolution the unlimited rule passed into the hands of defencists, the Mensheviks and the SR's. True enough, the Bolsheviks in the space of eight months conquered the overwhelming majority of the workers. But the decisive role in this conquest was played not by the refusal to defend the bourgeois fatherland but by the slogan: 'All Power to the Soviets!' And only by this revolutionary slogan! The criticism of imperialism, its militarism, the renunciation of the defence of bourgeois democracy and so on could have never conquered the overwhelming majority of the people to the side of the Bolsheviks...[22]

While Lenin used every opportunity to answer the flood of propaganda from the bourgeois and their apologists, who were lying through their teeth, he reserved his most brutal language for the *centrists*, who covered up their opportunism with radical phrases. This tendency was represented internationally by Kautsky, who, together with his centrist allies, Lenin regarded as the greatest danger facing the movement. There lay, after all, the greatest illusions. This was the main reason why Lenin adopted an extreme leftist approach, so as to differentiate the Bolsheviks from the politics of the centrist swamp.

'Nashe Slovo'

Whereas Lenin aimed his propaganda at the advanced layers, Trotsky and Martov were producing a *daily* newspaper in Paris, *Nashe Slovo*, which had a wide circulation and had replaced Martov's *Golos*. *Nashe Slovo* had a circle of collaborators, including Lunacharsky, David Ryazanov, Georgy Chicherin, Christian Rakovsky and Alexandra Kollontai. As a result, while they all opposed the war, their approach differed from Lenin's.

Trotsky, who was the real editor, was aiming at a broader audience and therefore did not make use of Lenin's slogan of revolutionary defeatism. Although he completely agreed with Lenin's opposition to defence of the fatherland, he understood that slogans such as "better the defeat of your own ruling class" could never influence or win over the masses, who would invariably interpret such views as support for the German Kaiser.

They adopted instead the slogan: 'Peace without indemnities or annexations, peace without conquerors or conquered'. They declared their unambiguous opposition to both imperialist camps; opposed voting for the war credits; opposed the 'civil peace'; and were for irreconcilable class struggle in time of war. They, like Lenin, argued for internationalism and for the overthrow of capitalism. In essence, the two views were identical, but Lenin was directing his arguments at a different audience altogether.

It should be noted that Lenin did not keep rigidly to his formula. When he returned to Russia in 1917, he changed his language, moving far closer to the position of Trotsky and Luxemburg. The reason was that, in 1917, *Lenin was addressing a very different audience*. He now began to write for mass consumption within Russia. It was no longer a question of talking to the cadres, but of preparing the masses for power. While basing himself on exactly the same Marxist principles as before, he took into consideration the mood among the masses and how they viewed things. Lenin therefore adapted his ideas to the real situation on the ground in 1917.

This change was explained in a piece he wrote on 7 April 1917, called 'The Tasks of the Proletariat in the Present Revolution':

This peculiar situation demands of us an ability to adapt ourselves to the *special* conditions of the Party work among unprecedentedly large masses of proletarians who have just awakened to political life.[23]

This shows Lenin's great flexibility when faced with new conditions. The approach he adopted in 1917 was one of 'patient explanation' and he played down the call for civil war. He therefore attacked the "ravings" of those who "present my views as a call to 'civil war' in the midst of revolutionary democracy."[24] He stated:

In view of the undoubted honesty of those broad sections of the mass believers in revolutionary defencism who accept the war as a necessity, and not as a means of conquest, in view of the fact that they are being deceived by the bourgeoisie, *it is necessary with particular thoroughness, persistence and patience to explain their error to them...*[25]

Some years later, at the Third Congress of the Communist International, Lenin looked back at this experience:

At the beginning of the war we Bolsheviks adhered to a single slogan – that of civil war, and a ruthless one at that. We branded as a traitor everyone who did not support the idea of civil war. *But when we came back to Russia in March 1917 we changed our position entirely.* When we returned to Russia and spoke to the peasants and workers, we saw that they all stood for defence of the homeland, of course in quite a different sense from the Mensheviks, and we could not call these ordinary workers and peasants scoundrels and traitors. We described this as 'honest Defensism'. [...] Our original stand at the beginning of the war was correct: it was important then to form a definite and resolute core. Our subsequent stand was correct too. It proceeded from the assumption that the masses had to be won over.[26]

Lenin clearly explains the difference between 1914 and 1917. During the war period, Lenin's only consideration was to strengthen the Party and hold the line against chauvinism. That is why his writings from August 1914 to January 1917 sought to concentrate on the theoretical questions, especially the nature of the imperialist war and the betrayal of the Second International.

While the whole struggle centred around the question of the 'defence of the fatherland', Lenin argued that there must not be a shred of support for the bourgeoisie or social patriotism. In other words, the same laws of the class struggle operated in wartime as in peacetime.

"Ilyich deliberately put the case strongly in order to make it quite clear what line people were taking", explained Krupskaya.[27] This explained his sharpness at this time.

Duma deputies waver

Without doubt, the pressures on the revolutionary vanguard were truly immense. The Party had been decimated by arrests. As a result, even within the Bolshevik Party, there were those who wavered under such pressure. In November 1914, the five Bolshevik Duma deputies were arrested. In February 1915, with a further five Bolshevik leaders, they were put on trial for belonging to an illegal organisation.

Lenin expected the Bolshevik deputies to show courage at the trial and act as a beacon in Russia and internationally of anti-war forces. However, some of the deputies, with the notable exception of Muranov, were not totally convinced of Lenin's line of 'revolutionary defeatism' and began to prevaricate.

Kamenev, a member of the Central Committee, together with several others, equivocated and actually disavowed the Party's position. Kamenev told the court that the documents found in his possession, which outlined Lenin's position, did not coincide with his views on the war. Nevertheless, all eleven deputies – Bolshevik and Menshevik – which included Petrovsky, Muranov, Badayev, Samoilov and Shagov, together with Kamenev, were sentenced on 14 February 1915 to exile and penal servitude in the Siberian district of Turukhansk.

As explained, Roman Malinovsky, who had been a Bolshevik Duma deputy, had been recruited as an undercover agent for the Okhrana. But by now Malinovsky had become unreliable as an agent and so was forced to resign by his 'employers' just before the outbreak of war. They then forced him to go abroad, after having paid him off for his services with 6,000 roubles. As a result, he announced his resignation from the Duma, without any consultation with the Party. This caused a lot of deep resentment among the workers who had helped him to get elected. All was to be revealed after the police archives were opened following the October Revolution. Having been found out, when Malinovsky returned to Russia in 1918, he was tried, then sentenced and shot as a police informant.

The ambivalent conduct of the Bolshevik deputies at their trial drew criticism from the ranks of the Party. Shlyapnikov, in particular, recalled the feelings at that time:

... at meetings of the organised comrades and also from members of the Petersburg Committee I was to hear much dissatisfaction about the conduct of our Duma faction at their trial. Comrades condemned Kamenev especially severely.[28]

Lenin, too, was critical of the conduct of the Bolshevik deputies. He thought that they had made too many concessions under pressure from the Mensheviks, although he moderated the tone of his criticisms because the trial had just ended and the deputies had been sentenced to exile.

"What, then, has the trial of the Russian Social-Democratic Labour group proved?", asked Lenin, so as to draw out the lessons. "First of all, it has shown that this advance contingent of revolutionary Social-Democracy in Russia failed to display sufficient firmness at the trial." He said that "to prove one's solidarity with the social-patriot Mr Yordansky, as Rosenfeld [Kamenev] did, or one's disagreement with the Central Committee [...] is inexcusable from the standpoint of a revolutionary Social-Democrat."[29]

It was important to explain the truth because, in Lenin's words, the revolutionary party "is strong enough to openly criticise itself, and unequivocally call mistakes and weaknesses by their proper names."[30]

Lenin nevertheless highlighted the importance of the trial in his propaganda, drawing out its positive features. He particularly emphasised the importance of using the parliamentary tribune in spreading revolutionary ideas: "The trial has revealed a picture without precedent in world socialism – that of *revolutionary* Social-Democracy making use of parliamentarianism."[31] He went on:

Thanks to the trial, the words cited in the indictment: "The guns should be directed, not against our brothers, the wage slaves of other countries, but against the reactionary and bourgeois governments and parties of all countries" – these words will spread – and have already done so – all over Russia as a call for proletarian internationalism, for the proletarian revolution. Thanks to the trial, the class slogan of the vanguard of the workers of Russia has reached the masses. [...]

About forty thousand workers have been buying *Pravda*; far more read it. Even if war, prison, Siberia, and hard labour should destroy five or even ten times as many – this section of the workers cannot be annihilated. It is alive. It is imbued with the revolutionary spirit, is anti-chauvinist. It *alone* stands in the midst of the masses, with deep roots in the latter, as the champion of the internationalism of the toilers, the exploited, and the oppressed. It *alone* has held its ground in the general *débâcle*. It alone is leading the semi-proletarian elements *away* from the social-chauvinism of the Cadets, the Trudoviks, Plekhanov and *Nasha Zarya*, and *towards* socialism. Its existence, its ideas, its work, and its call for the 'brotherhood of wage slaves of other countries' have been revealed to the whole of Russia by the trial of the RSDL group.

It is with this section that we must work, and its unity must be defended against social-chauvinists. That is the only road along which the working-class movement of Russia can develop towards social revolution, and not towards national-liberalism of the 'European' type.[32]

The wavering over the war question did not end, however. It would return in early 1917, when Stalin and Kamenev gave support to the Provisional Government's defencism – but we will deal with that later.

17. The National Question and Zimmerwald

The world war brought the national question to the fore in a number of countries. The German militarists, while attacking Belgium and France, had launched a campaign to subjugate Serbia and crush the national movement of the Southern Slavs. The social patriots and centrists, in turn, were trying to use the national question to disguise and justify the war aims of imperialism. For them, the war was a 'just war' for 'national liberation' and 'self-determination', a view echoed by Kautsky.

The national question had long been considered a vital question for the Russian Party. The Russian Empire systematically oppressed the national minorities, which made up the majority of its population. This country, composed of 140 nationalities held under subjugation to the centralised autocratic Great Russian state of the tsars, was therefore rightly called by Lenin 'the prison house of nations', who were faced with humiliating conditions.

Ever since the Second Congress of the RSDLP, Paragraph 9 of the Party's Constitution supported the right of nations to self-determination, up to and including separation. In this way, a free and voluntary union of peoples would help eradicate national oppression. The Bolsheviks regarded this demand as a democratic right and a key part of the Social-Democratic programme.

However, this position had been strongly opposed by Rosa Luxemburg, who was from Poland, an oppressed nation part of the Russian Empire. She argued that the demand for self-determination was utopian under imperialism – given the domination of the major capitalist powers – and redundant under socialism, as borders would no longer exist. She therefore rejected the demand of self-determination as an irrelevant abstraction.

This led to a protracted controversy. Within Poland, the so-called Socialist Party of Józef Piłsudski, which was in fact a bourgeois nationalist party, came out for Polish independence. At the same time, the Polish Social-Democracy, led by Rosa Luxemburg, opposed the bourgeois nationalists and called for Poland's autonomy within a democratic Russia. She wrote a lengthy article, 'The National Question and Autonomy', that outlined her position, to which Lenin responded in a series of articles.

In arguing against Rosa Luxemburg, Lenin explained that, even under imperialism, national problems retain their full force and can even become intensified. The right of self-determination was simply a democratic principle applied to the national sphere, as with the right to vote, strike, free assembly, etc. No nation should be able to subjugate another and, likewise, no national minority should be forced into a union against its will. Whether a nationality wished to remain within a state or wished to separate from a state must be their choice alone. It must be the right of any people to determine their own affairs, free from coercion. This, as far as Lenin was concerned, was a basic democratic right that would unite Russian and Polish workers.

In order to safeguard against national oppression, Marxists argued for a nation's *right* to self-determination. Lenin, unlike the so-called Austro-Marxists led by Otto Bauer, regarded nationality not as an abstract entity, but connected to territory, economy, language, and national consciousness. The historic borders that cut across the living body of different nations cannot be regarded as sacrosanct. There must be a right to self-determination of each nation within a state. Where such nations exist within a state, they should be afforded the broadest autonomy, including the rights of each minority.

Lenin and Luxemburg both agreed that the nation state and private ownership were absolute fetters on the development of society and acted as a brake on the development of the productive forces. Ultimately, in a future classless society, the borders created by capitalism would cease to exist. In the meantime, however, Lenin believed that the national question could not be ignored or swept under the carpet, but should be turned towards revolutionary ends.

Following in the footsteps of Marx and Engels, he argued that the working class needed its own independent position on the national question, which

83. Territory of the Russian Empire in 1890

should be linked to the struggle for socialism. It was not for nothing that Lenin said the national question was a question of bread. In other words, as material conditions improved, the national question would recede. Under socialism, the colossal development of the productive forces and the dramatic rise in living standards would do away with national conflicts. The peoples of the world would live peacefully as one.

However, under capitalist crisis, the national question can assume extreme forms. Centrifugal tendencies take a hold. The correct approach can direct these forces away from nationalism and towards proletarian revolution. That was Lenin's approach: to separate out the progressive features from the reactionary ones and to fight against all forms of national oppression. This allowed the revolutionary party to undermine bourgeois nationalism and win over the oppressed.

However, this was only one side of Lenin's position on the national question. When it came to the workers' organisations, whose task it was to unify the class to achieve its emancipation, there could be no trace of any national divisions. Lenin stood firmly for the sacred unity of the proletariat, above all national, racial, religious or linguistic divisions. Capitalism could only be overthrown by a militant, class-conscious, and united working class. It was therefore the duty of all workers within a state, irrespective of their nationality, creed, colour, or religion, to unite into a single class organisation. The Bolshevik Party was based on this fundamental principle.

A concrete question

Lenin's views were diametrically opposed to those of the Austrian Social-Democrats, who took the view that nationality was not determined by territory, language or economy, but instead based on an abstract programme of 'national cultural autonomy'. This proposed that the citizens of one nationality, no matter where they lived, should be united across countries on the basis of a common culture. This was clearly a recipe for breaking up the working class on national lines within the same state. This reactionary idea was the opposite of proletarian internationalism and class unity, and reflected the ideals of the petty-bourgeois nationalists.

These ideas of 'cultural autonomy' did, however, find support in the Jewish Bund, which, as described, originally demanded a special federal place within the RSDLP. Lenin opposed 'cultural autonomy' as reactionary and pointed to the example of Russian schools to prove his point.

Within St. Petersburg, the composition of schools was of an extremely mixed character. Pupils were from a variety of backgrounds: Russian, Polish, Czech, Lithuanian, Lettish, Samogitian, French, Italian, Romanian, German, Swedish, Norwegian, Danish, Dutch, English, Armenian, Jewish, Georgian, Ossetian, Finnish, Karelian, Chud, Estonian, Samoyed, Tatar, Persian, Chinese and others. Therefore, any attempt to impose a separate 'cultural identity' on these school children would impose criminal divisions and reinforce an artificial separation. As Lenin explained:

> It is as clear as daylight that the advocacy of such a plan ['cultural-national autonomy' – *RS and AW*] means, *in fact*, pursuing or supporting the ideas of bourgeois nationalism, chauvinism and clericalism. The interests of democracy in general, and the interests of the working class in particular, demand the very opposite. We must strive to secure the *mixing* of the children of *all* nationalities in *uniform* schools in each locality… We must most emphatically oppose segregating the schools according to nationality, no matter what form it may take.

> It is not our business to segregate the nations in matters of education in any way; on the contrary, we must strive to create the fundamental democratic conditions for the peaceful coexistence of the nations on the basis of equal rights. We must not champion 'national culture', but expose the clerical and bourgeois character of this slogan in the name of the international culture of the world working-class movement. […]

> To preach the establishment of special national schools for every 'national culture' is reactionary.[1]

When it comes to the national question within a certain country, it should be viewed separately and concretely. It was false to look at it in terms of generalities or abstractions. Whether Marxists would support separation of a particular nationality was not something given in advance. That would depend on concrete circumstances. While the Bolsheviks were opposed to the forcible incorporation of an oppressed nation within an existing state, they were not 'evangels of separation'. They were certainly not obliged to support separation on every occasion, as Lenin explained:

> The Social Democratic Party must decide the latter question [of secession] exclusively on its merits in each particular case in conformity with the interests of social development as a whole and with the interests of the proletarian class struggle for socialism.[2]

And again:

> To accuse those who support freedom of self-determination, i.e. freedom to secede, of encouraging separation, is foolish and hypocritical as accusing those who advocate freedom of divorce of encouraging the destruction of family ties.[3]

He explained that the bourgeoisie always places its national demands in the forefront, in the most categorical fashion, while for the proletariat, national demands are subordinate to the interests of the class struggle.

This was how Marx had dealt with the national question. He believed that the national question should be subordinate to the 'general interests' of the working class, or the 'labour question'. This meant that Marx adopted different attitudes towards different national movements at different times.

For instance, in the case of Ireland, Marx in the 1840s and 1850s held the position that Ireland would gain her freedom through the victory of the English working class, and not through a national movement of the Irish. However, later, as the English workers fell under the influence of liberalism, and the Irish liberation movement grew stronger and assumed revolutionary proportions, he changed his mind. He advocated the separation of Ireland from England, "although federation may follow upon separation."[4]

In another example, Marx opposed the national movement of the Czechs and South Slavs, which he regarded as reactionary "Russian outposts", and concentrated his attack on Russian tsarism, the most reactionary power on the continent.[5] Lenin therefore believed:

> (1) that the interests of the liberation of a number of big and very big nations in Europe rate higher than the interests of the movement for liberation of small

nations; (2) that the demand for democracy must not be considered in isolation but on a European – today we should say a world – scale.

That is all there is to it.[6]

Lenin showed that Marx had always remained faithful to his principles – that no nation can be free if it oppresses other nations. Lenin also drew parallels with Marx's position on tsarism's domination of international politics in the nineteenth century. He explained that if some nations carried through a socialist revolution, and *other* nations were the main bulwarks of counter-revolution, it would be their duty to wage a revolutionary war against these reactionary powers.

The armies of the French Revolution were compelled to declare war on feudal Europe, which threatened to crush the Revolution. In the course of these revolutionary wars, the French forces had to suppress the reactionary uprising of the peasants in the backward Vendée region, which, under the pretext of a war of national liberation, was used by the monarchist and clerical forces as a potent weapon of the counter-revolution, organised and financed by England.

In the same way, Lenin stated that if a victorious proletarian revolution in Russia was confronted with similar reactionary national movements, he would be "in favour of crushing them, in favour of destroying all their outposts, no matter what small-nation movements arose in them."[7] He continued:

> In individual concrete cases, the part may contradict the whole; if so, it must be rejected. It is possible that the republican movement in one country may be merely an instrument of the clerical or financial-monarchist intrigues of other countries; if so, we must *not* support this particular, concrete movement, but it would be ridiculous to delete the demand for a republic from the programme of international Social-Democracy on these grounds.[8]

Lenin applied this view to the world war. If taken in isolation, the only real national conflict was the war between Serbia and Austria. But this conflict – leading to a world war – could not be taken in isolation, as it had much wider and catastrophic implications. As Lenin explained:

> If this war were an isolated one, i.e. if it were not connected with the general European war, with the selfish and predatory aims of Britain, Russia, etc., it would have been the *duty* of all socialists to desire the success of the Serbian *bourgeoisie* – this is the only correct and absolutely inevitable conclusion to be drawn from the national element in the present war.[9]

But this was not the case:

> The national element in the Serbo-Austrian war is not, and cannot be, of *any*
> serious significance in the general European war. If Germany wins, she will
> throttle Belgium, one more part of Poland, perhaps part of France, etc. If Russia
> wins, she will throttle Galicia, one more part of Poland, Armenia, etc. If the
> war ends in a 'draw', the old national oppression will remain. To Serbia, i.e.
> to perhaps one per cent or so of the participants in the present war, the war
> is a 'continuation of the politics' of the bourgeois liberation movement. To
> the other ninety-nine per cent, the war is a continuation of the politics of
> imperialism, i.e. of the decrepit bourgeoisie, which is capable only of raping
> nations, not freeing them. The Triple Entente, which is 'liberating' Serbia, is
> *selling* the interests of Serbian liberty to Italian imperialism in return for the
> latter's aid in robbing Austria.[10]

For the imperialist powers, the fate of small nations is of little consequence.
They are merely so much small change in their calculations.

But Lenin did not make a fetish of the national question. For him, it was
a concrete question, subordinate to the general interests of the working class
internationally. He repeatedly stressed that the programme on the national
question was essentially a negative one, that is to say, it was not a question of
what you are *for*, but what you are *against*.

It is sufficient to explain that we are all against forms of national oppression,
against the suppression of national culture, language, etc. But to go beyond
this would lead directly to the swamp of bourgeois nationalism, where one
nation seeks to gain at the expense of another.

Lenin warned the working class not to fall into the trap set by the
bourgeoisie of the oppressed nation, which constantly demands that the
working class support its demands unconditionally. He says:

> The demand for a 'yes' or 'no' reply to the question of secession in the case
> of every nation may seem a very 'practical' one. In reality it is absurd; it is
> metaphysical in theory, while in practice it leads to subordinating the proletariat
> to the bourgeoisie's policy. The bourgeoisie always places its national demands
> in the forefront, and does so in categorical fashion. With the proletariat,
> however, these demands are subordinated to the interests of the class struggle.
> [...] That is why the proletariat confines itself, so to speak, to the negative
> demand for recognition of the *right* to self-determination, without giving
> guarantees to any nation, and without undertaking to give *anything at the
> expense* of another nation.

This may not be 'practical', but it is in effect the best guarantee for the achievement of the most democratic of all possible solutions. [...]

The proletariat is opposed to such practicality. [...] This call for practicality is in fact merely a call for uncritical acceptance of bourgeois aspirations.[11]

He went on to stress the importance of the class question and class independence, which was always paramount:

While recognising equality and equal rights to a national state, it values above all and places foremost the alliance of the proletarians of all nations, and assesses any national demand, any national separation, *from the angle* of the workers' class struggle.[12]

'Leftist' critics

Rosa Luxemburg did not understand this nuanced position of Lenin. It is perfectly understandable why she took the stand she did. She was reacting against the nationalism of the so-called Polish Socialist Party – the party of the reactionary nationalist, Piłsudski.

But while it was correct to oppose bourgeois nationalism, it was a mistake to swing 180 degrees in the opposite direction and to abandon the *right* of national self-determination. This led her to adopt an abstract internationalism. If the Bolsheviks had adopted this line, it would have undermined support for the Russian Revolution among the peasantry and the majority of non-Russian peoples within its borders.

Lenin, however, also had 'leftist' critics inside the Bolshevik Party, led by Nikolai Bukharin, Georgy Pyatakov, Karl Radek and others, who simply repeated Luxemburg's arguments of the 'un-achievability' of self-determination under capitalism. These 'lefts' actually went even further in their arguments and rejected as futile the struggle for *all* democratic demands, stating that in the imperialist era they were 'unachievable'. In doing so, they demanded that the Party drop its demand for national self-determination. In taking this stand, they proclaimed they were defending 'genuine Bolshevism'. Lenin replied to this claim:

I attach no importance to this desire to cling to the word 'Bolshevism', for I know such 'old Bolsheviks' from whom God [must] save us.

I can only say that the author's proclamation of "Bolshevism on a West-European scale" is, I am deeply convinced, neither Bolshevism nor Marxism, but a minor variant of the same old Economism.[13]

84. Nikolai Bukharin   85. Georgy Pyatakov   86. Karl Radek

Furthermore, he stated: "Here, again there is not a grain of Marxism, not a grain of logic, save the *logic of imperialist Economism*."[14]

Whether a demand is realisable or not is not an abstract question, as the 'Lefts' proclaimed, but depends on the struggle of the working class. Reforms, as Marxists explained, were generally a product of the revolutionary struggle.

It is no accident that the Bukharin-Pyatakov-Radek grouping, who took an ultra-left position on the national question, was later to become part of the 'Left Communists' within the Party. With Kamenev lining up with the opportunist wing of the Bolshevik Party, Lenin would again repeat his remarks about the lamentable role of the 'old Bolsheviks' between March and April 1917.

We have to note that in this dispute over self-determination, the Polish Rosa Luxemburg was from an oppressed nation, while the opposition within the Bolshevik party was from the Great Russian oppressor nation. This explains why Lenin was so scathing towards the Russian Bolsheviks – "*every line is wrong!*", he wrote.[15]

For him, it was the elementary duty of Marxists of the oppressor nation to stress the *right* of the oppressed nation to self-determination, up to and including secession. Any trace of national oppression must be burned out. On the other hand, those revolutionaries from an oppressed nation should stress the *unity* of the working class across all frontiers and, in the case of Poland, between Polish and Russian workers.

87. Barricade during the Easter Rising

At the end of the day, in spite of some differences, Lenin and Luxemburg were united in fighting for internationalism and world revolution. That was always their starting point. However, it was Lenin who was able to skilfully link the struggle of the oppressed nations against tsarism with the socialist revolution. This was a key factor in its success.

The Easter Rising

As explained, the national question was very much linked to the struggle of the oppressed (colonial) nations against the imperialist powers. It is no accident that Lenin rushed to defend the Easter Rising in 1916, a rebellion in Ireland, within the British empire, against British rule and the imperialist war. James Connolly, the Irish Marxist and internationalist, who helped lead the uprising, was wounded and captured by the British. He was wheeled out from his hospital bed as he was unable to walk, strapped to a chair and executed by a firing squad. This was at the behest of the British General Staff and on the orders of a British War Cabinet that included the Labour leader Arthur Henderson.

Lenin attacked those who described the Easter Rising in Ireland in 1916 as a 'putsch' and regarded it as a picture of the coming revolutionary explosions elsewhere:

88. James Connolly   89. Inessa Armand

To imagine that social revolution is *conceivable* without revolts by small nations in the colonies and Europe, without revolutionary outbursts by a section of the petty bourgeoisie *with all its prejudices*, without a movement of the politically non-conscious proletarian and semi-proletarian masses against oppression by the landowners, the church, and the monarchy, against national oppression, etc. – to imagine all this is to *repudiate social revolution*. So one army lines up in one place and says, "We are for socialism", and another, somewhere else and says, "We are for imperialism", and that will be a socialist revolution! Only those who hold such a ridiculous pedantic view could vilify the Irish rebellion by calling it a 'putsch'.

Whoever expects a 'pure' social revolution will *never* live to see it. Such a person pays lip-service to revolution without understanding what revolution is.

The Russian Revolution of 1905 was a bourgeois-democratic revolution. It consisted of a series of battles in which *all* the discontented classes, groups and elements of the population participated. Among these there were masses imbued with the crudest prejudices, with the vaguest and most fantastic aims of struggle; there were small groups which accepted Japanese money, there were speculators and adventurers, etc. But *objectively*, the mass movement was breaking the back of tsarism and paving the way for democracy; for this reason the class-conscious workers led it.[16]

Lenin's only regret was that the Irish rebellion did not coincide with a general European uprising, which could have given it a much greater chance of success: "It is the misfortune of the Irish that they rose prematurely, before the European revolt of the proletariat had *had time* to mature."[17]

Lenin would again return to the national question and the problem of the colonial peoples in 1920 at the Second Congress of the Communist International, where, based on the experience of the October Revolution, new lessons would be drawn about the national question that confirmed Trotsky's theory of permanent revolution.

Underground conditions

As mentioned, within tsarist Russia the vicious state repression, assisted by police infiltration, had driven the Bolshevik Party underground. The repression resulted in widespread arrests, as well as the imprisonment and exile of thousands of known revolutionaries, including Kamenev, who was exiled to Siberia. The Bolshevik organisation was largely broken up, although the proletarian Vyborg District of Petrograd still remained an isolated bastion for the Party.

Following the government closure of *Pravda* in July 1914, the Party was without a publication. In October, a new paper, *Sotsial-Demokrat*, was established abroad. However, given the shortage of funds, it only appeared irregularly. More seriously, for the first eighteen months of the war, the 'Russian bureau' of the Central Committee, its key leadership within Russia, ceased to function as most of its members were in Siberia. Even when it was eventually re-established, communication with Lenin in Switzerland was at best intermittent.

During 1915, the Party began to slowly revive, which was reflected in the increased number of delegates attending committees and conferences. Lenin wrote to Shlyapnikov in August 1915:

> It is clear that the advanced section of Pravdist workers, the bulwark of our Party, has survived, in spite of terrible devastation in its ranks. It would be extremely important for leading groups to come together in two or three centres (*most conspiratively*), establish contact with us, restore a Bureau of the Central Committee (one exists, I think, in Petersburg already) and the CC itself in Russia. They should establish firm ties with us (*if necessary*, one or two persons should be brought to Sweden for this purpose). We would send news-sheets, leaflets, etc. The most important thing is firm and constant relations.[18]

Throughout this period, Lenin fought to retain such "relations". He attempted to utilise every opportunity and small opening to advance the Party. This even included making use of the War Industry Committees for propaganda. The government tried to use these Committees to bind the workers to the war effort, and so isolate them from Bolshevism. But the scheme backfired, as workers used its forums to organise mass meetings to put forward their demands.

In this way, the Bolshevik workers skilfully built up their influence. The following is one of the resolutions passed at a mass meeting of the New Lessner works in Petrograd and recorded by Shlyapnikov:

> We, workers at the New Lessner works, having discussed the question of participation in the War Industries Committees and the election of deputies to works committees, have resolved: the present world war has been hatched and is being waged exclusively in the interests of bourgeois-capitalist society. The proletariat has no interest in the current war. It will bring it nothing but millions of comrades fallen in the field, millions of cripples and destitute. Simultaneously with the declaration of war on the Central Empires, the commanding classes of Russia have declared a ruthless war upon the whole labouring class, the proletariat. They have strangled the workers' trade unions and destroyed the workers' press…Our reply can be one only: the proletariat will fight for the emancipation and liberation of the labouring masses of the population, whatever nationality they belong to. We reject any activity connected with support for the international bloodbath, or support for the commanding classes, who have crushed and oppressed the labouring population for centuries on end. We recognise that only the complete destruction of the capitalist police-autocratic regime will be able to bring the country out of the situation that has come about. We demand the immediate convening of an All-Russian Constituent Assembly elected on the basis of universal, direct, equal and secret suffrage. We demand the immediate restoration of all the proletariat's trade unions and cultural and educational organisations; we demand freedom of the press, freedoms of assembly and association. We regard the broad organisation of the working-class in trade union, cultural and educational, and strictly class political organisations to be the most pressing urgent task of the hour. The police-autocratic regime is pushing the country towards a whole series of catastrophes: having clapped our best comrades into heavy convicts' shackles, it still holds them to this day behind locked prison gates, in exile or hard labour – these, the fighters for our better future. We demand the immediate release of all those arrested, exiled and sentenced for political activity.[19]

As can be seen, every legal opening, no matter how small, was used by the Bolsheviks, including those platforms set up by the government for their own ends. Such openings also included insurance and friendly societies, which were both legal and provided a further avenue for semi-revolutionary work.

Despite the military censorship, news percolated through of a developing strike movement throughout the country. Once again, the Party intervened. Petrograd became the centre of Bolshevik activity, led by the Petersburg Committee, where economic demands quickly became political ones. On 9 January 1916, on the anniversary of Bloody Sunday, some 40,000 workers demonstrated in the capital, with the Vyborg District at its head. There was a "spontaneous growth of mass discontent", wrote Shlyapnikov. "It passed from the rear out to the front and, reinforced by the grievances of trench life, rebounded into the villages and towns…"[20]

At this time, with the growing ferment against the impositions of the war, the thirst for illegal socialist literature was steadily growing. To satisfy this demand, there were various kinds of manuscripts and type-written copies of articles from illegal publications circulating among the workers. Among these were copies of Lenin's pamphlet, *Socialism and War*, which were passed around from hand-to-hand in Moscow. Copies of *Sotsial-Demokrat* and *Kommunist* became sought after and people paid 50 kopeks or a rouble for such 'luxuries'.

Membership of the Party was starting to grow. In the south, the Volga region, central region and in Petrograd, local organisations were filling up with new recruits. By mid-1916 and early 1917, there were now 3,000 members in the capital, 500 of whom were in the Vyborg District.

Despite the progress, Lenin was very critical of the lack of contact with Russia. His growing frustration found expression in his correspondence. He wrote to Shlyapnikov in October 1916, urging him to make a trip to the interior:

> The most pressing question now is the weakness of contacts between us and leading workers in Russia!! No correspondence!! No one but James [Anna Ulyanova], and now he has gone!! We can't go on like that. We *cannot* organise either the publication of leaflets or transport, either agreement about manifestos or sending over their drafts, etc. etc. without *regular* secret correspondence. That is the key question![21]

He continued by stressing the need to make contacts:

Two-thirds of the contacts, as a minimum, in each city, should be with leading *workers*, i.e. they should *write* themselves, *themselves* master secret correspondence (artists are made, not born), should themselves each train up 1-2 'heirs' in case of arrest. This should not be entrusted to the intelligentsia alone. Certainly not. It can and must be done by the leading workers. Without this it is *impossible* to establish continuity and purpose in our work – and that is the main thing.[22]

International front

While he tried to keep abreast of events in Russia, much of Lenin's attention was drawn to the international front. Following the collapse of the International he was very conscious of the need to gather together the forces of genuine internationalism. The first attempt began with the Bolshevik intervention at an international socialist women's conference held in Bern in March 1915.

Given the war-time restrictions on movements, the conference was a very modest affair with twenty-nine delegates present from several countries. It nevertheless provided an important platform and a testing ground for their ideas. The Bolsheviks managed to send five delegates, made up of Krupskaya, Inessa Armand, Zlata Lilina, Elena Fedorovna Rozmirovich and Olga Ravich.

As was expected, the main resolution before the conference was largely of a pacifist character, which studiously evaded condemning social chauvinism. Most of the German delegates attending were part of the Liebknecht-Luxemburg grouping, and included Clara Zetkin, but they acted rather cautiously on the international stage. Luxemburg was not able to attend, as she was already in prison. They sought the widest unity against the war and therefore opposed the Bolsheviks' defeatist line.

The Bolshevik delegation submitted an alternative draft that stated, "the working woman will attain her aim" of ending the suffering caused by imperialist wars "only through a revolutionary mass movement, and a strengthening and sharpening of the socialist struggle."[23]

This amendment, however, was overwhelmingly rejected with only the Bolsheviks and the Polish delegate voting in favour. "Everyone criticised our 'splitting' policy", notes Krupskaya.[24] But it was a modest start that had at least put down a marker. Lenin was, as always, optimistic. "No matter that we are so few. We shall have millions with us", he proclaimed.[25]

This was followed in April by an intervention in the International Socialist Youth Conference, also in Bern. Once again, the Bolsheviks pressed for a revolutionary struggle against the war. But again, to no avail. Nevertheless, despite the limits, such interventions served to raise the banner of socialist internationalism against the imperialist war and were to bear fruit over time.

Revolutionary epoch

In the summer, Lenin wrote an extensive text, *The Collapse of the Second International*, which dealt with the crisis within Social-Democracy and the role of the 'centrists' around Kautsky, who, as Lenin stated, posed the greatest threat to the movement. As opposed to the pessimism from the rest of the left, Lenin raised a bold perspective. He showed that the contradictions arising from the war were sowing the seeds of revolutionary crises everywhere. "All governments are sleeping on a volcano", he wrote. "The conflagration is spreading; the political foundations of Europe are being shaken more and more; the sufferings of the masses are appalling…"[26] He continued:

> … we cited facts which prove that those who *fear* revolution – petty-bourgeois Christian parsons, the General Staffs and millionaires' newspapers – are compelled to admit that symptoms of a revolutionary situation exist in Europe.[27]

For the first time, Lenin clearly outlined the three main objective conditions for a revolutionary situation. Firstly, he explained that revolution begins, not at the bottom, but at the top, with a split in the ruling class, which was evident everywhere:

> (1) when it is impossible for the ruling classes to maintain their rule without any change; when there is a crisis, in one form or another, among the 'upper classes', a crisis in the policy of the ruling class, leading to a fissure through which the discontent and indignation of the oppressed classes burst forth. For a revolution to take place, it is usually insufficient for 'the lower classes not to want' to live in the old way; it is also necessary that 'the upper classes should be unable' to live in the old way; (2) when the suffering and want of the oppressed classes have grown more acute than usual; (3) when, as a consequence of the above causes, there is a considerable increase in the activity of the masses, who uncomplainingly allow themselves to be robbed in 'peace time', but, in turbulent times, are drawn both by all the circumstances of the crisis *and by the 'upper classes' themselves* into independent historical action.

> Without these objective changes, which are independent of the will, not only of individual groups and parties but even of individual classes, a revolution, as a general rule, is impossible. The totality of all these objective changes is called a revolutionary situation. Such a situation existed in 1905 in Russia…[28]

90. Sörenberg

From Bern, Lenin and Krupskaya moved to Sörenberg, a village in the Swiss Alps, surrounded by woods and mountains. This change was mainly due to Krupskaya's poor health at the time. Shortly afterwards, Inessa came to stay with them for a period. "He found he could work very well in Sörenberg", explains Krupskaya.[29] Fortunately for Lenin, the Swiss library service was very good, and so was the Swiss postal service, which allowed him to obtain the books he needed. As Krupskaya explained:

> We would get up early, and before dinner, which was served throughout Switzerland at 12 o'clock, each of us would work in different nooks of the garden. Inessa often played the piano during those hours, and it was very pleasant to work to the sounds of music drifting down into the garden. In the afternoon we used to go for walks in the mountains sometimes for the rest of the day. Ilyich loved the mountains – he liked to climb the spurs of Rothorn towards the evening, when one got a beautiful view from the heights with the rose-tinted mist curling below, or to roam about the Schrattenfluh (a mountain about two kilometres from us) which we translated as 'accursed steps'.[30]

In Germany, the anti-war grouping around Liebknecht and Luxemburg was beginning to grow. In March 1915, twenty-five SPD deputies voted against the war credits, which increased in August to thirty-six, and in December to forty-three. There were also important strikes, which were a sign of the changing conditions. In April 1915, Luxemburg and Liebknecht founded the *International* magazine, which was immediately suppressed. Luxemburg had by now written her anti-war *Junius Pamphlet*, but it was not published until the following January 1916. This step coincided with the launch of the Spartacus League.

This ferment in Germany pushed the likes of Kautsky, Bernstein and Hugo Haase to the left verbally, in order to counter the growing influence of Liebknecht and Luxemburg.

Zimmerwald Conference

As expected, the old leaders of the Second International, terrified of anything that would upset the war effort, worked strenuously to block any attempt to organise opposition to their pro-war policy. But small cracks soon began to appear, which eventually led to the Zimmerwald Conference of internationalists in September 1915.

This small but significant conference marked an important step in the gathering together of the internationalists. It took place in the mountain town of Zimmerwald, near Bern. The meeting consisted of thirty-eight delegates from eleven European countries, who represented different groups and organisations, the big majority of whom held pacifist or semi-pacifist views.

Delegates from the British Independent Labour Party and the British Socialist Party were blocked from attending by the military authorities. Alfred Rosmer and Pierre Monatte, the French delegates, were also stopped from participating. When the delegates finally arrived, such were their small numbers that Lenin joked that the internationalists worldwide could be squeezed into a few stage coaches.

The main task, as Lenin saw it, was to rescue and defend the traditions of genuine internationalism, not in the form of pacifism, but in the traditions of Marxism. But this was to prove an uphill struggle. There were different political tendencies present at Zimmerwald. There were those on the far left, represented by Lenin, who were in favour of splitting from the reformists.

Another group was composed of the moderate elements, who simply saw the conference as a call for peace. They were followed by those of the 'centre' who, while leaning to the left, were against a split and looked towards some kind of accommodation with the moderates. These were mostly of the pacifist persuasion.

91. Hotel Beau Séjour, location of the Zimmerwald conference
– a lithograph from 1864

Hugo Haase and Karl Kautsky, who were now making statements against the war, were invited, but they refused to attend. Karl Liebknecht, being held in prison for his anti-war stand, was not able to attend. The same was true of Rosa Luxemburg.

The Bolsheviks were determined to make the most of Zimmerwald and sent a delegation that included Lenin and Zinoviev to argue their case. Lenin arrived early to rally the left delegates – who became known as the 'Zimmerwald Left' – and who put forward their own draft resolutions to the conference.

The majority of those attending were very confused as to the real nature of the imperialist war. This led to their failure to adopt a clear revolutionary policy. Lenin did his best to cut across this confusion, but his supporters were in a minority.

Karl Liebknecht managed to send a message to the conference which attacked the chauvinist social-democratic leaders, as well as the 'centre' around Kautsky. "This current is a more dangerous enemy of the proletariat than the bourgeois advocates of imperialism", stated Liebknecht, which aligned with Lenin's views. "By misusing the banner of socialism, it can mislead the less conscious layers of the proletariat. A ruthless struggle against social imperialism is the first prerequisite for the revolutionary mobilisation of the proletariat and the restoration of the International." He went on: "Civil war, not 'civil peace', is our slogan!"[31] This came very close to Lenin's idea.

At the conference, the majority still defended the 'unity' of the old International, which in practice was now in pieces, and baulked at the idea of a Third International. In the debate, Alphonse Merrheim, a French trade union leader, attacked Lenin: "You, Comrade Lenin, are concerned with the desire to lay the foundation of a new International, not with the demand for peace. This is what divides us." Merrheim would move rapidly to the right and eventually break with the Zimmerwald movement.

Lenin intervened in the central debate and said that "it was inevitable that things here would have come to a struggle of opinion between Ledebour and us."[32] Georg Ledebour was a Reichstag deputy who stood on the moderate wing, but the majority present were centrists and beset by political vacillation and hesitation. In the end, the Zimmerwald Left gained a total of eight votes out of thirty-eight, almost 20 per cent of the vote.

Lenin entertained no illusions in the pacifist majority, but saw the conference as a step in the right direction, in which the ideas of the Zimmerwald Left had gained an echo and, more importantly, received a wider international circulation following the conference. The Bolsheviks handed out a German edition of their main pamphlet, *Socialism and War*.

Finally, after four days of debates, a manifesto drafted by Trotsky was endorsed, which had managed to skilfully breach most of the differences. Ledebour demanded that there be no amendments or he would refuse to sign it.

While the manifesto retained many important principles, it inevitably contained a number of weaknesses, consisting mostly of things which had been left out for the sake of unity. Despite this, the manifesto marked an important step forward. It contained the following:

> Piece by piece, the veil which has hidden the meaning of this world catastrophe from the understanding of the peoples is falling down. In every country, the capitalists who forge the gold of war profits from the blood of the people are declaring that the war is for national defence, democracy, and the liberation of the oppressed nationalities. THEY LIE! [...]
>
> Organised workers!
>
> Since the outbreak of the war, you have put your energies, your courage, your steadfastness at the service of the ruling classes. Now the task is to enter the lists for your own cause, for the sacred aims of socialism, for the salvation of the oppressed nations, and the enslaved classes, by means of irreconcilable working-class struggle.

It is the task and duty of the socialists of the belligerent countries to begin the struggle with all their power. It is the task and duty of the socialists of the neutral countries to support their brothers by all effective means in this fight against bloody barbarity.

Never in the history of the world, has there been any more urgent, and more noble, a more sublime task, the fulfilment of which must be our common work. No sacrifice is too great, no burden too heavy, to attain this end: establishment of peace among nations.

Working men and women! Mothers and fathers! Widows and orphans! Wounded and crippled! To all who are suffering from the war, or in consequence of the war, we cry out over the frontiers, over the smoking, battlefields, over the devastated cities and hamlets.

Workers of the world unite![33]

Trotsky wrote extensively about the Zimmerwald conference in his paper, *Nashe Slovo*, where he praised the draft resolution submitted by Lenin and Radek. He considered that it:

> … represented a giant step forward for authentic revolutionary-socialist internationalism… In this framework everything separating the position of *Sotsial-Demokrat* [the Bolsheviks] from *Nashe Slovo* was absent from the draft resolution. It only remained for the representative of *Nashe Slovo* to declare his solidarity with the basic theses of the resolution and to propose it be transmitted to the commission for a happier formulation. Unfortunately, the resolution did not obtain a majority.[34]

The Left's declaration

Following the conference, the Zimmerwald Left organised a bureau of their own to further their aims. They also issued their own declaration, which was included in the official report:

> The undersigned declare as follows:
>
> The manifesto adopted by the Conference does not give us complete satisfaction. It contains no pronouncement on either open opportunism, or opportunism that is hiding under radical phraseology – the opportunism which is not only the chief cause of the collapse of the International, but which strives to perpetrate that collapse. The manifesto contains no clear pronouncement as to the methods of fighting against the war.

We shall continue, as we have done heretofore, to advocate in the socialist press and at meetings of the International, a clear-cut Marxian position in regard to the tasks with which the epoch of imperialism has confronted the proletariat.

We vote for the manifesto because we regard it as a call to struggle and in this struggle we are anxious to march side-by-side with the other sections of the International.

We request that our present declaration be included in the official proceedings.

[Signed] N Lenin, G Zinoviev, Radek, Nerman, Höglund, Winter.[35]

A further declaration was signed by Roland-Holst and Trotsky, which read as follows:

Inasmuch as the adoption of our amendment (to the manifesto) demanding the vote against war appropriations might in any way endanger the success of the Conference, we do, under protest, withdraw our amendment and accept Ledebour's statement in the commission to the effect that the manifesto contains all that is implied in our proposition.

It may be added that Ledebour, as an ultimatum, demanded the rejection of the amendment, refusing to sign the manifesto otherwise.[36]

Lenin, despite his reservations, drew up a balance sheet of the Zimmerwald conference in which he stated:

In practice, the manifesto signifies a step towards an ideological and practical break with opportunism and social-chauvinism. At the same time, the manifesto, as any analysis will show, contains inconsistencies, and does not say everything that should be said.[37]

He then went on:

Was our Central Committee right in signing this manifesto, with all its inconsistency and timidity? We think it was.[38]

The Zimmerwald manifesto, despite being shrouded in a conspiracy of silence, had its effect on the war-torn movement internationally. As the war dragged on, opposition currents began to emerge within the ranks of the parties of the Second International. This ferment was also reflected in a growing number of strikes at home.

In early May 1916, eight months after Zimmerwald, another international conference took place in Kienthal. This time it was attended by forty-three delegates from around Europe, reflecting a small increase. Again, this was in spite of the fact that more than a dozen delegates, including Trotsky, were denied travel documents and were therefore unable to attend. The Left were stronger at Kienthal, where their arguments began to find more of an echo.

However, the balance of forces was still against them as the majority of the conference, as before, was made up of centrists. The final outcome was the adoption of another compromise resolution. Nevertheless, Kienthal represented an advance of the Left in comparison to Zimmerwald, where their vote had increased from eight to twelve, a 50 per cent rise.

It reflected a subterranean shift that was taking place. It was a harbinger of a growing split within social democracy, which in Germany was to lead to the creation of the Independent Social Democratic Party (USPD), a centrist party, in Easter 1917. But this is still some way off.

18. Lenin Sharpens his Weapons

Despite the intervention at Kienthal, Lenin was increasingly feeling the burden of being in exile. Money was in short supply and, as a result of the war-time inflation, was becoming more of a problem. By the beginning of 1916, Lenin was feeling the squeeze and was desperately looking for a cheaper place to live. In October of that year, he wrote:

> As regards myself personally, I will say that I need to earn. Otherwise we shall simply die of hunger, really and truly!! The cost of living is devilishly high, and there is nothing to live on.[1]

He repeatedly requested translation work to make ends meet: "If this is not organised, I really will not be able to hold out, this is absolutely serious, absolutely, absolutely."[2] Krupskaya could see that the chronic lack of funds troubled Lenin. Such complaints were to be commonplace up until they left for Russia in March 1917.

Looking back on things, what is truly remarkable is that, from a tiny minority within the space of only two years, Lenin and the Bolsheviks would be in power. This showed the speed of events that were beginning to unfold, accelerated by the horrors of war. But that was in the run-up to 1917.

At this time, however, Lenin and Krupskaya were feeling deeply isolated in Switzerland. Krupskaya summed up their mood:

> ... nothing could shake off this feeling of being cooped up in a petty-bourgeois democratic cage. Out there the revolutionary struggle was mounting, life was seething, but it was all so far away.[3]

Zinoviev writes:

> At this time, in the years 1915-17, he [Lenin] led a rather secluded life in
> Switzerland. The war and the collapse of the International had deeply affected him,
> and many, who knew him before, were surprised at the change which had taken
> place in him since the war. He never was very tender towards the bourgeoisie, but
> since the war his hatred of the bourgeoisie became concentrated and sharp like a
> dagger. He seemed to have changed even in his appearance.[4]

These were extremely difficult years for Lenin, simply holding things together
and inching forward. Despite some strikes, the class struggle was dead
compared to the past, suffocated by the fumes of war and class-collaboration.
"During the war there was a silence as of death among the workers", notes
Trotsky.[5]

The war seemed to be endlessly dragging on and workers were killing
one another on a daily basis. The International had collapsed and Lenin
was feeling trapped, but he remained firm. He approvingly quoted a French
philosopher, who once said:

> Dead ideas are those that appear in elegant garments, with no asperity or daring.
> They are dead because they are put into general circulation and become part of
> the ordinary intellectual baggage of the great army of philistines. Strong ideas are
> those that shock and scandalise, evoke indignation, anger, and animosity in some,
> and enthusiasm in others.[6]

This summed up Lenin's fighting spirit. Faced with a crisis, some people
are broken by the experience, but with others, they are tempered and
strengthened. "Like every crisis in the life of individuals or in the history
of nations, war oppresses and breaks some, steels and enlightens others",
Lenin explained.[7] He was one of those who was steeled and enlightened
by such events.

Marxist philosophy

While feeling isolated, "the autumn of 1915 found us busier than ever
in the libraries", explains Krupskaya.[8] Although between 1914 and 1916
Lenin had many problems to deal with, he did not allow them to distract
him from his important theoretical work that provided him with much
greater insights.

The world catastrophe in particular had made him think even more
deeply about Marxism as a science. He therefore turned his attention to

92. Georg Friedrich Wilhelm Hegel   93. Ludwig Feuerbach

Marxist philosophy and took time out to deepen his understanding with an in-depth study of Hegel, Aristotle and Feuerbach. Lenin always had an interest in this subject and had done extensive work on philosophy in answering the idealism of Bogdanov and his followers in *Materialism and Empirio-criticism*.

For Lenin, dialectical materialism was the cornerstone of Marxism, which in fact had originated with a struggle for materialist philosophy and in defence of dialectics. This provided Marx and Engels with a weapon to understand the world, "an integral world outlook irreconcilable with any form of superstition, reaction, or defence of bourgeois oppression."[9]

This method opens our eyes to the real relationships that exist, together with their contradictions. It allows us to understand how things continually move, develop and transform, which is a vital part of uncovering what the laws of society are, and therefore how to change them.

Dialectical materialism is a revolutionary philosophy which allows the working class to interpret the world and understand its place within it. It wages war against all forms of idealist philosophy that seeks to justify the status quo. After all, the ruling ideas in society are the ideas of the ruling class that seeks to defend its rule.

It was precisely the application of dialectical materialism that allowed Marx to understand the laws of capitalism as well as the development of class struggle and history. In this viewpoint, there is no place for God or the immortal soul, nor eternal norms. The dialectic is not an invention, but a recognition of the real processes unfolding in the material world.

Before the war Lenin had reviewed the *Marx-Engels Correspondence*, in which he said:

> If one were to attempt to define in a single word the focus, so to speak, of the whole correspondence, the central point at which the whole body of ideas expressed and discussed converges – that word would be *dialectics*. The application of materialist dialectics to the reshaping of all political economy from its foundations up, its application to history, natural science, philosophy and to the policy and tactics of the working class – that was what interested Marx and Engels most of all, that was where they contributed what was most essential and new, and that was what constituted the masterly advance they made in the history of revolutionary thought.[10]

Krupskaya notes:

> He [Lenin] tried to use every minute of the time the library was open, going there punctually at 9 am, sitting there till 12, coming home at ten past twelve to the minute (the library was closed 12 to 1), going back again after lunch and staying there until 6 pm.[11]

In early January 1915, Lenin addressed a letter to the editors of the *Granat Encyclopaedia*, regarding an article he had written about Karl Marx. He was asking if there was "still time for some corrections to the section on dialectics [...] It is a question I have been working on these last six weeks, and I think I could add something if there is still time." Unfortunately, there was no time and the corrections could not be included.

Nevertheless, Lenin continued his studies, which presented him with greater insights into many questions of a more immediate and concrete nature. His short but brilliant article, 'On the Question of Dialectics', written in 1915, provides a concise explanation of materialist dialectics that has arguably never been surpassed. It was the direct result of his careful study of Hegel's works.

Hegel had rediscovered dialectics from a profound study of the whole course of philosophy, starting with Heraclitus and Aristotle. Here we have a summing up of the entire content of previous philosophy, which Hegel raised to a new and higher level. But Hegel was an idealist and his dialectic was therefore expressed in a one-sided and mystical manner. Marx and Engels placed the dialectic of Hegel back on its feet.

Hegel pointed out that contradiction exists in everything, and is, in fact, the source of all motion, life and development. Lenin sees this as the very essence of dialectics:

> The splitting of a single whole and the cognition of its contradictory parts [...] is the *essence* (one of the 'essentials', one of the principal, if not the principal, characteristics or features) of dialectics.[12]

He continues:

> Dialectics as *living*, many-sided knowledge (with the number of sides eternally increasing), with an infinite number of shades of every approach and approximation to reality (with a philosophical system growing into a whole out of each shade) – here we have an immeasurably rich content as compared with 'metaphysical' materialism...*[13]

Materialist dialectics, Lenin stressed, lies at the heart of Marxism. It is the key to a general understanding and approach to complex processes.

'Science of Logic'

Lenin was able to penetrate beneath the idealistic appearance of Hegel and reveal the colossal profundity of his dialectical thought that lies concealed beneath the surface. He writes in his 'Conspectus of Hegel's *Science of Logic*':

> I am in general trying to read Hegel materialistically: Hegel is materialism which has been stood on its head (according to Engels) – that is to say, I cast aside for the most part God, the Absolute, the Pure Idea, etc.[14]

He explained there was much mysticism and pedantry in Hegel, but the basic underlying idea was one of pure genius. In his 'Conspectus of Hegel's *Science of Logic*', Lenin wrote the following:

> A river and the *drops* in this river. The position of *every* drop, its relation to the others; its connection with the others; the direction of its movement; its speed; the line of the movement – straight, curved, circular, etc. – upwards, downwards. The sum of the movement. [...] There you have *à peu près* [approximately] the picture of the world according to Hegel's *Logic*, – of course minus God and the Absolute.[15]

---

* 'Metaphysical' materialism or 'metaphysics' means formal logic. Dialectics does not deny formal logic, but its relation to dialectical thinking is similar to the relation of a motion picture to a still photograph. The motion picture combines a series of still photos according to the laws of motion. Dialectics allows us to appreciate an ever-changing world.

94. The page from Lenin's manuscript 'Conspectus of Hegel's *Science of Logic*' in which he provides his outline of dialectical development

And again:

1. The determination of the concept out of itself (the thing itself must be considered in its relations and in its development);

2. the contradictory nature of the thing itself (*das Andere seiner* [the other of itself]), the contradictory forces and tendencies in each phenomenon;

3. the union of analysis and synthesis. Such, apparently, are the elements of dialectics.

One could perhaps present these elements in greater detail as follows:

1. The *objectivity* of consideration (not examples, not divergences, but the Thing-in-itself).

2. The entire totality of the manifold *relations* of this thing to others.

3. The *development* of this thing, (phenomenon, respectively), its own movement, its own life.

4. The internally contradictory *tendencies* (*and* sides) in this thing.

5. The thing (phenomenon, etc.) as the sum *and unity of opposites.*

6. The *struggle*, respectively unfolding, of these opposites, contradictory strivings, etc.

7. The union of analysis and synthesis – the break-down of the separate parts and the totality, the summation of these parts.

8. The relations of each thing (phenomenon, etc.) are not only manifold, but general, universal. Each thing (phenomenon, process, etc.) is connected with *every other.*

9. The only the unity of opposites, but the *transitions* of *every* determination, quality, feature, side, property into *every* other (into its opposite?).

10. The endless process of the discovery of *new* sides, relations, etc.

11. The endless process of the deepening of man's knowledge of the thing, of phenomena, processes, etc., from appearance to essence and from less profound to more profound essence.

12. From co-existence to causality and from one form of connection and reciprocal dependence to another, deeper, more general form.

13. The repetition at a higher stage of certain features, properties, etc., of the lower and

14. the apparent return to the old (negation of the negation).

15. The struggle of content with form and conversely. The throwing off of the form, the transformation of the content.

16. The transition of quantity into quality and *vice versa.*[16]

Lenin's notes are full of such interesting observations about dialectical change and contradiction – unfortunately, too many to quote here. The extensive notes of these studies are contained in Volume 38 of Lenin's *Collected Works* and reflect a deepening of his knowledge of Marxist philosophy. These notes indicate that Lenin intended to write a book on materialist dialectics, but due to time and events, was unfortunately unable to carry this out.

Some may think it strange that when the world was literally being blown to pieces, Lenin was spending his time in a library poring over Hegel's *Science of Logic*. But in strengthening his knowledge of Marxist philosophy, he was sharpening the most important weapon in the revolutionary arsenal – theory. In this way, Lenin was preparing for the coming revolution.

According to Rappaport, Lenin's efforts in this field simply resulted in twenty-three notebooks "full of his political and economic musings". But any unbiased person who takes the trouble to read the contents of Lenin's philosophical notebooks cannot fail to be impressed by their marvellous profundity.

Despite their obviously unfinished character, these terse but insightful notes cannot, by any stretch of the imagination, be described as musings, except by the likes of Rappaport whose distaste for Lenin is only surpassed by her abysmal ignorance of philosophy.

The dialectical method is in complete contrast to the fixed categories and abstractions of formal logic, which involves stationary and unchanging quantities. It attempts to provide us with motionless imprints of reality, which consists of eternal motion. In fact, everything flows and is changing.

Dialectical thought provides us with an understanding of change, closer approximations, and a richness of content and flexibility. It even provides a certain succulence that brings them closer to the living phenomena.*

Of course, the dialectic was not a magic formula that explains everything. It does not replace concrete scientific analysis. However, it guides the analysis along correct lines, avoiding unnecessary pitfalls and blind alleys.

This side of Lenin, as a great theoretician of Marxism, has been ignored by his bourgeois biographers and even some of those who claim to be sympathetic to him. To those who are blind to dialectics, this is to be expected. Dialectics, for Lenin, was not a secondary matter. He set out not simply to understand but to *master* the method of Marxism, which others merely skated over and never fully understood.

Theory and practice

This also applied, it must be said, to the leaders of the Bolshevik Party, all of whom had their merits, but few were rounded out Marxists in the theoretical sense. This was especially the case with Bukharin. Lenin once referred to Bukharin as "the most valuable and major theorist of the party" as well as "rightly considered the favourite of the whole Party".[17] But Lenin also recognised Bukharin's great weakness:

> ... his theoretical views can be classified as fully Marxist only with great reserve, for there is something scholastic about him (he has never made a study of dialectics and, I think, never fully understood it).[18]

---

* A deeper explanation of dialectical materialism would take us too far off the subject. For those who wish to delve into this subject in greater detail, we would recommend *The History of Philosophy* by Alan Woods and *Reason in Revolt* by Woods and Ted Grant.

The inability to think dialectically is the real reason for many – if not all – of Bukharin's mistakes. They were mistakes that in the end destroyed him. At first, he politically adopted an 'ultra-left' position, only eventually to swing 180 degrees far to the right.

Bukharin's weaknesses were partially overcome under Lenin's leadership and guidance – including with some harsh polemics. But, without the guiding hand of Lenin, he would quickly drift rightwards, calling for the kulaks to "Get rich!", and for socialism to be achieved "at a snail's pace".

Incidentally, this comment about Bukharin was in marked contrast to the praise Lenin expressed in relation to Trotsky, who had a solid grasp of dialectics. In his 1922 article, 'On the Significance of Militant Materialism', Lenin begins by saying:

> Comrade Trotsky has already said everything necessary, and said it very well, about the general purposes of *Pod Znamenem Marksizma** in issue No. 1-2 of that journal.[19]

It was in this article that Lenin demanded that every Communist study dialectics and follow advances in the sciences.

> For our attitude towards this phenomenon to be a politically conscious one, it must be realised that no natural science and no materialism can hold its own in the struggle against the onslaught of bourgeois ideas and the restoration of the bourgeois world outlook unless it stands on solid philosophical ground. In order to hold his own in this struggle and carry it to a victorious finish, the natural scientist must be a modern materialist, a conscious adherent of the materialism represented by Marx, i.e. he must be a dialectical materialist.

Lenin went on to explain:

> In order to attain this aim, the contributors to *Pod Znamenem Marksizma* must arrange for the systematic study of Hegelian dialectics from a materialist standpoint, i.e. the dialectics which Marx applied practically in his *Capital* and in his historical and political works, and applied so successfully that now every day of the awakening to life and struggle of new classes in the East...
>
> Of course, this study, this interpretation, this propaganda of Hegelian dialectics is extremely difficult, and the first experiments in this direction will undoubtedly be accompanied by errors. But only he who never does anything never makes

---

* A philosophical and socio-economic journal published in Moscow from January 1922 with the purpose of popularising materialism.

mistakes. Taking as our basis Marx's method of applying materialistically conceived Hegelian dialectics, we can and should elaborate this dialectics from all aspects, print in the journal excerpts from Hegel's principal works, interpret them materialistically and comment on them with the help of examples of the way Marx applied dialectics, as well as of examples of dialectics in the sphere of economic and political relations, which recent history, especially modern imperialist war and revolution, provides in unusual abundance.[20]

Lenin held that Marxism was a science and needed to be studied seriously. Not for nothing did he write as far back as 1902: "Without revolutionary theory there can be no revolutionary movement".[21] Theory for Lenin was not mere window dressing, but the essence of the revolutionary Party, an expression of the vital unity between dialectical materialism and revolutionary practice. It was on this solid basis alone that Lenin was able to prepare and arm the Bolshevik Party for taking power in 1917.

'Imperialism, the Highest Stage of Capitalism'

In 1915, Lenin read and was favourably impressed by Bukharin's study, *Imperialism and the World Economy*, for which he wrote an introduction that contained an attack on Kautsky's theory of imperialism. But Lenin felt that Bukharin's analysis only went so far, and he needed to go deeper into the subject. His studies in dialectical materialism allowed him to undertake this task. So, at the end of 1915, he began collecting material for a new book on imperialism.

Lenin undertook extensive research in libraries and relied heavily on John Hobson's book, *Imperialism*, as well as Rudolf Hilferding's *Finance Capital*, for material. He referred to an enormous number of books and articles on the subject in order to write his book. According to the preface of Volume 39 of his *Collected Works*, which contains nearly 800 pages of his notes on imperialism, these references amounted to 148 books (106 in German, twenty-three in French, seventeen in English and two translations into Russian), and 232 articles (of which 206 were in German, thirteen in French and thirteen in English) from forty-nine periodicals (thirty-four German, seven French and eight English). From this source material, as well as a thorough knowledge of Marxism, Lenin was able to write his classic work, *Imperialism, the Highest Stage of Capitalism*.

However, in order to deceive the tsarist censor, Lenin had to make certain modifications. Looking back on the book in a new preface in April 1917, he explained:

It is painful, in these days of liberty, to re-read the passages of the pamphlet which have been distorted, cramped, compressed in an iron vice on account of the censor.[22]

In dealing with annexations, he was forced to avoid naming the imperialist ambitions of Russia and instead quote the example of Japan. "The careful reader will easily substitute Russia for Japan, and Finland, Poland, Courland, the Ukraine, Khiva, Bokhara, Estonia or other regions peopled by non-Russians, for Korea."[23]

Despite these restrictions, the book remains another major classic of Marxism, which accurately defines the imperialist epoch that we are living in. Under capitalism, free competition developed into monopoly and by the turn of the previous century, the world economy was dominated by giant monopolies and banks. The old period of capitalism "has been followed by a new epoch, comparatively more impetuous, full of abrupt changes, catastrophes, conflicts, an epoch that no longer appears to the toiling masses as horror without end but is an end full of horrors", explained Lenin in his introduction to Bukharin's *Imperialism and World Economy*.[24]

The capitalist world had been divided up between a handful of imperialist powers, which were engaged in intense rivalry for world markets, raw materials and spheres of interest. As this rivalry intensified, and as the world was already divided, any new *redivision* would inevitably mean imperialist conflict and war. Consequently, the imperialist epoch was one of imperialist wars and conflicts, which, in turn, laid the basis for civil wars and revolutions.

In the book, Lenin criticises Kautsky's view, which declared that imperialism was "merely a system of foreign policy" (namely, annexation), and was not a definite economic stage in the development of capitalism.[25] Kautsky's argument was false, since foreign policy is nothing more than the continuation of home policy. Lenin took the opposite view to that of Kautsky:

Economically, imperialism (or the 'era' of finance capital – it is not a matter of words) is the highest stage in the development of capitalism, one in which production has assumed such big, immense proportions that *free competition gives way to monopoly*. That is the *economic* essence of imperialism. Monopoly manifests itself in trusts, syndicates, etc. in the omnipotence of the giant banks, in the buying up of raw material sources, etc., in the concentration of banking capital, etc. Everything hinges on economic monopoly.[26]

In the run-up to the war, Kautsky put forward his new theory of 'ultra-imperialism', as opposed to simply imperialism, in an article published in the SPD's theoretical journal, *Neue Zeit*. He believed that ultra-imperialism would lead to a more stable and peaceful world, where the contradictions of capitalism could be overcome. Such speculation about capitalism entering a new "peaceful" phase, in which the power of the giant monopolies would allow it to replace rivalries and contradictions, was the very basis of reformism and opportunism. As Lenin explained:

> The statement that cartels can abolish crises is a fable spread by bourgeois economists who at all costs desire to place capitalism in a favourable light. On the contrary, the monopoly created in *certain* branches of industry increases and intensifies the anarchy inherent in capitalist production *as a whole*.[27]

Rather than predicting an epoch of wars and revolution, as Lenin did, the perspective of Kautsky and the reformists was the opposite. In doing so, they pushed the idea of a socialist revolution into the far distant future, if not burying it altogether. Kautsky's idea was taken up by the German economist, Werner Sombart, who began as a 'Marxist', but moved far to the right.

> Capitalism will continue to transform itself internally in the same direction in which it has already begun to transform itself, at the time of its apogee: as it grows older, it will become more and more calm, sedate, reasonable.[28]

These prophetic lines were written in 1928, a year before the Wall Street Crash and the beginning of the Great Depression.

Lenin's book on imperialism completely refutes this peaceful and tranquilising perspective and offers a picture of intense rivalries and conflicts. As he explained:

> Half a century ago Germany was a miserable, insignificant country, if her capitalist strength is compared with that of the Britain of that time; Japan compared with Russia in the same way. Is it 'conceivable' that in ten or twenty years' time the relative strength of the imperialist powers will have remained *un*changed? It is out of the question.
>
> Therefore, in the realities of the capitalist system, and not in the banal philistine fantasies of English parsons, or of the German 'Marxist', Kautsky, 'inter-imperialist' or 'ultra-imperialist' alliances, no matter what form they may assume, whether of one imperialist coalition against another, or of a general alliance embracing *all* the imperialist powers, are *inevitably* nothing more than a 'truce' in periods between wars. Peaceful alliances prepare the ground for wars, and in their turn grow out of wars; the one conditions the other, producing alternating forms of peaceful and

non-peaceful struggle on *one and the same* basis of imperialist connections and relations within world economics and world politics.[29]

Lenin's writing on imperialism is enormously important for understanding the world today. Since the Second World War, as a result of the revolt of the colonial peoples, the imperialists were forced to relinquish direct control of the colonies. But that only meant that the *form* of oppression had changed. The major imperialist powers still retain their dominance over the weaker powers, no longer through direct military-bureaucratic rule, but through indirect domination through the mechanisms of world trade and debt, and a thousand other means whereby the poorest countries are enslaved, robbed and oppressed by imperialism.

Today, the growing tensions between the powers, constant wars, instability and upheavals present an accurate picture of imperialism in its epoch of capitalist decline and decay. It was explained and anticipated in advance by Lenin long ago.

19. The February Revolution

In September 1916, Lenin and Krupskaya moved to Zurich, where they continued their work for the Party. On their arrival, Lenin spent a lot of time doing research in the local libraries, as was usual. However, within a matter of a few months, this routine would be turned upside down. Russia would be in the throes of revolution and the Bolshevik Party would be thrust onto centre stage.

The crisis within Russia had been gradually maturing during the war years. On the military front, Russia had entered the conflict as a second-rate partner of the Entente. The initial advances had given way to military setbacks. In May 1915, the Russians were driven out of Galicia; in August, the Germans seized Warsaw and occupied vast areas of Poland and Russia.

As the war dragged on, Russian forces, more accustomed to fighting the peoples of the Caucasus than a modern Germany, faced declining morale and increasing discontent, all of which added to the growing difficulties and misfortunes at the front.

To make matters worse, this was compounded by an overwhelming feeling of war-weariness amongst Russian troops. "The lower orders began the war with enthusiasm; but now they are weary, and with the continual retreats have lost faith in a victory", wrote Alexei Kuropatkin, former Minister of War and Commander of the Grenadier Corps.[1]

This led to an increase in desertions at the front, which even affected whole regiments made up of peasant soldiers. Many left the trenches and simply went home.

95. Tsarina Alexandra

Those considered 'malcontents' on the home front, affected by Bolshevism, were drafted to the military front. This, of course, solved nothing and only made matters worse in spreading the Bolshevik infection far and wide. As the war dragged on, officers feared being shot in the back by their own men.

"Chaos now reigns supreme", the Grand Duke Nicholas wrote in July 1916.[2] But this chaos stemmed directly from the top, from a regime plagued with paralysis, infighting and splits. The squabbling court cliques seeking greater and greater influence only added to this crisis.

At the pinnacle of this centuries-old regime stood the tsar and tsarina, who were oblivious to the approaching storm. "The Russian aristocracy lived in a world of its own", remarked Bruce Lockhart, the British agent in Russia. "To the aristocracy the complete absolutism of the Tsar was something more than a religion. It was the rock on which its own sheltered existence was built."[3]

The role of the tsarina, Alexandra Feodorovna, was especially destructive. She was extremely religious, steeped in mysticism, and had a vice-like hold over Nicholas. As a result, she ended up running the country on behalf of

96. Rasputin surrounded by admirers in 1914

her husband. She was even more fanatical than him, believing she had a divine mission to preserve the autocracy for her son. "Be more autocratic", she demanded of Nicholas, "never forget that you are an autocratic ruler and that you must remain one." For good measure, she added: "Russia loves to be caressed with a horse-whip – such is the nature of these people."

In her flights of fancy, Alexandra urged her husband: "Be an Emperor, be Peter the Great, be Ivan the Terrible, be the Emperor Paul. Crush them all… No, don't laugh at me, you wicked man…" She campaigned to banish all the tsar's ministers to Siberia: "Send Lvov to Siberia… Milyukov, Guchkov and Polivanov to Siberia as well." She even exclaimed hysterically to her husband: "Oh, could one but hang Guchkov!"[4] Yet Guchkov was certainly no liberal, but the head of one of the most reactionary bourgeois parties, the Octobrists.

These outbursts didn't ingratiate her to Russia's natural rulers, who were alarmed by these ravings. In turn, the tsarina was under the influence of the 'debauched monk' and lecherous drunkard, Grigori Rasputin. This holy man was credited with the miraculous gift of healing. He was able to exploit the fact that Alexei, the tsar's son and heir to the throne, suffered from haemophilia, for which there was no cure. Rasputin convinced the superstitious tsarina that without him, Alexei would die. Through her, the monk was able to exercise colossal power, where ministerial positions were changed according to his every whim.

Decadence at the top of the regime was openly on display, with its drunkenness, superstition, moral corruption and obscurantism. As the war progressed, Rasputin's meddling in military matters increased, staunchly supported by the tsarina. She, in turn, believed that military victory could be delivered by the application of greater repression and cruelty. The actions of Rasputin and the tsarina only served to push the regime towards the abyss.

As the court cliques fought among themselves over her influence, the regime became increasingly divorced from reality. Consequently, rumours of a palace coup became more pronounced as fears grew of an impending collapse.

The mayhem at the top was accompanied by a deepening economic crisis below, brought on by a near-collapse of the transport system, especially the railways. This, in turn, created chronic food and fuel shortages, leading to mounting discontent. To cover the government's deficits, paper money was printed in increasing amounts, which only eroded the value of the ruble and increased inflation. The regime only managed to survive due to the loans granted by the Allies, which further increased Russia's reliance upon them. This, in turn, led to increased pressure on Russia to engage in greater, and more risky, military efforts on behalf of the Entente.

The assassination of Rasputin in December 1916 did nothing to solve the regime's problems. The whole Imperial edifice was crumbling. Rasputin's murder was a desperate gamble – the last throw of the dice – to save the old order, but it was far too late for that. The regime had become discredited and increasingly lacked social support. In a pathetic effort to change things, the feeble bourgeoisie went no further than engaging in a 'revolt on their knees'.

On 18 January 1917, the Okhrana reported on the situation to the Minister of Internal Affairs:

> The mood in the capital is extremely agitated. The wildest rumours are circulating in society, both as to the plans of the governing authority, for taking various kinds of reactionary measures, and as to the projected aims of groups and layers of the population hostile to the government, implying the possibility and likelihood of revolutionary initiatives and excesses. Everyone expects some sort of extraordinary actions either from one side or the other.[5]

In desperation, Rodzianko, the head of the Duma, sent a telegram to the tsar in late February, stating:

> The situation is becoming worse; measures must be taken immediately, for tomorrow will be too late. The last hour has come; the fate of our country and the dynasty is being decided.[6]

However, the tsar dismissed the advice and informed Count Vladimir Frederiks, the nobleman in charge of protocol: "Once again this Rodzianko has written me a lot of nonsense, which I won't even bother to answer."[7]

The Allies, growing ever more alarmed, attempted to intervene. Sir George Buchanan, the British Ambassador to Russia, spoke repeatedly to Nicholas about the serious state of the country, but to no avail. "If the Emperor continues to uphold his present reactionary advisers, a revolution is, I fear, inevitable", wrote Buchanan in his memoirs.[8] So desperate had things become, Buchanan revealed that plots were being hatched to murder the tsar and tsarina:

> A Palace revolution was openly spoken of, and at a dinner at the Embassy a Russian friend of mine, who had occupied a high position in the government, declared that it was a mere question whether both the Emperor and Empress or only the latter would be killed.[9]

The Ambassador added:

> A friend of mine, who was afterwards a member of the Provisional Government, sent me a message… to say that there would be a revolution before Easter.[10]

Lenin explained that revolution always begins at the top. Within the space of only ten weeks of Rasputin's death, revolution would arrive to sweep away the old regime.

In Switzerland, Lenin was largely oblivious to what was about to happen in Russia. He complained to Inessa Armand that the revolution was unfolding "extremely slowly and with difficulty".[11] At the end of December, he even applied for an extension of his Swiss residence permit until the end of 1917, not expecting much to happen.

'Pregnant with revolution'

On 22 January 1917, the anniversary of the 1905 Revolution, Lenin gave a lecture to a meeting of Swiss young socialists on the lessons of the Revolution.

In his speech, Lenin abandoned the idea of a 'democratic revolution' and outlined a future socialist perspective.

> ... the Russian revolution – precisely because of its proletarian character, in that particular sense of which I have spoken – is the *prologue* to the coming European revolution. Undoubtedly, this coming revolution can only be a proletarian revolution, and in an even more profound sense of the word: a proletarian revolution, socialist revolution in its content.[12]

This represented a fundamental change in Lenin's thinking, a profound break with the 'old Bolshevism', and the emergence of a new Bolshevik perspective for the Russian revolution.

> This coming revolution will show to an even greater degree, on the one hand, that only grim battles, only civil wars, can free humanity from the yoke of capital; on the other hand, that only class-conscious proletarians can and will give leadership to the vast majority of the exploited.

> We must not be deceived by the present grave-like stillness in Europe. Europe is pregnant with revolution.[13]

Lenin ended this speech by saying that he, as part of the older generation, "may not live to see the decisive battles of this coming revolution."[14] But great events were being prepared in Russia.

While Lenin was unaware of what was happening behind the scenes, the tsarist monarchy, which had all the police reports, was still blind to what was in store. In December 1916, three months before the regime was to be overthrown, the Empress Alexandra wrote to her husband, saying "a great and magnificent epoch is dawning for your reign."[15] However, "the approaching cataclysm was already in every mind, and on everybody's lips", wrote Bruce Lockhart.[16]

Within a relatively short time, tsarism fell and Russia was shaken by the February Revolution. As Lockhart noted, when it came, "the floodgates of three hundred years had been swept away."[17]

On 15 March, in Switzerland, Lenin heard the unexpected news that revolution had broken out in Russia, the tsar had abdicated, and a new Provisional Government had taken office. The revolution had finally arrived – a little earlier than expected!

Lenin scoured the newspapers for every scrap of information. He was forced to rely on reports in the foreign press to get as much up-to-date news as possible in order to help assist the Bolsheviks on the ground. But this was limited. He explained:

Information reaching Zurich from Russia at this moment, 17 March 1917, is so scanty, and events in our country are developing so rapidly, that any judgement of the situation must of need be very cautious.[18]

Nevertheless, he began to sketch out some preliminary, but important, observations, which he was to expand upon as time went on.

The Revolution begins

The year 1917 will stand out in history as the year of the successful Bolshevik Revolution in October, in which, for the first time in history, the working class seized and held onto power. However, the year began, at first, with the February Revolution, which swept away tsarism and introduced a regime of what Lenin described as 'dual power'. The October Revolution would consummate the February events by abolishing landlordism and capitalism. But that was nine months away, and between February and October was stormy period of revolution and counter-revolution.

The great February Revolution began with the protests of women textile workers, who went on strike on 8 March (23 February, Old Style) and called on other workers to support them. As Fyodor Raskolnikov explains in his memoirs, *Kronstadt and Petrograd in 1917*:

> "Today is Women's Day", it flashed through my mind on the morning of 23 February. "Will something happen in the streets today?" As things turned out, 'Women's Day' was fated to be the first day of the revolution. Working women, driven to despair by their hard conditions, a prey to the torments of hunger, were the first to come out onto the streets demanding "bread, freedom and peace".[19]

Their demands were, in fact, modest, but they soon led to the downfall of centuries of tsarism. The heroic role played by women in the Russian Revolution was foreseen some five months earlier when Lenin was drawing on the experiences of the Paris Commune:

> A certain bourgeois observer of the Paris Commune, writing to an English newspaper in May 1871, said: "If the French nation consisted entirely of women, what a terrible nation it would be!" Women and teenage children fought in the Paris Commune side by side with the men. It will be no different in the coming battles for the overthrow of the bourgeoisie. Proletarian women will not look on passively as poorly armed or unarmed workers are shot down by the well-armed forces of the bourgeoisie. They will take to arms, as they did in 1871, and from the cowed nations of today – or more correctly, from the present-day labour

97. International Women's Day demonstration in Petrograd, 1917

movement, disorganised more by the opportunists than by the governments – there will undoubtedly arise, sooner or later, but with absolute certainty, an international league of the 'terrible nations' of the revolutionary proletariat.[20]

He also praised the role of women workers in discussion with Clara Zetkin in 1920:

In Petrograd, here in Moscow, in other towns and industrial centres the women workers acted splendidly during the revolution. Without them we should not have been victorious. Or scarcely so. That is my opinion. How brave they were, how brave they still are![21]

Fyodor Raskolnikov went on to describe the scenes on that day of 8 March:

The trams were not running, which meant the streets were uncharacteristically empty and quiet. But at the corner of Bolshoi Prospekt and Gavanskaya Street groups of working women kept assembling. Mounted policemen tried to disperse them, roughly pushing them apart with the muzzles of their horses and hitting them with the flats of their drawn swords. When the tsarist *oprichniki* rode on to the pavement the crowd would, without losing composure, break up for the moment, heaping curses and threats upon them; but as soon as the mounted

СЛАВА ЖЕНЩИНАЪ БОРЦАМЪ ЗА СВОБОДУ

МАНИФЕСТАЦІЯ ЖЕНЩИНЪ

98. Another view of the demonstration

policemen had returned to the roadway, the crowd would close up again into a solid mass. In some of the groups we could see men, but the overwhelming majority consisted of working women and workers' wives.[22]

Morgan Philips Price, who was the Special Correspondent in Russia for the *Manchester Guardian*, wrote to his aunt in England expressing his excitement during the February events:

> Whole country is wild with joy, waving red flags and singing *Marseillaise*. It has surpassed my wildest dreams and I can hardly believe it is true. After two-and-a-half years of mental suffering and darkness I at last begin to see the light. Long live Great Russia, which has shown the world the road to freedom.[23]

As in all revolutions, events were moving at lightning speed. Consciousness was leaping ahead with every passing day. And as Lenin explained:

> Every revolution means a sharp turn in the lives of a vast number of people. Unless the time is ripe for such a turn, no real revolution can take place. And just as any turn in the life of an individual teaches him a great deal and brings rich experience and great emotional stress, so a revolution teaches an entire people very rich and valuable lessons in a short space of time. During a revolution, millions and tens

of millions of people learn in a week more than they do in a year of ordinary, somnolent life.[24]

The Bolsheviks in February

However, the Bolshevik Party, which would eventually lead the revolution, was in a very weak state compared to the pre-war period. There were only around 8,000 members nationally, with about a quarter of them concentrated in the capital, Petrograd.

According to the *Voprosy Istoriya KPSS*, the regional breakdown of Bolshevik Party members in February 1917 was approximately as follows: Petrograd: 2,000; Moscow: 600; Urals: 500; Yekaterinoslav: 400; Kiev: 200; Rostov: 170; Samara: 150; Kharkov: 200; Ivanovo-Voznesensk: 150-200.[25]

Things had become so difficult for the Party that the Petrograd Committee was unable to bring out a leaflet on the anniversary of Bloody Sunday. While this was mainly due to the unexpected loss of their underground print shop facilities, there were also financial problems that affected their ability to function. "Lack of financial resources greatly constrained the activity of the Central Committee Bureau", explained Shlyapnikov. "Contributions from the organisations were extremely modest."[26]

And yet, such was the abrupt turn of events that within a matter of months, the Party would experience a tenfold increase in membership.

At the beginning of 1917, however, with most of its experienced leaders in exile, it was the Bolshevik workers who directly intervened in the February Revolution. Many of them, schooled in Bolshevism over the years, played a leading role in the events. Trotsky explains:

> To the question, who led the February revolution? we can then answer definitely enough: Conscious and tempered workers educated for the most part by the party of Lenin.

> But we must here immediately add: This leadership proved sufficient to guarantee the victory of the insurrection, but it was not adequate to transfer immediately into the hands of the proletarian vanguard the leadership of the revolution.[27]

These rank-and-file worker Bolsheviks, however, were mainly individuals acting on their own initiative in the factories. In the absence of clear-minded and determined leaders, the Bolshevik Party failed to provide the necessary guidance in the initial stages.

The entry of the broad masses onto the scene in February, together with the fall of the old regime, created a power vacuum, which was spontaneously filled by the newly formed Petrograd Soviet. Although power was in its hands, the leadership of the Soviet itself was in the hands of the Mensheviks and Socialist-Revolutionaries, who had no perspective of, or interest in, taking power. They simply handed over the power like a hot potato to a shaky bourgeois Provisional Government.

Bolshevik vacillations

At that time, the majority of the Bolshevik Party leadership was either abroad, in prison, or in exile. This meant that the three leading figures present in Petrograd during the February events were relatively inexperienced or second-line cadres – Shlyapnikov, Vyacheslav Molotov and Pyotr Zalutsky. They saw their role as a provisional one: to hold the fort until other more experienced comrades arrived from abroad.

Shlyapnikov, who was in touch with Lenin before the February Revolution, was regarded as the principal figure on the ground. But he and the other leaders lacked the necessary experience, clear-headedness and political firmness needed in a revolutionary situation.

The excessive caution by the leadership was first evident when strikes were called for International Women's Day. The Bolshevik leaders, instead of promoting them, were urging restraint to avoid any premature bloody clashes.

However, 90,000 workers came out, as the strikes intensified. The striking workers from the Putilov Works took the lead and marched to the centre of the city. The following day, the strike movement spread. Then, on 10 March, a general strike developed and Petrograd soon resembled a besieged fortress. The Vyborg District, an area where the Bolsheviks were strong, was in the hands of the workers. However, when the masses demanded weapons, the Bolshevik leaders refused, fearing it would lead to a bloody clash. But the Russian workers were now feeling their strength.

Some factories were occupied, while other workers were locked out. The workers started creating barricades from tramcars, telegraph poles and anything they could get their hands on. Feeling the pressure and fearing for their lives, the demoralised police and troops took no action. This, in turn, added to the audacity of the masses.

A turning point came when panicking police fired on unarmed protesters. This provoked mutiny amongst the troops, who, in turn, fired on the police and set police stations on fire.

The Bolsheviks were clearly lagging behind events. They only managed to issue their first leaflet on 12 March, the day that fraternisation between

99. Demonstration of Putilov workers on the first day of the February Revolution

soldiers and workers became commonplace and the Petrograd garrison joined the insurrection. Mutinous troops and crowds of people burst open the prisons, freeing many socialists and victims of the regime. This signalled the end of tsarism, which was in a state of disorderly collapse.

When Philips Price heard about the revolution, he rushed back from the Caucasus to Moscow. He described the scene as follows:

As I crossed the great central plain of Russia by train from the Caucasus I could tell even from the railway stations that something tremendous was happening. At every station now there were offices of the Councils of Soldiers' Deputies, and the platforms were crowded with old peasants, eagerly asking for the latest news from Petrograd. What they chiefly wanted to know about was the prospect of new land laws and agrarian reforms.

The train reached Moscow in the early hours of the morning. I walked through the streets, and the first and most remarkable change I noticed was that not a single policeman or gendarme was to be seen. They had all been arrested. Moscow was without any police and seemed to be getting on quite happily without them. The next thing that struck me was the large number of meetings going on in the streets around the Kursk railway station. Street meetings in Tsarist Russia were hitherto unheard of things. But the air was full of uncertainty.[28]

100. Demonstration on Nevsky Prospekt, Petrograd, led by soldiers in March 1917

The first Bolshevik leaflet issued had called for the creation of a revolutionary provisional government, which arose from their old perspective of 'democratic dictatorship'. However, events had overtaken this demand with the creation of an actual bourgeois Provisional Government. Furthermore, following the traditions of 1905, the workers held meetings in the factories to elect delegates to the Petrograd Soviet of Workers' Deputies, creating a situation of 'dual power'. As Sukhanov, who was a leading left-wing Menshevik, observes:

> A new factor had emerged which had not been present before, a plenipotentiary organisation of the entire democracy of revolutionary Petersburg – an organisation ready for combat, hallowed by a glorious tradition, and ready to take the cause of the revolution, *its own cause, into its own hands*. This was the Soviet of Workers' Deputies.[29]

Very quickly, the Soviet drew in representatives from the factories and workshops and began to take charge of the capital. A Provisional Executive Committee of the Soviet was quickly formed, which guaranteed emergency supplies and organised its own military staff. The authority of the Soviet grew exponentially. Not only had it taken control of Petrograd within days, but many other towns and cities followed its example, including Moscow. Sukhanov states:

101. Mutinous soldiers in Petrograd

Members of the Ex[ecutive] Com[mittee] were summoned at every minute by every possible delegate from the most unexpected organisations and groups, who had demanded that they should be admitted to the Soviet. They all wanted to participate in the overturn and become part of the core of the revolutionary democracy. Officials from the Posts and Telegraphs came along, teachers, engineers, *Zemstvo* and municipal employees, representatives of the doctors, the lawyers, the 'Socialist officers', the artists – they all thought they belonged in the Soviet…

The popularisation of the Soviet was of course aided also by the fact that the virtual authority, or more accurately the real power, was in its hands, insofar as there was any authority at all at that time. And this was obvious to every man in the street.[30]

This gives us a glimpse of the attraction and power of the Soviet and the vacuum that existed following the disintegration of the old regime. The authority of the Soviet "went on growing like a snowball amongst the urban and rural masses."[31]

If the Soviet had wanted, it could have raised its little finger and assumed power without any significant resistance. But the Bolshevik leaflet had made no mention of the Soviet, as the Party leaders were still transfixed on the idea of the 'democratic dictatorship of proletariat and peasantry'.

As Trotsky correctly explains: "For Bolshevism the first months of the revolution had been a period of bewilderment and vacillation."[32] In a meeting

102. Lithuanian prison burned by revolutionaries, March 1917

with Maxim Gorky, Sukhanov gave his impressions of the leading Bolshevik figures at this time:

> Meanwhile some fairly responsible Bolshevik leaders came along. And their flatfootedness or, more properly, their incapacity to think their way into the political problem and formulate it, had a depressing effect on us.[33]

Sukhanov's appraisal of Shlyapnikov was hardly much better:

> A first-rate technical organiser, and practical trade unionist, as a politician he was quite incapable of grasping and generalising the essence of the conjuncture that had been created.[34]

While this may have been an exaggeration on Sukhanov's part, the Bolshevik leaders were certainly out of their depth, which only served to add to the confusion.

The Provisional Government

As the regime crumbled, feverish discussions took place behind the scenes about what to do. Sukhanov explained:

> Attempts were being made at deals with tsarism, the political game was in full swing. All this was not only independent of the popular movement but at the expense and obviously aimed at its destruction.

103. Burning of tsarist symbols in Petrograd, 27 February

At this moment the position of the bourgeoisie was quite clear: it was a position on the one hand of keeping their distance from the revolution and betraying it to tsarism, and on the other of exploiting it for their own manoeuvres.[35]

As one of those involved, the monarchist Vasily Shulgin pointed out, "if we do not take power, others will take it for us, those rotters who have already elected all sorts of scoundrels in the factories."[36] He wished to employ machine guns and bullets to deal with the unruly rabble.

> Machine guns – that is what I wanted, because I felt that the language of machine guns was the only language the mob could understand, and that lead alone could drive the fearsome monster that had broken loose back into his lair... Alas, this monster was... His Majesty the Russian People! [...]
>
> That which we had feared so much, that which we had desired to avoid at all costs, was already a fact. The revolution had begun.[37]

Meanwhile, the bourgeoisie, which played no role in the revolution, simply whispered in corners about maintaining the monarchy. But the tsarist government, suspended in mid-air, had no alternative but to resign. Very reluctantly, after much hesitation, the bourgeoisie had little choice but to

104. Parade of revolutionary troops at the Red Square, 4 March 1917

step into the breach. Alexander Lukomsky, a Lieutenant-General, who later deserted to the White Army following the October Revolution, explained:

> The rabble are beginning to gain the mastery of the situation, and the Committee of the State Duma, in order to prevent the extermination of officers and officials, and to calm the heated passions, has decided to take over the function of government.[38]

It was through these backdoor means, with the connivance of the Mensheviks and SRs who at this early stage of the revolution were the leadership of the soviets, that the bourgeoisie was able to establish a Provisional Government. But real power lay not in their hands, but in the streets – in the armed workers thrown up by the revolution. Above all, it was centred around the newly formed Soviet of Workers' Deputies, which soon began to control everything.

Under the prevailing conditions, few workers drew the distinction between the different socialist parties, especially between the 'moderate' (right-wing) socialists – the Mensheviks and SRs – and the Bolsheviks. The advantage of the 'moderates' was that they possessed a larger proportion of the intelligentsia in their ranks, who poured in from all sides and provided them with an

105. Prince Lvov   106. Pavel Milyukov   107. Alexander Guchkov

immense staff of agitators. This allowed the two 'Compromise' parties, the Mensheviks and SRs, to gain greater popularity and win a majority in the Soviet at this time. The Bolsheviks were, as yet, a small minority.

The Executive Committee of the Soviet was terrified of taking power, and quickly handed it over to the impotent Provisional Government of Prince Lvov, who acted as its President. All they asked for, in return, was freedom of propaganda – a very cheap price, under the circumstances.

The new Provisional Government took the grand title of 'Committee for the Re-establishment of Order and Relations with Public Institutions and Personages'. The name was a clear indication of its real role. This rested on a weak Duma, which was a shadow of a shadow. However, the government had no support among the masses, who instead placed their faith in the Soviet. Sukhanov states:

> The people were not gravitating toward the Duma, had no interest in it, and did not think of making it the centre of the movement either politically or technically. Our liberal politicians later spent all their energies representing the Duma as the banner, and its fate as the cause of the movement. But these attempts were all completely implausible.[39]

With the formation of the Provisional Government, an ill-assorted collection of bourgeois figures, who were fundamentally *opposed* to the revolution, were allowed to take the reins of power. Behind the figurehead of Prince Lvov stood Pavel Milyukov, the leader of the liberal Cadet Party, who was the lynchpin and largely determined government policy. But even now, the tsar had still not abdicated. Nicholas clung to the trappings of the throne with all the power of a determined limpet. This posed a grave dilemma for the bourgeoisie, who were wondering which way to jump. The bourgeois seemed to have little alternative, as Sukhanov explains:

> ... as long as tsarism was not conclusively done for, it was necessary to cling to it, *support* it, and construct any domestic or foreign programme of national liberalism on the *basis* of it. This was understood by every bourgeois element with any experience at all.

> But what was to be done when tsarism had *almost* fallen beneath the blows of the popular movement but its final fate was not known? Obviously, the natural solution was to maintain neutrality until the last minute and not burn one's boats. But in practice it was clear that there had to be definite limits to neutrality, beyond which neutrality itself would burn the boats on one side and perhaps on both. Here one must be specially clear-sighted, single, and agile.

Sukhanov continues:

> But the real tragedy began later. What was to be done after the popular revolution had wiped tsarism off the face of the earth? To take power out of the hands of tsarism was natural. To make an alliance with tsarism to smash the revolution, if it tried to sweep away both the bourgeoisie and tsarism in the same breath, was even more natural and absolutely inevitable. But what if, on the one hand, tsarism was hopeless, and on the other the *possibility of standing at the head of the revolution was not excluded? What if some prospects of 'using' it developed?* What was to be done then? Take the power out of the hands of the revolution and the democracy after they had become masters of the situation?[40]

Such dilemmas provoked a great deal of shuffling and manoeuvring at the top. But it soon became clear that the game was up – the Romanov monarchy was doomed. Nicholas, the limpet-king, soon came unstuck. On 15 March, he was forced to abdicate and tried to hand the crown to his brother, the Grand Duke Michael, who, in turn, even more reluctantly, refused it. Milyukov, Alexander Guchkov, and the other bourgeois ministers of the Provisional Government, were soon left with nothing to cling to. They had no alternative but to lean on the moderate socialists to save the situation.

Menshevik perspectives falsified

The February Revolution – to all intents and purposes, a bourgeois revolution led by the working class – clearly falsified the perspectives of the Mensheviks.

108. Alexander Kerensky

The overthrow of the old regime took place without the bourgeoisie. In fact, it took place *against* them and their intrigues to prop up tsarism. The Revolution confirmed in practice the perspectives of Lenin, Trotsky and the Bolsheviks regarding the leading role of the working class.

The problem was that the fruits of victory, won by the actions of the workers, were simply handed over by the Mensheviks and SRs to the bourgeois Provisional Government. This capitulation arose naturally from the logic of their standpoint: that the bourgeois revolution must be led by the bourgeoisie!

The head of government was Prince Lvov, an aristocrat, and the only individual of any 'socialist' colouration included in the cabinet was Alexander Kerensky, a lawyer who became the Minister of Justice. The remainder were all from the bourgeois parties.

The illusions of the Bolshevik leaders were revealed in the discussions between the different parties within the Soviet about the question of power. As Sukhanov explains:

> … the focus of the debate shifted to the conditions for the transfer of power to the Provisional Government formed by the Duma committee. As for the actual formation of a propertied regime, that was accepted as something already

decided, and as far as I remember not one voice was raised against it on behalf of a democratic regime. Yet there were present at the meeting from the very beginning the official Bolshevik Zalutsky and the unofficial one Krasikov, and a little later Shlyapnikov, who was going about here and there on party business, presented the new Bolshevik representative Molotov to the Ex[ecutive] Com[mittee].[41]

As can be seen from Sukhanov's account, "not one voice was raised" in opposition to the transfer of power to the bourgeoisie, meaning that the Bolshevik representatives went along with this proposal. Their position was identical to the Mensheviks and the Socialist-Revolutionaries.

As Shlyapnikov recalled: "We agreed with the Mensheviks that we were passing through the period of a breakdown of feudal relations, and that in their place would appear all kinds of 'freedoms' proper to bourgeois relations."[42] In its first issue following the revolution, *Pravda* stated: "The fundamental problem is to establish a democratic republic."[43]

Sukhanov, who, let us remember, stood on the internationalist wing of Menshevism, justified the support for the Provisional Government: "The Government that was to take the place of tsarism must be exclusively bourgeois... This was the solution to be aimed at. Otherwise the overturn would fail and the revolution perish." In continuing to outline the Menshevik view, he explained:

> In these circumstances a Socialist seizure of power would mean the inevitable and immediate failure of the revolution. At that moment, in February, the first revolutionary Government could only be a bourgeois one.[44]

This view of the revolution being a bourgeois revolution coloured the Soviet leaders' whole outlook, but also that of the leading Bolsheviks in Russia. It would take the return of Lenin to end this confusion and carry through the 'internal revolution' that would rearm the Party for the October Revolution.

20. Lenin's Response from Exile

The 'carnival' atmosphere of the revolution proved quite intoxicating in the first flush of victory. The Bolshevik leaders in Russia, instead of standing their ground, were being swept along by the dizzying speed of events and had succumbed to the generalised euphoria that surrounded the revolution.

There was enormous pressure for 'unity' which led them to support the Provisional Government, despite certain qualifications. In response to this, there were a growing number of complaints and protests about the leadership from Bolshevik rank-and-file members who had a natural distrust of the new bourgeois government.

In Switzerland, despite the scant information available to him, Lenin immediately tried to make sense of the new realities facing the Bolsheviks. In this, he showed great perspicacity and flexibility, and he refused to be tied down to the old formulas.

However, in Lenin's absence, the Bolshevik leaders on the ground were incapable of reassessing the situation independently and, in practice, trailed behind the 'moderate' socialists, who, in turn, clung to the coat-tails of the bourgeoisie. Trotsky explains, referring to the Bolshevik leaders:

> They behaved not like representatives of a proletarian party preparing an independent struggle for power, but like the left wing of a democracy, which, having announced its principles, intended for an indefinite time to play the part of loyal opposition.[1]

Raskolnikov confirmed:

It must be confessed that before his [Lenin's] arrival there was rather a lot of confusion in the Party. There was no definite, consistent line. The task of taking state power was depicted by the majority as a sort of distant ideal and not, as a rule, presented as a close, urgent and immediate aim. It was considered sufficient to support the Provisional Government, using one formula or another, with these or those reservations and, of course, retaining the right to apply the widest criticism. Inside the Party there was no unity of thought: vacillation and disunity were typical, everyday phenomena especially showing themselves at broad Party and fraction meetings. The Party had no authoritative leader to weld it into unity and draw it behind him.[2]

This lack of leadership was not confined to the Bolsheviks, but affected all the left parties and groups. As Sukhanov explained: "there were no authoritative leaders on the spot in any of the parties, almost without exception. They were in exile, in prison, or abroad."[3]

Lenin's appraisal

Lenin, still in exile, basing himself on limited information from the newspapers, had nevertheless begun to form a clear picture of what was happening. He outlined a bold internationalist and class perspective in his 'Draft Theses' of 17 March:

> ... that the new government that has seized power in St. Petersburg, or, more correctly, wrested it from the proletariat, which has waged a victorious, heroic and fierce struggle, consists of liberal bourgeois and landlords whose lead is being followed by Kerensky [...]

> The new government cannot give peace, because it represents the capitalists and landlords and because it is tied to the English and French capitalists by treaties and financial commitments.[4]

What was required to bring peace, bread and full freedom was "a workers' government, acting in alliance with, first, the poorest section of the rural population, and, second, the revolutionary workers of all countries in the war."[5] Lenin explained: "The working class must therefore continue its fight for socialism and peace, utilising for this purpose the new situation and explaining it as widely as possible among the masses."[6]

He pointed to the importance of the Soviet of Workers' Deputies, which, he said, should be armed. He believed that the Soviet example should be extended to the armed forces as well as the rural areas.

Only by making the truth known to the widest masses of the population, only by organising them, can we guarantee full victory in the next stage of the revolution and the winning of power by a workers' government.[7]

Lenin now began to talk of a "next stage" of the revolution.[8] What is clearly absent from Lenin's 'Draft Theses' was the old position of the 'democratic dictatorship of proletariat and peasantry', which had been replaced with a "workers' government" and "socialism". This position began to resemble Trotsky's theory of the permanent revolution.

Two days later, on 19 March, gripped with alarm at the positions taken by the Party leaders in Russia, Lenin sent a telegram to the Bolsheviks leaving for Russia and copied to those in the interior. It simply read:

Our tactics: no trust in and no support of the new government; Kerensky is especially suspect; arming of the proletariat is the only guarantee; immediate elections to the Petrograd City Council [the Duma]; no rapprochement with other parties. Telegraph this to Petrograd.[9]

To those in Russia, the telegram came like a bombshell. It was sharp, telescopic, and expressed things clearly in a few words. Its aim was to stiffen up the Bolsheviks, who had become intoxicated by the revolution.

The only point mentioned by Lenin that was no longer relevant was the call for "immediate elections" to the Petrograd Duma. With the rise of the Petrograd Soviet, elections to the Duma lost all real significance and soon fell by the wayside. The other telegraphic points retained their full force and indicated the direction of Lenin's policy.

This was swiftly followed days later with the first in a series of directives in the form of letters for publication in *Pravda*, called *Letters from Afar*, which analysed the situation and outlined the new tactics flowing from it. In his first letter on 20 March, after examining the new bourgeois Provisional Government, Lenin went on to look at the importance of the soviets, which he defined "*as the embryo of a workers' government*":[10]

Side by side with this government – which as regards the *present* war is but the agent of the billion-dollar 'firm' 'England and France' – there has arisen the chief, unofficial, as yet undeveloped and comparatively weak *workers' government*, which expresses the interests of the proletariat and of the entire poor section of the urban and rural population. This is the *Soviet of Workers' Deputies* in Petrograd, which is seeking connections with the soldiers and peasants, and also with the agricultural workers, with the latter particularly and primarily, of course, more than with the peasants.

109. First page of Lenin's manuscript for his second *Letter from Afar*

Such is the *actual* political situation, which we must first endeavour to define with the greatest possible objective precision, in order that Marxist tactics may be based upon the only possible solid foundation – the foundation of *facts*.[11]

'Letters from Afar'

Lenin brushed aside all abstractions and focused exclusively on the concrete realities of the situation, which had thrown up new problems and challenges not envisaged before now:

The Soviet of Workers' Deputies is an organisation of the workers, the embryo of a workers' government, the representative of the interests of the entire mass of the *poor* section of the population, i.e. of nine-tenths of the population, which is striving for *peace*, *bread* and *freedom*.[12]

This posed the immediate need to transition from the first stage of the revolution, which was now completed, to the second stage. Lenin did not hold back when he wrote:

He who says that the workers must *support* the new government in the interests of the struggle against tsarist reaction (and apparently this is being said by the Potresovs, Gvozdvovs, Chkhenkelis and also, all *evasiveness* notwithstanding, by *Chkheidze*) is a traitor to the workers, a traitor to the cause of the proletariat, to the cause of peace and freedom.[13]

This was strong language, essentially branding the conciliators within the Bolshevik Party, especially its leaders, as "traitors to the cause" for their support of the Provisional Government. He then went on to denounce the sugary words and promises from the bourgeois ministers, which he described as "mere phrase-mongering and lies, self-deception on the part of the politicians of the liberal and radical camp, fraudulent trickery."[14]

Lenin continued: "Ours is a bourgeois revolution, *therefore*, the workers must support the bourgeoisie, say the Potresovs, Gvozdyovs and Chkheidzes, as Plekhanov said yesterday."[15] But, he explained:

Ours is a bourgeois revolution, we Marxists say, *therefore* the workers must open the eyes of the people to the deception practised by the bourgeois politicians, teach them to put no faith in words, to depend entirely on their *own* strength, their *own* organisation, their *own* unity, and their own *weapons*.[16]

A second *Letter from Afar* was written on 22 March, based on even more up-to-date information. This time, he analysed the support granted by the Soviet majority to the Provisional Government:

The manifesto declares that all democrats must 'support' the new government and that the Soviet of Workers' Deputies requests and authorises Kerensky to enter the Provisional Government [with] a committee consisting of members of the Soviet of Workers' Deputies and of 'military men' to supervise the activities of the Provisional Government.[17]

Lenin continues:

The appointment of the Russian Louis Blanc, Kerensky, and the appeal to support the new government is, one may say, a classical example of betrayal of the cause of the revolution and the cause of the proletariat, a betrayal which doomed a number of nineteenth-century revolutions, irrespective of how sincere and devoted to socialism the leaders and supporters of such a policy may have been.

The proletariat cannot and must not support a war government, a restoration government.[18]

Lenin censored

Lenin's articles, which he wrote almost every day, were intended for publication in *Pravda*, which, given the collapse of censorship, had just resumed publication. However, the editors of *Pravda*, who now included Kamenev and Stalin who had returned from exile, censored, cut and delayed their publication.

Lenin sent the first two *Letters* to *Pravda* via Kollontai in Oslo. On 30 March, he asked if the editors had received them. The first *Letter* then duly appeared in *Pravda* on 3 and 4 April, but with significant abridgements – about 20 per cent was deleted. The full text was not published until 1949.

The changes introduced by the *Pravda* editors were cuts where Lenin described the Menshevik and SR leaders as conciliators and flunkeys. The editors wanted to tone down Lenin's criticisms. Therefore, edits were made to warnings about supporting "the Cadet-Octobrist imperialism, which […] is as abominable as tsarist imperialism."[19] Another cut was made when Lenin went on to describe Kerensky as "a balalaika on which they [the bourgeois leaders of the Provisional Government] play to deceive the workers and peasants" and declared that "he who says the workers must *support* the new Government […] is a traitor to the workers."[20]

These omissions and abridgements showed the deep-seated opposition to Lenin's position that existed within the Party leadership. The following third and fourth letters were not published at all in 1917, while the fifth was unfinished, but the ideas it contained were developed in other later writings.

The third letter was particularly instructive. It deals with the state, defined classically as the 'armed bodies of men'. Lenin explains:

> Comrade workers! You performed miracles of proletarian heroism yesterday in overthrowing the tsarist monarchy. In the more or less near future (perhaps even now, as these lines are being written) you will again have to perform the same miracles of heroism to overthrow the rule of the landlords and capitalists, who are waging the imperialist war. You will not achieve *durable victory* in this next 'real' revolution if you do not perform *miracles of proletarian organisation!*[21]

He continued:

> We need revolutionary *government*, we need (for a certain transitional period) a *state*. This is what distinguishes us from the anarchists. […]
>
> We need a state. But *not the kind* of state the bourgeoisie has created everywhere, from constitutional monarchies to the most democratic republics. And in this we

differ from the opportunists and Kautskyites of the old, and decaying, socialist parties, who have distorted, or have forgotten, the lessons of the Paris Commune and the analysis of these lessons made by Marx and Engels.

We need a state, but *not* the kind the bourgeoisie needs, with organs of government in the shape of a police force, an army and a bureaucracy (officialdom) separate from and opposed to the people. All bourgeois revolutions merely perfected *this* state machine, merely transferred it from the hands of one party to those of another.

The proletariat, on the other hand, if it wants to uphold the gains of the present revolution and proceed further, to win peace, bread and freedom, must 'smash', to use Marx's expression, this 'ready-made' state machine and substitute a new one for it by *merging* the police force, the army and the bureaucracy with *the entire armed people*. Following the path indicated by the experience of the Paris Commune of 1871 and the Russian Revolution of 1905, the proletariat, must organise and arm *all* the poor, exploited sections of the population in order that they *themselves* should take the organs of state power directly into their own hands, in order that *they themselves should constitute* these organs of state power.

And the workers of Russia have already *taken* this path in the first stage of the first revolution, in February – March 1917. The whole task now is clearly to understand what this new path is, to proceed along it further, boldly, firmly and perseveringly.[22]

The fourth letter goes on to expose the real class nature of the Provisional Government, as a government of the capitalists and landlords, incapable of confronting the most urgent problems of the workers and peasants, especially the achievement of peace and giving land to the peasants.

The fifth letter is only a fragment outlining a programme for the working class, which was never finished by Lenin. Nevertheless, in the letter he hammered home once again the question of the state, stressing that the "government must be organised on the model of the Soviets of Workers' and Peasants' Deputies". Its immediate tasks must be to smash the old state machine, the army, the police force and bureaucracy. In its place must be "a universal organisation of the entire armed people". Only in this way will it be possible to bring about, not an imperialist peace, "but a really lasting and democratic peace, which cannot be achieved without a proletarian revolution in a number of countries."[23]

Such a regime would have all the features of the Paris Commune, that is, a regime described by Engels as a workers' state. In Lenin's words, "In their entirety and in their development these steps will mark the *transition to socialism*".[24] The programme of demands was "based on an appraisal of the class forces in the Russian and world revolution, and also on the experience of 1871 and 1905."[25]

These *Letters from Afar* graphically reveal Lenin's struggle to correct the line of the Bolshevik leaders in Russia and marked the first attempt by him to reorientate the Party towards a second revolution and the conquest of power by the working class. This would be completed on his return to Russia.

Journey to Russia

When Lenin received news of the Revolution, he was excited and eager to return to Russia. Back in 1905, he arrived in November, almost at the tail end of the Revolution. This time, he was determined to arrive as early as possible. But there was a problem. As a result of the wartime conditions, there was no way of travelling from Switzerland to Russia by legal means. The British and French governments would never allow Lenin and his comrades permission to travel through Allied territory. It was therefore necessary to find another route out.

Lenin was frustrated that he had not left Switzerland sooner. He wrote to Inessa Armand on 15 March: "I'm beside myself at the thought that I cannot go to Scandinavia! I cannot forgive myself for not having risked going there in 1915."[26]

However, within a few days, Lenin attended a meeting of Russian émigrés, called to discuss possible plans to return home. Various schemes were put forward, but doubts were raised about each one. Then Martov made the suggestion that they contact the Petrograd Soviet to ask them to offer the German government repatriation of prisoners of war in exchange for the revolutionaries' safe passage through Germany. Lenin immediately seized upon the idea as the most promising, which was heartedly supported by everyone present. Given the sensitivities of travelling through enemy territory, they decided to work through an intermediary. Robert Grimm, the Swiss socialist, was chosen for this role. But given his ambivalent attitude, Fritz Pattern, a Left Zimmerwaldist and secretary of the Swiss Social-Democratic Party, took over the negotiations on behalf of the émigrés.

Of course, any attempt by the Russians to cross German territory in wartime would be inevitably used by their political enemies. But given the urgency of them returning to Russia, this problem was quickly dismissed. The negotiations dragged on as it became evident that the Provisional

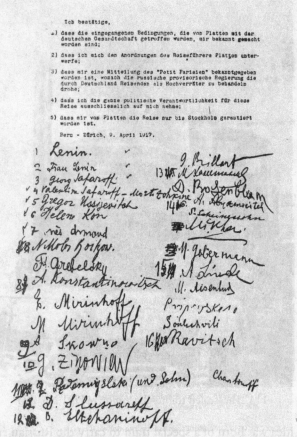

Ich bestätige,

1) dass die eingegangenen Bedingungen, die von Platten mit der deutschen Gesandtschaft getroffen wurden, mir bekannt gemacht worden sind;

2) dass ich mich den Anordnungen des Reiseführers Platten unterwerfe;

3) dass mir eine Mitteilung des "Petit Parisien" bekanntgegeben worden ist, wonach die russische provisorische Regierung die durch Deutschland Reisenden als Hochverräter zu behandeln drohe;

4) dass ich die ganze politische Verantwortlichkeit für diese Reise ausschliesslich auf mich nehme;

5) dass mir von Platten die Reise nur bis Stockholm garantiert worden ist.

Bern - Zürich, 9. April 1917.

110. Signatures of the passengers on the 'sealed train' through Germany

Government in Petrograd was not too eager to see the return of these revolutionary internationalists. An eventual agreement was reached through the German Foreign Office, which, for its own purposes, was eager for this to happen. One factor behind this urgency was the entry of the United States into the war on the side of the Allies in February 1917. Lenin sent an urgent telegram to the intermediary on 31 March:

> Our Party has decided to accept without reservations the proposal that the Russian émigrés should travel through Germany, and to organise this journey at once. We already expect to have more than ten participants in the journey.

> We absolutely decline responsibility for any further delay, resolutely protest against it and are going alone. We earnestly request you to make the arrangements immediately and, if possible, let us know the decision tomorrow.[27]

111. The 'sealed train' – Locomotive Hk1 No. 293

Thus, the idea was born of a special train to carry the Russian émigrés back home. The means of transport went down in history as the 'sealed train', as it was agreed that nobody would have the right to enter or leave the train on its journey and there would be no passport checks. The émigrés would also need Swedish visas, as they would be travelling through Sweden to Finland. On 5 April, the protocol for the group's travel came through and there was a mad dash on the part of the Russians to get everything ready in time.

In the end, a group of nineteen Bolsheviks, six members of the Bund and three supporters of *Nashe Slovo* left Bern that afternoon. Following a delay of a few days, they finally departed from Switzerland on 9 April. They would reach Sassnitz on the Baltic seaboard, then transfer to a cargo vessel on their way to the port of Trelleborg, then after four-day's journey, finally arrive in Stockholm on 13 April.

As Lenin was in a hurry to get back to Russia the very next morning, not to waste any time, he picked up a few items of new clothing and departed.

112. Lenin in Stockholm with Nerman and Lindhagen, 13 April 1917

There is a famous picture of Lenin, with his new hat, new shoes, coat and umbrella, in Stockholm crossing the Vasagatan, in conversation with Ture Nerman. The group was en route to Petrograd.

On the day they departed from Switzerland, a statement was drawn up on behalf of the Russian revolutionaries and signed in Stockholm by the Swedish left Social-Democrats Carl Lindhagen, Fredrik Ström, CN Carleson, Karl Kilbom and Ture Nerman, and by the Norwegian Left Social-Democrat Arvid Hansen. The statement read in part as follows:

> We the undersigned are aware of the obstacles that the Entente governments have created to the return of the Russian internationalists. We are aware of the terms on which the German government has permitted their journey to Sweden… The undersigned internationalists of France, Switzerland, Poland, Germany, Sweden and Norway, believe that our Russian comrades not only have the right, but also the obligation to avail themselves of this opportunity to return to Russia. We wish them every success in the struggle against the imperialist policy of the Russian

113. Lenin's route from Switzerland to Russia

bourgeoisie – a struggle that is part of a common fight for the emancipation of the working-class and for the socialist revolution.[28]

This statement appeared in the Swedish Left Social-Democratic *Politiken* of 15 April 1917, just as Lenin finally crossed the border into Russia. Krupskaya recalled the affair as follows:

> The defencists raised a terrible hullabaloo about the Bolsheviks travelling through Germany. Naturally, the German government gave permission for us to travel through Germany in the belief that revolution was a disaster to a country, and that by allowing emigrant internationalists to return to their country they were helping to spread the revolution in Russia. The Bolsheviks, for their part, considered it their duty to develop revolutionary agitation in Russia, and made it their aim

to bring about a victorious proletarian revolution. They did not care what the German bourgeois government thought about it. They knew that the defencists would start a mud-slinging campaign against them, but that the masses in the long run would follow their lead. At that time, on 27 March [4 April, New Style], the Bolsheviks were the only ones to take the risk of going that way. A month later, over two hundred emigrants, including Martov and other Mensheviks, followed the same route through Germany.[29]

The former Conservative Prime Minister Winston Churchill, whose hatred for Bolshevism is well-known, later summed up the move by the Germans in his usual toxic style: "They turned upon Russia the most grisly of weapons. They transported Lenin in a sealed truck like a plague bacillus."[30] Churchill's hatred of the Bolsheviks was only matched by his love for Mussolini and fascism in the 1930s, until they clashed with the interests of British imperialism, when Churchill suddenly discovered his 'democratic' credentials. The same was true of the pro-fascist British Royal Family. All these matters are well documented facts. However, sadly, they fall outside the scope of the present work.

Which side gained more from the transaction of the 'sealed train'? That can be demonstrated by subsequent events. While the Bolsheviks took power on 7 November 1917 (25 October, Old Style), creating the first workers' state in history, the regime of Kaiser Wilhelm was swept away by the German Revolution in November 1918. Therefore, it proved to be a price worth paying.

The day before they left Switzerland, Lenin had read out a 'Farewell Address to Swiss Workers', in which he again outlined the perspective of socialist revolution:

Our Party was formed and developed in the struggle for these ideas, which have been fully confirmed by the experience of 1905 and the spring of 1917, in the uncompromising struggle against all the other parties; and we shall continue to fight for these ideas. [...]

Single-handed, the Russian proletariat cannot bring the socialist revolution to a *victorious conclusion*. But it can give the Russian revolution a mighty sweep that would create the most favourable conditions for a socialist revolution, and would, in a sense, *start* it. It can facilitate the rise of a situation in which its *chief*, its most trustworthy and most reliable collaborator, the *European* and American *socialist* proletariat, could join the decisive battles.

Let the sceptics despair because of the temporary triumph within the European socialist movement of such disgusting lackeys of the imperialist bourgeoisie as the

Scheidemanns, Legiens, Davids and Co. in Germany; Sembat, Guesde, Renaudel and Co. in France; the Fabians and the Labourites in England. We are firmly convinced that this filthy froth on the surface of the world labour movement will be soon swept away by the waves of revolution. [...]

The future belongs to the trend that has given us Karl Liebknecht, created the Spartacus group, has carried on its propaganda in the Bremen *Arbeiterpolitik*.

The objective circumstances of the imperialist war make it certain that the revolution will not be limited to the first stage of the Russian revolution, that the revolution will not be limited to Russia.

The German proletariat is the most trustworthy, the most reliable ally of the Russian and the world proletarian revolution.[31]

He ended his message with:

Long live the proletarian revolution that is *beginning* in Europe!"

[Signed] On behalf of the departing comrades, members of the RSDLP (united under the Central Committee), who approved this letter at a meeting held 8 April (new style), 1917.[32]

Lenin's view of the socialist revolution in Russia and worldwide now becomes crystal clear. From now on, his sights were firmly on the conquest of power by the working class as the first blow on the road to the world proletarian revolution.

21. Rearming the Bolsheviks

The perspective outlined by Lenin in *Letters from Afar* marked a clear break with the idea of a bourgeois republic, which was replaced by a new second revolution and the establishment of Soviet power. This was a far cry from the position adopted by the leading Bolsheviks within Russia, who were bending to the pressures and swept along helplessly by events.

The arrival of Kamenev and Stalin from exile changed nothing. If anything, they were even more conservative than those they replaced. The old editors were unceremoniously elbowed aside and the newcomers took hold of the reins of *Pravda*. Kamenev and Stalin were then reinforced by Muranov, a former Bolshevik Duma deputy, who had also returned from exile. Muranov's stature had grown after his firm stand at the 1915 trial of deputies. But he used his newfound authority as a political cover for Kamenev, who stood on the right wing of the Party. Stalin, the practico, on the other hand, was simply carried along by the prevailing mood.

The newcomers collectively pushed the Party further to the right, seeing their main role as defending the cause of the bourgeois-democratic republic, together with its government. They then covered their support for the Provisional Government with the qualification: "in so far as it struggles against reaction or counter-revolution", a meaningless phrase open to a wide interpretation.[1]

On 27 March, two days after the return of these new leaders, Stalin published a short article in which he called on the workers to rally to the Soviet because "the rights won must be upheld so as to destroy completely the old forces and… further advance the Russian revolution."[2] The article contained not a single word of criticism of the Mensheviks and SRs in the Soviet or the attitude of the bourgeois Provisional Government.

The next day, *Pravda* carried an announcement of the changes to the editorial board and on its front page carried the proclamation of the Petrograd Soviet, 'To the Peoples of the Whole World', which announced that "we shall stoutly defend our liberty" and that "the Russian revolution will not flinch before the bayonets of the aggressors".[3] This was then followed by a signed article by Kamenev, who openly rejected Lenin's idea of revolutionary defeatism:

> When army faces army it would be the most insane policy to suggest to one of the armies to lay down its arms and go home. This would not be a policy of peace, but a policy of slavery, which would be rejected with disgust by a free people.[4]

A free people could only "answer bullet with bullet, shell with shell".[5] While Stalin tried to distance himself from Kamenev's wholehearted endorsement of national defence, *Pravda* still refused to wage any fundamental attack on the Provisional Government or its pro-war policy.

These 'old Bolsheviks' utterly failed to grasp that, despite the fall of tsarism and the emergence of the Provisional Government, it did not alter the imperialist character of the war.

As a result, the editorials in *Pravda* mirrored the position of the Mensheviks and SRs, the defencists in the Soviet. Stalin wrote, for instance, that what was needed was "to bring pressure on the Provisional Government to make it declare its consent to start peace negotiations immediately." Meanwhile, it was "unquestionable" that "the stark slogan 'Down with war!'" was "absolutely unsuitable as a practical means".[6] All this was happening while the publication of Lenin's articles from Switzerland was delayed and truncated, especially his criticism of the conciliators. In effect, *Pravda* had disavowed him, and not for the first time.

The whole policy of Kamenev and Stalin was to support the Provisional Government 'insofar' as it struggles against reaction, while paying lip service to 'the ultimate goal of socialism'. But this was simply a fig leaf to cover up their capitulation to the Soviet's defencist majority.

No rapprochement

Lenin in contrast took a hard line, wanting to cut through this subterfuge. On 11 April, he wrote a letter from Zurich to Jakub Hanecki (also known as Kuba) in Stockholm, a member of the Bureau Abroad of the Central

Committee, sharply denouncing the deception of the Mensheviks and SRs, starting with Kerensky and Nikoloz Chkheidze. He asked for the letter to be urgently sent to Petrograd and *Pravda*. He wrote:

> Our Party would disgrace itself for ever, commit political suicide, if it tolerated such a deception [...] that any rapprochement with those who are wobbling in the direction of social-patriotism and have taken up the profoundly mistaken, profoundly harmful social-pacifist, Kautskian, position of Chkheidze and Co. is, I am deeply convinced, *harmful* for the working class, *dangerous, inadmissible*.[7]

He continued even more firmly and threatened to politically break with his comrades, including those editing *Pravda*:

> ... I shall prefer even an immediate split with anyone in our Party, whoever it may be, to making concessions to the social patriotism of Kerensky and Co. or the social-pacifism and Kautskyism of Chkheidze and Co.[8]

Lenin then went on:

> The workers must be told the *truth*. We have to say that the government of Guchkov-Milyukov and Co. is an imperialist government [...] *all* state power [must be transferred] into the hands of the working class, the enemy of capital, the enemy of imperialist war, and only then will they have the *right* to appeal for the overthrow of *all* kings and *all* bourgeois governments.
>
> For God's sake try and deliver all this to Petrograd and to *Pravda*, to Muranov and Kamenev and the others. For God's sake make every effort to send this with a most reliable person. It would be best of all if a reliable sensible chap like Kuba went (he would perform a great service to the whole world working-class movement) and help our friends in Petrograd!! I hope you will do this!! Do everything in your power.
>
> Conditions in Petrograd are exceptionally difficult. The republican patriots are straining *every* effort. They are trying to drown our Party in slander and dirt...[9]

He concluded in his letter with the clear instruction:

> No rapprochement with other parties, any of them! Not a shadow of confidence in or support for the government of Guchkov-Milyukov and Co.!! The most irreconcilable propaganda of internationalism and of struggle with republican chauvinism and social-chauvinism everywhere, both in the press and within the Soviet of Workers' Deputies; the organisation of *our* Party: this is the essential. Kamenev must realise that he bears a *world*-historic responsibility.[10]

The content of this letter leaves no doubt as to where Lenin stood. He instinctively connected with the advanced workers and their views. This fact, namely Lenin's correct political assessment of the real situation in Russia, made from far away Switzerland, destroys the false idea (mainly coming from the 'lefts') that you always have to be on the ground to understand what is happening. Those 'on the ground' were simply swept along by the prevailing mood and had lost their bearings.

Pravda's soft line towards the compromiser-socialists – the Mensheviks and SRs – was creating opposition among the worker-militants. The conciliatory tone of the Bolshevik leaders towards the government was noted elsewhere among the bourgeois elements and moderate socialists. According to Shlyapnikov, "the whole of the Tauride Palace, from the members of the Committee of the Duma to the Executive Committee, the heart of revolutionary democracy, was full of news – the victory of the moderate, reasonable Bolsheviks over the extremists".[11]

The Bolshevik rank and file became increasingly indignant at the policies of capitulation of *Pravda*. Shlyapnikov states:

> The indignation in the party locals was enormous and when the proletarians found out that *Pravda* had been seized by three former editors arriving from Siberia they demanded their expulsion from the party.[12]

A few days before Lenin's return, the Bolshevik Party held a special conference in Petrograd, which opened on 9 April. By this time, the revolution was already a month old. The confusions introduced by the editors of *Pravda* stemmed from the old contradictory slogan of 'democratic dictatorship of proletariat and peasantry', which had now led them into the swamp of support for the Provisional Government.

On the first day, 10 April, Stalin gave a report on the Party's attitude towards the new Government, which talked about the leading role of the Soviet "controlling" the government. Although confused, the bourgeois Government, he said, "takes the role of fortifier of those conquests of the people, which they have already seized [...] It is not to our advantage at present to force events, hastening the process of repelling the bourgeois layers..."[13]

After the debate, a resolution was passed that called on the revolutionary democracy, that is, the Soviet majority, to "exercise a vigilant control over the activities of the Provisional Government in the centre and in the provinces, urging it on towards a most energetic struggle for the complete liquidation of the old regime".[14]

Therefore, before Lenin's arrival, the majority of the conference had lined up behind the position of Kamenev and Stalin, including their faith in the progressive nature of the bourgeois Provisional Government.

The question of unification

This was followed by a joint session of the Bolsheviks and Mensheviks called to discuss their attitude to the war and other questions. Mikhail Liber, the leading Menshevik, argued, "we must do away with the old division between Bolsheviks and Mensheviks, and speak only of our attitude towards war."[15]

After a debate, a decision was taken narrowly to support the defencist position of the Soviet's Executive Committee, which caused some Bolsheviks to walk out.

Following this, the conference then considered the proposal of the Menshevik Tsereteli for a fusion of Bolsheviks and Mensheviks. The fact that this proposal was being considered after so many discussions about the nature of Menshevism shows how far they had departed from Lenin.

Later, Stalin intervened in the discussion and spoke firmly in favour of Tsereteli's unity proposals: "We ought to go. It is necessary to define our proposal as to the terms of unification. Unification is possible along the lines of Zimmerwald-Kienthal."[16] In reply to those who expressed opposition, Stalin argued:

> There is no use running ahead and anticipating disagreements. There is no party life without disagreements. We will live down trivial disagreements within the party. But there is one question – it is impossible to unite what cannot be united. We will have a single party with those who agree on Zimmerwald and Kienthal...[17]

But what Stalin regarded as merely 'trivial' disagreements were, in fact, questions of fundamental principles. To take just one: he argued that unity with the Mensheviks could be achieved on the basis of the policies of Zimmerwald and Kienthal. But those were not Bolshevik policies, but the kind of confused *centrist* policies that Lenin had denounced repeatedly. "... Zimmerwald should be buried at all costs", he wrote.[18]

Yet here was Stalin advocating unity with the Mensheviks precisely on that basis. His entire argument was aimed against Lenin's struggle to separate Bolshevism from social-patriotism and pacifism, which Stalin light-mindedly dismissed as "trivial". After all, what was the reason for separate organisations when *Pravda* was giving support to the Provisional Government?

114. Finland Station, Petrograd, c. 1913

Lenin addresses the workers

While the conference was still taking place, Lenin arrived at the Finland Station in Petrograd, on the evening of 16 April. A very large crowd, together with armoured cars and banners, had assembled at the station to greet Lenin, including the editorial board of *Pravda*. Lenin had already seen several copies of *Pravda* and was outraged at what he read. When his train had made a scheduled stop on the outskirts of Petrograd, workers from Sestroretsk and some of the Bolshevik leaders, including Kamenev, boarded the train to greet him.

"Hardly had he entered the compartment and sat down when Vladimir Ilyich turned on Kamenev", explained Raskolnikov. "What's this you're writing in *Pravda*? We've seen several issues, and really swore at you…"[19] This was Lenin's opening shot as he stepped foot in Russia. He then made light of it, but it set the tone for things to come.

Sukhanov vividly describes the scene on Lenin's arrival at the Finland Station:

> Shlyapnikov, acting as master of ceremonies, appeared in the doorway, portentously hurrying, with the air of a faithful old police chief announcing the Governor's arrival. Without any apparent necessity he kept crying out fussily: "Please, Comrades, please! Make way there! Comrades, make way!"

Behind Shlyapnikov, at the head of a small cluster of people behind whom the door slammed again at once, Lenin came, or rather ran, into the room. He wore a round cap, his face looked frozen, and there was a magnificent bouquet in his hands. Running to the middle of the room, he stopped in front of Chkheidze as though colliding with a completely unexpected obstacle. And Chkheidze, still glum, pronounced the following 'speech of welcome' with not only the spirit and wording but also the tone of a sermon.

"Comrade Lenin, in the name of the Petersburg Soviet and of the whole revolution we welcome you to Russia ... But – we think that the principal task of the revolutionary democracy is now the defence of the revolution from any encroachments either from within or from without. We consider that what this goal requires is not disunion, but the closing of the ranks of the democratic ranks. We hope you will pursue these goals together with us."[20]

But Lenin looked away from the official delegation and Chkheidze and turned to the assembled crowd, which he addressed directly:

Dear comrades, soldiers, sailors and workers! I am happy to greet in your persons the victorious Russian revolution, and greet you as the vanguard of the worldwide proletarian army... The piratical imperialist war is the beginning of civil war throughout Europe... The hour is not far distant when at the call of our comrade, Karl Liebknecht, the peoples will turn their arms against their own capitalist exploiters... The worldwide Socialist revolution has already dawned... Germany is seething... Any day now the whole of European capitalism may crash. The Russian revolution accomplished by you has prepared the way and opened a new epoch. Long live the worldwide Socialist revolution![21]

There was not a single word from Lenin about the bourgeois revolution, or 'democratic dictatorship', but only the world socialist revolution.

Lenin then set off for the Party headquarters, the former palatial home of the tsar's favourite ballerina, Kshesinskaya, which had been taken over during the February Revolution. He addressed a huge crowd of workers from the first-floor balcony about the prospects for world revolution. Later, he listened to speeches of welcome from his comrades, old friends who had been separated for years by prison or emigration. Raskolnikov recalls the occasion:

Ilyich sat and listened with a smile to all the speeches, waiting impatiently for them to finish.

When the list of speakers was exhausted, Ilyich at once came to life, got to his feet and set to work. He resolutely assailed the tactics which the leading Party groups and individual comrades had been pursuing before his return. He caustically ridiculed the notorious formula of support for the Provisional Government 'in so far as ... to that extent', and gave out the slogan, 'No support whatsoever to the government of capitalists', at the same time calling on the Party to fight for power to be taken over by the Soviets, for a socialist revolution.

Using a few striking examples, Comrade Lenin brilliantly demonstrated the whole falsity of the policy of the Provisional Government, the glaring contradiction between its promises and its actions, between words and deeds, emphasising that it was our duty to expose ruthlessly its counter-revolutionary and anti-democratic pretensions and conduct. Comrade Lenin's speech lasted nearly an hour. The audience remained fixed in intense, unweakening attention. The most responsible Party workers were represented here, but even for them what Ilyich said constituted a veritable revelation.[22]

Lenin's improvised speech had hit the mark, as intended, and made an unforgettable impression on everyone present, for which he was given a prolonged and stormy applause. According to Sukhanov:

I shall never forget that thunder-like speech, which startled and amazed not only me, a heretic who had accidentally dropped in, but all the true believers. I am certain that no one had expected anything of the sort.[23]

Kamenev then summed up the meeting with some final greetings, in which he diplomatically referred to the clear political differences:

We may or may not agree with Comrade Lenin's views, we may differ from him in our evaluation of one proposition or another, but, in any case, there has returned to Russia in the person of Comrade Lenin the brilliant and acknowledged leader of our Party and we shall go forward together with him, towards socialism.[24]

The 'April Theses'

A joint meeting was later organised of all Social-Democrats – Bolsheviks, Mensheviks and independents – in the Tauride Palace. When Lenin took the floor and outlined his views about the revolution, he held nothing back. He made sure that there could be no more talk of unification with these men of moderate views. His opponents were aghast. There was no longer the politeness of the earlier meeting at the Party headquarters.

For instance, Bogdanov, who had become a Menshevik, and was now the secretary of the Soviet Executive Committee, shouted at Lenin angrily: "This is the raving of a madman! It's indecent to applaud this clap-trap!" Livid with

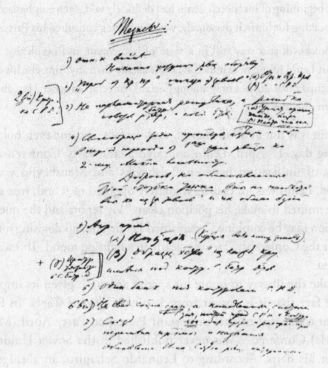

115. Initial draft of Lenin's *April Theses*

rage and contempt, he turned to the audience. "You ought to be ashamed of yourselves! Marxists!"[25] Then the old Social-Democrat, IP Goldenberg, a Menshevik leader, denounced Lenin's supposed anarchism:

> Lenin has now made himself a candidate for one European throne that has been vacant for thirty years – the throne of Bakunin! Lenin's new words echo something old – the superannuated truths of primitive anarchism.[26]

Plekhanov also denounced Lenin's speech as "raving". Zenzinov, an SR leader, recalled that Lenin's speech was greeted "not so much with indignation as with jeers, so stupid and fantastic did it sound". And when the speech was reported to the Cadet leader Milyukov later that day, he remarked he had little to fear from such "lunatic ideas".[27]

Lenin felt quite isolated, even within his own Party. But this was not a new situation for Lenin. At every important turning point in the Party, when a sharp turn was necessary, he often found himself in a minority, sometimes a minority of one. At this point, he was speaking for himself alone. Sukhanov reports:

At the beginning of his speech Lenin had definitely said, even emphasised, that he was speaking for himself personally, without having consulted his Party.

The Bolshevik sect was still in a state of bafflement and perplexity. And the support Lenin found may underline more clearly than anything else his complete intellectual isolation, not only among Social-Democrats in general but also among his own disciples.[28]

But Lenin was not at all dismayed, and, in fact, became even bolder. The following day, 17 April, Lenin appeared at the Party Conference where the idea of unification between Bolsheviks and Mensheviks was being discussed. Lenin was, of course, resolutely opposed to it and, true to form, was determined to make his position clear. "My report and the question of unification may be combined", explained Lenin, after apologising for his late arrival at the Conference. He was clearly in a fighting mood. This was Lenin at his best.

We take the liberty to quote his speech at length given its importance and the fact that it is absent from Lenin's *Collected Works*. In fact, the verbatim transcript of this important Petrograd Party April (March in Old Style) Conference was never published in the Soviet Union under Stalin or his heirs. According to Leonardo Schapiro, an abridged copy had survived in the Marx-Engels-Lenin Institute archives.[29] However, a full transcript was given to Trotsky by Zinoviev and Kamenev, following their break with Stalin, and was later published by Trotsky along with other banned documents in *The Stalin School of Falsification*, from where the speech is taken.

To begin with, in his 'First Thesis', Lenin took up their attitude to the question of the war, which was like a bombshell exploding amid the Conference:

The new Government, like its preceding one, is imperialist, despite the promise of a republic. It is imperialist through and through.

[As a result] it is impermissible to make the slightest concession to 'revolutionary defencism'.[30]

He explained that they could give consent to a revolutionary war only when power was transferred to the working class. For now, it was important, with "...patience, to explain" that "...without the overthrow of capitalism, it is impossible to conclude the war with a really democratic, non-oppressive peace."[31]

In reading the resolution of the Soviet of Workers' Deputies, one is amazed that people who call themselves socialists could have adopted such a resolution. [...]

The war can be terminated only through a complete break with international capitalism. [...]

The peculiarity of the present moment in Russia consists in the *transition* from the first stage of the revolution, which gave power to the bourgeoisie on account of the inadequate organisation of the proletariat, to the second stage, which must give power to the proletariat and the poorest layers of the peasantry.[32]

"Why didn't you seize power?" asked Lenin in his 'Second Thesis':[33]

Steklov says it was because of this and that, and something or other. That's nonsense. The reason is that the proletariat is not sufficiently conscious and sufficiently organised. That we have to acknowledge. The material force is in the hands of the proletariat, but the bourgeoisie was conscious and ready. That is the monstrous fact. But it is necessary to acknowledge frankly, and say to the people straight out that we did not seize power because we were unorganised and not conscious.[34]

Revolutionary intoxication

Lenin then spoke of the current role of the Party:

Even our Bolsheviks show confidence in the Government. That can only be explained by the intoxication incidental to revolution. That is the death of socialism. You, comrades, have confidence in the government. If that's your position, our ways part. I prefer to remain in the minority. One Liebknecht is worth more than 110 defencists of the Steklov and Chkheidze type. If you are in sympathy with Liebknecht and extend even a finger to the defencists – this will be a betrayal of international socialism. [...] If we draw away from these people, all the oppressed will come to us, because the war will bring them to us. They have no other way out.[35]

He continued in his 'Third Thesis':

No support to the Provisional Government. We must explain the utter falsity of all its promises, particularly its renunciation of annexations. There must be exposure instead of impermissible illusion-breeding 'demand' that this Government, the government of the capitalists, cease being imperialistic.

Pravda demands of the *Government* that it renounces annexation. To demand of the Government of the capitalists that it renounce annexations – nonsense! Flagrant mockery of ... [break in original]

From the scientific standpoint, it is such a fog of deceit, which the entire international proletariat, the entire… [break in original] It is high time to admit the mistake. Have done with greetings and resolutions! It's time to get down to business. We must proceed with a business-like, sober… [break in original][36]

Lenin went on in his 'Fourth Thesis' to state that in the Soviet, the Bolsheviks were a small minority "in the face of the bloc of all petty bourgeois opportunist elements".[37] The Bolsheviks needed to explain that the only possible form of revolutionary government was the Soviet one:

So as long as we remain in the minority, we carry on the work of criticism and explaining errors, advocating all along the necessity of transferring the entire state power to the Soviets of Workers' Deputies, so that the masses may learn from experience how to rid themselves of their errors. [...]

The Manifesto of the Soviet of Workers' Deputies – there isn't a word in it imbued with class-consciousness. There is nothing to it but phrases. The one thing that can ruin everything revolutionary is the phrase – this flattery of the revolutionary people. All of Marxism teaches us not to succumb to the revolutionary phrase, especially at the moment when it is particularly current.

Thesis 5. Not a parliamentary republic – a return to it from the Soviet of Workers' Deputies would be a step backward – but a Republic of Soviets of Workers', Farmhands' and Peasants' Deputies, from top to bottom.[38]

Lenin then went on to draw the important lessons of the Paris Commune:

Abolition of the police, the army and the officialdom.*

Salaries of all functionaries not to exceed the average wage of a competent worker; all functionaries to be elected and to be subject to recall at any time.

This is the lesson taught us by the French Commune, a lesson forgotten by Kautsky, but taught by the workers in the years 1905 and 1917. The experience of these years teaches us that… we must not permit the re-establishment of the police, we must not permit the re-establishment of the old army. We must change our programme; it is antiquated. The Soviet of Workers' and Soldiers' Deputies is a step toward socialism. No police, no army, no officialdom. The Constituent Assembly must be convoked – but by whom? [...] I would be glad to see the Constituent Assembly convened tomorrow, but it is naïve to believe that Guchkov will convoke the Constituent Assembly. All this prattle about

---

* Note by Lenin: I.e. the replacement of the standing army by the universal arming of the people.

compelling the Provisional Government to convoke the Constituent Assembly is hollow, wholesale deception. There were revolutions in the past, but the police has remained; there were revolutions in the past, but all the functionaries remained and the rest have remained. Therein lies the reason for the ruin of the revolutions. The Soviet of Workers' Deputies is the only government that can convoke this Assembly. We have all embraced the Soviets but we have failed to grasp their meaning. From this form of government we are pulling back to the International, which drags at the tail of the bourgeoisie. [...]

The art of ruling cannot be gleaned from any books. You must experiment, make mistakes and learn how to rule. [...]

Thesis 8. Not the 'introduction' of socialism as our immediate task, but the immediate placing of social production and the distribution of goods under the *control* of the Soviet of Workers' Deputies.

Life and revolution are pushing the Constituent Assembly into the background. It is not important who writes the laws down on paper, but it is important who puts them into effect. A dictatorship of the proletariat exists, but nobody knows what to do with it (Marx... [break in original] only that which has matured into actuality). Capitalism has become state capitalism.

Thesis 9. The party tasks:

1. Immediate party Congress.
2. Change the party programme, chiefly:
    a. on imperialism,
    b. on the attitude to the state, and our demand for a 'Commune-State',*
    c. amend our outdated minimum program.
3. Change the party name.** [39]

Lenin, who drew every drop of experience from what was happening, proposed a fundamental break with the past – the 'old Bolshevism'. A new name, a new clean banner was needed and the old one discarded. Again, he spoke for himself alone:

Personally and speaking for myself alone, I propose that we change the name of the Party, that we call it the *Communist Party*. The people will understand the name 'Communist'. The majority of the official Social-Democrats have betrayed

* Note by Lenin: A state model for which we had in the Paris Commune.
** Note by Lenin: Instead of 'Social-Democracy', the official leaders of which have betrayed socialism the world over by going over to the bourgeoisie ('the defencists' and the vacillating Kautskyans), we must call ourselves the Communist Party.

socialism. Liebknecht is the only Social-Democrat. You are afraid to go back on your old memories? But to change our linen, we've got to take off the dirty shirt and put on a clean one. [...]

The name social democrat is inaccurate. Don't hang on to an old name which is rotten through and through. Have the will to build a new party... and all the oppressed will come to you.

In Zimmerwald and Kienthal the Centre, *Rabochaya Gazeta*, predominated. We shall prove to you what the entire experience has shown. We declare that we have formed a left and have broken with the centre. Either you talk of the International, and then you must carry on... [break in original] or you... [break in original]

The Left Zimmerwald tendency exists in all countries of the world. The masses must realise that socialism has split throughout the world. The defencists have renounced socialism. Liebknecht alone... the future is his.[40]

Lenin then directed his strongest remarks to the vacillating leadership within the Bolshevik Party, which contained a clear threat. He warned that, if he was in a minority at the Conference, he would take his criticisms to the ranks of the Party, even if he was completely alone. He then slammed the idea of unification with the Menshevik-SR 'Compromisers'.

I hear that in Russia there is a trend toward unification. Unification with the defencists – that is a betrayal of socialism. I think that it is better to stand alone like Liebknecht – one against 110.[41]

Hostility to Lenin

A public *Theses* based on Lenin's speech was published in *Pravda* three days after the Conference. However, the editors of *Pravda* were at pains to point out that it was published only under Lenin's name.

The following day, Kamenev published another article entitled *Our Disagreements*, in which he dissociated himself, the editors and the Bureau of the Central Committee from Lenin's theses. It was a clear statement of their position which opposed any socialist perspective – a position held just six months before the October Revolution was to take place. Kamenev wrote:

As for Comrade Lenin's general scheme, it appears to us unacceptable, inasmuch as it proceeds from the assumption that the bourgeois-democratic revolution is *completed* and builds on the immediate transformation of this revolution into a socialist revolution.[42]

The idea that the revolution in Russia was a bourgeois revolution, and nothing more, had been ingrained in the Party. As mentioned, the problem was the old slogan of 'democratic dictatorship of proletariat and peasantry', which, given its algebraic formulation, opened up the danger of supporting the Provisional Government. Shamefully, this was exactly what had happened.

Boris Avilov, for example, at a meeting of the Bolshevik Petersburg Committee, put forward the case for supporting the Provisional Government by referring to old articles and resolutions. According to Raskolnikov:

> … he unmercifully quoted from old articles of his own, he cited in their support excerpts from the resolutions of Party Congresses, and all this merely so as to substantiate the typically Menshevik proposition that we were experiencing a bourgeois revolution and that therefore the task of the proletariat consisted in giving support, fully and wholly, not from fear but for conscience's sake, to the Provisional Government.

Raskolnikov admits that such views were not uncommon, including in the leadership:

> The leading nucleus of the Petersburg Committee then shared the view of which the fundamental thesis was that, in so far as the Provisional Government was carrying out the tasks of the revolution and upholding its conquests against counter-revolutionary infringements, to that extent our Party ought to give it support, struggling against it only in so far as it retreated from the programme of the revolution.[43]

He went on:

> Vladimir Ilyich's arrival marked in general a decisive turning point in our Party's tactics. It must be confessed that before his arrival there was rather a lot of confusion in the Party. There was no definite, consistent line. The task of taking state power was depicted by the majority as a sort of distant idea and not, as a rule, presented as a close, urgent and immediate aim. It was considered sufficient to support the Provisional Government, using one formula or another, with these or those reservations and, of course, retaining the right to apply the widest criticism. Inside the Party there was no unity of thought: vacillation and disunity were typical, everyday phenomena especially showing themselves at broad Party and faction meetings…

> After Comrade Lenin's arrival I did not see Avilov again, even on the threshold of our Party institutions. The Right-wing Bolsheviks were swept away as though by

a mop. By the current life they were cast into the camp of the 'in-between' *Novaya Zhizn*.* All the rest of the comrades were quickly united under Lenin's leadership and the Party became of one mind, gradually and not without internal struggle and wavering, adopting Comrade Lenin's slogans and tactics.[44]

If anything, Raskolnikov's statement fails to convey an adequate impression of the deep-seated and hostile opposition to Lenin's *April Theses*. At a meeting of the Bureau of the Central Committee on 19 April, both Kamenev and Stalin spoke against the *Theses*, while the Petrograd Committee rejected it by thirteen votes to two, with one abstention.

Radical break

Letters from Afar and the *April Theses* constituted a complete break from the position that had been previously held for many years, which had now been superseded by the experience of the February Revolution. Concretely, events had turned out differently. Lenin recognised this change and drew the necessary conclusions. In doing so, Lenin had returned to a position he had held in the aftermath of the 1905 Revolution, where he talked of "uninterrupted revolution".[45]

From then on, Lenin carried out a blistering defence of his ideas. He declared war on those who rigidly stuck to the old position. This began with an article, *Letters on Tactics*, written between 8 and 13 April:

> Marxism requires of us a strictly exact and objectively verifiable analysis of the relations of classes and of the concrete features peculiar to each historical situation. We Bolsheviks have always tried to meet this requirement, which is absolutely essential for giving a scientific foundation to policy.
>
> "Our theory is not a dogma, but a guide to action",** Marx and Engels always said, rightly ridiculing the mere memorising and repetition of 'formulas', that at best are capable only of marking out *general* tasks, which are necessarily modifiable by the *concrete* economic and political conditions of each particular *period* of the historical process. [...]
>
> Before the February – March revolution of 1917, state power in Russia was in the hands of one old class, namely, the feudal landed nobility, headed by Nicholas Romanov.
>
> After the revolution, the power is in the hands of a *different* class, a new class, namely, the *bourgeoisie*.

---

* Paper of the Menshevik-Internationalists, edited by Gorky.
** Note by Lenin: See Engels, 'Letter to FA Sorge', 29 November 1886.

The passing of state power from one *class* to another is the first, the principal, the basic sign of a *revolution*, both in the strictly scientific and in the practical political meaning of that term.

To this extent, the bourgeois, or the bourgeois-democratic, revolution in Russia is *completed*.

But at this point we hear a clamour of protest from people who readily call themselves 'old Bolsheviks'. Didn't we always maintain, they say, that the bourgeois-democratic revolution is completed only by the 'revolutionary-democratic dictatorship of the proletariat and the peasantry'? Is the agrarian revolution, which is also a bourgeois-democratic revolution, completed? Is it not a fact, on the contrary, that it has *not even* started?

My answer is: The Bolshevik slogans and ideas *on the whole* have been confirmed by history; but *concretely* things have worked out differently; they are more original, more peculiar, more variegated than anyone could have expected.

To ignore or overlook this fact would mean taking after those 'old Bolsheviks' who more than once already have played so regrettable a role in the history of our Party by reiterating formulas senselessly *learned by rote* instead of *studying* the specific features of the new and living reality.

'The revolutionary-democratic dictatorship of the proletariat and the peasantry' has *already* become a reality* in the Russian revolution, for this 'formula' envisages only a *relation of classes*, and not a *concrete political institution implementing* this relation, this co-operation. 'The Soviet of Workers' and Soldiers' Deputies' – there you have the 'revolutionary-democratic dictatorship of the proletariat and the peasantry' already accomplished in reality.

This formula is already antiquated. Events have moved it from the realm of formulas into the realm of reality, clothed it with flesh and bone, concretised it and *thereby* modified it. [...]

The person who *now* speaks only of a 'revolutionary-democratic dictatorship of the proletariat and the peasantry' is behind the times, consequently, he has in effect *gone over* to the petty bourgeoisie against the proletarian class struggle; that person should be consigned to the archive of 'Bolshevik' pre-revolutionary antiques (it may be called the archive of 'old Bolsheviks').

The revolutionary-democratic dictatorship of the proletariat and the peasantry has already been realised, but in a highly original manner, and with a number of extremely important modifications. I shall deal with them separately in one of my

---

* Note by Lenin: In a certain form and to a certain extent.

next letters. For the present, it is essential to grasp the incontestable truth that a Marxist must take cognisance of real life, of the true facts of *reality*, and not cling to a theory of yesterday, which, like all theories, at best only outlines the main and the general, only *comes near* to embracing life in all its complexity.

"Theory, my friend, is grey, but green is the eternal tree of life."*

To deal with the question of 'completion' of the bourgeois revolution *in the old way* is to sacrifice living Marxism to the dead letter.[46]

When the situation changes, then the Party must change too. This stand brought out the real Lenin, who saw the need to radically change direction and was prepared to fight for it every inch of the way. Ever the realist, Lenin explained:

> In real life, however, things have *already* turned out *differently*; there has been an extremely original, novel and unprecedented *interlacing of the one with the other*.[47]

Dual power

He went on to describe the situation of 'dual power' which existed between the Provisional Government (the rule of the bourgeoisie), on the one hand, and the soviets of workers (the embryo of workers' power) on the other:

> We have side by side, existing together, simultaneously, *both* the rule of the bourgeoisie (the government of Lvov and Guchkov) and a revolutionary-democratic dictatorship of the proletariat and the peasantry, which is *voluntarily* ceding power to the bourgeoisie, voluntarily making itself an appendage of the bourgeoisie.
>
> For it must not be forgotten that actually, in Petrograd, the power is in the hands of the workers and soldiers; the new government is *not* using and cannot use violence against them, because *there is no* police, *no* army standing apart from the people, *no* officialdom standing all-powerful *above* the people. This is a fact, the kind of fact that is characteristic of a state of the Paris Commune type. This fact does not fit into the old schemes. One must know how to adapt schemes to facts, instead of reiterating the now meaningless words about a 'dictatorship of the proletariat and the peasantry' *in general*.
>
> To throw more light on this question let us approach it from another angle.
>
> A Marxist must not abandon the ground of careful analysis of class relations. The bourgeoisie is in power. But is not the mass of the peasants *also* a bourgeoisie,

---

* From Goethe's *Faust*.

only of a different social stratum, of a different kind, of a different character? Whence does it follow that *this* stratum *cannot* come to power, thus 'completing' the bourgeois-democratic revolution? Why should this be impossible?

This is how the old Bolsheviks often argue.

My reply is that it is quite possible. But, in assessing a given situation, a Marxist must proceed *not* from what is possible, but from what is real.[48]

Furthermore, Lenin again slammed Kamenev's reliance on the old, outdated slogan of 'democratic dictatorship', which had become reactionary in the present situation. For Lenin, it therefore needed to be completely discarded. Kamenev wrote an article in *Pravda* rejecting Lenin's position. We have already quoted it, but it is worth repeating:

> As for Comrade Lenin's general scheme, it appears to us unacceptable, inasmuch as it proceeds from the assumption that the bourgeois-democratic revolution is *completed*, and builds on the immediate transformation of this revolution into a socialist revolution.[49]

Lenin then replied:

> There are two big mistakes here.

> First. The question of 'completion' of the bourgeois-democratic revolution is *stated* wrongly. The question is put in an abstract, simple, so to speak one-colour, way, which does not correspond to the objective reality. To put the question *this way*, to ask *now* "whether the bourgeois-democratic revolution is completed" and say *no more*, is to prevent oneself from seeing the exceedingly complex reality, which is at least two-coloured. This is in theory. In practice, it means surrendering helplessly to *petty-bourgeois revolutionism*.

> Indeed, reality shows us *both* the passing of power into the hands of the bourgeoisie (a 'completed' bourgeois-democratic revolution of the usual type) and, side by side with the real government, the existence of a parallel government which represents the 'revolutionary-democratic dictatorship of the proletariat and the peasantry'. This 'second-government' has *itself* ceded the power to the bourgeoisie, has chained *itself* to the bourgeois government.

> Is this reality covered by Comrade Kamenev's old-Bolshevik formula, which says that "the bourgeois-democratic revolution is not completed"?

> It is not. The formula is obsolete. It is no good at all. It is dead. And it is no use trying to revive it.[50]

'Old Bolshevism'

Lenin forcefully argued that it was necessary to break with this theoretical inertia and ideological routinism. It was time to face up to the realities of the new situation, 'the tree of life', as he liked to call it, and this required fresh tactics. To simply cling to the old was to treat Marxism as a dogma and not a guide to action. In his conclusion, Lenin ended with the bold statement: "Old Bolshevism should be discarded."[51]

Lenin was forced to battle with the 'old Bolsheviks', who repeated everything by rote, without understanding what was meant. In effect, they were treating Marxism, not as a method, but as a fetish. They even accused Lenin of 'Trotskyism' and simply relied upon what was said or written before, without taking into consideration the changed situation.

Leninism or Marxism was not a set of biblical texts, but a scientific doctrine and method. Lenin explained that it was a guide to action many times. What Lenin had written or said in 1905 or 1906 was not necessarily applicable to 1917. On the contrary, many of these things were out-of-date as the situation had completely changed. Therefore, many ideas previously expressed needed to be modified or even abandoned altogether, depending on the current concrete situation.

That was Lenin's method. He never made a strait-jacket out of his tactical formulas or writings of yesterday, but displayed the greatest degree of flexibility in regard to tactics.

From a position of extreme isolation, Lenin's ideas nevertheless found an echo in the rank and file. His remarks had the ear of the Bolshevik workers, who in turn were in touch with the workers in the factories and soldiers in the barracks. His ideas of a second revolution to put power in the hands of the working class were readily supported.

Towards the end of April, a general City Conference of the Bolsheviks was held in Petrograd, at which Lenin's views were endorsed, although even then a significant minority was against. His resolution that "the Russian Revolution is only the first phase of the first of many proletarian revolutions inevitably engendered by the war" was only passed by seventy-one votes to thirty-nine, with eight abstentions.

Moreover, on the motion calling for the Bolsheviks to participate in an International Conference of Zimmerwaldists in Stockholm, there was a single vote against – that of Lenin – who thought the Bolsheviks were too tolerant of opportunism. Lenin, unlike Stalin, wanted a complete break with Zimmerwald, which was associated with centrism and pacifism, and to strike out in a completely new direction. This reflected Lenin's boldness; this was the real Lenin in action.

Within three weeks, after a short but sharp struggle, Lenin had won over the majority of the Bolshevik Party. No longer were they simply committed to a bourgeois republic, the old perspective of Bolshevism, but to the fight for a new regime, similar to the Paris Commune, based on the soviets.

"It laid down a 'Rubicon' between the tactics of yesterday and those of today", remarks Raskolnikov.[52] This whole episode became known as 'rearming the Party'. Lenin's eventual victory at the April Conference would put the Party on course for the October Revolution.

Trotsky's perspective

Of all the old Social-Democratic leaders at this time, the only one whose ideas corresponded completely with Lenin's was Leon Trotsky.

Trotsky, who had been expelled from France by the authorities in 1916, then deported from Spain, found himself in New York. There he engaged in revolutionary activity with Bukharin, who himself had been deported from Scandinavia. Trotsky wrote a series of articles in the paper *Novy Mir* (*New World*) in March 1917, which reflected Lenin's *Letters from Afar*. Completely independent of Lenin, he argued for the same position: for the working class to seize power in a second revolution.

As the 'old Bolsheviks' moved further away from Lenin, he himself drew closer to Trotsky's position. On all the principal questions – attitude to the bourgeoisie, the Provisional Government, the peasantry, world war and world revolution – their views were identical.

Kollontai, who had broken with Menshevism and joined the Bolsheviks, was also in New York, and to demonstrate her new Bolshevik credentials she sent a stream of letters to Lenin containing false information about Trotsky. This was quite dishonest, but her only saving grace was that on Lenin's return from exile, she alone supported Lenin's *April Theses*.[53]

On his way back to Russia, Trotsky was interned in a concentration camp by the British in Canada. On 4 May 1917, having been released, he finally arrived back in Russia. From that very moment, he spoke and acted in complete solidarity with the Bolsheviks. Raskolnikov writes:

> Lev Davidovich [Trotsky] was not at that time formally a member of our Party, but as a matter of fact he worked within it continually from the day of his arrival from America. At any rate, immediately after his first speech in the Soviet, we all looked upon him as one of our party leaders.[54]

116. Trotsky arriving in Petrograd, 4   117. Aleksandra Kollontai, c.
                May 1917   1900

From then on, the paths of Lenin and Trotsky coincide. 1917 marked a
decisive turning point. Lenin had revised his position and accepted, in essence,
Trotsky's idea of permanent revolution, while Trotsky had fully adopted
Lenin's views on the party. The old formula of 'democratic dictatorship
of proletariat and peasantry' was ditched in favour of workers' power, and
despite past differences, which the revolution made irrelevant, they were now
at one politically. Raskolnikov notes:

> The echoes of the past disagreements during the pre-war period had completely
> disappeared. No differences existed between the tactical line of Lenin and Trotsky.
> That fusion, already observable during the war, was completely and definitely
> achieved from the moment of Trotsky's return to Russia. From his first public
> speech all of us old Leninists felt he was ours.[55]

From then on, their names were inseparable. With Lenin's complete
agreement, Trotsky did not immediately join the Bolshevik Party, but
instead joined the 4,000-strong Petrograd Inter-District Committee – the
Mezhraiontsy – in order to win them over to Bolshevism. Trotsky writes:

> I arranged with Comrade Kamenev to meet the editors of *Pravda* a few days after
> my return. I think I went to see them on 5 May or 6 May. I told Lenin that I was
> in complete agreement with his *April Theses* and with the whole course which the

Party had taken since his arrival, and that I saw before me two possibilities: either to join the Party of my own – 'individually' – or to attempt to bring into it the best of the 'Unionists' [Mezhraiontsy], among whom in Petersburg alone there were 3,000 workers and allied with them a whole *pléiade* of inestimable revolutionaries like Uritsky, Lunacharsky, Joffe, Vladimirov, Manuilsky, Karakhan, Yurenev, Posern, Litkens, and others. Antonov-Ovseyenko had by that time already joined the Party; so did Sokolnikov, I believe…

Having met with Lenin's tacit and general approval, I personally refrained from forcing the course of events. We had a common policy.[56]

On 23 May, Lenin personally attended a meeting of the Mezhraiontsy and offered them a seat on the editorial board of *Pravda*, as well as on the organising committee for the forthcoming Party Congress. Under Trotsky's influence, they soon joined the Bolsheviks, with their membership recorded as when they first joined their party. "Accordingly", wrote Trotsky in *Pravda*, "there are no motives which justify the separate existence of these organisations."[57]

Later, Lenin was to remark that, in 1917, "Bolshevism […] drew to itself all that was best in the trends of socialist thought akin to it…"[58] These remarks were clearly referring to Trotsky and the Mezhraiontsy.

In these revolutionary times, the doors of the Bolshevik Party were thrown open to the working class. According to Raskolnikov: "Enrolment as a Party member was very greatly simplified at this time. It was enough to give the secretary one or two acceptable recommendations and anyone who wanted would be given a Party card without delay."[59] As a result, membership in Petrograd jumped from 2,000 to 16,000 between February and the April conference.

With the Bolshevik Party now rearmed under Lenin's leadership, it began to make significant advances inside and outside the Soviets. With the Mensheviks and SRs increasingly exposing themselves, prospects for Bolshevism looked very promising. "Here is a revolution which has not said its last word yet", stated Lenin at the end of May 1917.[60] The next six months would be decisive.

Glossary

Cadets – Acronym for Constitutional Democrats, the main bourgeois liberal party in Russia which emerged from the earlier Liberation (Osvobozhdeniye in Russian) League.

Duma – An ancient Russian word, virtually synonymous with soviet, meaning a council. During the reign of Nicholas II the State Duma was the name given to the national parliament. There were also local dumas, the equivalent of local councils.

Kulak – A rich peasant. The word actually means 'a fist', probably an ironic reference to the tightfistedness of these elements.

Muzhik – Russian name for a peasant. Sometimes used colloquially to mean 'a man'.

Okhrana – Short for Okhrananoye Otdyelyeniye or Department of Safety. It was the tsarist secret police, founded in 1881, which operated a vast network of spies, informers, and agents provocateurs who infiltrated the revolutionary movement and whose operations extended to many countries.

Pogrom – A racially motivated attack in which mobs, usually organised and directed by agents of the state, attack minorities. The victims were most often Jews, but also included other minorities, such as the Armenians in Azerbaijan.

Socialist-Revolutionaries (SRs) – A petty-bourgeois party, descended from the Narodniks, which advocated a kind of 'peasant socialism'. They split into a right and left in 1917. The Left supported the October Revolution and for a time were in a coalition government with the Bolsheviks.

Zemstvo (Russian plural, zemstva) – Semi-official local organs of self-government. Control of the zemstvos was in the hands of the rural gentry. They had virtually no powers and were dependent on the whims of the local governor, who was appointed by the central government.

A name glossary has been compiled for this book, available online at:

wellred-books.com/in-defence-of-lenin-glossary

References

Preface

1. Lenin, 'The Present Political Situation, *Vperyod*, No. 3, 28 May 1906, *Lenin Collected Works*, (henceforth referred to as *LCW*), Vol. 10, p. 485
2. Krupskaya, *Memories of Lenin*, p. 115
3. Martin Sandbu, 'From Lenin to Lehman', *Financial Times*, 15 August 2017
4. 'A better form of capitalism is possible', editorial, *Financial Times*, 30 December 2020
5. Quoted in Sarah O'Connor, 'Iceland gives Christmas frosty reception', *Financial Times*, 23 December 2008
6. McLachan, *In the Chair: Barrington-Ward of 'The Times', 1927-1948*, p. 206, footnote

Introduction

1. Quoted in Alexievich, *Second-hand Time*, p. 123
2. Quoted ibid, p. 219
3. Krupskaya, *Reminiscences of Lenin*, p. 376
4. Foner, *The Bolshevik Revolution*, p. 29
5. Hoover, *Masters of Deceit*, quoted in LeBlanc, *Lenin and the Revolutionary Party*, pp. 2-3
6. Churchill, *The World Crisis*, p. 74
7. Rappaport, *Conspirator*, p. 8
8. Montefiore, *Young Stalin*, p. 150
9. Quoted in Trotsky, *The Young Lenin*, p. 197
10. Carlyle, *Cromwell's Letters and Speeches*, p. 13
11. Kershaw, *Personality and Power*, p. 46
12. Volkogonov, *Lenin*, p. 259
13. Serge, *From Lenin to Stalin*, pp. 9-10
14. Ibid., p. 9
15. *New York Evening Call*, 22 December 1917
16. Milton, *John Maclean*, p. 152
17. Read, *The World on Fire*, p. 51
18. Ibid., p. 101
19. Ibid., p. 58
20. Ibid., p. 193
21. Ibid., p. vii
22. Steffens, *The Autobiography of Lincoln Steffens*, Vol. 2, p. 799
23. Williams, *Lenin*, p. 120
24. Chaplin, *My Trip Abroad*, p. 37
25. Quoted in Prashad, 'The Political Life And Cinema Of Comrade Charlie Chaplin', *The Wire*, 29 July 2017
26. Ransome, *The Truth About Russia, Six Weeks in Russia in 1919*, p. 34
27. Ibid., pp. 57-8
28. Ibid., p. 118

29. *Manchester Guardian*, 2 September 1918
30. Russell, 'Lenin: An Impression', *The New Leader*, 23 January 1924
31. Russell, *The Practice and Theory of Bolshevism*, p. 6
32. Russell, *Autobiography*, pp. 109-10
33. Ransome, *Six Weeks in Russia*, pp. 119-20
34. Gorky, *Days with Lenin*, p. 38
35. Lenin, 'To the Library of the Rumyantsev Museum', 1 September 1920, *LCW*, Vol. 35, p. 454, emphasis in original
36. Lunacharsky, *Revolutionary Silhouettes*, p. 41
37. Wells, 'The Dreamer in the Kremlin', *The New York Times*, 5 December 1920, *Russia in the Shadows*, p. 123
38. Ibid., p. 135
39. Quoted in Trotsky, *On Lenin*, p. 148
40. Lenin, 'To AA Joffe', 17 March 1921, *LCW*, Vol. 45, p. 99, emphasis in original
41. Lenin, *The State and Revolution*, August – September 1917, *LCW*, Vol. 25, p. 390
42. Applebaum, *The Washington Post*, 6 November 2017
43. *The Independent*, 7 November 2019
44. 'Report on US Attitudes Towards Socialism, Communism, and Collectivism', conducted by YouGov
45. *Bloomberg*, 9 May 2022
46. Marx and Engels, *Manifesto of the Communist Party*, *MECW*, Vol. 6, p. 519, emphasis in original

1. Lenin's Roots

1. Trotsky, *The Young Lenin*, p. 3
2. Quoted in Figes, *A People's Tragedy*, p. 54
3. Lenin, 'The Fiftieth Anniversary of the Fall of Serfdom', *Rabochaya Gazeta*, No. 3, 8 (21) February 1911, *LCW*, Vol. 17, p. 88, emphasis in original
4. Lockhart, *Memoirs of a British Agent*, p. 165
5. Carr, *The Bolshevik Revolution, 1917-*

1923, Vol. 1, p. 4
6. Quoted in Figes, *A People's Tragedy*, p. 131
7. Krupskaya, *Memories of Lenin*, p. 204
8. Ibid., p. 199
9. Quoted in Volkogonov, *Lenin*, p. 13
10. Ulyanova, 'Preface to *Letters to Relatives*', 1930, *LCW*, Vol. 37, p. 28
11. Quoted in Deutscher, *Lenin's Childhood*, p. 25
12. Trotsky, *The Young Lenin*, p. 12
13. Ibid., p. 24
14. Lenin, *What Is to Be Done?*, March 1902, *LCW*, Vol. 5, p. 517
15. Quoted in Lenin, 'Revolutionary Adventurism', *Iskra*, No. 23, 1 August 1902, *LCW*, Vol. 6, p. 193
16. Trotsky, *The Young Lenin*, p. 49
17. Quoted in Serge, *Year One of the Russian Revolution*, p. 26
18. Lenin, 'Revolutionary Adventurism', Part 1, *Iskra* No. 23, 1 August 1902, *LCW*, Vol. 6, p. 193
19. Ibid., p. 191, emphasis in original
20. Alexander III, 'Manifesto of 29 April 1881', *Documents in Russian History*, 26 March 2002, available at: academic.shu.edu/russianhistory/index.php/Alexander_III,_Proclamation_of_April_29,_1881 (accessed 21 July 2023)
21. Trotsky, *The Young Lenin*, p. 36
22. Maria Ulyanova, 'Preface to *Letters to Relatives*', 1930, *LCW*, Vol. 37, p. 62
23. Quoted in Deutscher, *Lenin's Childhood*, p. 37
24. Wilson, *To the Finland Station*, p. 360
25. Quoted in Deutscher, *Lenin's Childhood*, pp. 39-40
26. Quoted in Zinoviev, *History of the Bolshevik Party*, p. 34
27. Ibid., pp. 33-4
28. Trotsky, *The Young Lenin*, p. 65
29. Quoted in Deutscher, *Lenin's Childhood*, p. 61
30. Quoted in Liebman, *Leninism Under Lenin*, p. 35
31. Rappaport, *Conspirator*, p. xxi
32. Krupskaya, *Reminiscences of Lenin*, p. 14

33. Ibid., p. 15
34. Ibid.
35. Krupskaya, *Memories of Lenin*, p. 4
36. Trotsky, 'Leon Trotsky on Lenin', *Encyclopedia Britannica*, 22 Nov 2022, available at: www.britannica.com/topic/Leon-Trotsky-on-Lenin-1983748 (accessed 20 October 2023)
37. Krupskaya, *Reminiscences of Lenin*, p. 15
38. Trotsky, *The Young Lenin*, p. 118

2. The Early Years

1. Quoted in Clark, *Lenin*, p. 20
2. Quoted in Popov, *Outline History of the Communist Party of the Soviet Union*, p. 52
3. Zinoviev, *Lenin*, p. 9
4. Quoted in Trotsky, *The Young Lenin*, p. 144
5. Trotsky, *History of the Russian Revolution*, Vol. 1, p. 32
6. Quoted in Zinoviev, *History of the Bolshevik Party*, p. 35
7. Plekhanov, *Selected Philosophical Works*, Vol. 1, p. 90
8. Engels, 'Letter to Plekhanov', 8 February 1895, *MECW*, Vol. 50, pp. 439-40, emphasis in original
9. Lenin, 'From the History of the Workers' Press in Russia', *Rabochy*, No. 1, 22 April 1914, *LCW*, Vol. 20, p. 247
10. Marx and Engels, 'Preface to the Second Russian Edition of the *Manifesto of the Communist Party*', *MECW*, Vol. 24, p. 426
11. Quoted in Lenin, *What Is to Be Done?*, March 1902, *LCW*, Vol. 5, p. 409
12. Trotsky, *The Young Lenin*, p. 130
13. Figes, *A People's Tragedy*, p. 144
14. Quoted in Vodovozov, *Moe Znakomstvo s Leninym* (*My Acquaintance with Lenin*), p. 176
15. Pipes, *The Russian Revolution, 1899-1919*, pp. 350-1
16. Wilson, *To the Finland Station*, p. 371
17. Quoted in Trotsky, *The Young Lenin*, p. 174
18. Ibid., p. 173

19. Figes, *A People's Tragedy*, p. 144
20. Lenin, 'Adventurism', *Rabochy*, No. 7, 9 June 1914, *LCW*, Vol. 20, p. 358
21. Trotsky, *On Lenin*, pp. 192-3
22. Trotsky, *The Young Lenin*, p. 188

3. St. Petersburg

1. Quoted in Trotsky, *The Young Lenin*, p. 202
2. Ibid., pp. 206-7
3. Ibid., p. 186
4. Quoted in Cliff, *Lenin*, Vol. 1, p. 35
5. Quoted in Lenin, *What Is to Be Done?*, March 1902, *LCW*, Vol. 5, p. 372
6. Lenin, 'To his Mother', 5 October 1893, *LCW*, Vol. 37, pp. 65-6
7. Lenin, 'To Maria', 13 December 1894, ibid., p. 68
8. Lenin, 'To his Mother', 20 May 1895, ibid., p. 73
9. Maria Ulyanova, 'Preface to *Letters to Relatives*', 1930, ibid., p. 26
10. Lenin, 'To his Mother', 7 or 8 December 1909, ibid., p. 442
11. Maria Ulyanova, 'Preface to *Letters to Relatives*', 1930, ibid., p. 40
12. Krupskaya, *Reminiscences of Lenin*, p. 52
13. Lenin, *What Is to Be Done?*, March 1902, *LCW*, Vol. 5, p. 491
14. Trotsky, *My Life*, pp. 94-5
15. Lenin, *What the 'Friends of the People' Are and How They Fight the Social-Democrats*, 1894, *LCW*, Vol. 1, pp. 298-9, emphasis in original
16. Ibid., p. 300, emphasis in original
17. Plekhanov, *Selected Philosophical Writings*, p. 16
18. Quoted in Clark, *Lenin*, p. 38
19. Lenin, 'To his Mother', 10 August 1895, *LCW*, Vol. 37, p. 77
20. Lenin, 'Friedrich Engels', 1895, *LCW*, Vol. 2, p. 27
21. Quoted in Pipes, *The Russian Revolution, 1899-1919*, p. 348
22. Quoted in Shub, *Lenin*, p. 43
23. Krupskaya, *Reminiscences of Lenin*, p. 23
24. Ibid., p. 26

25. Ibid., p. 20
26. Ibid., p. 27
27. Ibid., p. 28
28. Ibid., p. 28

4. Exile to Siberia

1. Arnot, *A Short History of the Russian Revolution*, Part 1, Chapter 2, 1937, available at: www.marxists.org/archive/arnot-page/1937/russ_rev_1/01.htm#exr (accessed 1 September 2023)
2. Lenin, 'To his Mother', 2 March 1897, *LCW*, Vol. 37, p. 92
3. Lenin, 'To his Mother', 10 May 1898, ibid., p. 171
4. Lenin, 'To his Mother', 14 June 1898, ibid., p. 176
5. Lenin, 'Lenin and Krupskaya to Lenin's Mother', 14 June 1898, ibid., p. 287
6. Lenin, 'To AN Potresov', 27 June 1899, *LCW*, Vol. 34, p. 41
7. Lenin, 'Lenin and Krupskaya to Lenin's Mother', 27 June 1907, *LCW*, Vol. 37, p. 366
8. Lenin, 'To his Mother and Anna', 25 May 1897, ibid., p. 112
9. Lenin, *The Development of Capitalism in Russia*, 1899, *LCW*, Vol. 3, p. 25
10. Krupskaya, *Reminiscences of Lenin*, p. 44
11. Lenin, *The Tasks of Russian Social-Democrats*, 1898, *LCW*, Vol. 2, p. 345
12. Ibid., p. 347
13. Lenin, 'To PB Axelrod', 16 August 1897, *LCW*, Vol. 34, p. 24
14. Quoted in Zinoviev, *History of the Bolshevik Party*, p. 53
15. Quoted in Carr, *The Bolshevik Revolution, 1917-1923*, Vol. 1, p. 4
16. Lenin, 'To AN Potresov', 27 April 1899, *LCW*, Vol. 34, p. 32
17. Lenin, 'To his Brother-in-law', 28 February 1899, *LCW*, Vol. 37, p. 241
18. Lenin, 'To his Mother', 1 September 1899, ibid., pp. 281-2
19. Quoted in Zinoviev, *History of the Bolshevik Party*, p. 42
20. Lenin, *What the 'Friends of the People' Are and How They Fight the Social-Democrats*, 1894, *LCW*, Vol. 1, p. 326
21. Lenin, *What Is to Be Done?*, March 1902, *LCW*, Vol. 5, p. 361, emphasis in original
22. Lenin, 'Interview with Arthur Ransome, *Manchester Guardian* Correspondent', *Manchester Guardian*, No. 23797, 22 November 1922, *LCW*, Vol. 33, p. 400
23. Rimlinger, *The Management of Labor Protest in Russia: 1870-1905*, p. 229
24. Lenin, 'To Nadezhda Krupskaya', prior to 25 August 1900, *LCW*, Vol. 34, p. 46
25. Lenin, *What Is to Be Done?*, March 1902, *LCW*, Vol. 5, p. 474
26. Lenin, 'To his Mother', 5 May 1900, *LCW*, Vol. 37, p. 293
27. Quoted in Lenin, 'To Nadezhda Krupskaya', 24 August 1900, *LCW*, Vol. 34, p. 45
28. Lenin, 'How the *Spark* Was Nearly Extinguished', September 1900, *LCW*, Vol. 4, p. 340
29. Ibid., p. 348

5. 'Iskra' Launched

1. Krupskaya, *Reminiscences of Lenin*, p. 55
2. Zinoviev, *History of the Bolshevik Party*, p. 73
3. Lenin, 'How the *Spark* Was Nearly Extinguished', September 1900, *LCW*, Vol. 4, p. 348
4. Lenin, 'The Urgent Tasks of Our Movement', *Iskra*, No. 1, December 1900, *LCW*, Vol. 4, pp. 370-1
5. Lenin, 'Draft of a Declaration of the Editorial Board of *Iskra* and *Zarya*', 1900, ibid., p. 327
6. Lenin, 'On Strikes', 1899, *LCW*, Vol. 4, pp. 314-5
7. Ibid., p. 316
8. Ibid., p. 317
9. Piatnitsky, *Memoirs of a Bolshevik*, p. 57
10. Quoted in Clark, *Lenin*, p. 63
11. Lenin, *What Is to Be Done?*, March 1902, *LCW*, Vol. 5, p. 350, emphasis in original

12. Lenin, 'An Urgent Question', 1899, *LCW*, Vol. 4, p. 221
13. Lenin, 'A Letter to a Comrade on Our Organisational Tasks', September 1902, *LCW*, Vol. 6, pp. 246-7, emphasis in original
14. Lenin, 'Where to Begin?', *Iskra*, No. 4, May 1901, *LCW*, Vol. 5, p. 22-3
15. Lenin, 'Declaration of the Editorial Board of *Iskra*', September 1900, published as a separate leaflet by *Iskra*, *LCW*, Vol. 4, pp. 352-3, emphasis in original
16. Ibid., p. 354, emphasis added
17. Ibid., pp. 354-5
18. Lenin, *What Is to Be Done?*, March 1902, *LCW*, Vol. 5, p. 472, emphasis in original
19. Ibid., p. 470, emphasis in original
20. Quoted in Rappaport, *Conspirator*, p. 43
21. Trotsky, *Stalin*, pp. 71-2
22. Lenin, *What Is to Be Done?*, March 1902, *LCW*, Vol. 5, p. 467
23. Lenin, 'Where to Begin', *LCW*, Vol. 5, p. 18
24. Lenin, 'To Apollinaria Yakubova', 26 October 1900, *LCW*, Vol. 34, p. 53, emphasis in original
25. Quoted in Lenin, 'A Talk With Defenders of Economism', *Iskra*, No. 12, 6 December 1901, *LCW*, Vol. 5, p. 314
26. Ibid., p. 319
27. Lassalle, 'Letter to Marx', 24 June 1852, quoted ibid., p. 320
28. Lenin, 'A Talk With Defenders of Economism', *Iskra*, No. 12, 6 December 1901, *LCW*, Vol. 5, p. 320
29. Lenin, 'To Lyubov Axelrod', 17 December 1901, *LCW*, Vol. 43, p. 75
30. Lenin, 'To NE Bauman', 24 May 1901, *LCW*, Vol. 34, p. 65
31. Lenin, 'To LY Galperin', 18 or 24 June 1901, ibid., p. 72
32. Quoted in Clark, *Lenin*, p. 66
33. Lenin, 'To PB Axelrod', 26 July 1901, *LCW*, Vol. 34, p. 83-4
34. Trotsky, *On Lenin*, p. 57
35. Lenin, 'To the Iskra Organisations in Russia', prior to 18 December 1901, *LCW*, Vol. 34, p. 90, emphasis in original
36. Figes, *A People's Tragedy*, p. 151
37. Ibid., p. 150
38. Lenin, 'Preface to the Collection *Twelve Years*', September 1907, *LCW*, Vol. 13, p. 102
39. Quoted in Krupskaya, *Reminiscences of Lenin*, p. 66
40. Lenin, 'Preface to the Collection *Twelve Years*', September 1907, *LCW*, Vol. 13, p. 107
41. Lenin, *What Is to Be Done?*, March 1902, *LCW*, Vol. 5, p. 369, emphasis in original
42. Ibid., p. 446
43. Lenin, 'Revolutionary Adventurism', Part 1, *Iskra*, No. 23, 1 August 1902, *LCW* Vol. 6, p. 186
44. Lenin, *What Is to Be Done?*, March 1902, *LCW*, Vol. 5, p. 355, emphasis in original
45. *1903*, 9th session, pp. 169-70
46. Krupskaya, *Memories of Lenin*, p. 65
47. Lenin, *What Is to Be Done?*, March 1902, *LCW*, Vol. 5, p. 372

6. The Work of 'Iskra' Progresses

1. Krupskaya, *Reminiscences of Lenin*, p. 90
2. Krupskaya, *Memories of Lenin*, p. 66
3. Lenin, 'Notes on Plekhanov's Second Draft Programme', Februrary – March 1902, *LCW*, Vol. 6, p. 35, emphasis in original
4. Beer, *Fifty Years of International Socialism*, pp. 144-5
5. Lenin, 'Harry Quelch', *Pravda Truda*, No. 1, 11 September 1913, *LCW*, Vol. 19, p. 371
6. Krupskaya, *Reminiscences of Lenin*, p. 70
7. Ibid., p. 75
8. Volkogonov, *Lenin*, p. 51
9. Ibid., p. 62
10. Krupskaya, *Memories of Lenin*, 1930, p. 87
11. Lenin, 'To his Mother', 4 February

1903, *LCW*, Vol. 37, p. 355

12. Lenin, 'To his Mother', 29 March 1903, ibid., p. 358, emphasis in original

13. Krupskaya, *Reminiscences of Lenin*, p. 75

14. Lenin, 'To GV Plekhanov', 14 May 1902, *LCW*, Vol. 34, p. 103

15. Lenin, 'To GV Plekhanov', 23 June 1902, ibid., p. 105

16. Quoted in Trotsky, *On Lenin*, pp. 35-6

17. Trotsky, *Notebooks 1933-1935*, p. 81

18. Ibid

19. Quoted in Rothstein, *Lenin in Britain*, p. 15

20. Quoted ibid., pp. 13-14

21. Krupskaya, *Memories of Lenin*, pp. 84-6

22. Trotsky, *My Life*, p. 124

23. Krupskaya, *Memories of Lenin*, 1930, p. 89

24. Lenin, 'To GV Plekhanov', 2 March 1903, *LCW*, Vol. 43, pp. 110-1

25. Krupskaya, *Memories of Lenin*, p. 92

26. Ibid., p. 88

27. Krupskaya, *Reminiscences of Lenin*, p. 89

28. Ibid.

7. The Second Congress and its Myths

1. Service, *Lenin*, p. 157

2. Popov, *Outline History of the Communist Party of the Soviet Union*, Vol. 1, p. 103

3. Lenin, 'The Historical Meaning of the Inter-Party Struggle in Russia', *Diskussionny Listok*, No. 3, 29 April (12 May) 1911, *LCW*, Vol. 16, p. 380

4. Lenin, *One Step Forward, Two Steps Back*, May 1904, *LCW*, Vol. 7, p. 209

5. *1903*, 1st session, pp. 27-8

6. Trotsky, *Political Profiles*, p. 88

7. *1903*, p. 76, footnote, Article 2

8. Ibid., p. 105

9. Service, *Lenin*, p. 154

10. See Rubenstein, *Leon Trotsky*, p. 33

11. Trotsky, *My Life*, p. 139

12. *1903*, 16th session, p. 220

13. Krupskaya, *Reminiscences of Lenin*, p. 91

14. Lenin, *The Proletarian Revolution and the Renegade Kautsky*, October – November 1918, *LCW*, Vol. 28, p. 280, emphasis in original

15. *1903*, 9th session, p. 158-9

16. Ibid., pp. 171-2

17. Ibid., p. 168

18. Ibid., Appendix XI, 'Draft Organisational Rules of the RSDLP Moved at the Congress by Lenin', p. 511, emphasis added

19. Ibid., 'Organisational Rules of the Russian Social-Democratic Labour Party adopted at the Party's Second Congress', p. 10, emphasis added

20. Lenin, *One Step Forward, Two Steps Back*, *LCW*, Vol. 7, p. 258

21. *1903*, 22nd session p. 311

22. Ibid., 31st session, p. 435

23. Ibid., 23rd session, p. 326, emphasis added

24. Ibid., emphasis in original

25. Ibid., pp. 326-7

26. Service, *Lenin*, p. 154

27. Ibid., p. 155

28. Ibid., p. 157

29. Quoted in Lenin, *LCW*, Vol. 6, p. 546, footnote

30. *1903*, 23rd session, p. 321

31. Service, *Lenin*, p. 155

32. Krupskaya, *Memories of Lenin*, p. 99

33. Trotsky, *My Life*, p. 140

34. *1903*, 10th session, p. 179

35. Wolfe, *Three Who Made a Revolution*, p. 278

36. *1903*, p. 422, footnote

37. Ibid., 30th session, p. 427

38. Ibid., 31st session, p. 431

39. Ibid., p. 432

40. Ibid., p. 435, emphasis in original

41. Lenin, *One Step Forward, Two Steps Back*, *LCW*, Vol. 7, pp. 410-1

42. Trotsky, *On Lenin*, p. 53

43. Lenin, *One Step Forward, Two Steps Back*, *LCW*, Vol. 7, pp. 344-5, footnote

44. Krupskaya, *Reminiscences of Lenin*, p. 95

8. Aftermath of the 1903 Split

1. Pipes, *The Russian Revolution*, p. 349
2. Quoted in Henderson, *The Spark that Lit the Revolution*, p. 109
3. Trotsky, *My Life*, p. 141
4. Lenin, 'To AN Potresov', 13 September 1903, *LCW*, Vol. 34, p. 166
5. Engels, 'To A Bebel', 20 June 1873, *Marx and Engels Selected Correspondence*, p. 285
6. Engels, 'To E Bernstein', 20 October 1882, ibid., p. 353, emphasis in original
7. Quoted in Lenin, *One Step Forward, Two Steps Back*, *LCW*, Vol. 7, p. 312
8. Ibid., emphasis in original
9. Quoted ibid., pp. 312-3, emphasis in original
10. Trotsky, *My Life*, p. 141
11. Krupskaya, *Reminiscences of Lenin*, p. 95
12. Ibid., p. 97
13. Quoted in *LCW*, Vol. 34, p. 196
14. Lenin, *One Step Forward, Two Steps Back*, *LCW*, Vol. 7, p. 350, emphasis in original
15. Lenin, 'To Alexandra Kalmykova', 7 September 1903, *LCW*, Vol. 34, p. 161
16. Ibid., p. 163
17. Lenin, *One Step Forward, Two Steps Back*, *LCW*, Vol. 7, p. 253
18. Lenin, 'Account of the Second Congress of the RSDLP', September 1903, ibid., p. 34, emphasis in original
19. Lenin, 'Letter to *Iskra*', *Iskra*, No. 53, 25 November 1903, ibid., p. 114, emphasis added
20. Lenin, 'To AN Potresov', 13 September 1903, *LCW*, Vol. 34, pp. 164-5, emphasis added
21. Ibid., p. 166
22. Rappaport, *Conspirator*, pp. 86-7
23. Lenin, 'To GM Krzhizhanovsky', 10 to 14 September 1903, *LCW*, Vol. 34, p. 167
24. Krupskaya, *Reminiscences of Lenin*, p. 99
25. Gorky, *Days With Lenin*, p. 54
26. Lunacharsky, *Revolutionary Silhouettes*, p. 36
27. Lenin, 'To GM Krzhizhanovsky', 8 November 1903, *LCW*, Vol. 34, p. 191
28. Ibid.
29. Lenin, 'To GM Krzhizhanovsky', 8 November 1903, *LCW*, Vol. 34, p. 191
30. Krupskaya, *Reminiscences of Lenin*, p. 104
31. Ibid., p. 102
32. Lenin, 'To AA Bogdanov, Rozalia Zemlyachka and MM Litvinov', 3 December 1904, *LCW*, Vol. 34, pp. 271-2
33. Trotsky, *Stalin*, p. 83
34. Trotsky, *Our Political Tasks*, p. 77
35. Lenin, *One Step Forward, Two Steps Back*, *LCW*, Vol. 7, p. 204
36. Ibid., pp. 204-5
37. Trotsky, *Stalin*, p. 66
38. Lenin, 'To Karl Kautsky', 10 October 1904, *LCW*, Vol. 43, p. 127
39. Lenin, 'What Are We Working For', July 1904, *LCW*, Vol. 7, p. 445
40. Lenin, '*One Step Forward, Two Steps Back* – Reply by N Lenin to Rosa Luxemburg', September 1904, ibid., p. 472
41. Luxemburg, 'Organisational Questions of the Russian Social Democracy' (later retitled 'Leninism or Marxism?'), p. 10

9. The Revolution Begins

1. Quoted in Zinoviev, *History of the Bolshevik Party*, p. 103
2. Lenin, 'The Fall of Port Arthur', *Vperyod*, No. 2, 14 (1) January 1905, *LCW*, Vol. 8, pp. 54-5
3. Wolfe, *Three Who Made a Revolution*, pp. 323-4
4. Figes, *A People's Tragedy*, p. 177
5. Lenin, 'Lecture on the 1905 Revolution' 22 January 1925, *LCW*, Vol. 23, p. 237
6. Lenin, '"Left-Wing" Communism – An Infantile Disorder', 1920, *LCW*, Vol. 31, p. 27
7. Lenin, *Fifth All-Russia Congress of the Soviets of Workers', Peasants', Soldiers' and Red Army Deputies*, 6 July 1918, *LCW*,

Vol. 27, p. 511

8. Lunacharsky, *Revolutionary Silhouettes*, p. 46

9. Lenin, 'Time to Call a Halt!', *Vperyod*, No. 1, 4 January 1905, *LCW*, Vol. 8, p. 37

10. Lenin, *Revolutionary Days*, *Vperyod*, No. 4, 31 (18) January 1905, ibid., pp. 118-9

11. Ibid., p. 104

12. Lenin, 'The Beginning of the Revolution in Russia', *Vperyod*, No, 3, 25 (12) January 1905, *LCW*, Vol. 8, pp. 97-8

13. Lenin, '*Left-Wing' Communism: An Infantile Disorder*, June 1920, *LCW*, Vol. 31, p. 27

14. Trotsky, 'The Events in Petersburg', 20 January 1905, *Our Revolution*, pp. 55-6, emphasis in original

15. Lenin, '"Our Father the Tsar" and the Barricades', *LCW*, Vol. 8, p. 97

16. Lenin, 'The Beginning of the Revolution in Russia', *Vperyod*, No, 3, 25 (12) January 1905, *LCW*, Vol. 8, p. 97

17. Lenin, 'To AA Bogdanov', 10 January 1905, *LCW*, Vol. 8, p. 46, emphasis in original

18. Pipes, *The Russian Revolution, 1899-1919*, p. 361

19. Krupskaya, *Reminiscences of Lenin*, pp. 111-2

20. Lenin, 'Should We Organise the Revolution?', *Vperyod*, No. 7, 21 (8) February 1905, *LCW*, Vol. 8, p. 167

21. Lenin, 'The First Lessons', prior to 1 (14) February 1905, ibid., p. 138

22. Ibid.

23. Lenin, 'A Letter to AA Bogdanov and SI Gusev', 11 February 1905, ibid., p. 143-4

24. Ibid., p. 145

25. Ibid.

26. Ibid., p. 146

27. Ibid.

28. Lenin, *Revolutionary Days*, *Vperyod*, No. 4, 31 (18) January 1905, ibid., p. 104

29. Lenin, 'A Letter to the Organisations in Russia', 28 February 1905, ibid., p. 182

30. Quoted in Trotsky, *Stalin*, p. 91

31. Krupskaya, *Reminiscences of Lenin*, p. 124

32. Ibid., p. 125

33. Ibid., p. 125

34. Lenin, 'New Tasks and New Forces', *Vperyod*, No. 9, 8 March (23 February) 1905, *LCW*, Vol. 8, pp. 217-9, emphasis in original

35. Ibid., p. 220

36. Liebman, *Leninism Under Lenin*, pp. 46-7

37. Lenin, 'To the Odessa Committee of the RSDLP', 25 March 1905, *LCW*, Vol. 34, p. 307, emphasis in original

38. Lenin, 'Speech on the Question of the Relations Between Workers and Intellectuals Within the Social-Democratic Organisations', 20 April (3 May) 1905, *The Third Congress of the RSDLP*, *LCW*, Vol. 8, p. 408

39. Lenin, 'A Remark During the Discussion of the Resolution on the Relations Between Workers and Intellectuals Within the Social-Democratic Organisations', 22 April (5 May) 1905, ibid., p. 411

40. Trotsky, The Revolution Betrayed, p. 206

41. Henderson, *The Spark that Lit the Revolution*, p. 123

42. Ibid., p. 128

43. Ibid., p. 132

44. Lenin, 'To AA Bogdanov', 10 January 1905, *LCW*, Vol. 8, p. 44, emphasis in original

45. Read, *The World on Fire*, pp. 3-4

46. Lenin, 'The First of May', prior to 12 (25) April 1905, *LCW*, Vol. 8, pp. 348-50

47. Lenin, 'The Struggle of the Proletariat and the Servility of the Bourgeoisie', *Proletary*, No. 6, 3 July (20 June) 1905, ibid, p. 538

48. Lenin, 'The Reorganisation of the Party', Part 1, *Novaya Zhizn*, No. 9, 10 November 1905, *LCW*, Vol. 10, p. 32

49. Ibid., p. 29

50. Ibid., p. 32

51. Ibid., emphasis added

52. Lenin, 'The Lessons of the Revolution', *Rabochaya Gazeta*, No. 1, 30 October (12 November) 1910, *LCW*, Vol. 16, pp. 301-2, emphasis in original

53. Lenin, 'Differences in the European Labour Movement', *Zvezda*, No. 1, 16 December 1910, ibid., p. 348

54. Lenin, 'Lecture on the 1905 Revolution', prior to 9 (2) January 1917, *LCW*, Vol. 23, p. 241

55. Ibid., p. 238

56. Lenin, *The Victory of the Cadets and the Tasks of the Workers Party*, April 1906, *LCW*, Vol. 10, p. 252

57. Lenin, 'Let the Workers Decide', *Vperyod*, No. 6, 1 June 1906, ibid., pp. 502-3, emphasis in original

58. Pipes, *The Russian Revolution, 1899-1919*, p. 361

59. Figes, *A People's Tragedy*, p. 154

60. Liebman, *Leninism Under Lenin*, p. 47

10. Perspectives for the Russian Revolution

1. Quoted in Zinoviev, *History of the Bolshevik Party*, pp. 107-8

2. Lenin, 'Working-class and Bourgeois Democracy', *Vperyod*, No. 3, 24 (11) January 1905, *LCW*, Vol. 8, p. 82

3. Krupskaya, *Memories of Lenin*, p. 199

4. Quoted in Lenin, *Two Tactics of Social-Democracy in the Democratic Revolution*, July 1905, *LCW*, Vol. 9, p. 134

5. Lenin, 'The Historical Meaning of the Inner-Party Struggle in Russia', after September 1910, *LCW*, Vol. 16, p. 375

6. Lenin, *Two Tactics of Social-Democracy in the Democratic Revolution*, July 1905, *LCW*, Vol. 9, p. 56

7. Ibid.

8. Ibid.

9. Ibid., p. 56 and p. 58

10. Ibid., p. 57

11. Ibid., p. 82

12. Lenin, 'The Stages, the Trend and the Prospects of the Revolution', prior to early 1906, *LCW*, Vol. 10, p. 92, emphasis in original

13. Lenin, *Two Tactics of Social-Democracy in the Democratic Revolution*, July 1905, *LCW*, Vol. 9, p. 107

14. Ibid., p. 113

15. Marx and Engels, 'Address of the Central Authority to the League', March 1850, *MECW*, p. 287

16. Trotsky, *The Permanent Revolution, The Permanent Revolution & Results and Prospects*, pp. 76-7

17. See Lenin, 'The Aim of Proletarian Struggle in Our Revolution', *LCW*, Vol. 15, pp. 370-4

18. See Lenin, 'Social-Democracy's Attitude Towards the Peasant Movement', *Proletary*, No. 16, 14 (1) September 1905, *LCW*, Vol. 9, pp. 237

19. Lenin, 'On the Two Lines in the Revolution', *Sotsial-Demokrat*, No. 48, 20 November 1915, *LCW*, Vol. 21, p. 419, emphasis added

20. Ibid., p. 420, emphasis added

21. Lenin, 'On Compromises', *Rabochy Put*, No. 3, 19 (6) September 1917, *LCW*, Vol. 25, p. 310

11. The St. Petersburg Soviet

1. Quoted in Figes, *A People's Tragedy*, p. 186

2. See Alexis de Tocqueville, *L'Ancien régime*

3. Quoted in Trotsky, *My Life*, p. 158

4. Lunacharsky, *Revolutionary Silhouettes*, p. 60

5. Lenin, 'To PA Krasikov', 27 (14) September 1905, *LCW*, Vol. 34, pp. 339-40

6. Trotsky, *1905*, p. 265

7. Ibid., p. 267

8. Ibid., p. 242

9. Lenin, 'Our Tasks and the Soviet of Workers' Deputies', 2 to 4 November 1905, *LCW*, Vol. 10, p. 21

10. Trotsky, *1905*, p. 266

11. Quoted in Liebman, *Leninism Under Lenin*, p. 88

12. Quoted ibid., p. 86

13. Lenin, 'Our Tasks and the Soviet of Workers' Deputies', 2 to 4 November 1905, *LCW*, Vol. 10, p. 19, emphasis

in original

14. Ibid., p. 21, emphasis in original
15. Pipes, *The Russian Revolution, 1899-1919*, p. 363
16. *History of the Communist Party of the Soviet Union (Short Course)*, 1938, pp. 96-7
17. Wolfe, *The Three Who Made a Revolution*, p. 366
18. Lenin, *The Victory of the Cadets and the Tasks of the Workers' Party*, April 1906, *LCW*, Vol. 10, p. 252
19. Engels, *Revolution and Counter-Revolution in Germany*, *MECW*, Vol. 11, p. 85
20. Lenin, 'The Revolutionary Army and the Revolutionary Government', *Proletary*, No. 7, 10 July 1905, *LCW*, Vol. 8, p. 565
21. Lenin, 'To the Combat Committee of the St. Petersburg Committee', 16 October 1905, *LCW*, Vol. 9, p. 344
22. Andreyeva, *Encounters With Lenin*, Lenin and Gorky, *Letters, Reminiscences, Articles*, p. 334
23. Quoted in Lenin, 'Preface to the Russian Translation of *Karl Marx's Letters to Dr Kugelmann*', *LCW*, Vol. 12, p. 108
24. Lenin, ibid., emphasis in original
25. Ibid., emphasis in original
26. Lenin, 'The Revolutionary Upswing', *Sotsial-Demokrat*, No. 27, 17 (4) June 1912, *LCW*, Vol. 18, p. 107, emphasis in original
27. Krupskaya, *Reminiscences of Lenin*, p. 57
28. Lunacharsky, *Revolutionary Silhouettes*, p. 61
29. Ibid., p. 46
30. Quoted in Woods, *Bolshevism: The Road to Revolution*, p. 85
31. Lenin, 'The Crisis of Menshevism', *Proletary*, No. 9, 7 December 1906, *LCW*, Vol. 11, p. 359, emphasis in original
32. Ibid., footnote, emphasis in original
33. Lenin, 'The Reorganisation of the Party', Part 3, *Novaya Zhizn*, No. 14, 16 November 1905, *LCW*, Vol. 10, p.

38, emphasis in original
34. Lenin, 'To GV Plekhanov', October 1905, *LCW*, Vol. 34, p. 365, emphasis in original
35. Krupskaya, *Reminiscences of Lenin*, p. 145
36. Lenin, *The Victory of the Cadets and the Tasks of the Workers' Party*, April 1906, *LCW*, Vol. 10, pp. 251-2
37. Lenin, '"Left-Wing" Communism – An Infantile Disorder', 12 May 1920, *LCW*, Vol. 31, p. 35
38. Sukhanov, *The Russian Revolution 1917*, p. 230
39. Stalin, *Works*, Vol. 6, p. 56

12. The 'Unity' Congress

1. Krupskaya, *Reminiscences of Lenin*, p. 147
2. Lenin, 'Speech in Reply to the Debate on the Agrarian Question', *The Unity Congress of the RSDLP*, 10 (23) April to 25 April (8 May) 1906, *LCW*, Vol. 10, p. 280
3. Lenin, 'An Appeal to the Party by Delegates to the Unity Congress Who Belonged to the Former 'Bolshevik' Group', 25 to 26 April 1906, ibid., p. 314
4. Lenin, *Report on the Unity Congress of the RSDLP*, June 1906, ibid., p. 380
5. Ibid., pp. 380-1
6. Lenin, 'The Present Political Situation, *Vperyod*, No. 3, 28 May 1906, ibid., p. 485
7. Lenin, 'The Crisis of Menshevism', *Proletary*, No. 9, 7 December 1906, *LCW*, Vol. 11, p. 364
8. Figes, *A People's Tragedy*, p. 196
9. Ibid., pp. 197-8
10. Lenin, 'The Crisis of Menshevism', *Proletary*, No. 9, 7 December 1906, *LCW*, Vol. 11, p. 351, emphasis in original
11. Ibid., emphasis in original
12. Quoted ibid., p. 348
13. Ibid., pp. 361-2, emphasis in original
14. Ibid., pp. 354-5, emphasis in original
15. Lenin, 'Closing Speech on the Political

Report of the CC of the RCP(B)', 28 March 1922, *Eleventh Congress of the RCP(B)*, *LCW*, Vol. 33, p. 318

16. Quoted in Henderson, *The Spark that Lit the Revolution*, p. 163

17. Quoted in Rappaport, *Conspirator: Lenin in Exile*, p. 148

18. Lenin, 'Speech on the Attitude Towards Bourgeois Parties', 12 (25) May 1907, *The Fifth Congress of the RSDLP*, *LCW*, Vol. 12, p. 463

19. Lenin, 'Concluding Remarks on the Report on the Attitude Towards Bourgeois Parties', 14 (27) May, *The Fifth Congress of the RSDLP*, *LCW*, Vol. 12, p. 470

20. Lenin, 'To Maxim Gorky', 13 February 1908, *LCW*, Vol. 34, p. 386

21. Lenin, 'Objections to Trotsky's Amendments to the Bolshevik Resolution on the Attitude Towards Bourgeois Parties, Adopted by the Congress', 15-16 (28-29) May 1907, *The Fifth Congress of the RSDLP*, *LCW*, Vol. 12, p. 479, emphasis in original

22. Lenin, 'The Attitude Towards the Bourgeois Parties', 1907, ibid., p. 500

23. Quoted in Lenin, 'Strike Statistics in Russia', Part 1, *Mysl*, No. 1, December 1910, *LCW*, Vol. 16, p. 406

24. Lenin, 'Against Boycott', 26 June 1907, *LCW*, Vol. 13, p. 42

25. Lenin, 'The Revolutionary Phrase', *Pravda*, No. 31, 21 February 1918, *LCW*, Vol. 27, p. 29

26. Lenin, 'The International Socialist Congress in Stuttgart', September 1907, *LCW*, Vol. 13, p. 85

27. Ibid., p. 79

28. Riddell (ed.), *Lenin's Struggle for a Revolutionary International*, p. 35

29. Lenin, *'Left-Wing' Communism: An Infantile Disorder*, June 1920, *LCW*, Vol. 31, p. 35-6

30. Ibid., p. 32, emphasis in original

31. Lenin, 'On to the Straight Road', *Proletary*, No. 26, 19 March (1 April) 1908, *LCW*, Vol. 15, p. 17

32. Quoted ibid., p. 18

33. Quoted in Lenin, 'The Assessment of the Russian Revolution', *Proletary*, No. 30, 10 (23) May 1908, *LCW*, Vol. 15, p. 53, emphasis in original

34. Ibid., emphasis in original

35. Krupskaya, *Reminiscences of Lenin*, p. 162

36. Quoted ibid.

13. Years of Disintegration

1. Krupskaya, *Reminiscences of Lenin*, p. 169

2. Ibid., p. 176

3. Lenin, 'Two Letters', *Proletary*, No. 39, 13 (26) November 1908, *LCW*, Vol. 15, p. 290

4. Krupskaya, *Reminiscences of Lenin*, p. 169

5. Lenin, 'On the Road', *Sotsial-Demokrat*, No. 2, 28 January (10 February) 1909, *LCW*, Vol. 15, p. 345, emphasis in original

6. Ibid.

7. Ibid., pp. 351-2

8. Ibid., p. 346

9. Lenin, 'On the Article "Questions of the Day"', *Proletary*, No. 42, 12 (25) February 1909, ibid., p. 357, emphasis in original

10. Ibid., pp. 358-9, emphasis in original

11. Lenin, 'The Liquidation of Liquidationism', *Proletary*, No. 46, 11 (24) July 1909, ibid., pp. 458-9

12. Trotsky, *Crisis of the French Section*, p. 69

13. Woods, *Bolshevism*, pp. 361-2

14. Lenin, 'To Maxim Gorky', prior to 8 January 1913, *LCW*, Vol. 35, p. 71

15. Lenin, 'On the Question of Dialectics', 1915, *LCW*, Vol. 38, p. 363

16. Lenin, 'To Maxim Gorky', 13 February 1908, *LCW*, Vol. 34, p. 386

17. Krupskaya, *Reminiscences of Lenin*, p. 183

18. Lenin, *Materialism and Empirio-criticism*, May 1909, *LCW*, Vol. 14, p. 20

19. Lenin, 'The *Vperyod* Faction', *Sotsial-Demokrat* No. 15-16, 30 August (12 September) 1910, *LCW*, Vol. 16, p.

270, emphasis in original

20. Lenin, 'A Letter to AM Gorky', 25 February 1908, *LCW*, Vol. 13, p. 450

21. Krupskaya, *Reminiscences of Lenin*, p. 189

22. Ibid., p. 64

23. Ibid., p. 75, emphasis in original

24. Quoted ibid., p. 82

25. Ibid., p. 185

26. Ibid., p. 358

27. Trotsky, 'Leon Trotsky on Lenin', *Encyclopedia Britannica*, 22 Nov 2022, available at: www.britannica.com/topic/Leon-Trotsky-on-Lenin-1983748 (accessed 20 October 2023)

28. Krupskaya, *Reminiscences of Lenin*, p. 183

29. Ibid., p. 193

30. Lenin, 'To VV Vorovsky', 1 July 1908, *LCW*, Vol. 34, p. 395

31. Ibid.

32. Lenin, 'Announcement on the Publication of *Rabochaya Gazeta*', October 1910, *LCW*, Vol. 16, p. 289

33. Lenin, 'To Maxim Gorky', 16 April 1908, *LCW*, Vol. 34, p. 393, emphasis in original

34. Lenin, 'To Maxim Gorky', 11 April 1910, *LCW*, Vol. 34, p. 421

35. Ibid., pp. 421-2, emphasis in original

36. Krupskaya, *Reminiscences of Lenin*, p. 206

14. Factions Disbanded

1. Lenin, 'To his Sister Anna', 1 February 1910, *LCW*, Vol. 37, p. 451, emphasis in original

2. Lenin, 'To Maxim Gorky', 11 April 1910, *LCW*, Vol. 34, p. 420

3. Krupskaya, *Reminiscences of Lenin*, p. 224

4. Lenin, '*Left-Wing' Communism: An Infantile Disorder*, June 1920, *LCW*, Vol. 31, pp. 27-8

5. Lenin, 'To NY Vilonov', 27 March 1910, *LCW*, Vol. 34, p. 414

6. Lenin, 'The Beginning of Demonstrations', *Rabochaya Gazeta*, No. 2, 18 (31) December 1910, *LCW*,

Vol. 16, p. 356, emphasis in original

7. Quoted in Lenin, 'The Liquidators Exposed', *Proletary*, Nos. 47-8, 5 (18) September 1909, ibid, p. 16

8. Quoted ibid., p. 20

9. Quoted in Zinoviev, *History of the Bolshevik Party*, p. 157

10. Lenin, 'To Maxim Gorky', 27 May 1911, *LCW*, Vol. 34, p. 447, emphasis in original

11. Lenin, 'To GL Shklovsky', 14 October 1910, ibid, p. 430, emphasis in original

12. Lenin, 'Those Who Would Liquidate Us', *Mysl*, Nos. 2-3, January – February 1911, *LCW*, Vol. 17, pp. 72-3, emphasis in original

13. Lenin, 'To Maxim Gorky', 13 February 1908, *LCW*, Vol. 34, p. 385

14. Lenin, 'The New Faction of Conciliators, or the Virtuous', *Sotsial-Demokrat*, No. 24, 18 (31) October 1911, *LCW*, Vol. 17, p. 258, emphasis in original

15. Krupskaya, *Reminiscences of Lenin*, p. 211

16. Lenin, 'The Beginning of Demonstrations', *Rabochaya Gazeta*, No. 2, 18 (31) December 1910, *LCW*, Vol. 16, p. 358

17. Krupskaya, *Reminiscences of Lenin*, p. 216

18. Lenin, *The Sixth (Prague) All-Russia Conference of the RSDLP*, 'Resolutions of the Conference', January 1912, *LCW*, Vol. 17, p. 481

19. Krupskaya, *Reminiscences of Lenin*, p. 232-3

20. Trotsky, *In Defence of Marxism*, p. 184-5

21. Quoted in Trotsky, *Stalin*, p. 169

22. Lenin, 'To GK Orjonikidze, SS Spandayan and Yelena Stasova', April 1912, *LCW*, Vol. 35, p. 33

23. Lenin, 'To the Editor of *Pravda*', 1 August 1912, *LCW*, Vol. 35, p. 47, emphasis in original

24. Lenin, 'To the Editor of *Pravda*', 3 October 1912, *LCW*, Vol. 36, p. 198

25. Lenin, 'To the Bolshevik Deputies of the Fourth Duma', 7 February (25

January) 1913, *LCW*, Vol. 43, p. 335

26. Lenin, 'To the Editors of *Za Pravda*', not earlier than 27 October 1913, ibid., p. 361

27. Lenin, *Controversial Issues*, Part 1, *Pravda*, No. 85, 12 April 1913, *LCW*, Vol. 19, pp. 150-1, emphasis in original, brackets are Lenin's

28. Lenin, 'The Question of Mr Bogdanov and the *Vperyod* Group (For the Editors of *Pravda*)', 3 (16) June 1913, *LCW*, Vol. 19, pp. 173-4, emphasis in original

29. Lenin, 'Material on the Conflict Within the Social-Democratic Duma Group', *Za Pravda*, No. 22, 29 October 1913, ibid., p. 461, emphasis in original

30. Lenin, *Resolutions of the Summer, 1913, Joint Conference of the Central Committee of the RSDLP and Party Officials*, ibid., p. 423

31. Ibid.

32. Lenin, 'How Vera Zasulich Demolishes Liquidationsim', *Prosveshcheniye*, No. 9, September 1913, p. 406

33. Quoted in Trotsky, *Stalin*, pp. 207-8

34. Ibid.

35. Lenin, *Socialism and War*, July – August 1915, *LCW*, Vol. 21, p. 319

36. Braunthal, *History of the International*, Vol. 2, p. 30

15. War and the Collapse of the Second International

1. Lenin, *Imperialism, the Highest Stage of Capitalism*, January – June 1916, *LCW*, Vol. 22, p. 254, emphasis in original

2. Clausewitz, *On War*, p. 119

3. Krupskaya, *Reminiscences of Lenin*, p. 277

4. Zinoviev, *Lenin*, p. 33

5. *Lenin's Struggle for a Revolutionary International*, p. 104

6. Trotsky, *My Life*, p. 208

7. Braunthal, *History of the International*, Vol. 2, p. 7

8. Lenin, The International Socialist Congress in Stuttgart', September 1907, *LCW*, Vol. 13, p. 85

9. Zinoviev, *Lenin*, p. 33

10. Broué, *The German Revolution*, p. 15

11. Quoted in Lenin, 'Notes of a Publicist', February 1922, *LCW*, Vol. 33, p. 210

12. Lenin, 'The Position and Tasks of the Socialist International', *Sotsial-Demokrat*, No. 33, 1 November 1914, *LCW*, Vol. 21, p. 40

13. Ibid.

14. Lenin, 'To AG Shlyapnikov', 17 October 1914, *LCW*, Vol. 35, p. 162, emphasis in original

15. Lenin, 'To AG Shlyapnikov', 27 October 1914, ibid., pp. 167-8

16. Lenin, 'The European War and International Socialism', August – September 1914, p. 20

17. Ibid., p. 21, emphasis in original

18. Ibid., p. 22, emphasis in original

19. Lenin, 'The "Disarmament" Slogan', October 1916, *LCW*, Vol. 23, p. 97

20. Quoted in Trotsky, *My Life*, p. 216

21. Lenin, *Sochineniya*, Vol. 21, p. 21

22. Krupskaya, *Reminiscences of Lenin*, pp. 285-6

23. Ibid.

16. Lenin's Revolutionary Position

1. Lenin, The Tasks of the Revolutionary Social-Democracy in the European War', 25 August (6 September) 1914, *LCW*, Vol. 21, pp. 15-6

2. Ibid., p. 16

3. Ibid.

4. Ibid., p. 18

5. Ibid.

6. Lenin, 'The Conference of the RSDLP Groups Abroad', 19 February (4 March) 1915, ibid., p. 162

7. Lenin, 'The War and Russian Social-Democracy', 28 September (11 October) 1914, ibid., p. 34

8. Shlyapnikov, *On the Eve of 1917*, p. 26

9. Lenin, 'The Position and Tasks of the Socialist International', *Sotsial-Demokrat*, No. 33, 1 November 1914, *LCW*, Vol. 21, p. 40

10. Ibid.

11. Ibid., pp. 40-1
12. Lenin, Proposals Submitted by the Central Committee of the RSDLP to the Second Socialist Conference', February – March 1916, *LCW*, Vol. 22, p. 176
13. Krupskaya, *Reminiscences of Lenin*, p. 294
14. Clausewitz, *On War*, p. 101
15. Lenin, 'The Junius Pamphlet', July 1916, *LCW*, Vol. 22, p. 306
16. Lenin, 'The Conference of the RSDLP Groups Abroad', 19 February (4 March), *LCW*, Vol. 21, p. 159
17. Lenin, 'Appeal on the War', August 1915, ibid., pp. 367-8
18. Lenin, 'To the Participants in a Sitting of the Commission on Tactics of the Third Congress of the Comintern', 7 July 1921, *LCW*, Vol. 45, p. 203
19. Zinoviev, *History of the Bolshevik Party*, p. 183
20. Ibid., p. 190
21. Trotsky, 'Fighting Against the Stream, *Writings, 1938-39*, p. 328
22. Trotsky, 'Bonapartism, Fascism and War', *Writings, 1939-40*, pp. 546-7
23. Lenin, 'The Tasks of the Proletariat in the Present Revolution', *Pravda*, No. 26, 7 April 1917, *LCW*, Vol. 24, p. 22
24. Ibid., p. 25
25. Ibid., pp. 21-2, emphasis added
26. Lenin, *The Third Congress of the Communist International*, 'Speeches at a Meeting of Members of the German, Polish, Czechoslovak, Hungarian and Italian Delegations', 11 July 1921, *LCW*, Vol. 42, p. 325, emphasis added
27. Krupskaya, *Reminiscences of Lenin*, p. 290
28. Shlyapnikov, *On the Eve of 1917*, p. 98
29. Lenin, 'What Has Been Revealed by the Trial of the Russian Social-Democratic Labour Duma Group', *Sotsial-Demokrat*, No. 40, 29 March 1915, *LCW*, Vol. 21, p. 171
30. Ibid., p. 172
31. Ibid., p. 173, emphasis in original
32. Ibid., pp. 176-7, emphasis in original

17. The National Question and Zimmerwald

1. Lenin, 'The Nationality of Pupils in Russian Schools', *Proletarskaya Pravda*, No. 7, 14 December 1913, *LCW*, Vol. 19, pp. 532-3, emphasis in original
2. Lenin, *Resolutions of the Summer, 1913, Joint Conference of the Central Committee of the RSDLP and Party Officials*, 'Resolution on the National Question', September 1913, *LCW*, Vol. 19, p. 429
3. Lenin, *The Right of Nations to Self-Determination*, *Prosveshcheniye*, Nos. 4-6, April – June 1914, *LCW*, Vol. 20, p. 422
4. Marx, 'Letter to Engels', 2 November 1867, *MECW*, Vol. 42, p. 460
5. Quoted in Lenin, 'The Discussion on Self-Determination Summed Up', July 1916, *LCW*, Vol. 22, p. 340
6. Ibid., p. 341
7. Ibid.
8. Ibid., emphasis in original
9. Lenin, *The Collapse of the Second International*, *Kommunist*, Nos. 1-2, May – June 1915, p. 235, emphasis in original
10. Ibid., pp. 235-6, emphasis in original
11. Lenin, *The Right of Nations to Self-Determination*, *Prosveshcheniye*, Nos. 4-6, April – June 1914, *LCW*, Vol. 20, pp. 410-11, emphasis in original
12. Ibid., p. 411, emphasis in original
13. Lenin, 'Nascent Trend of Imperialist Economism', August – September 1916, *LCW*, Vol. 23, p. 20
14. Ibid., p. 17, emphasis in original
15. Lenin, 'Nascent Trend of Imperialist Economism', August – September 1916, *LCW*, Vol. 23, p. 16, emphasis in original
16. Lenin, *Lenin's Struggle for a Revolutionary International*, pp. 377-8, emphasis in original
17. Ibid., p. 379, emphasis in original
18. Lenin, 'To AG Shlyapnikov', 23 August 1915, *LCW*, Vol. 35, p. 205, emphasis in original

19. Quoted in Shlyapnikov, *On the Eve of 1917*, p. 75
20. Ibid., p. 87
21. Lenin, 'To AG Shlyapnikov', after 3 October 1916, *LCW*, Vol. 35, p. 235, emphasis in original
22. Ibid., emphasis in original
23. Quoted in *Lenin's Struggle for a Revolutionary International*, p. 277
24. Krupskaya, *Reminiscences of Lenin*, p. 302
25. Ibid., p. 303
26. Lenin, *The Collapse of the Second International*, *Kommunist*, Nos. 1-2, May – June 1915, *LCW*, Vol. 21, p. 215
27. Ibid., p. 216, emphasis in original
28. Ibid., pp. 213-4, emphasis in original
29. Krupskaya, *Reminiscences of Lenin*, p. 307
30. Ibid.
31. *Lenin's Struggle for a Revolutionary International*, pp. 298-9
32. Ibid., Documents: 1907-1916, pp. 303, 312
33. *The Age of Permanent Revolution: A Trotsky Anthology*, pp. 80, 83
34. Ibid., p. 329
35. *Sotsial-Demokrat*, No. 47, 13 October 1915, quoted in Trotsky, *The War and the International*, p. 90
36. Ibid.
37. Lenin, *Lenin's Struggle for a Revolutionary International*, p. 332
38. Ibid., p. 334

18. Lenin Sharpens his Weapons

1. Lenin, 'To AG Shlyapnikov', after 3 October 1916, *LCW*, Vol. 35, p. 236
2. Ibid.
3. Krupskaya, *Reminiscences of Lenin*, p. 312
4. Zinoviev, *Lenin*, p. 38
5. Trotsky, 'Fighting Against the Stream, *Writings, 1938-39*, p. 328
6. Quoted in Lenin, 'The Voice of an Honest French Socialist', *Kommunist*, Nos. 1-2, 1915, *LCW*, Vol. 21, p. 353
7. Lenin, 'Reply to P Kievsky (Y Pyatakov)', August – September 1916, *LCW*, Vol. 23, p. 22
8. Krupskaya, *Reminiscences of Lenin*, p. 312
9. Lenin, 'The Three Sources and Three Component Parts of Marxism', *Prosveshcheniye*, No. 3, March 1913, *LCW*, Vol. 19, p. 23
10. Lenin, 'The Marx–Engels Correspondence', 1913, ibid., p. 554
11. Krupskaya, *Reminiscences of Lenin*, p. 333
12. Lenin, 'On the Question of Dialectics', 1915, *LCW*, Vol. 38, p. 359, emphasis in original
13. Ibid., p. 362, emphasis in original
14. Lenin, 'Conspectus of Hegel's Book, *The Science of Logic*', ibid., p. 104
15. Ibid., p. 147, emphasis in original
16. Ibid., pp. 221-2, emphasis in original
17. Lenin, 'Letter to the Congress', 25 December 1922, *LCW*, Vol. 36, p. 595
18. Ibid.
19. Lenin, 'On the Significance of Militant Materialism', *Pod Znamenem Marksizma*, No. 3, March 1922, *LCW*, Vol. 33, p. 227
20. Ibid., pp. 233-4
21. Lenin, *What Is to Be Done?*, March 1902, *LCW*, Vol. 5, p. 369
22. Lenin, *Imperialism, the Highest Stage of Capitalism*, January – June 1916, *LCW*, Vol. 22, p. 187
23. Ibid., p. 188
24. Bukharin, *Imperialism and World Economy*, p. 10
25. Quoted in Lenin, 'A Caricature of Marxism and Imperialist Economism', August – October 1916, *LCW*, Vol. 23, p. 42
26. Ibid., emphasis in original
27. Lenin, *Imperialism, the Highest Stage of Capitalism*, January – June 1916, *LCW*, Vol. 22, p. 208
28. Quoted in Trotsky, *The Living Thoughts of Karl Marx*, p. 28
29. Lenin, *Imperialism, the Highest Stage of Capitalism*, January – June 1916, *LCW*, Vol. 22, p. 295, emphasis in original

19. The February Revolution

1. Quoted in Woods, _The First World War_, p. 104
2. Quoted in Liebman, _The Russian Revolution_, p. 77
3. Lockhart, _Memoirs of a British Agent_, p. 119-20
4. Quoted in Liebman, _The Russian Revolution_, p. 22, all quotes
5. Quoted in Clark, _Lenin_, p. 179
6. Quoted ibid., p. 181
7. Quoted ibid.
8. Buchanan, _My Mission to Russia_, Vol. 2, pp. 18-9
9. Ibid., p. 41
10. Ibid., p. 51
11. Lenin, 'To Inessa Armand', 25 December 1916, _LCW_, Vol. 35, p. 266
12. Lenin, 'Lecture on the 1905 Revolution', 9 (22) January 1917, _LCW_, Vol. 23, p. 252, emphasis in original
13. Ibid., pp. 252-3
14. Ibid., p. 253
15. Quoted in Liebman, _The Russian Revolution_, p. 44
16. Lockhart, _Memoirs of a British Agent_, p. 158
17. Ibid., p. 173
18. Lenin, 'Draft Theses', 4 (17) March 1917, _LCW_, Vol. 23, p. 287
19. Raskolnikov, _Kronstadt and Petrograd in 1917_, p. 1
20. Lenin, 'The Military Programme of the Proletarian Revolution', September 1916, _LCW_, Vol. 23, p. 82
21. Quoted in Zetkin, _Reminiscences of Lenin_, pp. 41-2
22. Raskolnikov, _Kronstadt and Petrograd in 1917_, pp. 1-2
23. Price, _Dispatches From the Revolution_, p. 30
24. Lenin, 'Lessons of the Revolution', July 1917, _LCW_, Vol. 25, p. 229
25. _Voprosy Istoriya KPSS_, 1957, No. 4, quoted in Woods, _Bolshevism_, p. 573 – a further source is _Ocherki ist._ MO KPSS, p. 214
26. Shlyapnikov, _On The Eve of 1917_, p. 215
27. Trotsky, _History of the Russian Revolution_, Vol. 1, p. 171
28. Price, _My Three Revolutions_, p. 51
29. Sukhanov, _The Russian Revolution 1917_, p. 38, emphasis in original
30. Ibid., p. 85
31. Ibid., p. 308
32. Trotsky, _History of the Russian Revolution_, Vol. 1, p. 300
33. Sukhanov, _The Russian Revolution 1917_, p. 24
34. Ibid., p. 43
35. Ibid., p. 18
36. Quoted in Liebman, _The Russian Revolution_, p. 112
37. Shulgin, _Days of the Russian Revolution_, Book VIII-XII, pp. 93 and 96
38. Lukomsky, _Reminiscences_, Vol. 2, p. 20
39. Sukhanov, _The Russian Revolution 1917_, p. 22
40. Ibid., pp. 54-5, emphasis in original
41. Ibid., pp. 107-8
42. Quoted in Trotsky, _History of the Russian Revolution_, Vol. 1, p. 302
43. Quoted ibid.
44. Sukhanov, _The Russian Revolution 1917_, pp. 6-8, all quotes

20. Lenin's Response from Exile

1. Trotsky, _History of the Russian Revolution_, Vol. 1, p. 300
2. Raskolnikov, _Kronstadt and Petrograd in 1917_, pp. 22-3
3. Sukhanov, _The Russian Revolution 1917_, p. 21
4. Lenin, 'Draft Theses', 4 (17) March 1917, _LCW_, Vol. 23, pp. 287-8
5. Ibid., p. 288
6. Ibid.
7. Ibid., p. 290
8. Ibid.
9. Lenin, 'Telegram to the Bolsheviks Leaving for Russia', 6 (19) March 1917, ibid., p. 292
10. Lenin, 'First Letter', 7 (20) March 1917, _Letters from Afar_, _LCW_, Vol. 23, p. 304, emphasis added
11. Ibid., emphasis in original

12. Ibid., emphasis in original
13. Ibid., p. 305, emphasis in original
14. Ibid.
15. Ibid., p. 306
16. Ibid., emphasis in original
17. Lenin, 'Second Letter', 9 (22) March 1917, ibid., p. 315-6
18. Ibid., p. 316
19. Lenin, 'First Letter', 7 (20) March 1917, ibid., p. 302
20. Ibid., p. 303 and 305, emphasis in original
21. Lenin, 'Third Letter', 11 (24) March 1917, ibid., p. 323, emphasis in original
22. Ibid., p. 325-6, emphasis in original
23. Lenin, 'Fifth Letter', 26 March (8 April) 1917, ibid., p. 340, all quotes
24. Ibid., p. 341, emphasis in original
25. Ibid.
26. Lenin, 'To Inessa Armand', 15 (2) March 1917, ibid, p. 416, footnote
27. Lenin, 'Telegram to Robert Grimm', 31 March 1917, *LCW*, Vol. 36, p. 427
28. *Politiken*, No. 86, 15 April 1917, quoted in *LCW*, Vol. 23, p. 417, footnote
29. Krupskaya, *Reminiscences of Lenin*, p. 345
30. Churchill, *The World Crisis*, Vol. 5, p. 73
31. Lenin, 'Farewell Letter to the Swiss Workers', 26 March (8 April) 1917, *LCW*, Vol. 23, pp. 371-3, emphasis in original
32. Ibid., p. 373

21. Rearming the Bolsheviks

1. *Pravda*, 15 March 1917, quoted in Trotsky, *History of the Russian Revolution*, Vol. 1, p. 305
2. Quoted in Leibman, *Leninism Under Lenin*, p. 122
3. Carr, *The Bolshevik Revolution, 1917-1923*, Vol. 1, p. 75
4. Quoted ibid., p. 75
5. Quoted ibid.
6. Quoted in Leibman, *Leninism Under Lenin*, p. 123

7. Lenin, 'To JS Hanecki', 39 March 1917, *LCW*, Vol. 35, p. 309, emphasis in original
8. Ibid., p. 310, emphasis in original
9. Ibid., p. 312, emphasis in original
10. Ibid., pp. 312-3, emphasis in original
11. Quoted in Leibman, *Leninism Under Lenin*, p. 123
12. Quoted in Trotsky, *History of the Russian Revolution*, Vol. 1, p. 306
13. Quoted in Trotsky, *Stalin School of Falsification*, p. 238
14. Quoted ibid., p. 300
15. Quoted ibid., p. 263
16. Quoted ibid., p. 274
17. Quoted ibid., p. 275
18. Lenin, 'To Karl Radek', 17 June 1917, *LCW*, Vol. 43, p. 635
19. Quoted in Raskolnikov, *Kronstadt and Petrograd in 1917*, p. 71
20. Sukhanov, *The Russian Revolution 1917*, pp. 272-3
21. Quoted ibid., p. 273
22. Raskolnikov, *Kronstadt and Petrograd in 1917*, p. 76
23. Sukhanov, *The Russian Revolution 1917*, p. 280
24. Raskolnikov, *Kronstadt and Petrograd in 1917*, p. 77
25. Quoted in Sukhanov, *The Russian Revolution 1917*, p. 286
26. Quoted ibid., p. 287
27. Quoted in Liebman, *The Russian Revolution*, p. 136, all quotes
28. Sukhanov, *The Russian Revolution 1917*, p. 287-8
29. See FI Drabkina, 'Vserossiiskoe soveshchanie bol'shevikov v Marte 1917 goda', in *Voprosy istorii*, No. 9, Moscow, 1956, pp. 4-16
30. Quoted in Trotsky, *Stalin School of Falsification*, p. 289
31. Quoted ibid., p. 290
32. Quoted ibid., p. 290-2, emphasis in original
33. Quoted ibid., p. 292
34. Quoted ibid.
35. Quoted ibid., p. 293
36. Quoted ibid., emphasis in original
37. Quoted ibid.

38. Quoted ibid., pp. 294-5
39. Quoted ibid., pp. 295-8
40. Quoted ibid., pp. 298-9
41. Quoted ibid., p. 299
42. Quoted in Lenin, 'Letters on Tactics', 8-13 (21-26) April 1917, *LCW*, Vol. 24, p. 50
43. Raskolnikov, *Kronstadt and Petrograd in 1917*, pp. 16-7
44. Ibid., pp. 33-3
45. See Lenin, 'Social-Democracy's Attitude Towards the Peasant Movement', *Proletary*, No. 16, 14 (1) September 1905, *LCW*, Vol. 9, pp. 237
46. Lenin, 'Letters on Tactics', 8-13 (21-26) April 1917, *LCW*, Vol. 24, pp. 43-5, emphasis in original
47. Ibid., p. 46, emphasis in original
48. Ibid., emphasis in original
49. Quoted ibid., p. 50
50. Ibid., emphasis in original
51. Ibid., p. 149
52. Raskolnikov, *Kronstadt and Petrograd in 1917*, p. 76
53. See Liebman, *Leninism Under Lenin*, p. 131
54. Ibid., p. 71
55. Ibid., p. 150
56. Trotsky, *On Lenin*, p. 69
57. Quoted in Carr, *The Bolshevik Revolution, 1917-1923*, Vol. 1, p. 89
58. Lenin, 'Greetings to Italian, French and German Communists', 10 October 1919, *LCW*, Vol. 30, pp. 55-6
59. Raskolnikov, *Kronstadt and Petrograd in 1917*, pp. 66-7
60. Lenin, 'War and Revolution', 14 (27) May 1917, *LCW*, Vol. 24, p. 413

Bibliography

Akhapkin, Yuri, *First Decrees of Soviet Power*, Lawrence & Wishart, 1970

Alexievich, Svetlana, *Second-hand Time*, Juggernaut Books, 2016

Ali, Tariq, *The Dilemmas of Lenin*, Verso, 2017

Arnot, Robin Page, *A Short History of the Russian Revolution*, Victor Gollancz, London, 1937

Astashkevich, Irina, *Gendered Violence: Jewish Women in the Pogroms of 1917 to 1921*, Academic Studies Press, 2018

Avrich, Paul, *The Russian Anarchists*, AK Press, 2005

Babel, Isaac, *Complete Works of Isaac Babel*, WW Norton & Co., 2002

Badayev, Alexei Y, *Bolsheviks in the Tsarist Duma*, Bookmarks, 1987

Balabanoff, Angelica, *Impressions of Lenin*, University of Michigan Press, 1964

Beer, Max, *Fifty Years of International Socialism*, Unwin Brothers, 1937

Brailsford, Henry Noel, *The Russian Workers' Republic*, George Allen & Unwin, 1921

Braunthal, Julius, *History of the International*, Thomas Nelson, 1967

Broué, Pierre, *The German Revolution*, Merlin Press, 2006
— *Le Parti bolchevique, historie du PC de l'URSS*, Les Editions de Minuit, 1971

Bryant, Louise, *Six Red Months in Russia,* Journeyman Press, 1982

Buchanan, George, *My Mission to Russia: And Other Diplomatic Memoirs*, Little, Brown & Co., 1923

Bukharin, Preobrarazhensky, *The ABC of Communism*, Penguin Classics, 1970

Buranov, Yuri, *Lenin's Will*, Prometheus, 1994

Carlyle, Thomas, *Cromwell's Letters and Speeches*, Harper & Brothers, 1860

Carr, Edward Hallett, *The Bolshevik Revolution, 1917-1923*, Macmillan, 1950
— *The Interregnum, 1923-1924*, MacMillan, 1954
— *What is History?*, Penguin, 1965

Chaplin, Charlie, *My Trip Abroad*, Harper & Brothers, 1922

Churchill, Winston, *The World Crisis: The Aftermath*, Thornton Butterworth, 1929

Clark, Ronald William, *Lenin: The Man Behind the Mask*, Faber & Faber, 1988

Clausewitz, Carl von, *On War*, Penguin Classics, 1983

Cliff, Tony, *Building the Party: Lenin, 1983-1914*, Bookmarks, 1986
— *Revolution Besieged: Lenin, 1917-1923*, Bookmarks, 1987
— *All Power to the Soviets: Lenin, 1914-1917*, Bookmarks, 1985

Degas (ed.), Jane, *The Communist International*, Routledge, 1971

Denikin, Anton, *Sketches of the Russian Revolt*, Paris, 1922

Deutscher, Isaac, *Lenin's Childhood*, Oxford University Press, 1970
— *Stalin: A Political Biography*, Oxford University Press, 1961
— *The Prophet Armed*, Oxford University Press, 1976
— *The Prophet Unarmed*, Oxford University Press, 1970

Dietzgen, Josef, *Philosophical Essays*, Social-Democratic Philosophy, Chicago, 1917

Dutt, Palme, *Lenin*, Hamish Hamilton, 1933

Erich, Wollenberg, *The Red Army*, New Park, 1978

Figes, Orlando, *A People's Tragedy: The Russian Revolution, 1891-1924*, Pimlico, 1996

Fischer, Louis, *Life of Lenin*, Harper & Row, 1964

Foner, Philip, *The Bolshevik Revolution: Its Impact on American Radicals, Liberals and Labor*, International Publishers, 1967

Fotieva, Lydia, *Pages from Lenin's Life*, Progressive Publishers, 1960

Gallacher, Willie, *Revolt on the Clyde*, Lawrence & Wishart, 1949

Goldman, Emma, *My Disillusionment in Russia*, Doubleday, Page & Co, 1923

Gorky, Maxim, *Days with Lenin*, Martin Lawrence, 1933
— *Vladimir Ilyich Lenin*, Leningrad: State Publishing House, 1924

Grant, Ted, *Russia: From Revolution to Counter-revolution*, Wellred Books, 2023
— *The Unbroken Thread*, Fortress, 1989

Grant, Ted and Silvermanm Roger, *Bureaucratism or Workers' Power*, 1967

Harding, Neil, *Lenin's Political Thought*, Vol. 1, MacMillan, 1977

Hegel, Georg Wilhelm Friedrich, *Hegel Selections*, The Modern Student's Library, 1929

Henderson, Robert, *The Spark that Lit the Revolution: Lenin in London and the Politics that Changed the World*, IB Tauris, 2020

Hill, Christopher, *God's Englishman*, Pelican, 1979
— *Lenin and the Russian Revolution*, Hodder & Stoughton, 1947

Hollis, Christopher, *Portrait of a Professional Revolutionary*, Longmans Green & Co., 1938

Horne, Alistair, *The Fall of Paris: The Siege and the Commune 1870-71*, Penguin, 1990

James, Cyril Lionel Robert, *World Revolution, 1917-1936*, Martin Secker & Warburg, 1937

Kershaw, Ian, *Personality and Power: Builders and Destroyers of Modern Europe*, Allen Lane, 2022

Kerzhentsev, Platon, *Life of Lenin*, Cooperative Publishing Society of Foreign Workers in the USSR, 1937

Krausz, Tamás, *Reconstructing Lenin: An Intellectual Biography*, Monthly Review Press, 2015

Krupskaya, Nadezhda, *Memories of Lenin*, Martin Lawrence, 1930
— *Reminiscences of Lenin*, International Publishers, 1979

Khrushchev, Nikita, *Khrushchev Remembers*, London, 1971

Lawton, Lancelot, *Economic History of Soviet Russia*, Macmillan, 1932

LeBlanc, Paul, *Lenin and the Revolutionary Party*, Haymarket Books, 1993

Lenin, Vladimir Ilyich, *Lenin Collected Works*, Lawrence & Wishart, 1960

Lenin, Vladimir Ilyich and Gorky, Maxim, *Letters, Reminiscences, Articles*, Progress Publishers, 1974

Lewin, Moshe, *Lenin's Last Struggle*, Pluto Press, 1973

Liebman, Marcel, *Leninism Under Lenin*, Merlin, 1980
— *The Russian Revolution*, Vintage Books, 1972

Lockhart, Robert Hamilton Bruce, *Memoirs of a British Agent*, Pan Books, 2002
— *Diaries*, Macmillan, 1973

Lukomsky, Alexander, *Reminiscences: Archives of the Russian Revolution*, Otto Kirchner & Co, 1922

Lunacharsky, Anatoly, *Revolutionary Silhouettes*, Allen Lane, 1967

Luxemburg, Rosa, *'Organisational Questions of the Russian Social Democracy' (later retitled 'Leninism or Marxism?')*, Pathfinder Press, 1971
— *Rosa Luxemburg Speaks*, Pathfinder Press, 1970

Maclean, John, *In the Rapids of Revolution*, Allison & Busby, 1978

McLachan, Donald, *In The Chair: Barrington-Ward of 'The Times', 1927-1948*, Weidenfeld and Nicolson, 1971

Marx, Karl and Engels, Friedrich, *Marx and Engels Collected Works*, Lawrence & Wishart, 1975
— *Marx and Engels Selected Correspondence*, Progress Publishers, 1965

Maxton, James, *Lenin*, Daily Express Publications, 1932

Medvedev, Roy, *Let History Judge*, MacMillan, 1972

Milton, Nan, *John Maclean*, Pluto Press, 1973

Montefiore, Simon Sebag, *The Romanovs*, Weidenfeld & Nicolson, 2017
— *Young Stalin*, Phoenix, 2008

Payne, Robert, *The Life and Death of Lenin*, Pan Books, 1967

Piatnitsky, Osip, *Memoirs of a Bolshevik*, International Publishers, 1926

Pipes, Richard, *The Russian Revolution, 1899-1919*, Harvill Press, 1997

Plekhanov, Georgi, *Selected Philosophical Works*, Progress Publishers, 1974

Polovtsev, Peter Alexandrovich, *Days of Eclipse*, Paris

Popov, Nicolai, *Outline History of the Communist Party of the Soviet Union*, Cooperative Publishing Society of Foreign Workers in the USSR, 1934

Price, Morgan Philips, *Dispatches From the Revolution: Russia 1916-18*, Pluto Press, 1997
— *My Three Revolutions: Russia, Germany, Britain, 1917-69*, Allen & Unwin, 1969

Rabinowitch, Alexander, *The Bolsheviks Come to Power: The Revolution of 1917 in Petrograd*, NLB, 1979

Ransome, Arthur, *Six Weeks in Russia in 1919*, Redwoods, 1992
— *The Crisis in Russia*, Redwords, 1992

Rappaport, Helen, *Conspirator: Lenin in Exile*, Windmill Books, 2010

Raskolnikov, Fyodor, *Kronstadt and Petrograd in 1917*, New Park, 1982

Read, Anthony, *The World on Fire: 1919 and the Battle with Bolshevism*, Jonathan Cape, 2008

Reed, John, *Ten Days That Shook the World*, Penguin, 1970

Rimlinger, Gaston V, *The Management of Labor Protest in Russia: 1870-1905*, Cambridge University Press, 1960

Roberts, John Peter and Weston, Fred, *Women, Family and the Russian Revolution*, Wellred Books, 2023

Rosmer, Alfred, *Lenin's Moscow*, Pluto Press, 1971

Ross, Edward Alsworth, *The Russian Soviet Republic*, George Allen & Unwin, 1923

Rogovin, Vadim Z, *1937: Stalin's Year of Terror*, Mehring Books, 1998

Rothstein, Andrew, *Lenin in Britain*, Communist Party of Great Britain, 1970

Rubenstein, Joshua, *Leon Trotsky: A Revolutionary Life*, Yale University Press, 2011

Russell, Bertrand, *Autobiography*, George Allen & Unwin, 1968
— *The Practice and Theory of Bolshevism*, Allen & Unwin, 1921

Santayana, George, *The Life of Reason*, Scribner, 1953

Schapiro, Leonard, *The Communist Party of the Soviet Union*, Methuen, 1964

Serge, Victor, *From Lenin to Stalin*, Monard Press, 1973
— *Memories of a Revolutionary, 1901-1941*, Oxford University Press, 1963
— *Year One of the Russian Revolution*, Allen Lane, 1972

Service, Robert, *Lenin: A Biography*, Macmillan, 2000
— *Lenin: A Political Life – Volume 3: The Iron Ring*, Palgrave Macmillan, 1995

Sewell, Rob, *In the Cause of Labour*, Wellred Books, 2003
— *Socialism or Barbarism: Germany 1918-1933*, Wellred Books, 2018

Shlyapnikov, Alexander, *On the Eve of 1917*, Allison & Busby, 1982

Shub, David, *Lenin: A Biography*, Penguin, 1969

Shulgin, Vasily, *Days of the Russian Revolution: Memoirs From the Right*, Russian
    Thought, Prague, 1922

Souvarine, Boris, *Stalin: A Critical Survey of Bolshevism*, Secker & Warburg, 1939

Stalin, Joseph, *Lenin and Leninism*, Foreign Languages Press, 1977
— *On the Opposition*, Foreign Language Press, 1974
— *The October Revolution*, Lawrence & Wishart, 1936
— *Works*, Foreign Languages Publishing House, 1954

Steffens, Lincoln, *The Autobiography of Lincoln Steffens*, Harcourt Brace Jovanovich, 1958

Stites, Richard, *Revolutionary Dreams: Utopian Vision and Experimental Life in the
    Russian Revolution*, Oxford University Press, 1989

Sukhanov, Nikolai Nikolaevich, *The Russian Revolution 1917*, Oxford University
    Press, 1955

Trepper, Leopold, *The Great Game*, Michael Joseph, 1977

Trotsky, Leon, *1905*, Penguin, 1973
— *Crisis of the French Section*, Pathfinder Press, 1977
— *Diary in Exile, 1935*, Faber and Faber, 1958
— *History of the Russian Revolution*, Wellred Books, 2022
— *How the Revolution Armed*, New Park, 1981
— *In Defence of Marxism*, Wellred Books, 2019

— *Lenin*, George G Harrap & Co., 1925
— *Lenin's Fight Against Stalinism*, Pathfinder, 1975
— *Military Writings of Leon Trotsky*, Merit Publishers, 1969
— *My Life: An Attempt at an Autobiography*, Wellred Books, 2018
— *Notebooks 1933-1935*, Columbia University Press, 1986
— *On Lenin: Notes Towards a Biography*, George Harrap, 1971
— *Our Political Tasks*, New Park, 1979
— *Our Revolution: Essays on Working-class and International Revolution, 1904-1917*, Henry Holt & Co., 1918
— *Political Profiles*, New Park, 1972
— *Stalin: An Appraisal of the Man and His Influence*, Wellred Books, 2016
— *Terrorism and Communism*, New Park, 1975
— *The Case of Leon Trotsky*, Merit Publishers, 1969
— *The Challenge of the Left Opposition*, Pathfinder, 1981
— *The First Five Years of the Communist International*, Wellred Books, 2020
— *The Living Thoughts of Karl Marx*, Fawcett Publications, 1963
— *The Permanent Revolution & Results and Prospects*, Wellred Books, 2020
— *The Revolution Betrayed*, Wellred Books, 2015
— *The Stalin School of Falsification*, Pioneer Publishers, 1937
— *The War and the International*, Colombo, 1971
— *The Young Lenin*, David & Charles, 1972
— *Their Morals and Ours*, New Park, 1968
— *Writings of Leon Trotsky*, Pathfinder Press, 1969
— *Writings on Britain*, Wellred Books, 2023

Valentinov, Nikolay, *Encounters with Lenin*, Oxford University Press, 1968

Vodovozov, V, *Moe Znakomstvo s Leninym*, Prague, 1925

Volkogonov, Dmitri, *Lenin: A New Biography*, Free Press, 1994

Watt, Richard, *The Kings Depart*, The Literary Guild, 1969

Wells, Herbert George, *A Short History of the World*, The Labour Publishing Company, 1924
— *Russia in the Shadows*, Hodder & Stoughton, 1920

Wicks, HM, *Eclipse of October*, Holborn Publishing Company, 1957

Williams, Albert Rhys, *Lenin: The Man and His Work*, Scott and Seltzer, 1919

Wilson, Edmund, *To the Finland Station: A Study in the Writing and Acting of History*, The Fontana Library, 1968

Wolfe, Bertram David, *Three Who Made a Revolution*, Stein & Day, 1984

Wollenburg, Erich, *The Red Army*, New Park, 1978

Woods, Alan, *Bolshevism: The Road to Revolution*, Wellred Books, 2017
— *The First World War: A Marxist Analysis of the Great Slaughter*, Wellred Books, 2019

Woods, Alan and Grant, Ted, *Lenin and Trotsky: What They Really Stood For*, Wellred Books, 2000

Zagorsky, S, *Wages and Regulation of Conditions of Labour in the USSR*, Geneva, 1930

Zbarsky, Ilya, and Hutchinson, Samual, *Lenin's Embalmers*, Vintage, 1999

Zetkin, Clara, *Reminiscences of Lenin*, International Publishers, 1934

Zinoviev, Grigory, *History of the Bolshevik Party: A Popular Outline*, New Park, 1973
— *Lenin*, Socialist Labour League, 1966

Minutes and collections

1903: Second Congress of the RSDLP, New Park, 1978

Classics of Marxism: Volume Two, Wellred Books, 2015

Founding the Communist International, Riddell (ed.), Pathfinder, 1987

History of the Communist Party of the Soviet Union (Short Course), Foreign Languages Publishing House, 1948

Joseph Stalin: A Short Biography, Foreign Languages Publishing House, 1940

Lenin: A Biography, Progress Publishers, 1965

Lenin Through the Eyes of the World, Progress Publishers, 1969

Lenin and Trotsky on Kronstadt, Monad Press 1979

Lenin's Economic Writings, Desai (ed.), Lawrence & Wishart, 1989

Lenin's Fight Against Stalinism, Pathfinder, 1975

Lenin's Struggle for a Revolutionary International, Riddell (ed.), Monad Press, 1984

Moscow Trials Anthology, New Park, 1967

Not by Politics Alone: The Other Lenin, Deutscher, Tamara (ed.), Allen & Unwin, 1973

The German Revolution and the Debate on Soviet Power, Riddell (ed.), Pathfinder, 1986

The Age of Permanent Revolution: A Trotsky Anthology, Deutscher (ed.), Dell Publishing, 1964

The Bolsheviks and the October Revolution: Minutes of the Central Committee of the Russian Social-Democratic Labour Party (Bolsheviks), August 1917 to February 1918, Bone (trans.), Pluto Press, 1974

The Errors of Trotskyism: A Symposium, Communist Party of Great Britain, 1925

The History of the Civil War in the USSR, Lawrence & Wishart, 1937

The Trotsky Papers, 1917-1922, Meijer (ed.), The Hague, 1971

The Theory and Practice of Leninism, Communist Party of Great Britain, 1925

The Sixth Congress of the RSDLP(B), August 1917, Moscow, 1934

Workers of the World and Oppressed Peoples, Unite! Proceedings and Documents of the Second Congress of the Communist International, 1920, Riddell (ed.), Pathfinder, 1991

Papers and periodicals

East European Jewish Affairs
Encyclopedia Britannica
Financial Times
In Defence of Marxism
Manchester Guardian
New York Evening Call
The New Leader
The Russian Review
The Wire

Index

Titles by Wellred Books

Wellred Books is a publishing house specialising in works of Marxist theory. Among the titles we publish are:

Anti-Dühring, Friedrich Engels

Bolshevism: The Road to Revolution, Alan Woods

Chartist Revolution, Rob Sewell

China: From Permanent Revolution to Counter-Revolution, John Roberts

The Civil War in France, Karl Marx

Class Struggle in the Roman Republic, Alan Woods

The Class Struggles in France, 1848-1850, Karl Marx

The Classics of Marxism: Volumes One & Two, Various authors

Dialectics of Nature, Friedrich Engels

The Eighteenth Brumaire of Louis Bonaparte, Karl Marx

The First Five Years of the Communist International, Leon Trotsky

The First World War: A Marxist Analysis of the Great Slaughter, Alan Woods

Germany: From Revolution to Counter-Revolution, Rob Sewell

Germany 1918-1933: Socialism or Barbarism, Rob Sewell

History of British Trotskyism, Ted Grant

The History of Philosophy: A Marxist Perspective, Alan Woods

The History of the Russian Revolution: All Volumes, Leon Trotsky

The History of the Russian Revolution to Brest-Litovsk, Leon Trotsky

The Ideas of Karl Marx, Alan Woods

Imperialism: The Highest Stage of Capitalism, VI Lenin

In Defence of Lenin, Rob Sewell & Alan Woods

In Defence of Marxism, Leon Trotsky

In the Cause of Labour, Rob Sewell

Ireland: Republicanism and Revolution, Alan Woods

Lenin and Trotsky: What They Really Stood For, Alan Woods & Ted Grant

Lenin, Trotsky & the Theory of the Permanent Revolution, John Roberts

Marxism and Anarchism, Various authors

Marxism and the USA, Alan Woods

Materialism and Empirio-criticism, VI Lenin

My Life, Leon Trotsky

Not Guilty, Dewey Commission Report

The Origin of the Family, Private Property & the State, Friedrich Engels

The Permanent Revolution and Results & Prospects, Leon Trotsky

Permanent Revolution in Latin America, John Roberts & Jorge Martin

Reason in Revolt, Alan Woods & Ted Grant

Reformism or Revolution, Alan Woods

Revolution and Counter-Revolution in Spain, Felix Morrow

The Revolution Betrayed, Leon Trotsky

The Revolutionary Legacy of Rosa Luxemburg, Marie Frederiksen

The Revolutionary Philosophy of Marxism, John Peterson (Ed.)

Russia: From Revolution to Counter-Revolution, Ted Grant

Spain's Revolution Against Franco, Alan Woods

Stalin, Leon Trotsky

The State and Revolution, VI Lenin

Ted Grant: The Permanent Revolutionary, Alan Woods

Ted Grant Writings: Volumes One and Two, Ted Grant

Thawra hatta'l nasr! - Revolution until Victory!, Alan Woods & others

What Is Marxism?, Rob Sewell & Alan Woods

What Is to Be Done?, VI Lenin

Women, Family and the Russian Revolution, John Roberts & Fred Weston

Writings on Britain, Leon Trotsky

To make an order or for more information, visit wellred-books.com, email books@wellred-books.com or write to Wellred Books, 152-160 Kemp House, City Road, London, EC1V 2NX, United Kingdom.

Printed in the USA
CPSIA information can be obtained
at www.ICGtesting.com
CBHW011805280424
7690CB00017B/721

9 781913 026950